In and Out of Sight

MODERNIST LITERATURE & CULTURE

Kevin J. H. Dettmar & Mark Wollaeger, Series Editors

Consuming Traditions
Elizabeth Outka

Machine Age Comedy
Michael North

The Art of Scandal
Sean Latham

The Hypothetical Mandarin
Eric Hayot

Nations of Nothing But Poetry
Matthew Hart

Modernism & Copyright
Paul K. Saint-Amour

Accented America
Joshua L. Miller

Criminal Ingenuity
Ellen Levy

Modernism's Mythic Pose
Carrie J. Preston

Pragmatic Modernism
Lisa Schoenbach

Unseasonable Youth
Jed Esty

World Views
Jon Hegglund

Americanizing Britain
Genevieve Abravanel

Modernism and the New Spain
Gayle Rogers

At the Violet Hour
Sarah Cole

Fictions of Autonomy
Andrew Goldstone

The Great American Songbooks
T. Austin Graham

Without Copyrights
Robert Spoo

The Degenerate Muse
Robin Schulze

Commonwealth of Letters
Peter J. Kalliney

Modernism and Melancholia
Sanja Bahun

Digital Modernism
Jessica Pressman

In a Strange Room
David Sherman

Epic Negation
C. D. Blanton

Modernist Informatics
James Purdon

Blasphemous Modernism
Steven Pinkerton

The Poetry of the Americas
Harris Feinsod

The Modernist Art of Queer Survival
Benjamin Bateman

In and Out of Sight
Alix Beeston

In and Out of Sight

Modernist Writing and the Photographic Unseen

Alix Beeston

OXFORD
UNIVERSITY PRESS

Oxford University Press is a department of the University of Oxford. It furthers
the University's objective of excellence in research, scholarship, and education
by publishing worldwide. Oxford is a registered trade mark of Oxford University
Press in the UK and certain other countries.

Published in the United States of America by Oxford University Press
198 Madison Avenue, New York, NY 10016, United States of America.

© Oxford University Press 2018

CIP data is on file at the Library of Congress
ISBN 978–0–19–069016–8

9 8 7 6 5 4 3 2 1
Printed by Sheridan Books, Inc., United States of America

For Davey

Contents

Foreword ix
Acknowledgments xiii

Introduction: Things Normally Unseen   1

1. Bodies Bad and Gentle: The Surrealist Convulsions
   of Gertrude Stein's *Three Lives*   30

2. Black Flesh Is White Ash: Reframing Jean Toomer's *Cane*   66

3. Frozen in the Glassy, Bluestreaked Air: John Dos Passos's
   Photographic Metropolis   108

4. Torn, Burned, and Yet Dancing: F. Scott Fitzgerald's
   Hollywood Writing   147

   Coda: Shared Hallucinations   188

Notes 197
Works Cited 231
Index 253

Foreword

In his essay "If I Were Four-and-Twenty" (1919), W. B. Yeats writes, "One day when I was twenty-three or twenty-four this sentence seemed to form in my head, without my willing it, much as sentences form when we are half-asleep: 'Hammer your thoughts into unity.' For days I could think of nothing else, and for years I tested all I did by that sentence." Apparently Yeats's thoughts hammered themselves into unity, and when they had done so, they instructed him to go and do likewise. It's a baptismal moment for Yeats; shortly after leaving art school he receives his anointing and his calling—to be a modernist (though that's not the terminology he would have used). The goal of his art would be to transform T. S. Eliot's "immense panorama of futility and anarchy which is contemporary history" into Ezra Pound's "rose in the steel dust"—in part by using what Eliot, borrowing the term from James Joyce, called the "mythical method." And the rest, as they say, is literary history.

That's one myth of the modern: Alix Beeston's *In and Out of Sight: Modernist Writing and the Photographic Unseen* presents a very different narrative, one that our conventional accounts of the field have most often sought to suppress. In one of her most compact formulations, Beeston writes in the introduction, "the composite form of modernist writing disturbs, fragments, and shows as heterogeneous that which is imagined to consolidate the modernist field." Versions of this argument have of course been mounted before, suggesting that the monumental achievement and achievements of high modernism were never as articulate (or as monumental) as their makers made out. Nor, of course, could they have been: when Samuel Beckett, for instance, told Israel Shenker in 1956 that "there isn't a syllable that's superfluous" in all of Joyce's writing, it's a bit hard to reconcile with *Finnegans Wake*, the work that occupied most of Joyce's last two decades. Since at least the advent of the "new modernist studies" in the closing years of the last century, we've recognized that modernism never was all that its early practitioners and apologists claimed for it—"nor was meant to be," Prufrock might add. But through the kinds of heterogeneity embraced by Beeston, we've also learned that it was more.

In furthering and complicating this line of analysis, *In and Out of Sight* elegantly accomplishes something quite new: it suggests in very real, local, and material ways the intermedia synergies that animate various modernist art forms. Although the book's subtitle singles out photography, Beeston's remarkable chapter on John Dos Passos's *Manhattan Transfer* actually pushes back against the filmic intertext of that novel. That is, it's something of a cliché of Dos Passos scholarship to suggest that his writing was influenced by film; Dos Passos himself, late in his career and perhaps willing to say anything to attract attention to his writing, went along with this assessment. Beeston here persuasively demonstrates that claim to be ahistorical, showing that it's not cinematic montage but rather the ramshackle assemblage of the Ziegfeld Follies variety shows that helps explain the novel's strange stylistic and structural choices. When a version of this work was published in *PMLA* (May 2016), it was titled "A 'Leg Show Dance' in a Skyscraper": and in Beeston's reading, it's upon and by means of those glamorous, disarticulated limbs that the covert work of aesthetic disarticulation gets carried out. As she explains it early in her introduction, "This book maps the connective and disconnective tissue of modernist narration onto the conspicuous appearances and disappearances of female bodies that are constituted in, and constituent of, that narration." Such ontological oscillation, Beeston shows, is fundamental to modernist articulations of race as well as gender.

Thus when it comes to Gertrude Stein's controversial 1909 novellas, Beeston writes, "In its bad bodies and its bad form, *Three Lives* achieves a Surrealist convulsion of gendered, nativist, and racialist oppositions that have served to withhold subjecthood and power to its female characters." In its stylized gestures toward photography, she argues, Stein's neorealism "not only recognizes its complicity in racialist and nativist taxonomies, but . . . tells the traumatic stories of the female bodies that are the objects of those taxonomies through silence, the end of discourse." When she turns her attention to Jean Toomer's *Cane*—among modernism's most notoriously fragmentary narratives—Beeston argues that "the representation of black women as an act of violence" and the obscenity of "the ritualized scene of lynching" necessitate "taking back the camera, tearing apart the image, giving it a new frame."

Because Beeston moves so deftly and persuasively through her literary texts, it's easy to miss just how extraordinary that archive is: one of the subtler delights of this book is its theoretically informed archival work. Too often these, the "theoretically informed" and the "archival," form two different camps; but Beeston arrives at the archive with a fully formed and informed theoretical apparatus already in place, helping her to discover things that the mere bibliophile would never imagine to look for. Her results are frequently a revelation.

In and Out of Sight weaves compelling close readings of literary form into a complex fabric of secondary literature in several vibrant fields; it brings to light a wide range of unexamined or underexamined archival materials; its collation of primary texts and authors cuts a wide swath through the first half of the twentieth century and allows for a tightly argued yet wide-ranging examination of the topic; and the argument hits central questions in literary modernism while rippling outward into several adjacent fields (for example, feminism, visual culture studies, American and African American studies, cinema studies), making original contributions to these as well.

We're pleased to be able to bring Alix Beeston's challenging and rewarding new work to you.

Kevin Dettmar
Mark Wollaeger

Acknowledgments

I always love reading the acknowledgment sections of scholarly books: those few pages that store all the warm, living stuff that sustains the labor of writing. Among other things (so many other things, probably too many other things), this book wants to keep its ends loose, its scholarly debts on the table, by a composite method that traces and extends the web of contributions and kindnesses—scholarly or otherwise—that conditioned it in the first place. As much as the active assistance and input of colleagues, institutions, friends, and family that it honors, this note of acknowledgment is an essential part of this book's work.

This book began as a doctoral dissertation in the Department of English at the University of Sydney under the brilliant supervision of my mentor, friend, and champion, Sarah Gleeson-White—a model of intellectual and interpersonal generosity whom I hope to spend my life emulating. Many other scholars in the English Department have supported me since the first time I entered a lecture hall in the Woolley building as a coffee-carrying, backpack-wielding undergraduate student with a bad haircut and a nascent love for the discipline, now over a decade ago. I am especially grateful to Paul Giles, Peter Marks, Melissa Hardie, Kate Lilley, David Kelly, Mark Byron, Vanessa Smith, Liam Semler, and Matthew Sussman, for their scholarly interest, practical help, and corridor chats.

Alongside government support for my PhD research through the Australian Postgraduate Award, the University of Sydney enabled me to conduct the archival research that forms the basis of this study through the Postgraduate Research Support Scheme and the award of a Postgraduate Research Travel Grant. Many librarians and curators offered knowledgeable and prompt assistance at the Beinecke Rare Book and Manuscript Library at Yale University, the Department of Rare Books and Special Collections at Princeton University Library, and the Special Collections Library at the University of Virginia. Hoke Perkins and the staff at the Harrison Institute at this last institution, where I worked for a month in 2012 as the Lillian Gary Taylor Fellow in American Literature, were especially supportive of my work on Dos Passos.

In very real terms, the completion of this book was made possible by the School of English, Communication, and Philosophy at Cardiff University, which warmly welcomed me as a new member of faculty in October 2017—and, previously, the United States Studies Centre at the University of Sydney and Anglican Deaconess Ministries (ADM) in Sydney. I was affiliated as a postdoctoral researcher at these last two institutions in 2016 and 2017, and ADM, in particular, provided a calm and collegial home for me to revise, revise, and revise some more. I am especially obliged to Kate Harrison Brennan and Annette Pierdziwol, for their belief in this project and in the importance of the humanities in Australia. For their help in sourcing the beautiful images included in this book and securing the permissions for their reproduction—a labyrinthine task that tested my patience but somehow, seemingly, never theirs—I am grateful to Subhadra Das at the Galton Collection, University College London; Lauren Lean at George Eastman House; Jocelyne Dudding at the Museum of Archaeology and Anthropology, University of Cambridge; Eben English at Boston Public Library; Claire Guttinger at Collège de France Archives; Erika Babatz at the Bauhaus-Archiv (and Pepper Stetler for leading me in the right direction with regards to László Moholy-Nagy's work); Jule Schaffer at the August Sander Archiv; Glen Menzies at Viscopy; Liz Kurtulik Mercuri at Art Resource; Nicholas Keyzer at Schaeffer Fine Arts Library, University of Sydney; Mark Rogovin at the Rogovin Collection; Jignasa Ghaghda at Getty Images; Melissa Barton at the Beinecke; Thomas Lisanti at the New York Public Library; Jacklyn Burns at the J. Paul Getty Museum; Todd Ifft at Photofest; and Jeri Wagner at the Metropolitan Museum of Art. There would not have been any images at all in this book without the financial support of the Department of English at the University of Sydney, which provided a small grant for image costs, and the Australian Academy of the Humanities, which provided a larger one through the 2017 Publication Subsidy Scheme. My thanks to both organizations.

Early drafts of sections from this book were presented as papers at many venues, including the Modernist Studies Association conference (with the support of Travel Grants in 2015 and 2016); the Pacific Ancient and Modern Language Association conference (with the support of a Graduate Student Scholarship in 2012); the Australian and New Zealand American Studies Association conference;

the Australian Modernist Studies Network Symposium; the Workshop Series at the Centre for Modernism Studies in Australia; and, at the University of Sydney, the Department of English Research Seminar Series and the American Cultures Workshop. I am very appreciative of Jed Evans and Lucas Thompson who, like Sarah Gleeson-White, read the book in manuscript in one or more of its many iterations, and whose thoughtful comments made it immeasurably better than it would have been. This is also true of the manuscript reports by the anonymous readers for Oxford University Press, and, before that, the PhD examination reports of Paula Rabinowitz, Michael North, and Mark Goble—all of which offered shrewd insights that helped me to see much more clearly what this project is actually about.

The quality and substance of my writing were vastly improved by the rigorous process of peer review at *PMLA* and *Modernism/modernity*; I would like to thank the anonymous readers and the members of these journals' editorial boards for their serious, constructive consideration of my work. A version of a section of this book's third chapter appears as "A 'Leg Show Dance' in a Skyscraper: The Sequenced Mechanics of John Dos Passos's *Manhattan Transfer*," in *PMLA* 131.3 (2016), and abridged sections from the Introduction and Chapter 1 were published as "Images in Crisis: *Three Lives*'s Vanishing Women" on the Print Plus platform of *Modernism/modernity* in May 2017. The book's coda discussion of Walker Evans is expanded into a much wider treatment of *American Photographs*—in the context of Evans's and James Agee's classic 1941 documentary work *Let Us Now Praise Famous Men*—in "Icons of Depression," *Arizona Quarterly: A Journal of American Literature, Culture, and Theory* 73.2 (2017).

I owe tremendous thanks to Kevin Dettmar and Mark Wollaeger, the hugely gracious editors of the Modernist Literature and Culture Series, for making this book possible. I was so buoyed by our first meeting at the MSA in Boston—and so thrilled at the possibility of being a part of your incredible series—that I immediately went out and bought myself the leather biker jacket I had been coveting for years. This was, admittedly, a preemptive celebration, so thanks for justifying it by backing this book all the way into print. I am thankful also to Brendan O'Neill, for his early interest in the project (and the gin and tonics), and to my editor Sarah Pirovitz and her assistant Abigail Johnson, who, alongside members of the production teams at Oxford and at Newgen Knowledge Works, have handled every stage of this project with expertise and enthusiasm. Particular thanks are due to Victoria Danahy, whose copyediting work on the book in manuscript was light and meticulous—an artful combination, and one by which she demonstrated her clear understanding of the aims and spirit of this project.

I am deeply grateful to my family, especially my parents, Caron and Albert Baumgartner, and my sister and lifelong best friend, Lara Baumgartner, for all the big and small ways they care for me, as well as to the Beeston family, especially Lee and Allan, who have carved out a space for me to belong with them. In large part this book was written under the roof of Fitzroy Palace, the world's best share house, and with the support of Bel Clough, Stevie Barnard, and Alec Sewell— three of the biggest-hearted and most open-handed people I know. To this list of friends who are really family I must add my thanks to Nathanael van der Reyden, who shares all of their best qualities, as do Alison Moffitt, Matthew Moffitt, Esther Butcher, Owen Butcher, Lauren McCorquodale, Josh Tickell, Clare Woodley, and Natasha Moore. My church community at Christ Church Inner West has kept me alive, in many senses of the word, over the last six years; I am particularly thankful to Andrew Katay, Fiona Smartt, and Megan Winch—as well as to Paige Katay, who helped out with the more tedious tasks associated with turning a book project into a book.

My fullest gratitude is reserved for my husband, Davey, who lives more gently and kindly in this world than anyone I have ever met. This book is dedicated to him, whose laughing, cooking, cleaning, reassuring, abiding embrace enables me to be the person that I was made to be and to do the work that I was made to do.

In and Out of Sight

Introduction

Things Normally Unseen

In 1876, Francis Galton, the cousin of Charles Darwin and the founder of eugenics, reported to the Anthropological Institute of London his newest physiognomic method for uncovering and defining human "types." Galton's composite portraiture was an exercise in re-photography that co-opted the mechanical precision of the photograph for a pseudoscience of predetermined sociological and biological categories. Galton gathered sets of standardized quarter-length portraits of criminals and the infirm, as well as people defined by the indices of race, class, and gender, and layered them on top of one another, dividing the exposure time by the number of individual photographs. By evenly combining the images, he turned "irregularities" or inconsistencies among the faces into ghostly smudges, performing a series of erasures in the hope of isolating, capturing, and displaying "the central physiognomic type of any race or group."[1] The subject of the composite portrait became both less and more than a subject; the portrait depicted "no man in particular," as Galton wrote, but rather "an imaginary figure possessing the average features of any given group of men. These ideal faces have a surprising air of reality. Nobody who glanced at one of them for the first time would doubt its being the likeness of a living person" (see Figures I.1–I.3).[2]

Whatever vitality Galton perceived in his photographic portraits, the swimming form of these mathematically averaged and mashed-up faces is decidedly eerie. The portraits make the photographic surface into—or rather disclose its

Fig I.1 Francis Galton, Composite photograph of a family: a mother and two daughters, 1882. © University College London Galton Collection

status as—a palimpsest, a repository of mysterious remains. Far from effacing the particularities of the individual images that make up the composite whole, the shadows and tracings of those particularities are entrancingly apparent. The eye gropes for the residue of idiosyncrasy and individuality that Galton hoped to obscure. Etched in a hazy play of joinings and junctures, Galton's photographic figurations are riven with an interpretative vagueness and instability that belies their claims to the scientific knowing and controlling of the bodies of others through photographic mechanisms. They query, rather than codify, the discursive map of congenital essences that Galton imagines and images upon bodily surfaces.

Galton boasted that his composite portraits were "pictorial statistics," and more specifically "the equivalents of those large statistical tables whose total, divided by the number of cases, and entered in the bottom line, are the averages."[3] Intriguingly, he claims a metaphorical correspondence not between the composite portrait and the averages that line the bottom of "those large statistical tables," but between the portrait and the statistical table itself. Reaching to align the composite portrait with the props of scientific data, Galton's conception of the photographic image as a tabulated series allegorizes his efforts to recover perspicacity for it. These efforts involve exceeding the physical limits of the photograph—its arrested moment, its bounded

Fig I.2 Francis Galton, Composite photograph of a family: two sons, two daughters, father, and mother, 1882. © University College London Galton Collection

Fig I.3 Francis Galton, Composite photograph of a family: father and two sons, his brother, and his brother's son, 1882. © University College London Galton Collection

frame, its paper-thin surface—through processes of repetition and accumulation. But in calling attention to the material system of the image, its thickly embedded strata of profilmic shards, he promotes a reading of his composite portraiture that dismantles or decodes it. In effectively converting a technology of layered superimposition into one of orderly, listed juxtaposition, Galton's photograph-as-table implies both the susceptibility of the composite portrait to indexing and its status as an index. It lays bare the portrait's semihidden inventory of image-fragments, revealing the multiplicity measured in the interstices between its foliated parts. Rather than a genealogy of biological types, Galton's composite portraiture offers a genealogy of its own mediated technology: a history of textual reproduction.

Amid other photographic countenances, which appear and disappear across this book, the muddy and muddled faces of these nineteenth-century composite images provide a surprising but compelling model for the poetics and politics of modernist literary texts written in the early decades of the twentieth century. Looking at and through Galton's portraits permits a new theory of literary textuality in modernism—a theory that occasions a feminist reappraisal of its ethical possibilities. Galton, of course, already occupies a fairly prominent position in the literary history of the United States. His hereditarian projects, particularly his studies of twins in the 1870s and his attempts to develop a racial index for human fingerprints in the late 1880s and early 1890s, are the central context for reading Mark Twain's 1894 novella, *Pudd'nhead Wilson*—a tale of look-alikes switched at birth that has been called "the first post-Galtonian novel."[4] Yet there are less direct but equally pervasive lines of influence and equivalence connecting modernist writing to Galton's experiments in composite portraiture. This is especially true when these experiments are seen to exemplify photography as "a sequential, grammatical art,"[5] a technology defined from its beginnings by varied processes of assemblage that, by a visual syntax of spacing, do not so much compose the real as composite it.

As the faces of Galton's composite subjects dissolve and deliquesce into the edges of the photographic frame, they are relevant dialectically rather than strictly causally to the modernist literary texts I discuss in this book. Gertrude Stein's self-published first literary work, the 1909 short-story sequence *Three Lives*; Jean Toomer's 1923 poetry and prose admixture, *Cane*; John Dos Passos's experimental multilinear novel, *Manhattan Transfer*, published in 1925; and the writing that comprises the labor of the final year of F. Scott Fitzgerald's life, in Hollywood in 1940, the unfinished novel *The Last Tycoon* and the screenplay "Cosmopolitan": each of these texts encompass a number of generic borderlines. But they are all composite in form inasmuch as they operate in a segmented, serialized mode of narration and characterization that constructs narrative persons reiteratively, as aggregates or assemblages. These modernist literary texts share an intervallic structural, aesthetic, and narrative logic that retains—even mines—fissures and seams that are as diverting as those that define Galton's composite portraits.

More powerfully, the composite writing of Stein, Toomer, Dos Passos, and Fitzgerald is shaped by the figure and activity of what I conceptualize, after photography's densely laminous and sequenced bodies, as the woman-in-series. The reiterated, sutured body of the serialized woman in *Three Lives, Cane, Manhattan Transfer,* "Cosmopolitan," and *The Last Tycoon* is coextensive with the reiterated, sutured bodies of the texts she populates. Linked to and formulated through other female bodies along the linear track of the written word, the woman-in-series is made into one of many as she herself is "too many," which is the accusation of the physician Jeff Campbell to his patient–lover Melanctha Herbert in *Three Lives.*[6] Literary modernism's "too many" women are complex, taking the word as both an adjective and a noun: they are abstruse, convoluted, inscrutable, and they are multiple, compound, agglomerated.

This book maps the connective and disconnective tissue of modernist narration onto the conspicuous appearances and disappearances of female bodies that are constituted in, and constituent of, that narration. In a theoretical move that mimes the logic of incongruous juxtaposition that defines photography as form and practice, I bring new work in photography studies, and especially the cross-disciplinary discussions in what is known as the still–moving field, to bear on the study of modernist *écriture*. By interpreting composite modernist writing in relation to the aesthetic principles and ontological disclosures of serial or sequenced photography—or, in the case of Fitzgerald's Hollywood writing, its close cousin, the photogrammatic track of film—my discussion of several key modernist texts destabilizes oppositions of power and vulnerability as they relate to the interactions of subjects and objects in the representational realm. If, as Steve McCaffery claims, the textual fragment is "the mark of an absence previously present," the composite writing of Stein, Toomer, Dos Passos, and Fitzgerald might well manifest in and by its interstitial format the "presence–absence that constitutes the attraction and the fascination of the Sirens" that Maurice Blanchot associates with the photographic image.[7] Roland Barthes, in his classic work on photography, *Camera Lucida*, glosses Blanchot's formulation in terms of photography's casting of the human face in the future anterior tense. The photograph presents "death in the future" through the "absolute past of the pose"; it carries the "catastrophe" and "defeat of Time": "*that* is dead and *that* is going to die."[8] But what if, in refocusing our attention away from the melancholic temporality of the photograph, it turns out that photography's Sirens do more by their absent presence than lure and fascinate? What if their oscillation between these problematic states of being also sanctions their refusal to play the temptress—and, in the process, establishes alternative visions of female subjectivity before the camera?

These questions shape some of the best new studies of photography and visual culture, and they also gesture toward critical concerns for the study of literature. Modernist literary studies, specifically, must challenge the gendered and racialized logics of inclusion and exclusion that continue to define the limits of its inquiry, even after the proliferation of "new" modernisms over the last two decades.[9] We need new theoretical figurations of female subjectivity that, on the one hand, recognize the intersections of gender and other categories of social difference in the processes of objectification; and, on the other hand, work to exceed, diffuse, or overturn the usually hostile encounters between female subjects and those who "subjectify" them, to borrow Samira Kawash's term.[10] Recent work by feminist and queer studies scholars searches out the radical potential of the absent–present female body in photography and cinema by augmenting the psychoanalytic concept of femininity as an operation of masquerade, an elaborate "mask" or "decorative layer [that] conceals a non-identity."[11] Enfolding viewer and viewed "in a dense intermediate viewing space," this work substitutes a model of exchange and reciprocity between (male) subjects and (female) objects for the more unilateral model associated with the voyeuristic and fetishizing Mulveyan male gaze.[12] For Karen Beckman, for instance, it is the woman who vanishes in film and photography who, in posing "elusive vanishing and reappearance as alternatives to finite disappearance," radically questions her own status as spectacle.[13] In a similar vein, Ann Anlin Cheng, in her reading of Josephine Baker's glossy photographic self-fashioning, embraces Baker's body as a motile, eroticized surface on which we might appreciate "an injunction of injured subjectivity." Cheng locates the "agency" of "racialized subjects looking to free themselves from the burden of racial legibility" in the visual captivity of "the (specifically photographic) pleasure of suspension: that pause or delay before a person becomes a person and a thing a thing."[14]

The feminist reevaluation of the photographic and cinematographic image offers an opportunity for reconceiving subject–object relations in modernist literature, along with the ethical potentialities of its writing of the female body and its experiences. Part of a vast corpus of composite or serialized photography in the late nineteenth and early twentieth centuries, Galton's portraits are an especially striking instantiation of what Régis Durand calls "images *in crisis*," in which "[s]omething in them is always trying to run off, to vanish."[15] They emblematize the dissolution of the unitary, transcendental Cartesian subject propelled, in part, by the proliferation of technologies of mass reproduction. Hence the formal interstices that riddle and cleft Galton's composites are lauded as the material precondition for a tabulated biological essentialism even as they form the trace evidence of its tabulation and, ultimately, its failure. These images unveil the involved, politicized processes behind—and the stark limitations of—typological conceptions of identity. Simultaneously, they suggest that these conceptions are open to revision: to being undone, pulled to pieces. Divulging the essential lack at the base of taxonomies of representation organized around gender, race, ethnicity, and class, Galton's composites also turn that lack, that absence, into a locus of rich contingency, a metaphorical space of resistance to this representational order. It is in this way that the composite portraits illustrate the doubled function of the interstice in the composite modernist writing of Stein, Toomer, Dos Passos, and Fitzgerald. Commensurate to the operations of visual spacing in photographic projects in this period, ranging from the pseudoscientific to the fully artistic, the gap or interval in these writings signifies at once as a mark of trauma, the wounding of typologized representation, and as a vehicle for evading or defending against such trauma: a zone of withdrawal, incompliancy, or active recalcitrance, particularly for female characters. Just as the bodies in Galton's composite portraits seem to run off, in Durand's terms, outstripping and confounding eugenicist imperatives, so too do the bodies of the serialized women in the literary texts I analyze. From the subversive tactics of silence and disappearance actuated progressively through the repetitious lives and deaths of Anna, Melanctha, and Lena in Stein's *Three Lives*, to the visual and aural equivocality of Helen Wales in Fitzgerald's screenplay, "Cosmopolitan," the woman-in-series stages the insurrectionary potential of the visible–invisible, silent–speaking female subject in modernist writing.

Reading subjection with insurrection, and, sometimes, subjection as insurrection, my pivotal action is to transvalue gendered and racialized oppositions in order to reveal the radical potential of the subordinate terms: privileging absence over presence, disappearance over appearance, and silence over speech. No doubt this line of argument carries some significant risks. As much as I am haunted by the swampy figures and oblique gazes of Galton's composite images, I am also troubled by the prospect that this study might, by its recuperative posture, sentimentalize the narrative worlds of *Three Lives, Cane, Manhattan Transfer,* "Cosmopolitan," and *The Last Tycoon.* As literary scholars have demonstrated, each of these texts, in different ways, dramatizes the tragic and often violent subordination of female characters to the racist and patriarchal social order of modern life; and their authors, without exception, show marked tendencies toward essentialist thought, racialist, nativist, gendered, or otherwise.

Without ignoring how the texts I examine temper a wider narrative of feminist resistance in modernist literature, this book works to recognize the possibilities of resistance to the mechanisms of psychic, social, and physical domination even in texts that are preoccupied with—or complicit in—those mechanisms. In the essay "Nietzsche, Genealogy, History," Michel Foucault argues that the search for descent in genealogical study "is not the erecting of foundations: on the contrary, it disturbs what was previously considered immobile; it fragments what was thought unified; it shows the heterogeneity of what was imagined consistent with itself."[16] Galton's positivist dream of demarcated cultural norms and regulated social deviance is a case in point, as it is disrupted and defeated by the "messy contingency" of the photographic image that it sought to harness and tame.[17] As David Campany and other scholars of visual culture suggest, the photographic composite or sequence is primed not for the articulation but the disarticulation of teleological formulations and narrative syllogisms. Intrinsically elliptical, in that it both contains ellipses and is compiled elliptically, it is predisposed to be "allusive and tangential."[18] And, it finds its pleasures in substitutionary play, in conceptual slippages and inversions, and in ghostly apparitions that are always about to run off, to disappear into interstices and lacunae, circumventing the attentions and intrusions of those whose objectifying gaze is most ardent. Likewise, the composite form of modernist writing disturbs, fragments, and shows as heterogeneous that which is imagined to consolidate the modernist literary field. As women's bodies in Stein, Toomer, Dos Passos, and Fitzgerald move in and out of sight (or earshot), from presence to absence and back again, they perform a series of more-or-less evasive maneuvers in and through the intervals of the composite text. These textual openings can serve as sanctuaries from, or passageways out of, the social and political order whose injurious dictates they also materialize.

Writing That Still Moves

Within literary studies, the cultures and technologies of photography have usually served as a context for understanding the literature and society of the nineteenth century rather than those of the twentieth century. Nancy Armstrong, for instance, claims that photographic images supplied the mimetic standard for realist fiction in the Victorian era. Consequently, the abandoning of positivist commitments in modernist writing would seem to entail the rejection of photography.[19] However, as Michael North has pointed out, Armstrong's line of inquiry disregards the "distancing and aestheticizing effect" of photography from its earliest days and its function in producing a veritable "cabinet of wonders" of hitherto-unseen sights.[20] North's critique builds on the work of scholars such as Martin Jay and Karen Jacobs, which argues that the invention and dissemination of the photographic image served to erode the very scopic regime it seemed to validate.[21] Edgar Allan Poe may have been seduced, in 1840, by the "positively perfect mirror" of the daguerreotype, but, far from offering absolute verisimilitude, photography in its earliest forms could not reproduce color, and its long exposure times necessitated an artificial stiffness of pose in its subjects—as well as a surface multiplicity that was reconstructed, later in the century, in Galton's composites.[22] Walter Benjamin refers to this effect when he cites Bertolt Brecht in *The Arcades Project*: "With the older, less light sensitive apparatus, multiple expressions would appear on the plate, which was exposed for rather long periods of time." The "composed" face of early photography renders a "livelier and more universal expression" (see, for example, Figure I.4).[23]

Fig I.4 Daguerreotype of two unidentified women, twins, ca. 1855. Image courtesy of George Eastman Museum

With its open discrepancies of focus, perspective, and framing in relation to the actions of the human eye, the photograph played a critical role in undermining the claims of monocular Cartesian perspectivalism. It did not so much "erase all obstacles separating seeing from knowing" as instigate a crisis of belief in the continuity between the two.[24] In this light, Galton's composite subjects reflect the troubling of "the truth of the body as a sight," which resulted, paradoxically, from the proliferation of the photographic image from the mid-nineteenth century on.[25] What Mark Seltzer calls Galton's "standardizing schema" is scrambled by the photograph's lexical contiguity to "the absolute Particular, the sovereign Contingency," in Barthes's terms.[26] This perturbation of visual truth was compounded by the visual mistakes and puzzles attendant in photography's purchase on the world through its production of an endless series of homologous "notes on reality," as Susan Sontag suggests: the incongruous inversions and mergers of bodies and environs, of the animate and the inanimate, that comprise photography's surrealist practices of "dissociative seeing."[27] Ultimately, as Aaron Scharf writes with reference to the chronophotographic revelation of "phases of locomotion . . . which lay beyond the visual threshold," the uncovering of Benjamin's "unconscious" substratum of visual experience meant that the "meaning of the term 'truth to nature' lost its force: what was true could not always be seen, and what could be seen was not always true."[28]

In the evocative terms of the film critic Jean-Louis Comolli, the photograph represents both "the triumph and the grave of the eye. . . . Decentered, in panic, thrown into confusion by all this new magic of the visible, the human eye finds itself affected with a series of limits and doubts."[29] For North, accordingly, photography was a crucial resource and discursive interface for twentieth-century modernist writers and artists—and for nineteenth-century realist writers and artists—not for its fidelity to the "real" but for its implication of the "ignored and unexpected" aspects of the real.[30] What modernist writers admired in photography was its capacity to turn up to view the undersurface of the visual realm—and, in turn, the socialized physiology and slippery subjectivity of vision itself.

The reappraisal of the objective status of the photograph contradicts the persistent belief in an absolute split between nineteenth-century realism and twentieth-century modernism. Indeed, the continuities between realism and modernism are implied by the powerful consonance between two recent studies on writing and photography, both published in 2008. In the first instance, Daniel Novak's *Realism, Photography, and Nineteenth-Century Fiction* investigates the bizarre, distorted, and infinitely malleable bodies of Victorian photography. These bodies are fragmented through their collaged incorporation in photographic albums, a key vernacular use of photographic technology following the popularization of the *carte-de-visite* in the 1850s and bolstered by the development of paper roll film and the handheld Kodak camera in the 1880s. At the same time, these bodies were subject to retouching, combinatory, and other doctoring practices. Novak argues that it is precisely the abstracting properties of photography that shape the fictional bodies and narratives of nineteenth-century realist fiction. What he theorizes as realism's homogenized "novel bodies," bodies that are "merely a combination of interchangeable pieces or who are composite, abstract, and spectral types,"[31] is compatible with Stuart Burrows's trope of the "marvelous twins" in modernist American writing. According to Burrows's *A Familiar Strangeness*, the world of photography depicted in texts by Nathaniel Hawthorne, Henry James, William Faulkner, and Zora Neale Hurston is one of radical equivalence and "strangely indistinguishable subjects," in which every person is a reproducible type of every other person.[32] In spite of their different emphases, for both Novak and Burrows the unreality of photography produces a dilemma of resemblance and typicality that is proper to the episteme of doubt that emerges from the tensions between the "optical truths and visual pleasures," in Jacob's words, generated through photography's "documentary and visionary modalities."[33]

Like Novak and Burrows, I identify the "photography effect" in literary texts as a host of historical, theoretical, and representational problems in the late nineteenth and early twentieth centuries.[34] But I am interested in an unexplored valency of this effect in the modernist writing of Stein, Toomer, Dos Passos, and Fitzgerald. Burrows's "marvelous twins" are "characters whose relationship to one another is better understood according to a model of serial production rather than by the mimetic model of original and copy."[35] Burrows does not elaborate particularly on this "serial production," though ostensibly it is inherent to the actions of doubling and replication he details. I take as my focus the wider operations of seriality and repetition latent in this account.[36] The photography effect subsists in *Three Lives*, *Cane*, and *Manhattan Transfer*—and, as I will explain, the photogram effect in *The Last Tycoon* and "Cosmopolitan"—in their privileging of equivocality, ambiguity, and incongruity through their textual principle of sequenced assemblage and juxtaposition. According to this principle, formal interstices and gaps are raised as signposts to the limits of the eye and of language and, by extension, to the limits of visual and discursive objectification itself. In this sense, modernist writing is photographic in its connective and disconnective structuration, its tensile relation between the singular and the multiple, which extends into a dynamic interplay between coherence and incoherence, continuity and discontinuity, and movement and stasis.

In conjoining photographic praxis and discourse to a composite mode of writing in the early twentieth century, this book represents the first full-length study to apply the insights of the still–moving field in the detailed analysis of modernist literary texts.[37] Named for the double dialectical relation from which a slew of

Fig I.5 Unknown photographer, "High-class" and "low-class" Māoris, ca. 1879. © Museum of Archaeology and Anthropology, University of Cambridge

studies published in the last decade take their key terms of reference, this field of study offers an affirmative critique of the interactions and relays between the photographic and the cinematographic.[38] The interdependence and reciprocity of the two media are derived, in the first instance, from their shared technological basis: the use of chemical processes for recording images of reality on a translucent negative medium and of machineries of light projection and enlargement in reproduction. Much as with my own formalist pulling-apart of the photographic pieces that comprise Galton's swampy composite subjects, still–moving scholars disarrange the photograph in conceiving of it as torn "between narrativity and stasis," as George Baker writes.[39] Barthes wanted to distinguish the temporality of the "simple photograph" from that of the film still according to what he described as the photograph's lack of a "diegetic horizon, the possibility of configuration" that corresponds to the cinema's "permutational unfolding."[40] But for Baker and others, what is most suggestive about Barthes's attempts to separate the photographic and the cinematic is his difficulty in doing so. This is evidenced, first, in Barthes's location of the "filmic" in an analysis of film stills from Sergei Eisenstein, and second, in his location of the "photographic" in a quality of movement onward and away from the image: the *punctum*, the "sting, speck, cut, little hole" that tears open the photographic *studium*.[41]

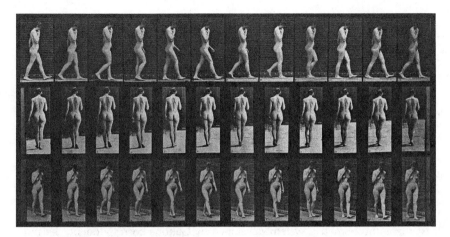

Fig I.6 Eadweard Muybridge, Woman walking, right hand at chin, plate 14 in *Animal Locomotion: An Electro-Photographic Investigation of Consecutive Phases of Animal Movements, 1872–1885*, 1887. Image courtesy of the Trustees of Boston Public Library

Baker finds the "unfolding of an unavoidable discursivity" that Barthes reserves for the cinematographic embedded in the social and the artistic uses of photography by the early part of the twentieth century, including those uses that entailed the photograph's "aesthetic organization into sequence and series."[42] In fact, as David Campany explains, the development of photography was organized around the conceits of "time and movement" through varied "procedures of assembly" deployed in the production of albums, archives, montages, collages, slideshows, and so on, long before cinema animated it at a rate of twenty-four stills per second.[43] With the advent of the era of photography's "industrial madness,"[44] ushered in by the introduction of negative–positive printing processes and collodion-coated glass negatives, a host of photographic experiments in the sciences and the arts in the second half of the nineteenth century sought to defy the conceptual deficiency embodied in the basic singularity of the photograph. Anthropologists, for example, distributed photographic images into spatial maps or grids in sociological storyboards that tracked narratives of racialized evolutionary development, as in the image of "high-class" and "low-class" Māoris, likely made for the 1879 Sydney International Exhibition, the first World's Fair in the Southern Hemisphere (Figure I.5).[45] Similarly, in the few decades prior to the invention of the cinema, the chronophotographic movement studies of Eadweard Muybridge, Étienne-Jules Marey, and Ottomar Anschütz worked to expand photography's revelatory powers by recording multiple images of a moving object or body on one or more photographic plate. These images were published or projected as long, juxtaposed bands or serialized patterns (see, for example, Figure I.6).

In phrasing the instant as a kind of incarceration from which the photograph must be liberated, Galton's composite portraits, his "equivalents of those large statistical tables," share a strong resemblance to these more straightforwardly tabulated photographic forms. "If many photographs of a person were taken at different times, perhaps even years apart," Galton once surmised, "their composite would possess that in which a single photograph is deficient."[46] For Allan Sekula, Galton's composite portraiture functions as a "collapsed version" of the vast, hierarchized "shadow archive" of photographic images, a bureaucratic paradigm by which the panoptic principle is brought to bear on everyday life from the second half of the nineteenth century on. Like other nineteenth-century uses of photography in taxonomic disciplines including physiognomy, phrenology, and criminology—not least the anthropometric system developed by Galton's correspondent, the pioneering criminologist Alphonse Bertillon—the composites manifest a statistical passion for quantification and numeral ranking in their attempt to command the "authority . . . of the general, abstract proposition."[47] Thus the same principle of temporal and spatial compression that animated the chronophotographers' racing pursuit of the technicalities of human and animal locomotion also defined Galton's (slower) push against the representational limits of the photographic portrait. This formal consistency is nowhere more evident than in the case of single-plate chronophotography, such as that produced by Marey during the 1880s at the Station Physiologique in Paris, which presented in a single image the phases of gestural movements as marked intervals within a layered series or a blurry arc (see, for example, Figure I.7). In each instance, dynamism, relationality, and depth are solicited through the compilation or collision of moments in time and space: instant is pitted against instant, whether next to or on top of one another.

Miles Orvell sums up the history of photography as "the history of the countless efforts to overcome the limitations of the medium, to expand upon what a representation of reality might be."[48] But rather than the fullest challenge or highest aim of photographic practice, the irrepressible movement of photography toward multiplicity and sequentiality might well be understood as its elemental property. As the art historian Joel Smith has explained, an overemphasis on the individual, isolated image and its moment of exposure in photography studies has "diverted attention from the longer-term modes of thoughtful effort that go into making photographs," the "acts of attention and accumulation" that compose photography's "editorial phases."[49] In recent years, however, as the "discourse networks" of modern technology have come into focus, scholars increasingly examine photography in its many serialized incarnations—as subject to combinatory processes for scientific or artistic purposes, adapted to social practices such as portrait

Fig I.7 Étienne-Jules Marey, Fixed-plate chronophotograph of a long jump from a standing-still position, ca. 1882. Image courtesy of Collège de France Archives

photography, enrolled in larger, integral bodies of imagery, and so on.[50] Certainly, for the Russian photographer and painter László Moholy-Nagy, writing in 1936, the photographic sequence, which transforms an individual image into "a detail of assembly" within a "concatenation of . . . separate but inseparable parts," is "the log-ical culmination" of the technology, securing its dual function as "the most potent weapon and the tenderest lyric."[51] Beginning in 1921, when Moholy-Nagy made his first successful photograms by placing objects directly on photosensitive paper, the artist—along with others associated with the Bauhaus school—experimented extensively with photographic sequencing and photomontage. Central to his 1925 treatise on photography, *Malerei, Fotografie, Film* [*Painting, Photography, Film*], is a series of over seventy photographs collected from scientific and popular books and periodicals. In their "continuity," the images were intended to produce "a state of increased activity in the observer" commensurate to the "new vision," the trans-formed mode of human perception, which Moholy-Nagy believed was enabled by the photographic camera.[52] With images printed in different directions, and incorporating a vast range of subject matter and techniques—from science to entertainment, from objective portraiture to trick photography—Moholy-Nagy's photographic sequence is deliberately disorienting, but it still works through con-ceptual or visual unities, doublings, and reversals. See, for instance, a page spread hinged by a Muybridgean fascination for the still–moving human body and its technologies, featuring a Charlotte Rudolf photograph of the dancer Gret Palucca, mid-leap, and an image of a speeding motorcyclist (Figure I.8).[53]

In a contemporary postdigital media landscape that is ceaselessly tracked with feeds and streams of images, photography's still–moving formats and contexts have become impossible to ignore. But more than a hundred years ago, at the turn of the twentieth century, the photographer, writer, and inventor Félix Nadar was already describing Paris as a "photographopolis"—a term that, Eduardo Cadava notes, refers not only to "a city that is entirely photographic . . . but to a world that, having become a series of images, is increasingly composed of proliferating copies, repetitions, reproductions, and simulacra."[54] As the dominance of photography only increased in the first half of the new century, especially through the growth in mass media photography, Siegfried Kracauer declared in 1927 that under the conditions of the "blizzard of photographs," "[t]he world itself has taken on a 'photographic face.'"[55] In this period, many of Moholy-Nagy's contemporaries in Europe, North America, and elsewhere began to assemble cumulative photographic archives of that face, notably Eugène Atget's sprawling, idiosyncratic documentation of Paris (1890s–1927) and August Sander's epic portrait project, *Menschen des 20. Jahrhunderts* [*People of the Twentieth Century*] (1910–1950s).[56]

Fig I.8 Page spread, László Moholy-Nagy, *Malerei, Fotografie, Film*, 1925. © Bauhaus-Archiv © Charlotte Rudolph. VG Bild Kunst/Licensed by Viscopy, 2017

Sander, in particular, sought to uncover *Antlitz der Zeit* [*The Face of Our Time*], as he announced in the title of his first book of photographs, published in 1929. He believed that the "existing social order" conformed to a cyclical pattern of distinct social groups that ascended and descended in stages throughout history, beginning with the "earthbound man" upward through to the "representatives of the highest civilization," before returning "back again to the idiot."[57] To make this social order visible, he exploited photography's capacity for mass reproduction in a standardized and serialized form, compiling an atlas of portraits organized into dozens of carefully arranged portfolios. The portfolio "The Woman," for instance, forms a matrix of social relationships out of portraits of working-class and society women (see Figures I.9 and I.10). "A successful photo is only a preliminary step toward the intelligent use of photography," Sander said in a letter of 1951, reflecting on his sequencing of the sixty portraits in *Antlitz der Zeit*. "Photography is like a mosaic that becomes a synthesis only when it is presented en masse."[58]

"The path my feet took was lined with images, whole gardens of pictures," the American photographer and poet Minor White once wrote. "With exposures I picked bouquets, each more vivid than the previous." As for Sander, White, who from the 1940s through the 1960s displayed and published his images in finely wrought sequences, the subject matter of the individual images was less significant than their collective effect. Whether pictures of rocks or people, "[t]he meaning appears in the space between the images. . . . The flow of the sequence eddies in the river of [the viewer's] associations as he [*sic*] passes from picture to picture."[59] This eddying flow of meaning is precisely the effect described by the art historian Blake Stimson in his discussion of the twentieth-century genre of the photographic essay—which includes White's sequences along with seminal works such as Walker Evans's *American Photographs* (1938) and Robert Frank's *The Americans* (1958)—as a version of Theodor Adorno's theory of the essay. In Adorno's terms, the essay, which like photographic technologies is split between art and science from its origins, is a series of linguistic elements that "crystallize as a configuration through their motion."[60] Likewise, Stimson suggests, the photographic essay is a "performative unfolding" that gives up its meaning "in the movement from one picture to the next."[61] For Stimson, the unfolding of serial photography from chronophotography onward involves a conservation of the instant that is displaced, all the way along the line, through the mechanization of the film strip. Sequenced uses of photography leave open "the moment of science," "the space between subject and object, between hypothesis and empirical investigation, between theory and praxis." Their intervallic pauses permit the analysis of "hidden structures."[62]

Fig I.9 August Sander, Mother and daughter: farmer's wife and miner's wife, 1912. © Die Photographische Sammlung/SK Stiftung Kultur–August Sander Archiv, Köln. VG Bild-Kunst/Licensed by Viscopy, 2017

Fig I.10 August Sander, Society lady, ca. 1930. © Die Photographische Sammlung/SK Stiftung Kultur–August Sander Archiv, Köln. VG Bild-Kunst/Licensed by Viscopy, 2017

This is the territory occupied by the virgule in still–moving concepts of the photograph as a "suspended thing" that complies by a neither–nor logical conjunction, conceived by Baker, after Rosalind Krauss, as a "hiccup of indecision, whether fusion or disruption," between *not-narrative* and *not-stasis*.[63] Emily

Dickinson once described herself as one of the "lingering *bad* ones" at the foyers of religious orthodoxy, slinking away to "pause, and ponder, and ponder, and pause."[64] In Dickinson's poetics, the lexicon of this pondering pause is the variable range of long and short, horizontal and vertical dashes that notate the circumnavigatory telling of indefinite, unutterable, "slant" truths: the dash as both a stroke of thought and a chasm of thought.[65] Similarly, for Stimson, the hidden structures of the social and political world are visible in the gaps and fissures of serial photography—recalling Kracauer's proposition that one of photography's most compelling characteristics is its capacity to "reveal things normally unseen," including "the transient," "the small and the big," and the "blind spots of the mind" that "habit and prejudice prevent us from seeing."[66] For Kracauer, as Miriam Hansen explains, "photographic representation has the perplexing ability not only to resemble the world it depicts but also to render it strange, to destroy habitual fictions of self-identity and familiarity."[67]

In Sander's work and in the photographic sequences made by Muybridge and others in the previous century, the visual comparisons activated by the serialized images externalize the discursive and ontological multivalence that is internal to the photograph proper. Although Sander's theory of the circular formation and deformation of civilization more or less coherently defines the system of his portfolios, the photographic portraits themselves do not necessarily support it. As Ulrich Keller argues, the "heroic aspect" of the portraits queries Sander's claim that his "vagrants," vagabonds, and beggars are "infected by decadence" and that the higher-class city dwellers are marred by "brokenness" or "uprootedness."[68] When it comes to Muybridge's studies of human movement, it is no doubt true, as Marta Braun has suggested, that the sequence is a "scientific" form powerfully associated with logic, order, and progression.[69] Yet, although movement is connoted through this form, it is exactly movement that is not captured in the frame-by-frame series of still images. The practical limits of Muybridge's work were not lost on Marey, who, according to Mary Ann Doane, was troubled by the fact that "the positions of the figures were too far apart—it was often impossible to determine how the figure moved from one position to the next. Too much time was lost."[70] Muybridge's scientific purpose is further undermined by the overdetermined *mise-en-scène* of the sequences featuring women's bodies in motion, which are fetishized, as Linda Williams notes, in their "surplus aestheticism" (see, for example, Figure I.11).[71] The spaces between the images, the repeating black lines that form a graphed network on the page, track the conceptual boundaries and terms of Muybridge's sequences.[72] As with the latticed folds and foibles of Galton's physiognomic intrigue, the photographic sequence instantiates the epistemological

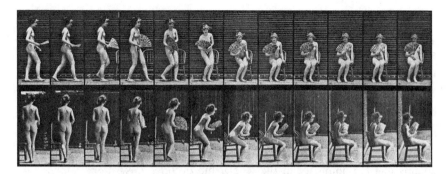

Fig I.11 Eadweard Muybridge, Woman sitting down on chair and opening fan, plate 237 in *Animal Locomotion: An Electro-Photographic Investigation of Consecutive Phases of Animal Movements, 1872–1885*, 1887. Image courtesy of the Trustees of Boston Public Library

crisis associated with the proliferation of photographic technologies in modernity. But in its serialized unfolding, its oscillation in and out of sight, it reveals the photographic unseen: Kracauer's "blind spots of the mind," which productively attenuate totalizing accounts of experience, history, and culture—the movement of human bodies, for Muybridge, or of entire human societies, for Sander.

Reading in the Gaps

This book aligns composite modernist writing to serial photography and the photogrammatic track in order to destabilize a host of gendered and racialized assumptions that have shaped the scholarship of the work of Stein, Toomer, Dos Passos, and Fitzgerald. More provocatively, it argues that this modernist writing confronts and interrogates these assumptions in ways that remain unacknowledged, unseen, because of a failure to attend to their intervallic form. In different but comparable ways, the elision of the gap or interval in scholarly understandings of *Three Lives, Cane, Manhattan Transfer, The Last Tycoon,* and "Cosmopolitan" is mutually constitutive of an elision of women in these texts—or, more precisely, of the subversive potential of the serialized female bodies represented in their serialized narrative worlds. Like composite photography, composite modernist writing affords spaces for equivocation and critical thought: Stimson's moment of science, Baker's hiccup of indecision, Dickinson's pondering pause. In these spaces, the secret and confounding histories of the vacillations, exchanges, and fusions between subjects and objects are shared. "Because the eye of the camera cannot overlook what the mind's eye chooses not to see," writes Elizabeth Abel, "it opens up a more democratic signifying field in which the repressed can have its say (or see)."[73] This is the kind of signifying field that finds its coordinates in the structuring gaps and intervals of composite modernist writing.

In the case of each of the texts I examine, the intervallic, denaturalizing logic of photography and cinema revealed in the still–moving field occasions a shift of focus within the multifaceted "relations of interdependence" in Pierre Bourdieu's "field of cultural production."[74] Departing from the artistic or technological paradigms that are dominant in the scholarship of *Three Lives*, *Cane*, *Manhattan Transfer*, and *The Last Tycoon* and "Cosmopolitan," respectively, I establish various historicized facets and uses of photographic technology—or, with regard to Fitzgerald's Hollywood writing, filmic technology—as alternative aesthetic analogues and traveling discourses to these writings. In the still–moving field, the recovery of motion in still images is the theoretical counterpoint to the presence and persistence of stasis in moving ones. Although film theory has tended to play photography and cinema against one another by relegating them to one or the other side of the still–moving dyad, scholars in recent years have argued that it is precisely the vexations within this dyad that inhere as "a material attribute and a founding myth" within the cinematic medium.[75] At the first public unveiling of the Lumière Cinématographe in 1895, a still image of a factory entrance appeared for a time on the surface of the projection screen before being set in motion. With the cranking of the apparatus, a crowd of workers suddenly spilled onto the busy street; "all at once," according to one enthralled spectator of an early cinematographic screening, "the image stirred itself and came alive."[76]

In spite of the implementation of the cinema's basic technical paradox at the introduction of the medium, the photographic dimension of film has conventionally been suppressed. This is at least partly due to the emphasis on the cinema as the absolute expression of movement in early film theory and criticism. But what was for Henri Bergson in 1907 the negative charge of the "cinematographic model," the sheer stiffness of its schematic representation and interpretation of mobility via an engineered succession of (photographic) fixities or immobilities, is lately accepted by scholars as the essential substructure of the medium.[77] Thus Garrett Stewart, in *Between Film and Screen*, moves in and along the photogrammatic track in an effort to "thematerialize" the filmic in the cinematic, trespassing the "terra incognita" of traditional film theory by naming the individual photographic frame as the "cinematic unthought."[78] For Stewart, the ever-vanishing photogram haunts the cinema, making its absence felt in the interruption of its finessed, mechanized invisibility—and indivisibility—in the form of freeze frames or panned photographic quotations on-screen. Stewart summons up cinema's photogrammatic undertext in a larger theory of modernist inscriptive practice that claims a measure of morphophonemic equivalence, however rough, between the photogram and the lexical phonogram of modernist literature. The profound resemblance between "the film track's flitting litter of images" and "the flack and static of an increasingly 'technologized' literary technique" in the early twentieth century is cued by the operation of each "as the contributory increment that disappears in process into the net effect of the representational function."[79]

Stewart's formulation of the dictates of "continuous and laminated" lineation of script and strip flags the way in which the still–moving field provides new points of reference for the historicized understanding of modernist writing in relation to the cinema—the technology that remains the privileged trope in discussions of literary modernism.[80] It has become a critical commonplace to assert an analogous relation between modernist literary strategies of episodic fragmentation and the montage effects of avant-garde film in the early twentieth century.[81] Although this tendency would seem to contradict the anti-technological bias that Sara Danius and others have distinguished in modernist studies, it actually preserves the oppositions that hinge this bias: beauty and utility, the organic and the mechanical, and the aesthetic and the social. Each of these play into, and resemble, the categorical distinction between high and low art that buttresses the "great divide" in modernist thinking, which for Andreas Huyssen exhibits a "paranoid" resistance to a mass culture that is insistently and pejoratively gendered.[82] The identification of a historical precursor, conceptual stimulus, and aesthetic correspondent for modernist writing in the pioneering work of Soviet filmmakers such as Eisenstein and Dziga Vertov elides mainstream, popular cinema—from the early "attractions" projected in the nickelodeons and on the vaudeville stage to the distinctive forms of narrative film that filled theater bills in the silent era and in classical Hollywood.[83]

Among the literary texts I examine, this scholarly tendency finds its fullest example in the history of criticism of *Manhattan Transfer*. As I explain in Chapter Three, Dos Passos's episodic, fragmentary 1925 novel has been consistently read as a model of Eisensteinian montage technique, in spite of the ahistoricity of this argument and the prominence of photography and its allusions in the novel.[84] Yet recognizing cinematographic and photographic technologies as deeply imbricated in their development, as well as mutually interfering and migratory in their practice, serves to augment our understanding of their phenomenological and generic dynamics in such a way as to overhaul accepted narratives around the complex exchanges between modern visual technologies and modernist writing.

Still–moving scholarship recalibrates film's range of significations as an artistic analogue to modernist writing in bearing to the surface, in Stewart's terms, cinema's "bridgework of disjunction," the "jagged seriality" of its photogrammatic gaps, joins, and seams that conduces "the unruffled flow" of screen action.[85] It not only widens the definition of the cinema's interstitial properties to include mainstream film alongside the avant-garde but, in so doing, offers a vantage point for spying the photographic element that this received account of aesthetic convergence between film and writing surreptitiously includes.

Therefore, where avant-garde cinema has frequently furnished the terms for the analysis of *Manhattan Transfer*, I understand Dos Passos's segmented narration and characterization to be consonant with the refiguring of female bodies through the photographic apparatus of advertisement and celebrity ancillary to popular Broadway entertainments in the early twentieth century. In unpacking the image of Dos Passos's central character, Ellen Thatcher, as a photograph at the end of the multilinear novel, "frozen into a single gesture," I account for his critique of the dominations of the male gaze and the complicity of photographic technologies as mechanisms of surveillance and social control in the specular economy of the modern city.[86] Ellen's photographic glaciation under the force of the sinister, crawling, sticky gazes of the men who surround her registers both her imprisonment to that gaze and her resistance to those who are ethnically and socially other to her. It is an encasement produced by the male gaze and a kind of cultural shield. Even so, at the novel's conclusion, Ellen's momentary identification with the working-class daughter of Jewish immigrants, Anna Cohen, undercuts her derogatory stance toward those she deems her social others—and Dos Passos's serialized construction of the female characters in *Manhattan Transfer* effaces any essentialized difference between Ellen and those around her.

Similarly, where the formal repetition and fragmentation of *Three Lives* has been interpreted analogously to the prismatic perspectival surfaces of Cubist painting, in Chapter One I read Stein's short-story sequence in terms of the deconstructive syntax of spacing and doubling in surrealist photography. This is the syntax of even the most vernacular of photographic collections, which are, as Susan Sontag suggests, exercises "in Surrealist montage and the Surrealist abbreviation of history."[87] Much as the Surrealists attended to the photographic frame as "a rupture that issues into sequence," in order to imprint the "spacings and doublings" of the represented "real," in Rosalind Krauss's formulation, the narrative frame in Stein's text constitutes its realist narration as narration, and, more specifically, as a typological system of discourse.[88] Anna, Melanctha, and Lena, the title characters in Stein's three prose pieces, form a characterological lineage that accumulates or accretes rather than develops along teleological or hierarchical lines. For these women-in-series, to be narrated typologically is to be silenced and killed—but Stein also recasts silence and deathly disappearance as a means of resistance, an intransigent acting out of type that is metaphorically reticulated in the blank interstices that separate and bridge these lives.

The gaps and absences that in *Three Lives* bespeak the trauma of representational typologies of race, ethnicity, and gender also puncture the generically mixed textual body of Toomer's *Cane*, which is the focus of Chapter Two. The scholarship of this 1923 composite text has been shaped by an emphasis on oral and musical traditions within African American culture. This emphasis reflects the separation and ghettoization of the cultural productions of the Harlem Renaissance from a high modernism closely associated with and discursively structured by whiteness. Rather than listening for the folk songs of the "singing tree" in *Cane*, this chapter looks at that tree and the lynched black bodies suspended upon it.[89] Toomer's tactics of poetic and narrative visualization correspond in striking ways to the strategic reappropriation of lynching photographs by African American political activists in the first decades of the twentieth century. *Cane* is therefore configured in line with the ontological multivalence of the photography and bears witness to the deep antinomy embedded in the photographic archive of white supremacy. Through the confluence of its ruptured, gap-ridden female figures and its ruptured, gap-ridden form, *Cane* reframes and restages the ritualized scene of lynching. It reveals the egregious contiguity between "black flesh" and "white ash"—that is, black bodies as burned by, and for, white bodies.[90]

Like the preceding chapters, Chapter Four contemplates the absent presence of the woman-in-series—but it does so with reference to different forms of composite textuality and to the seriality of the cinematic photogram rather than of the photograph per se. This final chapter considers the two major projects that Fitzgerald worked on interchangeably while living in Hollywood in 1940: "Cosmopolitan," a screenplay based on Fitzgerald's 1931 short story "Babylon Revisited," commissioned by the independent producer Lester Cowan, and *The Last Tycoon*, a novel of and about studio-era Hollywood that was unfinished when Fitzgerald died of a heart attack four days before Christmas. The unfinished text and the screenplay are variations on the fragmentary literary mode that is my overall focus in this book. In addition, they compose a textual sequence: they are, in Susan Stanford Friedman's terms, "distinct parts of a larger composite 'text.'"[91] In Fitzgerald's Hollywood writing, as in *Three Lives, Cane,* and *Manhattan Transfer*, the hauntings and tracings of Stewart's "jagged seriality" are loaded into the figure of the serialized woman.[92] However, Fitzgerald modifies this trope in concert with the "generalized logic of substitution, citationality, and seriality" of Hollywood film production.[93] Ultimately derived from the basic seriality of the photogrammatic track, this logic is incarnated by the characters of Helen Wales, in "Cosmopolitan," and Kathleen Moore, in *The Last Tycoon*, who each evince Hollywood celebrity in the 1930s as a photographic phenomenon, much like Broadway celebrity in Dos Passos's New York.

Alongside the other composite writing I examine, Fitzgerald's reworking of the woman-in-series suggests the centrality of this fleeting figure to literary modernism. At once, his Hollywood writing discloses and disrupts the looming role of women as instruments of the "continuity style" that was consolidated in the narrative films of 1930s Hollywood. In his work on Faulkner's modernism, Richard Moreland has argued that the writer's practice of "revisionary repetition," the repurposing of plots, episodes, and characters across diverse textual forms, amplifies the voices not merely of the poor, white, male characters that have traditionally preoccupied his readers but of "critically different" subjects, including black people and women. These "concealed" voices, Moreland contends, "throw into relief the fact that modernism's supposedly universal consciousness was a consciousness primarily middle-class, white, and male."[94] To similar effect, the rebellious voices of the female characters in Fitzgerald's textual sequence rupture the illusory conceits of smooth, seamless fictional narration in classical Hollywood—and its equally seamless discourse of femininity—that are conspiratorially secured by the mechanisms of continuity editing and acousmatic synchronization. Helen and Kathleen refuse to remain silent substitutes for other women or to be substituted silently by other women. They refuse to stay still and keep quiet in their replaceable place on the photogrammatic track. Here, again, is the attenuation of narrative syllogisms, the disturbing and fragmenting, in Foucault's terms, of what is imagined to be immobile, unified, and internally consistent, in studio-era Hollywood and, in fact, in the wider field of modernist writing and its study. Fitzgerald's work comes up against the gendered and racialized limits of modernism's consciousness, and, in the process, unravels one of the myths that nourishes and sustains it: the fable of the (middle-class, white, male) solitary author and the singular, bounded literary text.

My scholarly diction in this book foreshadows and models the collaborative, corporate authorship I enumerate in the final chapter on Fitzgerald. Self-consciously composite in form, this book is made in acts of critical superimposition, appropriation, and accumulation. In navigating the specular economy of studio-era Hollywood in *The Last Tycoon* and "Cosmopolitan" and of Broadway entertainments in *Manhattan Transfer*, and examining the specular imperatives of popular typologies of ethnicity, class, and race in *Cane* and *Three Lives*, I draw upon a wide range of critical methods and languages, including gender studies, visual culture studies, disability studies, and the industrial histories of performance and film. "Method: literary montage," Benjamin asserted as he set out, in *The Arcades Project*, to "appropriate no ingenious formulations" in allowing the "rags, the refuse . . . to come into their own: by making use of them."[95] Yet scholarly writing is most often a genre that strains for "ingenious formulations" and that is exceptionally well attuned to the theoretical excising of holes and gaps. As Jani Scandura suggests, scholarly writing is designed to expunge the evidence of "false starts and elisions . . . the costs, passions, and fatigue" that configure its labor—not to mention the collective, collegial, and institutional contexts in which it occurs.[96] But if intervallic openings serve as textual sites in which social and political laws are critically negotiated, it raises the question as to what preconceptions and prejudices inform my own uneven attempts at hermetically sealing this work of scholarship. What might I steal away from view as I move through the ambulatory relations of objects and subjects? How might I accidentally or stealthily underwrite the gendered and racialized discourses I want to interrogate?

It is in response to these issues that I draw together a wide and miscellaneous range of photographic projects and traditions with the writing of Stein, Toomer, Dos Passos, and Fitzgerald, and gather up Barthes, Kracauer, and many other scholars of photography and of literature, through a Benjaminian-with-a-difference process of theoretical combination and accrual. Coextensive with my argument, this method of citational reading is the most apt form for explicating the composite modality of literary modernism, and, more crucially, for leaving open intervals in which the operations of power might be exposed and revised. One recent essay collection exploring the interplay of writing and photography suggests that the coexistence of the two forms "has always generated a kind of uncertain energy, the kind of energy we find in the realm of the experiment, the crossed border, and the bastard outcomes of surprising encounters."[97] In this study, writing and photography is a "crossed border," even as both writing and photography comprise and contain crossed borders. And it constructs its own intervallic bridgework: a composite diction that bears its gaps and reiterations, its associative and additive logic, on the page, in the hope that it too might generate unexpected, bastard outcomes.

Seeing Absence, Hearing Silence, Feeling Images

Sontag, for one, was always skeptical of photography's ethical capacities. Across her work, she tended to draw attention to the disconnective force of photography, by which the momentary real is transformed into a series of slim, separable objects and thereby conferred "the character of a mystery." However, what she laments as the "very narrow relation" of dissociated photographic moments "to the needs of understanding" and truth-telling is now reassessed by scholars for whom the aphasiac or less legible qualities of photography are the germ, not the end point, of its ethical possibilities.[98] For Shawn Michelle Smith, what James Elkins has chronicled as the "stunted" or "imperfect visibility" of photography is an opportunity to grasp that which lingers "at the edge of sight," at the literal, metaphorical, and ideological edge of the photographic frame.[99] Smith's elegant extension of visual culture studies that "show seeing," as W. J. T. Mitchell describes it, by also showing "not seeing," resonates with Elspeth Brown and Thy Phu's 2014 essay collection, *Feeling Photography*, which eschews traditional emphases on issues of presence and memory for "the nuances of absence and forgetting."[100] In this view, the photograph's unseeable, unspeakable revelations approximate the *la vérité folle* [mad truth] of delirium, in Julia Kristeva's terms, which is "true in a different way than objective reality because it speaks to a certain subjective truth, instead of a presumed objective truth."[101]

For Barthes, near the end of *Camera Lucida*, the composite images in which Galton sought the visual contours of criminality or insanity evoke instead the photograph's *la vérité folle*, "that crazy point where affect (love, compassion, grief, enthusiasm, desire) is a guarantee of Being." As the subjects seem to stare Barthes "straight in the eye," the photograph "becomes a bizarre *medium*, a new form of hallucination." "I entered crazily into the spectacle, into the image," writes Barthes, "taking into my arms what is dead . . . gone mad for Pity's sake."[102] In the light of the radical presence of the photographic subject, Barthes newly conceptualizes the relationship of viewer and viewed as an experience of propinquity. As Smith explains, "Entering into the photograph, one might embrace its subject, allowing one's self to be touched, without demanding reference or representation. One might identify without subsuming or consuming the other."[103]

Such a haptic engagement with photography often coincides, as Margaret Olin points out, with the sensation that the photographed subject might somehow manage to touch back.[104] Barthes proclaims in *Camera Lucida*, "I wanted to explore [photography] not as a question (a theme) but as a wound: I see, I feel, hence I notice, I observe, and I think."[105] He wants, in other words, to dwell in Stimson's liminal zone "between subject and object, between hypothesis and empirical investigation, between theory and praxis." If the composite modernist texts I discuss are like still–moving photography because they also inhabit this conceptual space, then my own analytic is attuned to desires autologous to them: to feel, and feel around for, an untamed, intersubjective madness; to run my hands over representational skins that are permeable interfaces between outside and inside, between viewer and viewed; to accommodate subjects who look at or even touch those who picture them. When Barthes asserts that photography "has something to do with resurrection,"[106] I take him to mean that the photograph circulates as an object of loss and as a portal for ghostly returns and reappearances. This, too, is the scandal of composite modernist literary texts, as they—and their serialized women—move in and out of sight.

1. Bodies Bad and Gentle

The Surrealist Convulsions of Gertrude Stein's Three Lives

Gertrude Stein's *Three Lives* opens with a series of social exchanges in which "the good Anna" presides over tradesmen, dogs, and underservants in the fictional town of Bridgepoint. To "conquer," as Anna does, is to broker transactions, to arrange matters, and, especially, to supervise bodies and spaces.[1] The "high ideals for canine chastity and discipline" that regulate her strict governing of her three dogs, along with the town's transient creatures, parody Anna's management of Miss Mathilda's house, which equates to her mismanagement of a series of servant women. "For five years Anna managed the little house for Miss Mathilda," we are told. "In these five years there were four different under servants." Lizzie, a "pretty, cheerful Irish girl," is "[t]he one who comes first" (*TL*, 5). She is "succeeded" by three German women: the "melancholy Molly," the "heavy, ugly, short and rough" Old Katy, and—after a period of months during which many unnamed underservants come and go—Sallie, a "pretty blonde and smiling german girl" who is "stupid and a little silly" (7, 9).

The pace at which these women are replaced undermines the aggressive adamancy of their characterization according to typologies of ethnicity and class. There is, *Three Lives* implies, a degree of similitude between the untenable demands of Anna's superintendence, which effectively scolds the underservants into sequence, and that of the crude nativist code that structures her managerial conduct—and, at once, the narration of "The Good Anna." By the end of the first part of this prose piece, Stein foregrounds the relegation of the underservants to type through the description of "the cheerful Lizzies, the melancholy Mollies, the rough old Katies and the stupid Sallies" with whom Miss Mathilda sometimes rallies in the face of Anna's reprimands (12).

Made multiple and lumped together as a company of "rebels" against Anna's cause, these crowded women embody the collision of the individual and the collective that defines *Three Lives* as a composite whole. Indeed, for all Anna's vigorous choreographing of other women's bodies, it is she who is most properly the "one who comes first" in the sequenced unfolding of the three short stories or novellas that comprise Stein's 1909 book. As the good Anna emerges as the progenitor and forerunner of Melanctha and the "gentle" Lena, Stein's three central characters form a genealogical pattern that reflects the writer's habitual mode of "gradualism, accretion, continuity, and recontextualization," in Lisi Schoenbach's terms.[2] In *Three Lives*, as the satire of the language of succession in "The Good Anna" suggests, she who succeeds is not she who prospers or evolves, but she who follows.

Three Lives originates with a procession of bodies that prefigures the fractional, sequential arrangement of its narrative and narrative persons. It shares with earlier regional short-story sequences such as Hamlin Garland's *Main-Travelled Roads* (1891) and Sarah Orne Jewett's *The Country of the Pointed Firs* (1896) its displacement of the realist and novelistic logic of temporal chronology for a governing unity of place. Yet *Three Lives* is rarely evaluated as a short-story sequence. Rather, scholars tend to take its long middle prose piece, "Melanctha," as their privileged object of study, more or less completely ignoring "The Good Anna" and "The Gentle Lena." The scholarly preoccupation with "Melanctha" reflects a belief in its special importance as a literary experiment—a belief Stein encouraged when, in *The Autobiography of Alice B. Toklas* (1933), she lauded the story as "the first definite step away from the nineteenth century and into the twentieth century in literature."[3] This is not to mention the understanding that "Melanctha" bears a special relation to Stein herself, as a revision of her earlier, semi-autobiographical *Q.E.D. [Quod Erat Demonstrandum]* (1903).

Not surprisingly, contextualist or biographical readings of "Melanctha" have scrambled its meaning in the composite schema of *Three Lives*. When scholars like Sonia Saldívar-Hull receive Melanctha's lover, Jeff Campbell, as "a mouthpiece for Stein,"[4] Jeff's exasperation at Melanctha's inability to "remember right" or "to tell a story wholly" without "leav[ing] out big pieces" is automatically imported onto the structural and narrative registers of the short-story sequence (*TL*, 70). As Rebecca Emily Berne points out, this results in the conclusion that the text "values unity above all else."[5] But the unities to which Stein's poetics aspire are loose ones, resembling the "slowly wobbling," "mushy mass of independent dependent being with a skin holding it together from flowing away" that is Martha Hersland in Stein's (itself lumpy, massive, flowing away) *The Making of Americans* (1906–1908). If Martha Hersland is a "whole one," it is only insofar as her flabby, fluctuating mass, her "lax condition," is held together by the epidermal encasement of her skin.[6] The lack of "firmness" inherent to these "mushy masses" leads Sianne Ngai to oppose Stein's model of textual (in)coherence to Fredric Jameson's definition of postmodern cultural productions as "heaps of fragments," which, Jameson claims, arise from "a practice of the randomly heterogeneous and fragmentary and the aleatory."[7] In Ngai's reading, Jameson's heap of fragments emphasizes "the process in which wholes break down into parts," whereas Stein is more interested in "the way in which parts might be made to cohere or agglutinate." Unlike Jameson, Stein permits heaping as a viable organization of textual matter. Her "strategy of agglutination" in *The Making of Americans* casts formal fragmentation as a process of congealing and accumulating rather than one of disintegration and dissolution.[8]

The wobbly, whole-ish bodies and stories of *Three Lives* come into focus when we attend to the "big pieces" gaping at both Melanctha's storytelling and Stein's sequence more broadly. To read "Melanctha" apart from and in distinction to the prose pieces that precede and follow it is, as Mary Wilson notes, to transform one of Stein's "lives" into the "metonymic equivalent of all three."[9] It is to treat the textual fragment as a whole and, implicitly, to redouble the fixation of the physician Dr. Jeff Campbell in "Melanctha" with coherent and closed-off stories and bodies; to doctor Melanctha as Jeff does, performing a kind of curative patchwork that effaces and ameliorates wounds, recesses, and fissures. By contrast, when *Three Lives* is read in sequence, it is precisely these lesions and holes that appear to view—and with them, the deficiency and the damages of the typological diagnostics performed by Jeff's and Stein's narrators alike. The openings and intervals that are disregarded in readings of "Melanctha" without "The Good Anna" and "The Gentle Lena" are crucial to an understanding of the neorealism—or, after Emily Dickinson, the slant realism—of *Three Lives*. Thus Berne, in analyzing *Three Lives* as a short-story sequence, recovers the text's dialogic engagement with the typological imperatives of realist representation, brokered primarily through a "blackening" motif that thematizes the formation and propagation of racial types in "Melanctha" and its companion pieces.[10] Likewise, when Nancy Glazener considers "The Gentle Lena" as the final prose piece in *Three Lives*, she appreciates the text's creation of both a "version (a loyal, but not identical, repetition) and a subversion (a critical version, a version that lurks beneath the surface of realism) of the realist marriage plot."[11]

In this chapter, I place the "too many" Melanctha within a text that is likewise "too many" by interpreting *Three Lives* in relation to the intervallic form and denaturalizing function of composite or serialized photography. Discerning a measure of convergence between Stein's neorealist representation and the photograph in sequence gives definition to what Marianne DeKoven acknowledges as the chaotic, ambivalent operations of race in Stein's text—and, I would add, of ethnicity, class, and gender. Like the photograph, which is both naturalist and stylized, "real" and "unreal," *Three Lives* is caught between the individual and the type and is, at once, antiracist and racist, subversive and conservative.[12] It evinces in and through its composite form the great vanishing act performed by visual technologies in modernity: the search that came up empty for essentialized racial and cultural truths upon the surfaces of human bodies. More specifically, the fragmentary, repetitive recalcitrance of *Three Lives* conforms to the logic of "connection and separation" that Rosalind Krauss identifies in Surrealist photography. Like the Surrealists' acts of juxtaposition and sequencing in the 1920s and 1930s, Stein's use of the narrative frame—as a structuring principle for the text and in the repetitive circulations of its diction—reveals the "spacings and doublings" of the represented real.[13] In *Three Lives*, these spacings and doublings structure the reductive, typologizing discourses in which its narration participates.

Not only does Stein's short-story sequence mime the photographic revelation of "things normally unseen," the "blind spots of the mind," by its structural and thematic effects of fragmentation and juxtaposition, but the text also did so in the event of its first publication.[14] As is evident in the earliest reviews of *Three Lives* published in newspapers and magazines in North America, Stein's first readers participated in typological structures of thought that became intertwined with ideas of race, ethnicity, gender, and class as they gained currency from the middle of the nineteenth century onward. The popular notion of type developed alongside the legitimation of the older pseudosciences of physiognomy and phrenology by technological developments, especially in photography. Where the photograph was conscripted to shore up popular typologies by virtue of its claims to documentary verisimilitude, Stein's representation of immigrant and African American working-class women seemed, to its early readers, to clarify and fix ideas about sociobiological and cultural difference in the intensity of its realism. Yet, as I argue in the first part of this chapter, the early reviews of *Three Lives* ultimately open up the possibility of a "madly" disruptive, ethically charged embrace between Stein's characters and her readers, such as that experienced by Roland Barthes in the face(s) of Francis Galton's mug shots.

These disruptive possibilities are also raised by the formal and narrative registers of Stein's text, which together divulge the interactions of narrator to narrated person as effects of social power that might be revolutionized, overturned—or dispelled altogether, as in Barthes's photographic encounter. By its interstitial construction, which enlists the interstice as both joining and cleft, *Three Lives* enacts the deformation of the female body by her typological narration. Through a chain of "blue" talk that displaces the experiences of Anna, Melanctha, and Lena into the utterance of another, into rumor, it self-reflexively exposes the action of realist representation: not so much to allow women to speak as to silence them; not so much to picture women as to make them vanish. But the blank spaces that separate and bridge these serialized lives and deaths are more than just the abandoned graves of Stein's devastated, discarded women-in-series. They represent a productive ground in which deathly disappearance is metaphorically recuperated as a means of resistance.

In this way, *Three Lives* constructs and deconstructs racial, social, and gendered typologies through the charged correspondence of its fractured form and the epistemological fractiousness of its female characters—what I call, following Douglas Mao and Rebecca Walkowitz's "bad modernism," its bad form and its bad bodies.[15] If Stein is bad in the racialist and nativist oscillations of her discourse, she is also bad in a converse way, joining Emily Dickinson as a "lingering *bad* one" who haunts the margins of orthodoxy. As *Three Lives*, like Dickinson's poetry, slinks in and out of liminal spaces to "pause, and ponder, and ponder, and pause" over the destructive and imprisoning frames of the represented real, Stein's "bodies in jeopardy" index a "violence always in ascendance," in Houston Baker and Dana Nelson's formulation.[16] Nevertheless, Stein's bad female bodies, in the sequenced unfolding of her badly formed composite text, also demonstrate that those who seem most irreparably impaired by their typologized representation bear a radical potential for enduring and curtailing its violence. This is exemplified, finally, in the silently dissenting descent of Stein's last serialized woman, the gentle Lena, into the white space in which she—and *Three Lives*—terminates.

Looking and Looking at *Three Lives*

In her 1933 surprise bestseller, *The Autobiography of Alice B. Toklas*, Gertrude Stein writing "as" Alice Toklas describes her purchase, with Stein's brother, Leo, of "a big Cézanne" that proves "important . . . because in looking and looking at this picture Gertrude Stein wrote *Three Lives*."[17] Following Stein's lead, and responding to her close involvement with the host of important modern visual artists who frequented her Paris salon during the period when she was writing *Three Lives*, a diverse range of scholars has sought to understand the influence of modern visual art on her 1909 book.[18] In one of the only articles that interrogates *Three Lives* as a composite text, for instance, Philip Heldrich claims the relationship of part to whole as intrinsic to the structure of *Three Lives* with reference to Stein's interest in what she referred to, in a 1946 interview, as Paul Cézanne's "idea of composition" wherein "one thing was as important as another thing."[19]

Notwithstanding the relevance of the Cubist fragmentation of the subject and the foregrounding of perspectival surfaces to *Three Lives*, Stein's description of her "looking and looking" at "Madame Cézanne in a red armchair" has screened other kinds of looking in and around *Three Lives*.[20] Her description is, to borrow the terms of John Whittier-Ferguson, one of the "obstacles" that she "deliberately place[s] in the paths of our remembrances" of her.[21] In actual fact, the literary "looking" performed by the first readers of Stein's book in North America was substantially defined in relation to the ocular norms and standards of photography, not of modern painting. In the early reviews of the short-story sequence, published in the period 1909–1914 and collected in a clipping book by Stein and Toklas, Stein's readers ascribe to her writing an accuracy of descriptive realism that is understood to document popular social and cultural typologies that were similarly—and equally superficially—reinforced by photographic technologies during this period. The reviews, which are on the whole markedly negative, disdain the difficulties of Stein's composition precisely to the extent that her writing is imagined to trace the intellectual "crudity" and moral "depravity" of its characters. "The literary style, if it may be dignified with that phrase," wrote the reviewer for the Pittsburg *Post* in January 1910, "is suggestive of the speech of the German immigrant after he [*sic*] has acquired a partial knowledge of the English language. The thought is exceedingly rudimentary, and therein it may be regarded as typical of the brain processes of the characters."[22] A month earlier, the reviewer for the Rochester, New York *Post Express* despaired of the "pages devoted to the habits of dogs and of maid-servants" as "both tedious and distasteful."[23]

Bored and disgusted, the first North American readers of *Three Lives* articulate its indignities in terms that bond the eccentricities and laboriousness of its style to the types of bodies that it depicts. They thereby deny literary subjecthood to female, working-class, immigrant, or African American characters. This point is made clear in a *Washington Herald* review dated December 12, 1909:

> The thing is novel, in that it departs from traditional lines, the method of
> the great masters in this respect being one of summing up, or statement of
> ultimate and fixed condition, rather than a detailed showing of the repeated

thoughts in the brain by which such conditions are arrived at. Of course, it must be admitted that such repetition does occur, even in cultivated and brilliant minds, but it is a question if the mind-working of such persons as Miss Stein has chosen could be made interesting by any process whatsoever. If she should attempt the same thing with minds of a higher caliber, the result might be more entertaining.[24]

The *Herald* review distinguishes between the interest and entertainments of "great" literature and the (paradoxically) tedious novelty of Stein's writing by balancing discipline against disorderliness, moderation against excess, and stasis against flux—categories deployed to measure the "caliber" of her characters' "mind-working." Like the designation of the "rudimentary" cognitive function of Stein's characters in the Pittsburg *Post*, and the slightness of the difference, for the *Post Express*, between the "habits" of animals and underservants in *Three Lives*, the twin questions of caliber and cultivation work euphemistically to inscribe racial and social taxonomies. "Miss Stein's people are unfinished things," according to a Boston reviewer, writing in January 1910. "They are unable to express themselves except in crude, half-uttered thoughts," because of the "limitations" of their "analytic" faculties and the "persistency of their elemental feelings."[25] This description of the half-finished persons and half-uttered speech acts of *Three Lives* reflects what Maria Damon has recognized as the racialist dimension of Stein's writing. As Damon argues, Stein's own racial otherness, her Jewishness, is symbolically central to her language praxis. As a racial and religious "minority discourse," her writing valorizes repetitive, imprecise, and fragmentary verbal forms that were "despised as primitive, and . . . were literally thought to mark the speaker or writer as less than fully human."[26] It is difficult not to discern the inflection of Darwinian thought adapted to racist ends in the reviewer's scorning of Stein's characters as "things" that remain as incomplete and deficient as their "elemental," abortive patterns of thought and speech. The same is true of the following account of Stein's writing, published in a Baltimore newspaper in 1909: "[I]n each story the whole style is colored by what is characteristic of the protagonist of the story . . . . It is to be hoped that if Miss Stein devotes herself to literature she will work out a better process of artistic selection."[27] The unconventionality of Stein's subjects and prose style is made referable to a problem around "color" and "selection" that is resolved in a call to a form of literary eugenics: to the reproduction of certain subjects, and certain forms of utterance, over others.

The pitch of this call was raised by the reviewers' conception of the documentary facticity of Stein's short-story sequence. Variously called "accurately reproductive studies of actual persons," "verbatim transcripts from life," or "human documents" portraying "painstakingly, conscientiously, exactly what happened,"[28] Stein's writing was received "not as a story, but as a serious picture of life," in the words of a December 1909 review in the *Boston Evening Globe*.[29] It was apprehended as a kind of photographic sequence: a series of snapshots of racially and ethnically defined working-class subjects, commensurate to, for example, Jacob Riis's photographs of urban poverty in New York City's Lower East Side slums. Publicized in newspaper reports and lantern-slide lectures in the late 1880s and in his first book, *How the Other Half Lives* (1890), Riis's reform images helped to embroil photographic technologies in discourses of social–scientific "fact" (see, for example, Figure 1.1).[30]

Yet Stein's study in social abjection, such as it is, does not produce in its readers the measure of "sympathetic feeling" for the impoverished working class or the broad affective transformation of the middle class sought by this reportage. Riis hoped that his work would improve the social conditions of the poor by instigating a movement, in middle-class viewers, from disgust at the "dirty stains" of immigrant life, to pity, indignation, and finally social activism.[31] By contrast, the lives documented in *Three Lives* deeply disturb Stein's readers—as does the feeling

Fig 1.1 Jacob A. Riis, Richard Hoe Lawrence, and Henry Granger Piffard, Three women bundled up in a boarding house, ca. 1890. © Museum of the City of New York. Image courtesy of Art Resource, New York

of closeness to those lives that the text's realism seems to engender. The readers suppose the interface between *Three Lives* and the documentary real to be so total that Stein's fiction must be nonfiction, or even memoir. According to the Baltimore reviewer, the reader "feels that Miss Stein had an intimate personal acquaintance with the 'good Anna,' 'Melanctha' and the 'gentle Lena.'" The anonymous reviewer for the *Boston Evening Globe* in December 1909 goes so far as to assert that *Three Lives* gives "expression to [Stein's] own temperament, to her own way of seeing the world." Imagining Stein as the body double of her characters, and specifically aligning her eyes, her "way of seeing," to theirs, these readers tacitly interpret Stein's geographical, sociocultural, and racial otherness as constitutive of that of her characters. In the apparent lucidity of its realist expression, *Three Lives* is a site for a troubling communion of bodies that transplants one person's vision for another's—even canceling out the difference between them. In a review published in both *The Nation* and the *New York Evening Post* in January 1910, Stein's text is said to bring its readers "very near real people. Too near, possibly. The present writer had an uncomfortable sense of being immured with a girl wife, a spinster, and a woman who is neither, between imprisoning walls which echoed exactly all thoughts and feelings."[32] In yielding effects of intimacy with bodies and experiences that are socially other to its reviewers, *Three Lives* catalyzes interaffective encounters that are seen to be nothing less than felonious. Stein's readers find themselves squeamishly proximate to immigrant, working-class, female bodies in the realist echo chamber of the text.

In spite of the readers' stubborn antipathy for these bodies, the transmedial envisioning of writing-as-photography in the reviews calls attention to its own contradictions. In ascribing an "extraordinary vitality" to *Three Lives*, the January 1910 reviews in *The Nation* and the *New York Evening Post* initiate a problem between insides and outsides, blurring the lines between fictional and real worlds as well as the limits of individual human bodies, narrated or otherwise. This is a problem that refers back to the unsolvable puzzle of visual surfaces and ontological depths that is central to pseudoscientific efforts to uncover sociobiological types in this period. At the same time, in the very vitality of its realist imperatives, *Three Lives* mimes the intense, irrefutable presence of the photographed subject that so fascinated and repulsed Barthes. "From a real body, which was there, proceed radiations which ultimately touch me, who am here," he writes in *Camera Lucida*. "A sort of umbilical cord links the body of the photographed thing to my gaze: light, though impalpable, is here a carnal medium, a skin I share with anyone who has been photographed."[33] This filial image follows Barthes's reading of a photograph of a slave market that he cut from a magazine as a child. What shocks Barthes about the image, as Shawn Michelle Smith notes, is not just that it bears witness to the institution of slavery but also that the institution of slavery touches Barthes. By instigating a "provocative shared corporeality" in which Barthes shares the "skin" of the enslaved, Smith observes, the photograph disrupts his status "as a free, white, self-possessed European viewer . . . for his 'shared skin' metonymically links him with slavery, blackness, and objectification under a white gaze."[34] At least momentarily, Barthes approaches Frantz Fanon's understanding of race as an "epidermal schema" irrevocably tethered to the modality of the visible.[35] The imaginative contact between the white skin of Barthes with the black skin of enslaved men and women unsettles the categories of white and black, self and other, and subject and object.

As such, and contra the labors of Francis Galton and many other photographic practitioners and artists from the mid-nineteenth century on, photographic indexicality—what Barthes calls the *what has been* of the photographic subject— does not incontrovertibly differentiate between types of persons. It evokes their radical nondifference. A January 1910 review in the *Boston Morning Herald* claims that Stein has managed, in "Melanctha," to "reproduce the Negro habit of thought" more "faithfully" than African American authors. "The Negro is not portrayed from the surface and with more or less gush of sentiment as is the case in many southern tales of Negro life, but from the inside," the reviewer declares. "Indeed, the reader begins to doubt ere long if there is really any other world than this world of the Negro. The book pulsates with the intensest realism."[36] This description begs the question how, exactly, Stein is able to "faithfully" represent African American experience—or, by the same token, how her (presumably white) readers are able to identify this representation as such. More than this, the association of the "intensest realism" with description beyond "surfaces," from the "inside" out, doubles back on itself. It unconsciously confirms that the basis of the reviewer's characterization of "the Negro" is nothing but surfaces.

The internal inconsistencies in the formulation, "The Negro is not portrayed from the surface," are made explicit in a remarkable article written by Stein's friend, the art historian Georgiana Goddard King, and published in the *International* in June 1913. "A Review of Two Worlds: Gertrude Stein" sums up the challenges of the formal experimentation of *Three Lives*:

> The business of genius is to do away with limitations; here the expression seeks to escape from the limitations of formulas and definitions and concrete recall of sense perceptions. If you strip humanity to its skins, how are you to know the banker from the cobbler? If you strip them to their souls,

how are you to know a man from a woman? If you reduce them to their actual thought, caught, so to speak, in cross section, how are you to know anybody from anybody else: Shakespeare from Nick Carter? Mostly you could not.[37]

As the Bard is made to rub shoulders with Nick Carter, a pulp fiction private detective hero who first appeared in a *New York Weekly* serial in 1886, King admires in Stein's writing its dissolution of types, its leveling of hierarchies: the exact opposite effect to that sought after by Stein's other readers. Rather than decrying the beneath-the-skin revelations of *Three Lives* as a distressing experience of incarceration, King extols them as emancipatory, offering a means of evading and denying surface "limitations."

To be sure, racial categories are notably absent from King's interrogation of the "formulas and definitions" derived from visual stimuli. And King remains somewhat invested in a racialized scheme of social difference when she replays, in a brighter key, earlier notions of Stein's "Negro" world: as she writes, Stein's "extraordinary power" involves not only "throwing herself into the class she wrote about, but also of carrying the reader into it. In reading *Melanctha Herbert* [sic] you were a Negro yourself."[38] Even so, King's series of rhetorical questions, previously cited, unravel the idea that bodily surfaces encrust sociobiological truths. To some measure, she anticipates that battering "objective examination" that Fanon would experience, years later, when he discovered his "blackness" in the stories of "tom-toms, cannibalism, intellectual deficiency, fetichism [sic], racial defects, slave-shapes" spun by white persons—and that Barthes would glimpse, years later again, in the photographic skins of "the slaves, in loincloths, sitting" about "the slavemaster, in a hat, standing."[39]

Crucially, King's skepticism about skin-deep disclosures arises in reading Stein's short-story sequence in relation to photography as art and practice. Her article discusses *Three Lives* alongside Stein's literary portraits of Pablo Picasso and Henri Matisse, which appeared for the first time in the United States in the summer 1912 edition of Alfred Stieglitz's photographic magazine, *Camera Works*. That the literary portraits of Picasso and Matisse were published in a magazine devoted to the championing of photography as art indicates the extent to which Stein's writing, even as it was imbricated with the reputations and aesthetic innovations of modern painters, circulated in dialogue with a broader spectrum of visual arts than has usually been recognized. King places *Three Lives* on a continuum with the literary portraits in suggesting that its "curious, intricate and yet simple" style is extended in the greater abstraction in Stein's later pieces, specifically through the portraits' "neglect of those grammatical constructions which are too sharp and too rigid to express the incessant flux, the perpetual becoming of consciousness."[40] Even as King's review demonstrates that *Three Lives* was progressively caught up with photography on the American scene, her preference for rhetorical formulations that approach the "incessant flux" of experience over "sharp" rigidity can be understood to reflect photography's tensile operations of speed and stasis, movement and stillness. Certainly, according to Stieglitz, Stein's literary portraits belonged fully with art photography in an intellectual and aesthetic movement sharply "at odds with our familiar traditions."[41] If Stein's writing was like photography, for Stieglitz, it was for its manipulations of the real, its participation in new perceptual modes, and the deconstructive representational strategies that manifest both. Likewise, the photographic frame of reference in King's account of *Three Lives* reflects the paradoxical episteme of the photographic age— an age in which, in her words, the "concrete recall of sense perceptions" becomes less, not more, concrete. Her sense of the unrecognizability of persons "caught" in "cross section" is an image that owes much to the uses of photographic technology in medical practice beginning in the mid-nineteenth century, and it grasps the way in which the new sights offered up by photography undo the ontology of the visual. Educated by Stein's literary experiments in *Three Lives* and the portraits, in the orbit of *Camera Works*, King appreciates what most of Stein's early readers could not: the logical gap inherent to attempts to read skins in order to get under them and that foils efforts to keep bankers separate from cobblers and Shakespeares separate from Carters.

Ulla Haselstein has argued that Stieglitz, in his eagerness to enlist Stein's literary portraits into the art movement organized in and around *Camera Works*, neglects a distinctive aspect of Stein's technique vis-à-vis avant-garde painting, namely, Stein's attention to the "transferential nature" of perception. Stein's "snapshots" of Matisse and Picasso rearticulate the performativity of the conventional portrait setting and redefine its encounter auto-referentially, that is, by "fus[ing] the subject and the object of portraiture."[42] This transferential mode of portraiture, like Barthes's "carnal medium" of photography, raises the possibility that observers might themselves be observed, subjects objectified. As the "umbilical cord" stretches out from Stein's series of photographically imaged women—those "accurately reproductive studies" and "verbatim transcripts from life"—it sparks an interaffective connection, what Silvan Tomkins would call a "contagion."[43] Just as the racialist and nativist (il)logic of differentiation in the early reviews of *Three Lives* defeats itself, Stein's short-story sequence engages Anne Anlin Cheng's "hermeneutics of susceptibility," in which the light that is meant to objectify the female body through photography "becomes a kind of prosthetic skin" that renders "the idea of skin itself as costume, prop, and surrogate."[44] Photographic light, Cheng suggests, can be as much a protective cladding as a fetishized surface. This dialogism defines the cultural work performed by Stein's short-story sequence as a circulated textual object at its initial publication, and, as I detail throughout the rest of this chapter, as a composite text.

Rupturing the Real

In the essay "Photography in the Service of Surrealism," Rosalind Krauss examines the photographic frame in Surrealist images made during Stein's lifetime as "a rupture that issues into sequence," abiding by a logic of "connection and separation" that constitutes and registers reality as a sign.[45] The photographic apparatus, Krauss explains, was exploited by the Surrealists in line with their core project, namely the "beautiful convulsion" of the real through the transformation of "presence . . . into absence, into representation, into spacing, into writing." Through juxtaposition or superimposition, the Surrealists manipulated the photograph as a "deposit" or "transfer" of the real in order to imprint the "spacings and doublings" of the real itself.[46]

This formulation of Surrealist photography has clear echoes in Jonathan Levin's description of "Melanctha" as structured around "the rise and fall of abruptly alternating moments of connection and separation."[47] Even more, Krauss's conception of the coding and configuring of the real in photographic Surrealism aligns with Michael North's sense that in *Three Lives*, "the very effort to nail language to a single unequivocal reality defeats itself, as if the very act of invoking the real over and over actually multiplied it."[48] Yet Stein distanced herself from the "sur-realist crowd," as she called it in *Paris France*, the autobiographical chronicle she composed in the early months of World War II. The "trouble" with the Surrealists, she wrote, was that "they missed their moment of becoming civilized, they used their revolt, not as a private but as a public thing, they wanted publicity not civilization, and so really they never succeeded in being peaceful and exciting."[49] Stein's dismissal of "uncivilized" people—highly poignant in the context of the racialist and nativist typologies in her writing—is a function of her distinction between, in Schoenbach's words, the "iconoclasm, rupture, and opposition" of the avant-garde and her "pragmatic" modernist mode.[50] Her desire to be "peaceful and exciting" where the Surrealists are only "exciting" inflects the remembered anecdote with which she begins *Paris France*:

> I was only four years old when I was first in Paris and talked french there and was photographed there and went to school there, and ate soup for early breakfast and had leg of mutton and spinach for lunch, I always liked

spinach, and a black cat jumped on my mother's back. That was more exciting than peaceful. I do not mind cats but I do not like them to jump on
my back.

Her taste for spinach and distaste for jumping cats are clarified in terms of her
preference for calmness over changeableness in the following paragraph, where
she describes the manner of French pedestrians. "Anybody leaving a sidewalk to
go on or walking anywhere goes on at a certain pace and that pace keeps up and
nothing startles them nothing frightens them," she writes. "If anybody jumps back
or jumps at all in the streets of Paris you can be sure they are foreign not french."[51]
As Schoenbach notes, this passage is suggestive in relation to Stein's experimental-
ism, which produces effects not of shock but rather of intensification through repetition.[52] But the brief mention of Stein's being "photographed" as a child remains
intriguing, especially because it is unclear where the photographic encounter
belongs within her lists of dislikes and likes. Is it "foreign" or "french"?

If photography provided a key context for the first readings of *Three Lives* in
North America, and if, as Susan Sontag suggests, all collections of photographs
perform a Surrealist "abbreviation of history,"[53] the relevance of Surrealist photography to Stein's writing praxis might well be greater than her "trouble" with the
movement implies. As it turns out, Stein's own mixed statements about the constructive and deconstructive propensities of repetitive literary composition align
with Krauss's definition of the convulsions of Surrealist photography. On the one
hand, according to Stein in her 1925 lecture "Composition as Explanation," there is
in "Melanctha" "a constant recurring and beginning . . . a marked direction in the
direction of being in the present although naturally I had been accustomed to past
present and future, and why, because the composition forming around me was a
prolonged present."[54] But Stein's comments in this lecture are in tension with others she made a decade later, which extol the fragmentation of queued formations
in modernism. Elaborating, in 1938, upon the way in which her literary project
aligns with Picasso's artistic project, Stein explains what she sees as the fundamental difference between the "reality" of the twentieth century and the century
that preceded it. The twentieth century "is a time when everything cracks, where
everything is destroyed, everything isolates itself, it is a more splendid thing than
a period where everything follows itself."[55]

The emphases of Stein's two accounts are different: the one on a prolonging and lay-
ering of momentary experience, the other on its violent splitting and rending. But both
encompass her temporal play, her distortion of the classic Aristotelian narrative structure of beginning, middle, and end, whether by protracting or curtailing the instant.

The "prolonged present" that "cracks" is comparable to the dual operations of photography in the Surrealist tradition, superimposing or juxtaposing bodies and things.

Successive and fractured, Stein's narration and diction augment her stylistic tendency toward parataxis, a figure of speech she avowed when, in a 1935 lecture at the University of Chicago, she championed the "Old Testament" as a prototype for "new" writing.[56] Defined by the coordination of conjunctions, the irrepressible and meditative returning to a base word, as well as the erasure of connectives, paratactical formulations are nonlinear and achronological. Serving to "disrupt and fragment conventional sequencing, causality, and perspective," as Susan Stanford Friedman notes, parataxis is linguistically opposite to hypotaxis and is as such "the opposite of hierarchical relationships of syntactical units."[57] The Old Testament appealed to Stein because in it, she declared, "there really was not any such thing there was not really any succession of anything . . . there is really no actual conclusion that anything is progressing that one thing is succeeding another thing."[58] At the same time, though, parataxis does incorporate a structure of subordination according to the spatial ordering attendant in the organization of sentences or syntactical blocks on the surface of the page. As is suggested by its etymological encoding of the notion of side-by-side arrangement, parataxis formulates sequences that are both continuous and fragmentary—or, as Stein would say, constant and cracked.

Stein gestures toward this kind of writing in "Composition as Explanation," when she describes her method of insistent repetition as a process of "beginning again and again and again, it was a series it was a list, it was a similarity and everything different it was a distribution and an equilibrium."[59] In Stein's terms, writing plays off assonance and dissonance as it agglomerates and disperses; like Anna's directive labor at the beginning of *Three Lives*, to write is to move through a series of beginnings that never really seem to stick. At the opening of Stein's 1909 book, the repetition of Anna's name implies the contingency of practices of classificatory naming; as Laura Doyle notes, the "stressing" of Anna's Germanness makes it "feel like an identity under stress."[60] This repetition also opens up into a topographic metaphor for these narrative acts:

> Anna led an arduous and troubled life.
>
> Anna managed the whole little house for Miss Mathilda. It was a funny little house, one of a whole row of all the same kind that made a close pile like a row of dominoes that a child knocks over, for they were built along a street which at this point came down a steep hill. They were funny little houses, two stories high, with red brick fronts and long white steps. (*TL*, 3)

As "one" in a "close pile" and a "row," Miss Mathilda's house—the site where Anna's underservants are serialized—is at once formed into a conglomerate mass with the other houses and lined up alongside them. Establishing Bridgepoint as a space of replication and substitution, the group and chain of "all the same kind" of hillside houses suggest the doubled function of repetition in *Three Lives*, which—like the parataxis with which this passage begins—integrates and separates its units of discourse in a syntactical hierarchy. Stein's repetition, then, works in compound and in sequence. These precarious "little houses" are "funny" in their fraught relation to one another as parts of a mass that is whole (a "close pile") and un-whole (a "row").

"The Good Anna" returns again and again to Anna's name, as well as to sentences like "Anna led an arduous and troubled life"—framing markers that, as Mary Wilson notes, "function in a manner quite similar to the threshold, which architecturally speaking both is and is not part of the space it defines."[61] According to Wilson, Anna is a threshold figure whose attempts to manage the boundaries of Miss Mathilda's house circle back to her own experiences of being policed by others according to axiomatic concepts of class, gender, and ethnicity. These threshold encounters are embedded, in turn, within the recursive form of *Three Lives*. As "The Good Anna" poses the multiplication of the underservants and the hillside houses as the bodily and architectural extensions of Anna's own relentless naming—as "german," as "good"—it dramatizes the dubious knowing of bodies and objects taxonomically, in kind. Moreover, the uncertain limits of the house in which Anna labors correspond to the uncertain limits of the discursive dwelling that is *Three Lives*, such that the textual thresholds in and across Stein's sequenced blocks of narration work to set typed and named bodies in motion. Across the narrative frame between "The Good Anna" and "Melanctha," the image of the about-to-topple houses is enfolded into and supplemented by the reiterative utterances and events that shape the second story in *Three Lives*, along with the irreducible complexity of its persons. When Jeff Campbell determines, vacillatingly, that his lover Melanctha is "too many" for him, he approaches the essential fabrication of Stein's composite text: Melanctha is a woman-in-series, separate from and grafted together with Anna and Lena, like the houses that only just stay upright on Bridgepoint's sloping hill. Although Jeff hopes to distinguish between what he sees as the two Melancthas, the "two kinds of girls" who are "certainly very different to one another" and who do not "seem to have much to do, to be together," Melanctha might well be said to be more than just two different girls (*TL*, 97).

Hysteric Doctors, Undoctorable Hysterics

The fractured flow of *Three Lives* achieves a fusing or inversion of subjects and objects akin to that produced by the photograph—that Barthesian effect of contiguity that scripts racial and social nondifference in the early written encounters with Stein's short-story sequence. Sharing in the quintessentially Surrealist "taste" for incongruous juxtaposition that Sontag suggests is proper to all photographic sequences, I want to explain this subversive merger in relation to Surrealist photography, and in particular, a specific image made in 1933—more than twenty years after *Three Lives* was first published in the United States, though, interestingly enough, in the same year that it was reissued as a Modern Library Classics paperback following the success of *The Autobiography of Alice B. Toklas*.[62] Salvador Dalí's *Le phénomène de l'extase* [*The Phenomenon of Ecstasy*] (Figure 1.2) is a collage of female faces mostly drawn from the nineteenth-century neurologist Jean-Martin Charcot's file of female hysterics. Bearing the parted lips and upturned eyes of the so-called *attitude passionelles*, the enraptured faces are interspersed with Art Nouveau sculptured figurines and cropped images of ears taken from a forensic anthropomorphic catalogue for identifying criminals, developed by the pioneering criminologist Alphonse Bertillon (Figure 1.3). Together, the fragments form what David Lomas calls a "panorama of *fin de siècle* visual culture."[63] For Krauss, Dalí's image exemplifies the Surrealist disruption of the "seamlessness of reality" that is usually declared by the indexical "trace" of the photograph. The real is infiltrated through the gridded system of the image, which works to "destroy the pure singularity of the first [image]" and to open up "the original to the effect of difference, of deferral, of one-thing-after-another."[64] Loading up the photographic field, Dalí's activity of assemblage pressurizes the frame that contains it so that it is "experienced as figurative, redrawing the elements inside it."[65]

Although Krauss underscores the "production of the language effect" in *Le phénomène de l'extase*, which establishes by its fractures and segments a visual grammar for "the world's constant production of erotic symbols,"[66] scholars hardly adjudge a revolutionary purpose in the gendered symbology of hysteria in Surrealist texts. With his collaged celebration of ecstasy, Dalí joined with Louis Aragon and André Breton in lauding hysteria as "the greatest poetic discovery of the end of the nineteenth century."[67] But the "aspect of Charcot's legacy" that most fully captivated the Surrealists, Susan Rubin Suleiman argues, was the figure of the "madwoman observed, theatricalized, photographed, eroticized."[68] This is the pivotal figure in Pierre André Brouillet's 1887 group tableau portrait showing Charcot giving a demonstration at the Iconographie photographique de la Salpêtrière, a women's hospital in Paris (Figure 1.4). As head physician at the Salpêtrière in the 1870s and 1880s, Charcot paraded his female patients before the camera and before audiences of medical doctors (including Sigmund Freud, who would later

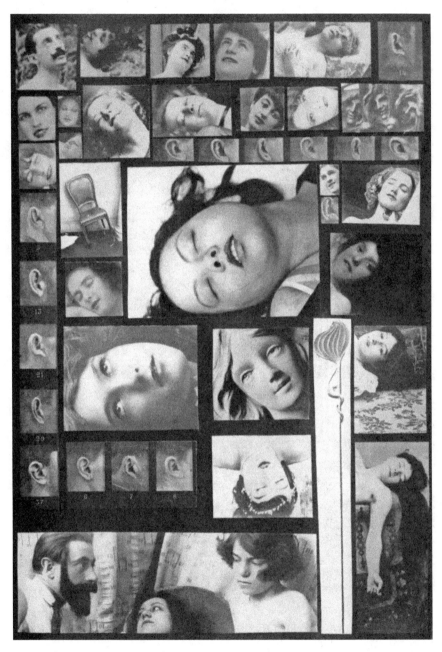

Fig 1.2 Salvador Dalí, *Le phénomène de l'extase* [*The Phenomenon of Ecstasy*], *Minotaure* 3–4 (December 12, 1933), p. 77. © Salvador Dalí, Fundació Gala-Salvador Dali/VEGAP. Licensed by Viscopy, 2017. Image courtesy of Schaeffer Fine Arts Library, University of Sydney

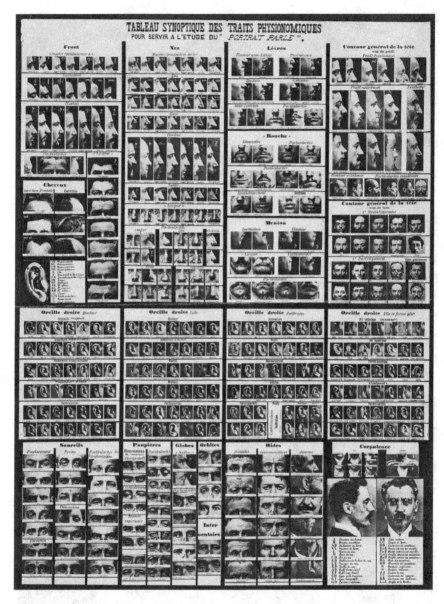

Fig 1.3 Alphonse Bertillon, *Tableau synoptic des traits physionomiques* [*Synoptic table of physiognomic features*], 1908. Image courtesy of Twentieth-Century Photography Fund, 2009, Metropolitan Museum of Art

revise Charcot's theory of hysteria) and members of high society at his famous "Tuesday Lessons."[69] Brouillet's painting underscores the centrality of the theatricalized madwoman to these events—and the role of photography in propagating her image—through its reproduction of the large charcoal drawing on the rear wall of the room, which depicts a convulsing woman in the classic hysteric's pose captured in Charcot's photographs, the *arc-in-circle* (that is, the back arched in a semicircle).

The psychiatric iconography redeployed by Dalí in 1933 was one produced by a policing, positivist gaze and steeped in emphatically gendered theatrics. As Lomas notes, Dalí's appropriation of the figure of the hysterical woman in accordance with the "dominant phallocentrism" of the Surrealist cult of desire replicates, in the visual realm, the incarceration of female patients at the Salpêtrière. Nevertheless, following Jean Baudrillard, Lomas identifies latent subversive operations in images of seduction, including *Le phénomène de l'extase*. If the seduction scene is "a guileful play of masks and artifice" that "thrives on (dis)semblance and inauthenticity," Lomas postulates, it opens up a "gap . . . between the apparent reality and immutability of sex and the staged performance of a gendered subjectivity," an indeterminate space in which "a productive confusion as regards masculine and feminine subject positions arises, and where the identities of male artist and female hysteric are liable to merge and exchange."[70]

In the psychiatric and Surrealist visions of female hysteria, the gaze of the male physician and the male artist is implicated within a circuitry of erotic power—and, importantly, is identifiable as such. As Allan Weiss points out, the serialized representation of ecstatic, "demoniacal" possession in *Le phénomène de l'extase* "is not merely a scenario of women possessed by demons, but also (and perhaps above

Fig 1.4 Pierre André Brouillet, A lesson on hysteria by Jean-Martin Charcot, 1887.
© Erich Lessing. Image courtesy of Art Resource, New York

all) of men possessed by the phantasms and images of the women they love, desire, or imagine. The Surrealist image is not simply that of the body deformed by desire; it is also the sign of desire informed by the body."[71] The essential doubleness or reciprocity of this scenario, its slippage between subject and object, is most fully thematized in the thick black lines of Dalí's image. In the conspicuous unevenness of the lines, as well as in the catalogued numbers from Bertillon's metrological archive visible on a number of the clipped images of ears, the fascinated labor of the male observer–artist leaves its marks.

Likewise, the medical encounter in Stein's "Melanctha" is a scene of social power in which subjects and objects are not clearly differentiated. It presents an abortive form of doctoring that, by its repetitions and recursions, its paratactical enframing, produces a diagnostic less of female malady than of its own discursive configuring. As a matter of fact, "Melanctha" has been read as a case study in the medical condition Aragon and Breton seized as a "poetic discovery." Scholars who identify in Melanctha the symptoms of hysteria or split personality disorder take on faith the normative psychological profile of Jeff Campbell and therefore the efficacy of his description of Melanctha acting like "two kinds of girls" who are "certainly very different to each other."[72] But Melanctha's supposed changeability is matched, rather than distilled or diffused, in the serial consultations of her lover and doctor. Immediately before Jeff tells Melanctha that she is "two kinds of girls," he sits by the fire in her parlor:

> At first his dark, open face was smiling, and he was rubbing the back of his black-brown hand over his mouth to help him in his smiling. Then he was thinking, and he frowned and rubbed his head hard, to help him in his thinking. Then he smiled again, but now his smiling was not very pleasant. His smile was now wavering on the edge of scorning. His smile changed more and more, and then he had a look as if he were deeply down, all disgusted. Now his face was darker, and he was bitter in his smiling, and he began, without looking from the fire to talk to Melanctha, who was now very tense with her watching. (TL, 96–97)

The short-circuiting of Jeff's diagnostic routines presents, so to say, in the conspicuous vacillations of his own physiognomy. A drama of his "thinking," the graduated transformation of the pose of his hand, the quality of his smile, and (most problematically) the palette of his skin directly undercuts his pronouncement of Melanctha's inconstancy.

A little later in the prose piece, at about its midpoint, the narrator tells us, "Jeff Campbell could not know any right way to think out what was inside Melanctha with her loving, he could not use any way now to reach inside her to find out if she was true in her loving." Capricious, convoluted, composite: Melanctha, before Jeff, is all impenetrable surfaces. Yet Melanctha's affective mystery parallels her affective abundance. As Jeff finds himself in a disquieting relation of dependence to Melanctha, as a "beggar" given alms "not of her need, but from her bounty," her emotional autonomy is posited as a threatening, overwhelming fullness that insists upon Jeff as auxiliary to her—that is, outside of her, unable to "reach inside her" (124). The deepest irony in the scene by the fireplace is that Melanctha remains inscrutable to Jeff, but his thought is ever more closely inscribed on his body—a reversal of patient and doctor that is emphasized by the contrast between Jeff's refusal to look up from the fire and Melanctha's own "tense" watching. The gently mocking narration in this section makes clear the discrepancy between Jeff's pro-tean patterns of thought and his pretensions to scientific empiricism: "He thought and thought, and always he did not seem to know any better what he wanted. At last he gave up his thinking.... Jefferson took out his book out of his pocket, and drew near to the lamp, and began with some hard scientific reading" (91). His "hard scientific reading" is a prop against, not for, thought; as he buries his face in his book, he seeks to mask the failure of medicalized rationality that marks his face before the fire.

As a symbol for his inability to name his desires or the "too many" woman who elicits them, the book pulled from Jeff's pocket is like Stein's book: a text that issues and incarnates, by its prolixity, the failure of typological "thinking and thinking." Repetition in *Three Lives*, as in *Le phénomène de l'extase*, interferes with reality by subverting its viewing relations and by disclosing its representational coding. Scaled to the pocketbook, the deficiency of Jeff's "thinking and thinking" is already implied by the superfluity and redundancy of its tautological descrip-tion. The "and" in between Jeff's thoughts is a rhythm of spacing that in Surrealist photography invokes "the sense of the linguistic hold on the real."[73] It is the inter-stice between signs, a stressed threshold, which points up the narration of Jeff's thinking as narration. Along with the repetitions of Stein's prose in *Three Lives* and the imaging of this stylistic aspect in the "row" and "pile" of houses at its outset, Jeff's "and" enacts the destabilizing operations of framing in the composite literary text as in Surrealist photography.

In 1930, the photographer, essayist, and poet Claude Cahun (born Lucy Schwob) published *Aveux non avenus*, a book of ten photomontages and ten chapters of text written over the previous decade. Released with Éditions du Carrefour, the house that published Max Ernst's Surrealist manifesto *La femme 100 têtes* in 1929, *Aveux non avenus* was ignored during Cahun's lifetime, but, after her work emerged from the shadows of art history in the 1990s, was republished in *Écrits* in 2002 and translated in English as *Disavowals, or, Cancelled Confessions* in 2008. The book is introduced as the "invisible adventure" of a photographer who wants to "trace the wake of vessels in the air, the pathway over the waters, the pupil's mirage"—"shadows" all, as Katharine Conley points out, not least the elusive "mirage" of another's vision: "a glimpse of self in the eyes of another or in the 'eye' of a camera or in a mirror."[74] *Aveux non avenus* participates in the Bretonian Surrealist project of "the failure of the category"; as Breton wrote in 1924, "Our brains are dulled by the incurable mania of wanting to make the unknown known, classifiable."[75] It is an exercise in *"un genre indéterminé,"* to borrow Cahun's description of angels in the book, combining photography with private letters, poems, diary entries, and previously published essays.[76] It is also authored and populated by such indeterminate, uncategorizable types. The photomontages are active collaborations, constructed under Cahun's directions by her stepsister and lover, Marcel Moore (born Suzanne Malherbe). Declaring, "My lover will not be the subject of my drama; s/he will be my collaborator," Cahun unsettles the traditional relationship between male artist and female subject, critiquing the masculinist and heteronormative culture of the Surrealist circle associated with Breton and Dalí.[77]

Aveux non avenus collapses the distinction between artist and collaborator, male and female, and subject and object, as it stages "a rough, brutal game . . . between Cahun as pursuer and pursued."[78] "I want to hunt myself down, struggle with myself," she claims at the outset, to find the "you who evade me."[79] These warring pronouns provide the key terms of reference for the photomontages, which "transform and recombine Cahun's face and body in a manner that problematizes any easy reading of Cahun's self."[80] This is especially true in *Portrait de Mademoiselle X* (Figure 1.5), an image of collaged female faces and body parts that anticipates Dalí's paean to female hysteria. Organized in a rough grid that visually enlarges the bars of the prison gate from which Cahun, in one of her many iterations, peers, the serial portraits scatter the meanings of the already ambiguous inscription in the upper-left corner of the work: *"Ici le bourreau prend des airs de victime. Mais tu sais à quoi t'en tenir"* ["Here the executioner takes on the air of a victim. But you know what to believe"].

As the executioner adopts the pose of the victim, Cahun's scenography of execution, like Charcot's scenography of psychiatry, embroils subject and object. The inscription assures us that we "know" this pose as a pose, but in the scheme of *Aveux non avenus*, all we know is that one pose cannot be disambiguated from another, any more than can the subject positions of pursuer and pursued. After all, Cahun is pictured covering her own ears in a gesture that makes the faculty of hearing central to this image—along with that of speech, signified through the collection of lips that are a precursor to Dalí's ears. Unhearing and unheard, the portrait of the nameless Mademoiselle turns on the willful negation of sensory

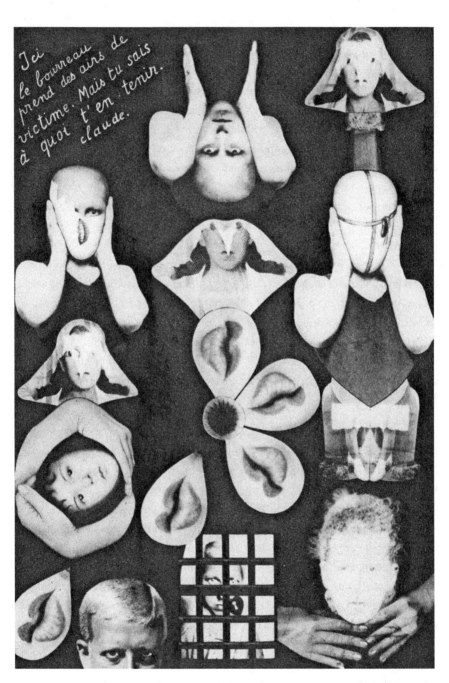

Fig 1.5 Claude Cahun, *Portrait de Mademoiselle X*, 1930. Image courtesy of George Eastman Museum

input and output. It depicts a soundless withdrawal from the realm of the social: a disavowing, and a canceling, such as that connoted in the book's title.[81]

Cahun's photomontage thus recasts the silence, absence, and death of the female self–other as a form of witness and presence. It initiates a "mute exchange" such as that associated with the photograph's "absence of language"—an absence that the image parodies in its assemblage of lips and its handwritten inscription. Although scholars have long considered the silence of photography to constitute its ethical failure, Karen Beckman has recently called for a theoretical "unleashing" of the photograph's "illegibility" in order to formulate "new, less bloodthirsty forms of responsibility" around the medium.[82] Stein's *Three Lives* shares the ominous overtones of *Portrait de Mademoiselle X* as of *Le phénomène de l'extase*, as Jeff Campbell doctors Melanctha and as Stein's narrators speak for and silence its women-in-series. But like Cahun's photomontage, *Three Lives* also opens up the ethical possibilities of silence and absence within an oppressive, masculinist world order. As I argue in the pages that follow, in moving narratively through the lives and deaths of Anna, Melanctha, and Lena, Stein's composite text revisions aural and visual formlessness or lack as the basis for an alternative signifying system and an alternative symbolic social body—a social body in which subject and object, narrator and narrated, merge in the mute communion of narrative (un)closure.

The Blue Speech of Bad Bodies

"Sometimes the thought of how all her world was made filled the complex, desiring Melanctha with despair," the narrator tells us near the end of "Melanctha." "She wondered often how she could go on living when she was so blue. Sometimes Melanctha thought she would just kill herself, for sometimes she thought this would be really the best thing to do" (*TL*, 149). Described repeatedly, Melanctha's "blue" state of mind is incorporated into a chain of female talk in Bridgepoint. According to the narrator at the beginning of the prose piece, her suicidal thoughts are culled from another woman's thoughts: "Melanctha told Rose one day how a woman whom she knew had killed herself because she was so blue. Melanctha said, sometimes, she thought this was the best thing for her herself to do." Blue utterance is passed from Melanctha's friend to Melanctha, and then from Melanctha to Rose Johnson, who co-opts and quarrels with its terms:

> I don't see Melanctha why you should talk like you would kill yourself just because you're blue. I'd never kill myself Melanctha just 'cause I was blue. I'd maybe kill somebody else Melanctha 'cause I was blue, but I'd never kill

myself. If I ever killed myself Melanctha it'd be by accident, and if I ever killed myself by accident Melanctha I'd be awful sorry. (60)

The comedy of Rose's response to her friend not only expresses her terrific lack of empathy but also trivializes the phraseology "being blue" and "killing yourself" so as to call attention to it as a construction of language—which is already implied by the inscription of Melanctha's blue affect as rumor, as story. As Rose's little speech obliquely detects and enacts the operation of blue utterance as echo or citation, it participates in and amplifies the larger procedures of silencing throughout the story. Where Rose's speech is given as a direct first-person speech act, Melanctha's blue thoughts are couched in and as narration—as they are in all of the mirroring passages in the story.

This narrative dubbing of Melanctha's feelings is further signaled through the contrivance of the overt rhyme "so blue"/"to do" and the stuttering diction of "her herself." The repetitive formulation of pronouns measures the distance between the narrator and Melanctha even as it emphatically asserts the intimate close-ness to her that occasions the narrating of her thoughts. In addition, the use of Melanctha's name as the pivot about which Rose's speech turns serves to unveil the intrusions of the representational by making a show of speaking of Melanctha. Through her naming and renaming, Melanctha is affiliated with and made equiv-alent to "being blue" and "killing yourself." She is transformed into an object and function of discourse.

"Melanctha" presents itself as an act of hearsay through the writing of its blue chain of utterance. This strategy is exemplified in the death scene that closes off the prose piece and opens it up into "The Gentle Lena" in *Three Lives*. Melanctha's last words in the story come from the mouth of Rose, who, having shrugged off Melanctha's friendship, tells "anybody" who asks her that she "certainly do think [Melanctha] will most kill herself some time, the way she always say it would be easy way for her to do. I never see nobody ever could be so awful blue." From the beginning to the end of the story, the "way" Melanctha "always say it" is the way Rose always says it. But it is the incessant "saying" of the narrator that is made most palpable through the translation of an anonymous woman's blue thoughts into the rumor of Melanctha's blue thoughts. The narrator propagates Rose's gos-sip: "But Melanctha Herbert never killed herself because she was so blue, though often she thought this would be really the best way she could do" (167). The short description of Melanctha's hospital death that follows, a scant two paragraphs later, is dominated and diminished by the blue talk of the narrator and Rose—talk that is problematized by the fact that Melanctha does not actually kill herself. There is, as Daylanne English notes, a great deal of ambiguity about what actually kills the three women in *Three Lives*.[83] Yet the way in which the reverberations of blue gossip hang over the scene of Melanctha's death implicitly connect the two: Melanctha dies in and through her being-spoken, her being-written; her death is a variation on and a logical extension of her being made to sound and look blue.

The ending of "Melanctha" largely repeats the ending of "The Good Anna," which concludes with the "word" of Anna's death—and of Anna's last words— passed from one woman to another: "'Dear Miss Mathilda,' wrote Mrs. Drehten, "Miss Annie died in the hospital yesterday after a hard operation. She was talking about you and Doctor and Miss Mary Wadsmith all the time. . . . Miss Annie died easy, Miss Mathilda, and sent you her love'" (*TL*, 56). The mysterious, "easy" deaths of Anna and Melanctha at the conclusion of the first two prose pieces are commensurate to their deformation into discourse, their devolution into "objects that can be symbolically possessed." This is Sontag's phrase, describing what she calls the "predatory" act of taking a photograph, a "soft murder" entailing a participation in "another person's (or thing's) mortality, vulnerability, mutability."[84] Along with Barthes's experience of a "micro-version of death" in the instant of being photographed ("I am neither subject nor object," he writes, "but a subject who feels he is becoming an object"),[85] Sontag's notion of the photograph as always *memento mori* is figured in the death-by-representation in "The Good Anna" and "Melanctha." At the end of the prose pieces, Stein's women become the dead things they always were: objects not subjects, absent not present, still not moving.

Or do they? When "Melanctha" is excised from *Three Lives*, the fate of its titular character more than justifies the lament of Aldon Lynn Nielson, among that of other scholars, that "Melanctha sings her blues and then simply dies away, fading from the white view behind the narrative veil, unable to answer for herself."[86] But although the white space that separates and bridges "Melanctha" and "The Gentle Lena" is a symbol of the death that yields (to) it, it is also a blankness that tersely represents—that represents by not representing—the catastrophe of Melanctha's typing. The break between the stories is a spatial version of Jeff Campbell's "and," a sequence-issuing rupture that reveals the signifying field for what it is. At once, because *Three Lives* as a composite text is by no means done with "awful blue" women, this structural "and" draws together Melanctha and Lena so as to complicate the notion of Melanctha's death as her ruination under the deadly force of the "white view." The subversive threat of the vanished woman, Beckman suggests, consists in the possibility that she might not remain vanished, instead shuttling "between the worlds of presence and absence."[87] As death repeatedly cedes to life across the threshold of the prose pieces in *Three Lives*, undercutting the apparent vulnerability of its typologized women, Stein's text dramatizes an essentially incomplete eradication of the female body, and so offers up a series of "potential moments of feminist resistance" and survival.[88] Slipping in and out of its textual gaps, Anna, Melanctha, and Lena—objects and subjects, still and moving, caught between presence and absence—bear the threat of *redivivus*, the woman returned: three lives phrased, structurally and narratively, as a series of reincarnations.

In one of the only readings to analyze *Three Lives* as a composite text, Nancy Glazener argues that "The Gentle Lena" hinges on an "implicit opposition between orderly living and desire." This opposition is developed in the composite text, first, through Anna's managerial efforts, and second, through the confrontation between Jeff's preference for "regular" living and Melanctha's insistence on "excitement," especially in her "wandering after wisdom" and "real experience," which take her all over Bridgepoint in the company of many different men (*TL*, 68). The characterization of Lena is calibrated through Stein's serial renditions of the *propre*, which, Glazener suggests, progressively enlarge its "deadening monologism and especially its capacity to set female subjectivity at odds with the female body."[89] The stillness of Melanctha's dead body, reifying the damages of blue talk, is transposed into Lena's supremely diminished subjectivity. Lena is patterned after the dead Melanctha as she becomes a "pale" figure of insentience. When she falls ill on the boat to America, Lena "just staid where she had been put, pale, and scared, and weak, and sick, and sure that she was going to die"; later, pregnant with her first child, she is overcome by this same fear: "She was scared and still and lifeless, and sure that every minute she would die" (*TL*, 177, 198). After she gives birth to three children, her husband Herman Kreder, much taken with his new role as father, simply stops thinking of her as she becomes "always more and more lifeless" (199).

"The Gentle Lena" ends with a death scene that, in Jayne Walker's words, "blurs the moment of passage from figurative to literal lifelessness."[90] "When the baby was come out at last, it was like its mother lifeless. While it was coming, Lena had grown very pale and sicker. When it was all over Lena had died, too, and nobody knew just how it had happened to her" (*TL*, 200). The conceptual holes that pull at this description, through its past-tense, passive-voice construction, work appositely to the death scene in "Melanctha." They are obfuscations testifying to the failure of realist narrative acts. For Lena, even more than Melanctha, is silenced and spoken for. Her interiority is witnessed through a relay of speech acts, primarily between the "good german cook" and the narrator—the former, like Rose in "Melanctha," serving as a confidante of and model for the latter.

Indeed, the narrator in "The Gentle Lena" frequently assures us that Lena has unconscious desires by naming what Lena does not know that she feels—an action that prompts Glazener to question whether the "stabilizing knowledge of Lena's feelings [has] sinister implications in a culture in which women are too often spoken for."[91] However, *Three Lives* works against this valid concern through the silent un-becoming of Lena and in the sequence of the text. From the perspective of her aunt, Lena's chief virtue is her astonishing passivity, the fact that "she would never want to do things her own way" (*TL*, 176). The subtitle to "Melanctha," "Each One As She May," echoes in this phrase, which is repeated in relation to Lena by several characters in "The Gentle Lena." When Herman's sister describes Lena as "never wanting her own way at all like some girls are always all the time to have it," it is Melanctha, with her wandering failure to "learn, what was the right way she should do," who dwells in this description (189, 167). At the same time, Anna's badly behaved underservants stand behind the cook's description of Lena as a "good girl" under her management. As the cook says, "I never had no trouble with her like I got with so many young girls nowadays, Mrs. Aldrich, and I never see any girl better to work right than our Lena" (196).

Even though the narration wants to set Lena's not-wanting at odds with Melanctha's wanting, and her working right against the underservants' working wrong, *Three Lives* finally suggests that Lena is far closer to Melanctha and the underservants than those around her imagine. Michael North has argued that Stein, in rewriting *Q.E.D.* as "Melanctha," crafts for herself a racial mask that serves to displace sexual difference into racial difference, much as Picasso performs a "figurative change of race" in his move to abstraction in *Les demoiselles d'Avignon* (1907). According to North, Picasso's use of the African mask in this painting—as well as in the portrait of Stein he painted (and painted over) in 1905 and 1906—was attractive to Stein for its enactment of a "tension . . . between mask and naked-ness" that "break[s] down the difference between surface and depth." As a result, Picasso's paintings turn gender into "a matter of role-playing rather than essence," and the gendered body from a biological fact into "something much more like clothes or—a mask." Likewise, for North, Stein's presentation of race as a "role" grants "an open invitation to consider it as culturally constituted."[92]

The defamiliarizing effects of masking correspond with those associated with the photograph, a textual skin that functions as a "guileful play of masks and arti-fice," as Lomas says of Surrealist images of female hysteria. Certainly, this was part of the reason that Cahun made photography and photomontage her privileged medium for materializing the constructedness of identity. Cahun's biographer, François Leperlier, records that throughout her life she played with masks, buying and wearing them regularly when among friends and visitors at her home.[93] In her unpublished self-portraits—as well as in the photomontages in *Aveux non avenus*, including *Portrait de Mademoiselle X*—masks ironically reference, in Dawn Ades's words, "the socially imposed shells of feminine and masculine identities."[94] In one self-portrait taken around 1928, for instance, Cahun's impassive gaze and scarf-wrapped, shaved head mocks, or is mocked by, the sculptural, hyperfeminine painted mask that hangs from the black backdrop behind her (Figure 1.6). Kept within the frame, the upper limits of this backdrop emphasize the performativity of the portrait scenario, which is depicted in the dark expanse between face and mask as a spectacle of masking and unmasking, of role-play and its exposure as play, as façade.

For Cahun, faces are themselves masks that might be removed. The final photomontage in *Aveux non avenus*, titled *I.O.U. (Self Pride)*, features a series of layered images of Cahun's face rising from a single neck, a citadel of the discontinuous, manifold self. It is framed by this inscription: "*Sous ce masque un autre masque. Je n'en finirai pas de soulever tous ces visages*" ["Under this mask another. I will never finish lifting up all these faces"] (Figure 1.7). The tower of faces irreverently reformulates Honoré de Balzac's eidolic theory of the daguerreotype, which holds that "each body in nature is composed of a series of specters, in infinitely superimposed layers, foliated into infinitesimal pellicules, in all directions in which the optic perceives the body," and that "every Daguerreian operation would catch, detach, and retain, by fixing onto itself, one of the layers of the photographed body."[95] In 1900, the photographer Félix Nadar would enlist Balzac's melancholic notion of photographic spectrality in his defense of the technology, celebrating how it "seized, grasped, fixed the intangible," "the impalpable specter that vanishes as soon as it is perceived."[96] What Nadar termed the "*la vision fugace*" of photography, its fleeting or fugitive vision, for Cahun entails specifically its capacity to envision the human face as a fugitive object of knowledge. In hunting herself down in *Aveux non avenus*, she aims to get at the "void bang down the middle" of the self.[97] So, whereas Balzac feared that for a body to lose one of its "specters" by being photographed was to lose "a part of its constitutive essence," Cahun sees a void where human essence should be and uses photography exactly to refract and multiply the specters of selfhood. Her archive of the self reflects its status as a limitless series of socially constituted, and therefore disposable, visages.

Stein's gentle Lena also treats her sociocultural otherness as a role that can be discarded, a covering that can be disrobed. But she does so in and by her increasing slovenliness, which is cast as a kind of seduction scene in reverse—or, to rework Mary Ann Doane's concept of feminine masquerade, an unflaunting of femininity

Fig 1.6 Claude Cahun, Self-portrait with mask, ca. 1928. © RMN-Grand Palais. Image courtesy of Art Resource, New York

that can rebuff the masculine gaze.[98] When the cook bemoans the fact that Lena has "let [herself] go" after giving birth, she endows to Lena a metaphor of mobility in describing what she sees as her woeful stagnation (*TL*, 195). The narrator, moreover, implies that Lena's passivity might be a kind of masquerade: "She just dragged around and was careless with all her clothes and all lifeless, and she acted

Fig 1.7 Claude Cahun, *I.O.U. (Self-Pride)*, ca. 1920–1930. © 2017 Museum Associates/
LACMA. Licensed by Art Resource, New York

always and lived on just as if she had no feeling" (198). If Lena's inaction is action in disguise, an act, then her becoming "more and more lifeless" is an intensification of her pantomime. As Victoria Rosner notes, the servant "moves between zones of cleanliness and filth, visibility and invisibility, with a power and responsibility to purge the house of dirt."[99] Refusing to purge either her house or her body of the muck of domestic life, Lena's changing comportment and dress is a form of protest: a refusal to continue to perform, sartorially or otherwise, to type. Where Melanctha wanders the streets of Bridgepoint, Lena infuses the act of just staying where she has been put with a dissenting energy.

Although Lena's "dragging around" is coded as a still–moving act of resistance, her demise still reinforces the oppressive dominations of the realist marriage plot and of ethnic and cultural taxonomies alike. The obvious difficulty with reading the death-defying (or at least death-agitating) motility of Anna, Melanctha, and Lena is, of course, that Stein's lives end with Lena's. And, if anything, Lena's dead body is buried more deeply than Anna's or Melanctha's in the narration of *Three Lives*. Where the final lines of "The Good Anna" and "Melanctha" are given over to the "word" of the women's deaths, "The Gentle Lena" ends with two paragraphs about how the cook is "the only one who ever missed" Lena and how "content" Lena's husband is without her (*TL*, 200). Even more than that of the previous two prose pieces, the ending of "The Gentle Lena" seems to corroborate Janice Doane's claim that the " 'meaning' of Stein's characters' lives is not revealed but lost in their abrupt deaths, which go unremarked and unmourned."[100]

Nevertheless, recent work in the philosophy and literary representation of pain offers a new context for reading the unremarked and unmourned ending of *Three Lives*. In Elaine Scarry's classic work, *The Body in Pain*, pain is "language-destroying," the "certainty" of its experience at stark odds with the "doubt" that marks its witnessing. The person in pain is regularly bypassed through the mistrusting and dismissal of their voice by medical physicians who perceive that voice to be "an 'unreliable narrator' of bodily events."[101] *Three Lives* clearly elaborates upon this notion of the physician as the certain voice of uncertainty and the patient as the uncertain voice of certainty; especially through Melanctha's relations with Jeff, Stein illustrates the gulf between the body and its apprehension, between experience and representation, and between the individual and the type. Yet the text also engages with a "wider range of relationships between pain and language" than those identified by Scarry and establishes what Susannah Mintz describes as a "vernacular of pain" that challenges the usually unquestioned belief that "pain obliterates everything but itself."[102] Taking Lena's passivity as resistant inactivity and her deathly absence as a defensive cloak, the fact that there is so little talk or "remembering" of her after her death—combined with the fact that, for once, Stein's narrator actually falls silent—signals the text's capitulation to her protest (*TL*, 200). Even in the most oppressive relations of power, Foucault maintained, there is always the "possibility of resistance": "a power can only be exercised over another to the extent that the latter still has the possibility of committing suicide, of jumping out of the window or of killing the other."[103] We might well ask, as Lois McNay does, exactly what kind of resistance is suicide or murder. But in the scene of Lena's death and the blank space that is its outgrowth, we see the individual's capacity "to resist the games played by others."[104]

In this light, the finality of Stein's final "FINIS" implies not the failure but the success of Lena's resistance to the normative injunctions of the textual world of Bridgepoint: her efforts to stop playing the game, and to end her own narration. Precisely by not carrying the same threat of return, the conclusion of *Three Lives* harmonizes Lena's spectral voice with that of the narrator. Lena's silent protest generates the silence of the text itself, a form of antirumor that, like the unhearing ears in Dalí's *Le phénomène de l'extase*, bears witness to female "ills" as social productions—as well as the latent power of the silenced to disturb that production, as in Cahun's *Portrait de Mademoiselle X*.

A Mute, Mad Embrace

In drawing the characters and narrators of *Three Lives* into a resounding, sonorous aphasia, curtailing their curative work, the ending of Stein's composite text represents a coming to terms between narrator and narrated, between subject and object. For Lennard Davis, the conventional novel form is complicit in structures of normalcy. Plot is "a form of pain control," its closure shoring up bourgeois identity by neutralizing the threat of aberrant and "abnormal" identities that are shaped by the cultural markers of disability, race, class, ethnicity, or gender.[105] But, Davis continues, this "desire to neutralize is ironic, since in a dialectic sense the fantasy of normality needs the abjection of disability to maintain a homeostatic system of binaries."[106] Cure narratives cannot cure; they simply replicate themselves, like Jeff's torturously repetitive treatment of Melanctha. But Stein's unconventional *Three Lives* plays up its own irresolution even as it resolves in silence. Moreover, although the text's fractured and flowing poetics to some extent replicate the harmful chain of Jeff's diagnostics and of blue talk, the wandering diction of *Three Lives* is pitched, dialogically, as utterance traumatized by and antithetical to this chattering speech. For James Snead, the shift from naturalism to modernism in Western literature—the exact moment in literary history at which Stein locates *Three Lives* by her self-aggrandizing claim that it is "the first definite step away from the nineteenth century and into the twentieth century"—marks the movement from a temporal theory of teleological linearity and progress toward a sense of time marked by repetition and return. The latter is exemplified in the black musician's practice of the "cut," which in jazz "continually 'cuts' back to the start, in the musical meaning of 'cut' as an abrupt, seemingly unmotivated break . . . with a series already in progress and a willed return to a prior series."[107] Calling attention to its own repetitions, the cut pulls against forward motion, much as Freud's repetition compulsion unendingly returns to an unresolved past event.[108] It structures the temporality of trauma, which is also the temporality of photography: "at once in motion and at a standstill, consisting of a recursive eventfulness, impervious to the linear rubrics of progress."[109] The cut, convulsed diction of *Three Lives* is the brace of and against the ideological violence of racialist, nativist, and gendered typologies. It cuts out and cuts away at its own taxonomies.

Summarizing Jacques Lacan's interpretation of Freud's reference, in *The Interpretation of Dreams*, to a father's nightmare about his dead son's burning body, Cathy Caruth explains that to "awaken" from the dream is "to awaken only to one's repetition of a previous failure to see in time. The force of the trauma is not the death alone, that is, but that, in his very attachment to the child, the father was not able to witness the child's dying as it occurred. *Awakening*, in Lacan's reading of the dream, *is itself the site of a trauma*."[110] For Caruth, however, the address of the dead child—"Father, don't you see I'm burning?"—is a ground for ethical response. "It is precisely the dead child, the child in its irreducible inaccessibility and otherness, who says to the father: *wake up, leave me, survive; survive to tell the story of my burning*."[111] Parataxis, as Friedman reminds us, features as a mechanism of Freudian dream work, "for the unconscious processes of disguised expression of the forbidden, indicating unresolved or conflicting desires."[112] By its formal and structural repetitions, then, Stein's neorealism awakens over and over again to its own deaths. It not only recognizes its complicity in racialist and nativist taxonomies but, with a twist on Caruth's reading of (Lacan's reading of) Freud, tells the traumatic stories of the female bodies that are the objects of those taxonomies through silence, the end of discourse.

Thus, when scholars follow the early reviewers of *Three Lives* in claiming the stylistic continuities between its narratorial voice and the voices of its immigrant and African American characters—when Janice Doane calls Stein's narrator "as inarticulate and 'illiterate' as her characters," or when Jayne Walker claims that the syntactically "deformed" patterns of the characters' speech "pervade the entire narrative"[113]—they appreciate only part of the composite text's widest narrative ploy.

Stein's narration, in its stylistic affinity with the characters' speech, foreshadows the larger sociality that is grafted out of Lena's death—with the damming, and damning, of the overflowing repetitions and recursions of its own discourse. "When it was all over" and "Lena had died, too," *Three Lives* depicts the extreme endpoint of Lena's shuffling, disheveled withdrawal from the social and political order of Bridgepoint and marks the moment of her incorporation into a new, unexpected form of community. This is the text's fullest iteration of Barthes's "mad" embrace of the other through the "carnal" and "bizarre medium" of photography: the narrator "[takes] into [her] arms what is dead, what is going to die" by the objectifying microdeath of representation.[114]

The standardizing logic of typological thought wreaks havoc with Stein's women-in-series, killing them off one by one. But in sequence, these women are not rehabilitated into this logic. Nor is Stein's (un)whole composite text. For the gaps in which its women disappear are spaces of revitalization as well as destruction, connection as well as disconnection—just as, for Stein, to heap textual fragments is to mold them together into wobbling, mushy masses. In its bad bodies and its bad form, *Three Lives* achieves a Surrealist convulsion of gendered, nativist, and racialist oppositions that have served to withhold subjecthood and power to female characters. As I will demonstrate in the next chapter, a similar transvaluation of oppositional terms is performed in and by Jean Toomer's sequence of images of African American women in *Cane*—a text that even more forcefully admonishes us, with Freud's dead son, to *"wake up, leave me, survive; survive to tell the story of my burning."*

2. Black Flesh Is White Ash

Reframing Jean Toomer's Cane

Much as with the deathly silence of the white spaces that separate and bridge the stories of Anna, Melanctha, and Lena in *Three Lives*, Jean Toomer's *Cane* (1923) is a composite text riven with traumatic "gaps and absences" that scholars, as George Hutchinson has pointed out, "have failed to make speak."[1] This chapter makes the intervallic constitution of this Harlem Renaissance text speak not by listening to it but by looking at it. The formal fragmentation of *Cane* and its aspects of conceptual obscurity or allusiveness have tended to be elided in scholarship that interprets the text in relation to Toomer's racial identity—which is to say his "blackness," his status as a "Negro." Toomer, with his mixed ancestry, consistently denied this identity. He instead presented himself as the prophet and prototype of what he would come to call "a new ideal of man," the first citizen of a transcendent new America in which "the old divisions into white, black, brown, red" are abolished.[2] Building on recent work by Mark Whalan and others to uncover Toomer's growing appreciation, from the late 1910s, of the raced body as a mediated object of sight, I argue that the photograph was crucial to the development of his understanding of racialization as a discursive and socialized process. In turn, *Cane* models photography in its fragmentary format and diction and models the photographic encounter in its thematic preoccupation with the "picturing" of the bodies of black women. Ruminating on the action of subjects to objects, Toomer's text poses the representation of black women as an act of violence. It reflects the ontological ambivalence and doubleness of photography, as it was exemplified in the political reappropriation of lynching photographs in the activist African American press during the first decades of the twentieth century. In sequence, *Cane* performs a comparable act of resistance to the production of racialized images as the props of white supremacy—and of patriarchy, as well. It dismantles the lynching scene as an apparatus of white, phallocentric power by reframing and restaging it: taking back the camera, tearing apart the image, giving it a new frame.

In what follows, I resist the urge to hear the folk songs and refrains of *Cane*'s "singing tree," calling out over dusk-hung Georgian valleys in the poem "Song of the Son," and instead work to apprehend the lynched bodies that are suspended upon the limbs of that same tree: "O Negro slaves, dark purple ripened plums,/ Squeezed, and bursting in the pine-wood air."[3] If "Song of the Son," and *Cane* as a composite text, turns out to sound less like a "swan song" for the African American pastoral—to take a phrase from Alice Walker's well-known essay on *Cane*[4]—and to look more like a lynching, then Toomer's text demands a move from the sonic to the visual register that complicates conventional understandings of African American literature and culture. Although visual culture is regularly pressed into service in the historicized study of modernist writing by white authors, "any visual accounting" of African American writing is problematic, as Sara Blair has noted, in the context of "a long-standing emphasis . . . on music as the privileged, uniquely authentic expressive form" in African American studies.[5] This neglect of expressive forms other than those related to oral or musical traditions in the field must be redressed.[6] As Katherine Henninger writes in relation to the American South, "In a culture where visual signs—the shape of a lip, a skin's shade, external sex characteristics, the carriage of one's body, the condition of one's clothing—determine 'place' (and may literally mean the difference between life and death), surely the visual may be said to reign supreme."[7]

In examining *Cane* in relation to this reigning visual order and its disciplines of surveillance and control, I approach the text's "blackness"—such as it is, given the complexity of Toomer's racial identifications—and its modernist experimentation as vastly entangled and mutually constitutive. The failure to acknowledge the intersections between African American writing and visual culture in modernism contributes toward the absence of the expressive art of the Harlem Renaissance in the "conventional maps of modernism." These maps are occupied, as Susan Stanford Friedman points out, with Picasso's "primitivism," Sherwood Anderson's "dark laughter," and William Faulkner's segregated Yoknapatawpha County. But there is somehow no space left over for African American artists and writers—despite the fact that the "linguistic and rhythmic experimentation, intertextual 'signifyin,' Africanist mythmaking, parodic mimicry, revolutionary fervor, and self-identification with the New" of African American art and literature fit neatly within modernism's formal and stylistic "definitional markers."[8] Yet as Laura Doyle argues, texts such as Stein's *Three Lives*, which fuses modernist literary experimentation with the overt racism of its narratorial "slurs," demonstrate that the terms "text" and "race" are co-formational in the English and American novelistic traditions.[9]

Like Stein's short-story sequence, which, in Michael North's words, reveals "the radical effect of racial difference on the representational schemes of modern art," Toomer's *Cane* instantiates and interrogates the way in which the "contaminations" of modernism's racialized discourses, tropes, and narrative logics are, as Ann Anlin Cheng writes, the "precondition and expression" of its formal and stylistic innovations.[10] The "misshapen, split-gut, tortured, twisted words" of the writer Ralph Kabnis in the final part of *Cane* inspires North's memorable description of Toomer's language as "submerged in slaughter" (*C*, 151–52).[11] It is not only the broken form of Kabnis's words that is inscribed with slaughter, but the broken form of *Cane* itself. The figural and formal gaps that define Toomer's text are the wounds of racialized trauma and, more profoundly, the trauma of racialization: the charged, ongoing interaction of "black flesh" and "white ash," to borrow from the pivotal line in one of the poems in the first part of *Cane*, by which whiteness produces and is produced by black death. These gaps are sites for revealing this ideological and physical violence—and, against all odds, for resisting it.

Circling Around *Cane*

In December 1922, just prior to the publication of *Cane*, Jean Toomer sent the full manuscript of the text to his friend and mentor, the author Waldo Frank. In the enclosed letter, Toomer defined the operations of his text as a series of circulations about aesthetic, geographic, and "spiritual" cores:

> From three angles, CANE's design is a circle. Aesthetically, from simple to complex forms, and back to simple forms. Regionally, from the South up into the North, and back into the South again. Or, From the North down into the South, and then a return North. From the point of view of the spiritual entity behind the work, the curve really starts with Bona and Paul (awakening), plunges into Kabnis, emerges in Karintha, etc., swings upward

into Theater and Box Seat, and ends (pauses) in Harvest Song. . . . Between
each of these sections, a curve. These to vaguely indicate the design.[12]

For many scholars, this brotherly missive has emerged from the archives as a gift,
an artistic confiding that yields clarity to the structural dynamics of Toomer's first
book. Toomer's circular mapping of Cane has suggested a means for conceiving of
the text as a psychospiritual Bildungsroman, the novel of an individual's coming-
of-age or self-cultivation, or Künstlerroman, the novel of an artist's development.
Bernard Bell, for instance, absorbs Toomer's terms of reference when he claims
that "Cane is the story of a metaphysical quest: a search for the truth about man,
God, and America that takes its nameless poet–narrator on a circular journey of
self-discovery and self-construction."[13] In accounts of Cane as a narrative expli-
cation of the poet–narrator's odyssey, the deployment of a first-person narrative
voice across the text is understood less as a trope and more as the key denotation
of a single and persistent source of utterance.

Epitomizing what J. Gerald Kennedy has called the "insistence on unity" that
shapes much of the scholarship around composite or generically mixed textual
forms, scholars have tended to assume that Cane represents the author's pursuit of
"identity through form."[14] Toomer's first publication is imagined as a transitional,
redemptive space in which the author's subjective, psychological, and sociocultural
wholeness is reckoned and measured through the writing of an organic textual
whole. This approach has a specifically racial dimension, reflecting the imperative
of "authenticity" that has traditionally been affixed to African American writing;
black expressive art has frequently been called upon, Michael Awkward writes, to
"right/write the race" by its affirmative representation of African American experience.[15] Wedded, in this line of thought, to identity politics, the writing of Cane is
conceived as a watershed moment in Toomer's literary career to the extent that it
entails an experience of racial clarity for its author: a back-to-roots encounter with
the African American past in rural Georgia.

Toomer did write a significant portion of the text pieces that comprise Cane
during a teaching stint he undertook in Sparta, Georgia, in 1921. After the publication of Cane, he publically attested to the "effects" upon his writing of the "strangely
rich and beautiful" Georgian setting and of the "rich and sad and joyous and
beautiful" spirituals sung by shack-dwelling, "back-country Negroes."[16] Because
of this, and because Cane is generally acknowledged to be Toomer's best work,
scholars have perceived a correspondence between the book's startling originality
and Toomer's immersion in a Georgian landscape overrun with the ghosts of his
African American ancestry. Cane is seen to document the apotheosis of Toomer's

racial consciousness. As follows, Toomer's literary career is interpreted through the rubric of his accelerating disengagement with normative discourses and practices of racialization, especially after 1924, when he refused to be identified publically as an African American. It seems to be with genuine lamentation that Robert Brinkmeyer claims, in relation to Toomer's writing after *Cane*, "Without the touch of the black soul, Jean Toomer was not an artist but a scribbler."[17]

When unity of form and identity is taken to be *Cane*'s highest aim, the fractured and gap-ridden shape of the composite text comes to signify a fractured and gap-ridden author and subject. "The first striking conclusion by an observer of Toomer's life," write Cynthia Earl Kerman and Richard Eldridge in their biography of Toomer, "is that it was a series of lives, a segmented sequence."[18] Kerman and Eldridge describe Toomer's life as riddled with lines of fracture that trace his appetite for an extraordinarily wide variety of interests and pursuits—an enthusiastic "neophytism," as Toomer once jokingly called it, that made him at different times a disciple of Bernarr Macfadden's physical culture movement, Gurdjieffian mysticism, and Quaker religiosity.[19] Mark Whalan interprets Toomer's faddish disposition in the context of his lifelong "belief in a capacity to reshape and reform his subjectivity, a view which takes subjectivity as a version of aesthetic formalism, something to be shaped and revised in relation to an ideal."[20] But Kerman and Eldridge make the "segmentations" of Toomer's life referable to a childhood and youth "fragmented by a checkerboard racial upbringing" that saw Toomer move "back and forth several times between the white and black cultures."[21] As the variegations of Toomer's career and his history of racial crossings are brought together in the metaphorical space of the checkerboard, patterned with boundary lines and points of juncture, the author's mixed occupations and affiliations are made equivalent to his mixed blood.

This conflation of Toomer's activities, literary or otherwise, and the problematics of racial identification plays into to the "discourse of failure" that has marked the study of Harlem Renaissance literature and art.[22] When, for example, Nellie McKay holds that *Cane* disappoints because Toomer "had not found personal liberation and unity in its meaning and could not accept, for himself, the identity that had caused him to write it," the formal complexities of the composite text are seen as evidence of its discursive and ideological deficiencies.[23] The composite form of Stein's *Three Lives* is elided through the substitution of part for whole, by the critical preoccupation with "Melanctha," but the opposite is true for *Cane*: whole is substituted for parts as the gaps and absences of Toomer's text are approached as mistakes to be excised through the creative resourcefulness of the critic. In each case, the temptation is to domesticate, tame, and fix the composite text.

Like the annulars of a carpenter's nail, a series of concentric grooves that improves holding power, Toomer's three circles have served to hold down *Cane*— much as Tom Burwell, with his hands "[s]trong . . . upon the ax or plow," tries to "hold" Louisa in "Blood-Burning Moon," the final text piece in the first section of *Cane* (*C*, 39). They have been used to sculpt narrative coherency out of *Cane*'s formal and thematic incoherence, streamlining its text pieces into one another and channeling its narrating chorus into a cantor. For Robert Jones, to take an especially idiosyncratic example, there is a correspondence between the arcs of Toomer's spiritual design and the formalized circular design of the mandala in Jungian thought. This correspondence, Jones alleges, illuminates *Cane* as a narrative of the spiritual awakening of "the author's self in art," but tracing it across Toomer's text requires some fancy interpretative footwork. Jones's narrative of *Cane* begins with the final story in its second part, "Bona and Paul," continues into the third and final section, "Kabnis," leapfrogs back to "Karintha," the first story in the first section, and ultimately finds an ending in the penultimate text piece in the second section of *Cane*, "Harvest Song."[24]

"I alone, as far as I know," wrote Toomer to John McClure of the little magazine *The Double Dealer* in 1922, "have striven for a spiritual fusion analogous to the fact of racial intermingling."[25] Yet, as Charles Scruggs suggests, the crucial ambiguities of *Cane* vis-à-vis such racial hybridity, along with Toomer's ever-increasing interest in post-identity, gives the lie to this boast.[26] To take Toomer at his word about the spiritual unity of his text, as well as about the mystical import of the Georgian landscape on the writing of *Cane*, is to disregard whatever commercial imperatives might have influenced Toomer's comments as a fledgling author promoting his writing in this period—and especially as an author who was identified, by others, as African American. That such imperatives at least partially directed Toomer's comments about the writing of *Cane* is implied by his correspondence with Sherwood Anderson in the years surrounding the book's publication. In 1922, Anderson wrote a brief letter to Toomer encouraging him on the publication of his short story "Nora" in *The Double Dealer*. This story was later included in *Cane* under the title "Calling Jesus." "It strikes a note," wrote Anderson to the younger writer, "I have long been wanting to hear come from one of your race."[27] Initially pleased with the attentions of an established author, Toomer responded by writing Anderson's influence into *Cane*'s origin-story. He told Anderson that he had read his 1919 short-story sequence *Winesburg, Ohio* just before going to Sparta, and that Anderson's follow-up volume, *The Triumph of the Egg* (1921), had "come to [him]" while he listened "to the old folk melodies that Negro women sang at sun-down." Both texts, Toomer claimed, were "elements of [his] growing" as a writer.[28]

In subsequent letters, Anderson repeatedly asserts Toomer's ability to speak for his race, to some degree adumbrating the famous manifesto of the Harlem Renaissance, Alain Locke's preface to *The New Negro* (1925), which determined to "let the Negro speak for himself."[29] At one point, Anderson calls Toomer's writing "the first Negro work I have seen that strikes me as really Negro."[30] Anderson was still singing the same tune in 1924, writing to Gertrude Stein to commend *Cane*'s "[r]eal color and splash—no fake Negro this time, I'm sure."[31] But his insistence on Toomer's "real" expression of an essentialized African American experience led directly to the cooling of their relationship. A frustrated Toomer wrote to Waldo Frank in 1923,

> Sherwood Anderson and I have exchanged a few letters. I don't think we will go very far. He limits me to Negro. As an approach, as a constant element (part of a larger whole) of interest, Negro is good. But to try to tie me to one of my parts is surely to loose me. My own letters have taken Negro as a point, and from there have circled out. Sherwood, for the most part, ignores the circle.[32]

Attesting to the restrictiveness of accounts of his work that make "Negro" an absolute category of analysis, Toomer's letter recasts his earlier remarks about Anderson's influence on *Cane* as evidence of his deft negotiation of literary and social networks as an aspiring young writer. In opposing Anderson's fixation with a "point" from which Toomer sees himself moving away, the language of the circle here signifies momentum over stasis, transformation over stagnation, and multiplicity over singularity. In Anderson's hands, the circle has become a bind, but for Toomer it is a structure of release and even of insurgency, as is intimated by the refractory spirit that foments his promise that attempts to tie him down will "loose" him.

Whatever exegetical force is wielded by Toomer's notion of the serial roundness of *Cane*, it is primarily for the opacity and diffuseness of this design. In his December 1922 letter to Frank, Toomer is careful to say that the curved symbols that demarcate the three sections of *Cane* only "vaguely indicate" the text's form. Because these arcs are not circles but segments of circles, they come to stand for the more vital openness of *Cane*'s aesthetic and thematic registers. This textual logic is plotted through *Cane*'s first text piece, "Karintha." Centering on a woman who belongs to the "dusk" and the "dust," terms that aurally loop about one another and shroud her body in a foggy haze, "Karintha" charts the quite literal dispersal of Karintha's body across the Georgian landscape through the death, we presume, of her illegitimate child upon a smoldering "pyramidal sawdust pile" at the nearby sawmill. "It is a year before one completely burns," we read at the end of the piece. "Meanwhile, the smoke curls up and hangs in odd wraiths about the trees. . . . Weeks after Karintha returned home the smoke was so heavy you tasted it in water" (*C*, 5). As Karintha's association with dusk and dust is made disturbingly concrete, the disintegration of the child's body into cloudy, uncontainable matter is mirrored by the reduction of the child to "one" who "burns." Part of the narrative's larger strategies of evasiveness, this abstraction initiates a play of concealment and disclosure that is itself a stylistic variation on dusk as a phenomenon of negation: marking the exhaustion of the day's light while always being in a process of extinguishing, fading and falling into night. "Her skin is like dusk on the eastern horizon," begins the verse that introduces "Karintha," "O cant you see it, O cant you see it" (3). At best, scholars treat this east-setting sun as a curiosity; more often it is dismissed as an error similar to that in "Beehive," a poem in the second section of *Cane*, in which it is the drone rather than the female worker bee who gleans pollen and nectar for the hive. Yet eastern sunsets and female worker bees are paradoxes appropriate to a text that proceeds from the dusk and subsists in its schisms and its silences.

Cane's focus on the enigmatic and the anomalous is made clear through the sequence of text pieces that begin its first section. In "Karintha," the town preacher convinces himself that Karintha, whom he has "caught at mischief," is nonetheless "as innocent as a November cotton flower" (4)—willfully ignoring her violent treatment of cows, dogs, and other children in aligning her with the prototypical Southern belle. The third text piece in *Cane* is named for the "November Cotton Flower," which "startles" the elderly with its "sudden" winter blooming (7). In its miraculous strangeness and seasonal inappropriateness, the November cotton flower summons up Karintha, whose skin encodes visual exigencies by its wrong-horizoned duskiness and whose voice is a solitary, shrill interruption to the momentary "hush" before the other women in the town begin their shared "supper-getting-ready songs" (3–4). Much like Melanctha in *Three Lives*, to whom the naming of Karintha is sometimes understood to refer, Karintha's inscrutableness is a sign for the socially unsanctioned space in which she lives: for her subsistence beyond the pale, as it were, upsetting standards of decency and transgressing the limits beyond which it is not permissible to go. The impossible image of the November cotton flower comes to represent the rift between Karintha and the Southern belle, between Karintha and the other women in her small Georgian town, and, most periphrastically, between "black" and "white" writing in modernism.

Cementing Karintha as an icon of anomalism, incongruity, and marginality, the November cotton flower images a void, a gap, that is constitutive of *Cane* rather than disruptive to or accidental within it. Hence Toomer's text gauges the inadequacy of gendered and racialized formulas and standards to order experience. After all, the point in "Blood-Burning Moon" is that it is "difficult" for Tom Burwell to "hold" Louisa with his "strong" hands (39). This phraseology is imported into the final section of *Cane*, "Kabnis," when Lewis says to Ralph Kabnis, "Cant hold them, can you? Master; slave. Soil; and the overarching heavens. Dusk; dawn. They fight and bastardize you" (148). "Blood-Burning Moon" and "Kabnis" are bridged in series through their shared governing image of racialized violence, as the horrific lynching of Tom Burwell in the factory in "Blood-Burning Moon," under the sign of "the full moon, an evil thing, an omen," is transmuted into the nightmare of Ralph Kabnis "yanked" beneath the court-house tower where "white minds . . . juggle justice and a nigger," washed in the moon's "dull silver" light (49, 115). As I discuss in detail later on, it is through the atrocious spectacle of lynching that *Cane* most fully stages the confusion of rhetorical and ideological distinctions. As Professor Layman says, in response to Kabnis's desperate protestation that the "white folks . . . wouldnt touch a gentleman," "Nigger's a nigger down this away. . . . An only two dividins: good an bad. An even they aint permanent categories. They sometimes mixes um up when it comes t lynchin. I've seen um do it" (120). Rather than marred by failure and abortiveness, *Cane* operates in a composite mode of paradox and allusiveness, in which racial and other categories are mixed up and impermanent. Seen in this way, the text's intervallic pauses and absences—of bodies, beginning with the disappearance of Karintha's child, and of connectives, in the formal register of its collage structure—manifest what Charles Scruggs and Lee VanDemarr call the "marvels" and mysteries of the "extraordinary seen," or, "the evidence of things not seen," which for them entails *Cane*'s "open secret" of violence and miscegenation.[33]

Scruggs and VanDemarr's description of "things not seen" calls up a crucial passage in the first part of Toomer's book, in which one of the narrators is confronted with a vision of "things unseen to men" in a Georgian cane field. It also echoes Siegfried Kracauer's remarks about the "things normally unseen" that appear to view through photographic representation. This juncture at the level of terminology speaks to a wider confluence between Toomer's writing and the ontology of photography, both of which broach the limits of the visual. *Cane*'s dilemma, as I subsequently argue, is a photographic one, concisely articulated in its first lyric: "O cant you see it, O cant you see it."

Machine Artistry

Toomer met the photographer Alfred Stieglitz, along with Stieglitz's partner, the painter Georgia O'Keeffe, shortly after the publication of *Cane* in 1923. In a letter to Stieglitz dated January 10, 1924, which began a twenty-year correspondence between the two men, Toomer describes a vision he saw through the frame of his bedroom window:

> This morning quite contrary to custom, I awoke early. For some reason my eyes were pulled to the window that frames a portion of the Woman's [sic] Day Court and adjoining prison. Usually, the buildings impinge, oppress, and bulk. Usually too the patch of sky between them is grey and leaden. But this morning as I looked, the patch was luminous, golden, crimson. And the somber masses seemed transfigured in this brightness. There came to me a vivid sense of your pure black. Last evening, the essence of it flushed me and for one moment I held a beauty as intense and clear as I've ever known.[34]

Toomer offers a parable of photographic illumination and representation: a framed vision of the "somber masses" is "transfigured" in "brightness," and a "portion" of the world is turned into an "intense and clear" object of sight. Toomer's allegory of Stieglitz's art is at least partly explained by the younger man's desire for approval from an artist commonly regarded as the grandfather of American modernism, much as with Toomer's early correspondence with Anderson. Toomer inculcates Stieglitz's artistic practices through a strategy of emulation, taking on the stance of the photographer. The initial letters shared by Toomer and Stieglitz, exchanged every few days in 1924, evince an infatuation between the two men; in this same letter, Toomer attests to finding himself in an emotional state in which he cannot differentiate between "I and you," between himself and Stieglitz.[35] In this sense, the "flush" of Stieglitz's "essence" of "pure black" gestures toward a moment of homoerotic union, in which the artistic endeavors of Toomer and Stieglitz—and the racial categories by which they are publically defined—coalesce and converge. Toomer is or possesses a white photographer; Stieglitz is or possesses "pure black."

This letter conjures what Ann Anlin Cheng calls the "dream of a second skin—of remaking one's self in the skin of the other," a fantasy shared by both modernist artists and racialized subjects, either in pursuit of the "pure surface" in modernist aesthetics and philosophy or in circumvention of the constraints of epidermal inscription.[36] Designating the reciprocal dreams of Toomer's "black" *Cane* and Stieglitz's "white" modernist art, Toomer's desire for the (photographing) body of Stieglitz indicates the critical importance of photography to Toomer's writing. In his letters to Stieglitz, Toomer repeatedly casts his thinking and writing as a series of visual fragments. "I've been thinking about you and O'Keeffe," he wrote in May 1924. "But the thoughts have been patches, almost without words. All of my thoughts are this way."[37] The resemblance between these "patches" and photographs is clarified in a letter Toomer wrote a little over a year later, in August 1925: "I wish my hand could fashion what my eyes could see. This is a country for the brush and camera."[38]

With few exceptions, scholars have taken up the connections between *Cane* and the brush rather than the camera—and, as in readings of *Three Lives*, have found an analogue for Toomer's writing in Cubist painting and its structure of separate but interlocked planes or facets of vision.[39] But Toomer's notion of the visual aspect of his work is signally informed by the camera, insofar as it worries over the ontological freight of images that straddle documentary and illusory modalities. Toomer believed that Stieglitz and O'Keeffe would have a privileged understanding of his writing precisely because they would know how to look at it. In a 1924 letter, Toomer told O'Keeffe that "Bona and Paul," the prose piece that concludes the second part of *Cane*, is analogous to Stieglitz's cloud photographs, the "Equivalents." "Most people cannot see this story because of the inhibitory baggage they bring with them," Toomer writes. "When I say 'white' they see a certain white man, when I say 'black,' they see a certain Negro. Just as they miss Stieglitz's intentions, achievements! because they see 'clouds.'"[40] For Toomer, the pen in his hand, like the camera in Stieglitz's, could "salvage color from the social world," as Martha Jane Nadell puts it.[41] But to "most people," these revelatory "achievements" are not readily apparent.

Toomer's sense of how pictures can be wrong, or wrongly seen, conditions his description of the "misunderstandings" around "the racial thing" that were perpetuated through the marketing of *Cane*. Toomer was disappointed with Waldo Frank's introduction to *Cane* because he believed it did not "explain" his "actuality" and, as a result, put an "erroneous picture" of him "in the minds of certain people."[42] The connection between Toomer's erroneous pictures and photography is implied in the writer's first letter to Stieglitz. That letter suggests that Stieglitz's photographs are capable of representing a "pure black," that is, black not as a material fact of social signification but purely as a color. Yet Toomer's dream of aesthetic transubstantiation, which depicts an illuminating brightness that generates blackness, is also a metaphor for the complicity of the photograph in processes of racialization. His writing, likewise, is an object of seeing and mis-seeing. "Bona and Paul," the prose piece that Toomer drew Stieglitz and O'Keeffe's attention to in 1924, revolves around rumors about the racial identity of its central character, Paul: "He is a harvest moon. He is an autumn leaf. He is a nigger" (*C*, 95). As Walter Benn Michaels points out, in the fascination with surfaces that change color in this piece, "Bona and Paul" destabilizes both black and white by "disconnecting color from race and insisting on the priority of color over race." Although Paul, whose "dark" skin turns "rosy" with desire for the "white" woman Bona, is not quite black, his friend Art is also not quite white: he is a "pale purple facsimile of a red-blooded Norwegian" (*C*, 103, 99). This description problematizes race, Michaels notes, "by making it available only in 'facsimile.'"[43] By its attentiveness to chromatic shifting, "Bona and Paul" approaches racial classifications as a substitution of facsimiles for persons, an effect of imaging by a technology of mechanical reproduction.

In Toomer's 1924 plans for a follow-up novel, he imagined his protagonist as a machine, capable of transforming "the crude energy of his material world into stuff of higher, rarer potency" in converting "racial consciousness" into an "inclusive art form."[44] This machine–artist bears a distinct resemblance to one of the central characters in *Cane*. In the final section of Toomer's text, as Kabnis roams his yard on a sleepless night, he "totters as a man would who for the first time uses artificial limbs. As a completely artificial man would" (*C*, 114). Awkwardly machine-like, Kabnis's body becomes a seeing apparatus:

> His gaze drifts down into the vale, across the swamp, up over the solid dusk bank of pines. . . . He forces himself to narrow to a cabin silhouetted on a knoll about a mile away. Peace. Negroes within it are content. They farm. They sing. They love. They sleep. Kabnis wonders if perhaps they can feel him. If perhaps he gives them bad dreams. Things are so immediate in Georgia. (115)

The moving, narrowing gaze of this artificial man is the action of a photographic or cinematographic camera, participating in the play of distances and scale enacted in its inventories of the visual world. As Kabnis imagines his nightmares seeping through the walls of the cabin and into the sleeping bodies, Toomer approaches an effect akin to what Walter Benjamin would later refer to as the unveiling of an optical unconscious through the camera's "lowerings and liftings, its interruptions and isolations, its extensions and accelerations, its enlargements and reductions." These mobile interventions in the real are preconditioned, for Benjamin, by the "desire of contemporary masses to bring things 'closer' spatially and humanly."[45] In "Kabnis," the immediacy of Georgia becomes a shorthand for the shrinking of space and the transgression of physical partitions—the cabin's walls, the skins of the family members—that make visible what is unseen by the human eye and make proximate what is separated by space and time.

"Kabnis" performs an act of returning to an earlier point in *Cane* that works to explicate the photographic configuration of Georgian immediacy in the text. Kabnis's sense of Georgia as a site of unorthodox communion and magical touching calls back to "Fern," a prose piece in *Cane*'s first part, in which the narrator is stirred by a "strange" feeling that summons up ghosts in the "purple haze" of the dusk-hued cane field: "I felt that things unseen to men were tangibly immediate.

It would not have surprised me had I had a vision. A black woman once saw the mother of Christ and drew her in charcoal on the courthouse wall. . . . When one is on the soil of one's ancestors, most anything can come to one" (*C*, 25). Full of buried ancestors poised to rise from the soil to share consciousness with the living, the cane field in "Fern" is imbued with a superstitious contiguity. The echo that carries from this field of "unseen things" to the knoll in "Kabnis" serves to ironize Kabnis's sense of the revelatory immediacy of Georgia, because the earlier story stages a critique of the narrator's visionary powers. The title character in "Fern" is an idol of passivity who spends her days "resting listless-like on the railing of her porch" (22). The male narrator attempts to interfere in her inertia by mobilizing, through his narration, the strangely aimless, desireless eyes that are its fullest symbol. He phrases Fern's porch side view as a series of narrative possibilities: "maybe they gazed at the grey cabin on the knoll," or maybe "they followed a cow that had been turned loose to roam," or maybe they settled "on some vague spot above the horizon" (22–23). Even as the narrator seeks to co-opt Fern's eyes, this narration-cum-speculation encodes the problem of sight ("O cant you see it") that is the fulcrum of the first part of *Cane*.

Throughout *Cane*'s first section, the objectifying intrusions and distortions of acts of narration are foregrounded by their formulation through the metaphor of the photographic encounter. Later in "Fern," the narrator maneuvers Fern through a series of spatial disturbances, asking the reader—who is, apparently, male—to "picture if you can, this cream-colored solitary girl sitting at a tenement window looking down on the indifferent throngs of Harlem," and to envision her "up North" and married to "a doctor or a lawyer," before sending her imaginatively to a Southern town as a "white man's concubine" or down a Chicago street as "out and out a prostitute" (23–24). The narrator is one who takes pictures and shares them around, a practice of homosocial collusion also evident in the following passage:

> I ask you, friend (it makes no difference if you sit in the Pullman or the Jim Crow as the train crosses her road), what thoughts would come to you— that is, after you'd finished with the thoughts that leap into men's minds at the sight of a pretty woman who will not deny them; what thoughts would come to you, had you seen her in a quick flash, keen and intuitively, as she sat there on her porch when your train thundered by? (24)

Whereas race supposedly "makes no difference," gender clearly does; as Laura Doyle has noted, "Fern" is framed as a "conversation between men" about women.[46] The train, of course, is a privileged symbol of modernity and as a technology of speed is frequently associated with the cinematic apparatus. In film lore, the movement of the train is entangled with the movement of film virtually from cinema's inception, as the rush of the train into the foreground of the Lumière brothers' *L'arrivée d'un train en gare de La Ciotat* [*The Arrival of a Train at the Ciotat Station*] elicits the (supposedly) terrified reactions of its first spectators in 1896.[47] The train paves the way for the cinema's mobilized gaze, instituting what Lynne Kirby calls a "panoramic perception" defined by scenic framing and a montage of passing, momentary images.[48] Yet at its first exhibition, *L'arrivée d'un train en gare de La Ciotat*—like *La sortie de l'Usine Lumière à Lyon* [*Workers Leaving the Lumière Factory in Lyon*], shown at the first public unveiling of the Lumière films in Paris on December 28, 1895—marked the introduction of film in its still–moving dialectic, as the frozen image of the train and the crowd at the station was set in motion on the screen. This passage in *Cane* posits the relation of male subjects to female objects through a still–moving cinematographic and photographic reference, as the static porch-side body of Fern is rendered in a "quick flash" from inside the train, its windows analogizing the camera's viewfinder and its "thundering" passage the speed of the camera shutter.

The narrator's encouragement to picture Fern is taken up by the other men in her town, who dream of one day rescuing her "from some unworthy fellow who had tricked her into marrying him." That the men hope for such "trickery" in the service of their heroic fantasies suggests the more sinister implications of seeing and narrating Fern. This is in keeping with the narrator's chummy acknowledgment, in the passage previously quoted, of the "thoughts that leap into men's minds at the sight of a pretty woman," which tightens the already close connection between the deeds of the men who see Fern and those of the men who are "everlastingly bringing her their bodies" (C, 22). It is through the narrator's movement from the first kind of deed to the second that the central drama of "Fern" is played out. Directly after making claim to Georgia's immediate visions, the narrator takes a resistant Fern into his arms and "does something" to her—and then asserts that he does not know what he has done in "the confusion of [his] emotion" (25). Embedding a silence in the text like that which screens the death of Karintha's baby, this "confusion" aligns his narration with outright falsehood. As such, when the men in the town are overcome by a "superstition" about Fern's "being somehow above them" and come to believe that "she was not to be approached by anyone. She became a virgin," the ascription of virginity is given as an ascription, which is to say, a lie (22). The act of sleeping with Fern is a kind of writing that can be effaced.

Together with the forgetting of the narrator in the cane field, the sexual unmarking of Fern paradoxically reveals her body as a palimpsest loaded with typological conceptions of femininity: a woman vaulted, with Karintha, onto a pedestal of small-town Southern gentility. "Fern" undermines the narrator's claim to intimacy with his ancestors and implies the violence of the racial past in their apparitions, which are paralleled with the "force of habit" that the narrator calls on to excuse his assault of Fern: "When one is on the soil of one's ancestors, most anything can come to one. . . . From force of habit, I suppose, I held Fern in my arms" (25). *Cane* therefore establishes an equivalence between the immediate visions experienced by the narrator in "Fern" and by Kabnis, which are each defined by their contingency, their failures to narrow in on an unseen optics beyond the racial consciousness that Toomer's machine–artist was designed to negate and overcome. However immediately or clearly Kabnis thinks he sees, his quixotic vision of the family through the walls is a romantic myth of the same order as that of the newly virginal Fern.

In Toomer's country, which is for the brush and the camera, the machine–artist captures the erroneous pictures with which Toomer took issue after *Cane's* publication. These are, to use the words of the text, the "facsimiles" of people in "Bona and Paul" and the "bad dreams" that Kabnis fears he might implant in the sleeping bodies across the knoll. From Fern, seen at her porch "in a quick flash" from a passing train, to the sight of Karintha, who as a child is "a wild flash" who darts past as "a bit of vivid color, like a black bird that flashes in light," the first section of Toomer's composite text presents a series of female bodies that is an expanded version of the various images fabricated out of Fern's idle form (24, 3). As *Cane's* women-in-series materialize and dematerialize in flashes of light, the text calls attention to—and challenges—the "habit" of "force" that defines the picturing of raced female bodies.

Uncanny Eclipses

In 1917, Stieglitz began producing a composite photographic portrait of O'Keeffe.[49] Compiled over more than twenty years, the portrait eventually included over 300 photographs (see, for example, Figures 2.1–2.3). Evoking a dialectic notion of female identity, the formal preoccupation of Stieglitz's composite portrait is the irreducible multiplicity and sheer volatility of O'Keeffe's body. In this visual itinerary of gestures and guises, postures and personas, O'Keeffe is "fertile and androgynous, open and self-contained, a creature of taut surfaces and cushiony ones."[50] Yet, as Marcia Brennan has suggested, the composite portrait exemplifies "the ways in which identity is itself constituted through an elaborate negotiation between self and others."[51] As O'Keeffe asserted, some sixty years after the last portrait was taken, "[Stieglitz] was always photographing himself."[52]

This remark tallies with Stieglitz's promotion of his 1921 exhibition at the Anderson Galleries in New York, which included the first images of the composite portrait; he saw this exhibition as an opportunity to present a kind of extended self-portrait through his images of O'Keeffe. As with the presence of the desiring Salvador Dalí in *Le phénomène de l'extase*, Stieglitz's presence in these photographs is, Brennan notes, "symbolic rather than iconographic . . . the camera lens is made to serve as a kind of transparent substitute for Stieglitz's own vision, assuming a position of propinquity to O'Keeffe's body that would only have been available to Stieglitz himself." As a number of the art critics who commented on these images after the 1921 exhibition recognized, "the aestheticized fragments of O'Keeffe's body actually functioned as symbols of Stieglitz himself, as agents of his sight and touch."[53]

Stieglitz's composite portrait represents a photographic scenario in which subjects and objects commingle, and in which the object of sight is liable to disappear in her very visibility. It is this kind of scenario that is staged in *Three Lives*, as we saw in the previous chapter—and it also shapes the subject–object encounters in Toomer's composite text. In arguing that archetypes of femininity are constructed and deconstructed through *Cane's* serialized women, Sally Bishop Shigley suggests that Toomer's text formulates a "composite female image" out of the "fragments of a real woman"—a woman who, because of her fragmentation, "cannot be captured in language" and so "can only exist in smoke, or reflected light, or rubble."[54] Given Toomer's close relationships with both Stieglitz and O'Keeffe—he had a brief romantic affair with O'Keeffe in the early 1930s—this portrayal of *Cane's* composite female image cannot help but recall the portrait of O'Keeffe (and of Stieglitz). Indeed, Shigley succinctly evokes the materiality and the mechanism of the photograph in her description of women's bodies appearing in "reflected light" as "fragments" of the "real." She also allows for a transferential mode of portraiture such as that which defines the composite portrait when she points out that the comparison between Karintha and the dusk on the eastern horizon suggests that Karintha "is not going down with the sun in the west and losing light, but reflecting the sun's light on the eastern horizon."[55]

Beginning with "Karintha," the first four text pieces in *Cane* reflect upon the actions of subjects to objects and of objects to subjects. The designation of Karintha as a "wild flash" and a "black bird" signifies her refusal to adhere to the town's codes of social conduct and, at once, the insistent efforts of others to devolve her into metaphor. These allegorical descriptions are the lexicon of symbolic acts of power, which seek to espy and categorize Karintha's running form at sunset, when "the pine-smoke from over by the sawmill hugged the earth, and you couldnt see more than a few feet in front" (*C*, 3). The narration of "Karintha" is conceived as a struggle to picture a moving body in smoky,

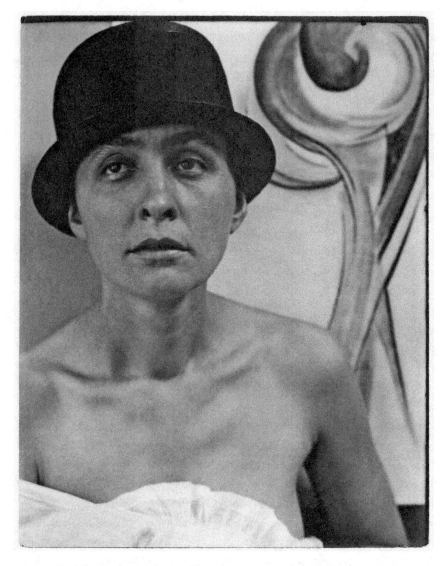

Fig 2.1 Alfred Stieglitz, Georgia O'Keeffe, 1918. © Georgia O'Keeffe Museum.
ARS/Licensed by Viscopy, 2017. Image courtesy of Art Resource, New York

low-light conditions. This ocular activity is clarified in "Reapers," the poem that
follows "Karintha." Upon its introduction to *Cane* in this poem, the narrative
"I" is twinned with the verb "see" (6). It bears witness to the sight of reapers
cutting through a field and unknowingly slaughtering a field rat in the process.
"Reapers" overdetermines the violence that is understated almost to the point of
nonstatement in "Karintha," by refiguring Karintha's child, who "falls" from the

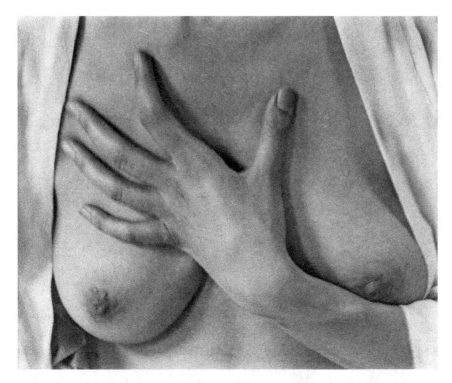

Fig 2.2 Alfred Stieglitz, Georgia O'Keeffe, 1919. © Georgia O'Keeffe Museum. ARS/Licensed by Viscopy, 2017. Image courtesy of Art Resource, New York

womb "onto a bed of pine-needles in the forest," in the description of the field rat with its "belly close to ground" (5, 6). The motif of grounded death is reformulated, a second time, in the next poem, "November Cotton Flower," when drought takes "[a]ll water from the streams" and "dead birds [are] found/In wells a hundred feet below the ground" (7).

Together, *Cane*'s first three text pieces establish the ground soil of the South as both death site and burial plot—a macabre antipastoral construction of the land as, in Jay Watson's words, "mulched and larded with African American organic material."[56] Unseen and seen, hidden and unhidden, the deaths in these first few text pieces are couched as effects of representation. The emergence of the "I" in a vision of violence establishes, as Catherine Gunther Kodat argues, a "parallel between the actual harvest of 'reapers' and Toomer's artistic 'harvest.'"[57] The "I" sees, and in seeing makes death. Thus, the move to the impersonal "one who burns" at the end of "Karintha" allegorizes the flashing transformation of the woman into a representation, an image—which is to say her vanishing, for, as Janet Whyde suggests,

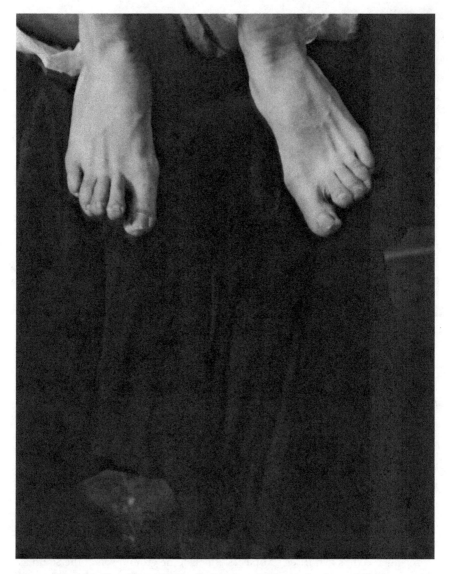

Fig 2.3 Alfred Stieglitz, Georgia O'Keeffe, feet, 1918. © The Art Institute of Chicago © Georgia O'Keeffe Museum. ARS/Licensed by Viscopy, 2017. Image courtesy of Art Resource, New York

Cane's women "disappear by being interpreted, transformed into the physical sign of a unifying abstraction."[58]

This process reaches its climax, in the overture of *Cane*, with the "[u]ncanny eclipse" that accompanies the death of Becky in the fourth text piece. A white woman with two African American sons, Becky is cast out by the Georgian community and into a single-room cabin "on a narrow strip of land between the railroad and the road" (C, 8). Her home is a theater of absence, "eye-shaped" and eyed-off by the passing trains. Once she enters the cabin she is never seen again; the only sign of life is the smoke curling from her leaning chimney, its "thin wraith" a token for her absent body. Finally, she disappears in a spectacle of ghostly origins and uncertain effects that replicates the death of Karintha's child, when the rumble of a "ghost train" causes the chimney to fall into the cabin (10). Although the narrator will later claim to tell the "true word" of Becky's death to the gawking, gossiping townsfolk, the narrator never actually sees Becky under the dusty mound (11). Approaching the cabin moments before it collapses, the narrator is disoriented: "Eyes left their sockets for the cabin. Ears burned and throbbed. Uncanny eclipse! fear closed my mind" (10). Becky's body is eclipsed, hidden in another crisis of perception articulated as a deprivation of light.

Even as the opening of Cane stages the injuries of representation through this event, the simultaneous eclipsing of Becky's body and the narrator's sight is laced with subversive potential—because, from "Karintha" on, to not be seen is to resist narration, and dusk and smoke are covers for women confounding the racist and patriarchal field of operations that defines their world. It is Karintha's "sudden darting" and running momentum that enables her to evade being apprehended. The extent to which she works against narrative efforts to stop and stabilize her is measured in the sensory confusion between visual and aural modes in the narrator's description of her running as a "whir" that has "the sound of the red dust that sometimes makes a spiral on the road" (3). Like these descriptive terms, Karintha is neither here nor there. In "Becky," too, as the narrator's eyes leave their sockets and he literally loses control of his faculty of sight, Becky's death both buries her in and liberates her from the exile of the town's design.

In the sequence of Cane, Karintha's and Becky's vanishing acts point up the impulse toward insurgency in Fern—a woman whose listlessness and enervation, whose stillness, is the sign for the sign into which she is made in the passing train's "quick flash." In resisting the narrator's advances in the cane field, she amplifies the single "groan" that is emitted from the eclipsed site in "Becky" (10):

> She sprang up. Rushed some distance from me. Fell to her knees, and began swaying, swaying. Her body was tortured with something it could not let out. Like boiling sap it flooded arms and fingers till she shook them as if they burned her. It found her throat, and spattered inarticulately in plaintive, convulsive sounds, mingled with calls to Jesus Christ. And then she sang, brokenly. A Jewish cantor singing with a broken voice. A child's voice, uncertain, or an old man's. Dusk hid her; I could only hear her song. It

seemed to me as though she were pounding her head in anguish upon the ground. I rushed to her. (26)

The last sentences in this passage represent a narratorial interference into women's experience and testimony that is already familiar in *Cane*, as Fern's physical "anguish" is subordinated to the narrator's sense of what "seems" to be happening under the cloak of dusk. All the same, Fern's broken song breaks through the dusk ("I could only hear her song"), suggesting its incendiary power in spite or because of its inarticulateness. The "convulsive" sounds of Fern's song correspond to the fracturing of her voice into multiplicity, singing as or for a Jewish cantor, a child, and an old man. As Fern's body is torturously distended with "something it could not let out," her song occasions a form of bodily contact that explodes the limits between her and others. It produces an intermediary relation that opens her up to a role of advocacy and activism. In this way, "Fern" records a means of revolutionizing the dynamic between photographic subjects and objects. By the end of the prose piece, the narrator again watches Fern at her porch from the window of the train. But by now the narrator himself has been implicated within the same myths of heroic "protection" that condition Fern's picturing. "There was talk about her fainting with me in the canefield," begins the final section of the prose piece. "And I got one or two ugly looks from town men who'd set themselves up to protect her. . . . They kept a watch-out for me" (26). As the watcher becomes the watched, *Cane* looks back at those who look.

Progressively revealed, these tactics of resistance emerge most powerfully in the prose piece "Esther," which dramatically revises the death scene in "Becky." In the earlier story, in a lexical variation on the formulation "Her skin" in the verse that begins "Karintha," Becky's features are catalogued as a list: "Her eyes were sunken, her neck stringy, her breasts fallen" (8). Esther's body is filed in a similar way, but with a more pointed emphasis on her lifeless pallor: "Esther's hair would be beautiful if there were more gloss to it. . . . Her cheeks are too flat and dead for a girl of nine" (29). After Esther grows up, "her face" is described as "the color of the gray dust that dances with dead cotton leaves," "her body" as "lean and beaten," and "her eyes" as "hardly see[ing]" the customers at the store where she works (33). Of all the women in the first part of *Cane*, then, Esther is most emphatically defined as a "flat and dead" image of a woman. Yet it is she who acts out the recalcitrance glimpsed in Karintha's wild, whirring form, and perceptible, by degrees, in Becky's groaning protest and Fern's paroxysmal song. When Esther is humiliated by King Barlo, the man she desires, he becomes "hideous" to her and she leaves the brothel: "She steps out. There is no air, no street, and the town has completely disappeared" (36). Crucially, this is not Barlo's first appearance in *Cane*; he, or someone with whom he shares his name, is the narrator's companion at the scene of Becky's death: "Barlo and I were pulled out of our seats . . . . Through the dust we saw the bricks in a mound upon the floor" (10). Because of this, the topographical void created by Esther symbolically redresses the damage done to the women in Toomer's text. Where Becky is disappeared by the town and before Barlo, Esther disappears the town along with Barlo.

As Whalan argues, the obliteration of the town is a result of Esther's "action of transgressing patriarchal codes" through her fantasy about bearing a bastard child with Barlo. It demonstrates the "constant, if limited, negotiation of power" exerted by women in *Cane* and, especially, "the destabilizing pressure [of] the illegitimate body."[59] It is striking, however, that Esther's eclipsing of the town is linked to an image—or, rather, a pair of images. Esther first becomes enamored of Barlo when, as a child, she sees him give a prophetic message on a street corner. Amid all the mythologizing around this day by the townsfolk in the years to come, "This much is certain: an inspired Negress, of wide reputation for being sanctified, drew a portrait of a black Madonna on the courthouse wall. And King Barlo left town. He left his image indelibly upon the mind of Esther. He became the starting point of the only living patterns that her mind was to know" (*C*, 31). Here the racial confusion set in motion by the black Madonna extends to a tension between two different images: the portrait imprinted on the courthouse wall, and the image of King Barlo imprinted on Esther's mind. Made interchangeable with the wall of the courthouse, Esther's mind becomes a repository for subversive messages in line with that of the "inspired Negress" who, as Rachel Farebrother notes, "inscribes the wall of a building that symbolizes white legal power with a figure that represents the suffering of black women, calling to question the courthouse's relationship with justice and legitimate control."[60] Just as the black Madonna transmutes that which is thought to be immutable—from the hegemony of white law to the materiality of race—these images animate Esther with "living patterns" that prompt her to revision Barlo as an "ugly and repulsive" drunkard awash in "thick licker fumes" (*C*, 36). Eventually, they lead her to the foot of a staircase that opens onto an empty un-landscape. Toomer's narrators are always covering over the violence of their representational acts with silence, but Esther uses their own devices against them, eradicating the town by an act of narrative defacement. By Esther's graffiti of expunction, she who is made into an image—a pale, mute, dead thing—is the only person left alive.

Acting in the black Madonna's image, Esther's narrative repossession tears the diegesis of *Cane*. bell hooks, who shares Foucault's belief in the "possibility of resistance" in even the most "unbalanced" relations of power, has argued that the gaze of the other can be returned and overturned by an "oppositional gaze": "Not only will I stare. I want my look to change reality."[61] Bearing this kind of reality-altering look, Esther realizes the incendiary—that is, inflammatory—potential of Fern, whose assault is ghosted by the same black Madonna: as the narrator of "Fern" remembers in the midst of his immediate Georgian epiphany, "A black woman once saw the mother of Christ and drew her in charcoal on the courthouse wall" (C, 25). Fern's body, "flooded" with "boiling sap" and burning to its extremities, undergoes a trauma of immolation in the canebrake that prefigures the death of Tom Burwell at the hands of a lynch mob in "Blood-Burning Moon," the final text piece in Cane's first section. And Esther also participates in this foreshadowing. Overcome by a fantasy of her town set "aflame" near the midpoint of the prose piece, Esther's body is flooded like Fern's, her veins swept with "a swift heat" as if they are "full of fired sun-bleached southern shanties" (32, 34). This dream of burning invites a reading of the town's final obliteration as an extinguishing by fire. There is, after all, "no more air" when Esther reaches the bottom of the stairs.

As Esther seeks to stave off the lynching death that will consume Tom Burwell in "Blood-Burning Moon," Cane suggests that the miscarriages of justice under white rule imaged by the black Madonna are, specifically, the racialized violence of lynching. But like Esther, who learns from this revisionist icon how to annex her own picturing, Toomer's composite text stages an intervention into the picturing of this violence. This intervention depends essentially on the epistemological slipperiness of the images that Toomer's machine–artistry emulates, and, as I argue in the next section, it takes as its standard the reappropriation of lynching photographs by African American activist groups in the early twentieth century.

Picturing the Black Body

Susan Sontag's critique of photography as "an act of non-intervention" in the 1970s casts a long shadow across the scholarship of the medium and its ethical potentialities in relation to acts of terror, war, and violence. When it comes to African American culture and history, Sontag's conviction that there is always "something predatory in the act of taking a picture" has held an awfully potent explanatory power. In the case of the lynching photograph, which developed in the wake of an increase in racialized lynchings in the 1890s and the rising popularity and accessibility of photographic technologies in this decade, the camera's status as a murderous "sublimation of the gun" exceeds its metaphorical limits in horrific ways.[62] The broad-based commercial trade in Kodak images of lynchings, printed on cheap postcard stock, sold in local stores and distributed through the post, served as an apparatus for the construction and persistence of white supremacy in the late nineteenth and early twentieth centuries. As Elizabeth Alexander writes, "Black bodies in pain for public consumption have been an American national spectacle for centuries."[63] It is therefore little wonder that in African American studies, as Blair notes, "photography has been—with certain sharp objections—framed as a blunt instrument or a coercive tool." The archive of lynching images from this period exemplifies "the participation—or at weak best, the studied neutrality—of the camera in the face of brutal murder."[64]

Sontag's final book, *Regarding the Pain of Others* (2003), supplements her earlier claims about the ways in which the "photograph has kept company with death."[65] Across Sontag's work, photographs turn the world into "a series of unrelated, freestanding particles," severed from historical meaning and damned to ethical failure: "Narratives can make us understand: photographs do something else," she writes in *Regarding the Pain of Others*. "They haunt us."[66] In recent years, Sontag's argument has come under scrutiny, notably by Judith Butler, who queries her sharp distinction between cognition and affect as well as the way in which these apparently split functions are, according to Sontag, represented by narrative prose and photography, respectively. In Butler's view, when Sontag asserts that photographs are capable of moving us only momentarily, she ignores the interpretative effects of the photographic frame and, in essence, "faults photography for not being writing."[67]

As Sontag reports at the outset of her final work, "During the fighting between the Serbs and Croats at the beginning of the recent Balkan wars, the same photographs of children killed in the shelling of a village were passed around at both Serb and Croat propaganda briefings. Alter the caption, and the children's deaths could be used and reused."[68] However, as Sharon Sliwinski points out, this example is not only a warning about the availability of these images to propagandistic recycling, but also a reminder of "the power of photography's refusal to explain." Instead of producing "a tyranny of non-action," the "mute refusal" of the photograph might open up a reflexive space in which the affective and political limitations of spectatorship can be appreciated: the "painful labor" of "interminably reaching toward the other's essential identity without ever grasping it."[69]

Karen Beckman takes this a step further. Refusing efforts to "tame the Photograph, to temper the madness which keeps threatening to explode in the face of whoever looks at it," she argues that photographs, by their "silent madness," their vital internal complexities, may in fact exceed what Butler terms the "forcible

Fig 2.4 Milton Rogovin, Unidentified African American woman sitting in a living room, Lower West Side, Buffalo, 1984. © Rogovin Collection/Center for Creative Photography, University of Arizona Foundation

frames" by which the dominant sociopolitical order demarcates its interpretation of the real.[70] Not only can we read against the photographic frame in the manner of hook's oppositional gaze, but the images themselves can act against their framing. As Beckman notes in relation to images of the so-called "war on terror," photographs "may not be—indeed may not be capable of being—fully in line with the perspective of the war effort."[71]

Cane models both the laborious encounter with the photograph Sliwinski describes and the explosive excess of the photograph theorized by Beckman. As it does so, it is patterned after a specific use of photography in the early decades of the twentieth century that complicates conventional readings of photography as a mute weapon of coercion and domination in African American culture. Through

Fig 2.5 Unknown photographer, African American family posed for portrait seated on lawn, ca. 1899–1900. Image courtesy of Library of Congress, Prints and Photographs Division, LC-USZ62-69913

processes of mechanical reproduction, the photograph transformed bodies and objects "into transportable simulacra" adapted to modernity's "systems of circulation," as Tom Gunning notes. But even as the photograph was conscripted as a "guarantor of identity" within the regulatory apparatus of criminology and surveillance from the second half of the nineteenth century on, it also served, by its very mobility, to "undermine traditional understandings of identity."[72] The dual operations of photography in circulation, closing down and opening up notions of identity, enable its revolutionary political use and reuse by marginalized subjects. It is because of this that hooks is able to locate the practice of exhibiting family photographs in the private spaces of African American homes in the twentieth century in a long tradition of self-affirming and redemptive African American photographic portraiture (see, for instance, the image of a woman sitting in a living room crowded with Polaroids and other photographs, taken in Buffalo, New York in the 1980s [Figure 2.4], which sits with the turn-of-the-century portrait of a family on a lawn in Georgia [Figure 2.5]). Family photographs, hooks says, create "ruptures" in the visual order of white supremacy, demonstrating the role of the camera in African American life as a "political instrument, a way to resist misrep-resentation as well as a means by which alternative images could be reproduced."[73]

This photographic lineage extends—in a more public and aggressive guise—to the political reappropriation of lynching photographs pioneered by the National Association for the Advancement of Colored People (NAACP) in the early decades of the twentieth century. An important tactic for a black press determined to garner a national audience for the issue of lynching and to galvanize the American peo-ple against its practice, the reappropriation of lynching images revealed the labor of white spectatorship and instantiated photography's conceptual lability. Toomer first published "Song of the Son," the poem I mentioned at the outset of this chap-ter, in the April 1922 issue of the *Crisis*, the NAACP's magazine.[74] Buoyed by the passing of the Dyer Anti-Lynching Bill through the House of Representatives in January of that year, the April 1922 *Crisis* bears witness to a moment of optimism in the antilynching movement. Epitomizing what Russ Castronovo has described as the "monthly confrontations" between aesthetics and social activism staged in the magazine, "Song of the Son" shares a double-page spread with a book review of Benjamin Brawley's *A Social History of the American Negro* (1921).[75] Written by the literary editor of the *Crisis*, Jessie Redmon Fauset, the review is imbued with a spirit of confidence, as it concludes, "When we see the arduous road we have followed and realize that always the struggle has been upward, we know that our hopes for the future are not in vain."[76]

To some extent, the juxtaposition of Toomer's poem with this review in the *Crisis* foregrounds the hopeful aspects of "Song of the Son," especially the "seed" that grows into the "everlasting song, a singing tree." The engendering of this song in the final stanza of the poem is also emphasized in readings that interpret it as a veneration of folk culture. Yet in the iconography of the first section of *Cane*, the "dark purple ripened plums" that hang from this tree have deeply ominous connotations. They are "Negro slaves," "[s]queezed and bursting in the pine-wood air" (*C*, 17–18), an image of lynched bodies that is firmly fixed through "Face" and "Portrait in Georgia," poems that precede and follow "Song of the Son" in the sequence of the text. These two poems mimic and revise the sixteenth-century poetic tradition of the blazon, performing a grossly literal rendition of its frag-mentation and enumeration of female bodies. Placed immediately after "Becky" in the text, "Face" critiques the blazon form by recovering the dead or dying female body in the previous prose piece as an experiential locus of pain instead of an object of beauty.[77] Rather than appropriating the woman's form for male appre-ciation, as in the classic blazon, in this poem the description of the woman's hair, brow, eyes, and muscles is diverted into metaphor in such a way as to destabilize its own symbolic claims. As "[h]air" becomes "streams of stars," and "eyes" become a "mist of tears," the poem's mode of inspection is imbued with pathos through the "quivering," "rippling," and "condensing" circulations of pain on the surface of the woman's body (C, 12). At the same time, Toomer's blazon of an already broken-up body exposes the latent violence of the rhetorical strategies of the blazon itself, which disfigures the female body through the overdetermination of single parts. The blazon, Nancy Vickers explains, "militate[s] against our seeing the 'entire and beautiful woman,'" such that "the body that is imagined in the most tactile and material of terms—that is partitioned, arranged, and rearranged under the scrutiny necessitated by the genre itself—ultimately vanishes."[78] (There are clear resonances, here, with Stieglitz's composite portrait of O'Keeffe, in which the objectifying force of the photographer's gaze fragments the female body—feet cut off at the ankles, a hand posed across a decontextualized torso—and subsumes it into a vision of male artistry.)

The slippage between representational and real violations of the female body is also central to "Portrait in Georgia," given here in full:

> Hair—braided chestnut,
>   coiled like a lyncher's rope,
> Eyes—fagots,
> Lips—old scars, or the first red blisters,
> Breath—the last sweet smell of cane,
> And her slim body, white as the ash
>   of black flesh after flame. (C, 38)

In this poem, the disassemblage at the heart of the blazon is aligned with the actual ripping apart of black bodies through the lynching ritual. Spectacle lynching often involved acts of molestation or dismemberment, which were commodified through the souvenir trade that, from the 1890s on, enabled spectators and participants to hoard charred remains, pieces of rope, or body parts along with lynching photographs.[79] Through the opening and closing descriptions of the woman's hair "coiled like a lyncher's rope" and her body "after flame," "Portrait in Georgia" educes the lynching scene that is more indirectly represented in the final lines of "Face": "And her channeled muscles/are cluster grapes of sorrow/purple in the evening sun/nearly ripe for worms" (C, 12).

Quite apart from the entrenchment of plums as a metaphor for lynching in the composite text, whatever promise is suggested by the "singing tree" in "Song of the Son" is radically undercut by the poem that immediately follows it in Cane. "Georgia Dusk" opens with the darkness of "night's barbecue,/A feast of moon and men and barking hounds," before establishing another image of lynching in the smoking "death" of the trees:

> Smoke from the pyramid sawdust pile
>> Curls up, blue ghosts of trees, tarrying low
>> Where only chips and stumps are left to show
> The solid proof of former domicile. (19)

The "chips and stumps" that are the remains of the amputated "blue ghost" trees are analogues for the pieces of black bodies collected in the aftermath of a lynching: the only traces of "former domicile," of now-extinguished life. The poem ends with "a chorus of the cane . . . caroling a vesper to the stars" (20), which joins with and ironizes the "everlasting song" in "Song of the Son." The "tarrying low" trees and the "singing tree" are the "solid proof" of the violence of white supremacy— like the visceral descriptions of the lynched bodies in "Face" and "Portrait in Georgia." Under the sign of the "pyramidal sawdust pile" from "Karintha," with its associations of (un)seen, (un)hidden death, these poems picture with revisionist intent, redoubling and deflating the logic of ritualized death.

By the same token, the optimistic gloss lent to "Song of the Son" in the *Crisis* redounds to the activist capacities that the NAACP identified in the public, photographed spectacle of lynching. The image of the lynched body is the subtext for the journal as a whole and for the April 1922 edition in particular. Within a year of its first issue, the *Crisis* ran a cropped, uncaptioned photograph of an unidentified lynching as the accompaniment to a short story by NAACP founder, W. E. B. Du Bois, titled "Jesus Christ in Georgia." From then on, the *Crisis*'s strategic re-contextualization of lynching photographs impelled readers across the United States to interpret the images oppositionally, distancing themselves from the white persons who had taken and posed for the photographs, and so shifting, as Amy Louise Wood writes, "from the position of spectator to moral witness" of white injustice and brutality.[80] Inverting the categories of victim and perpetrator, lynching photographs evidenced the monstrosity not of African American men but of white lynch mobs.

Replicating and repudiating the circulations of lynching postcards through the United States Postal Service, the NAACP's publication of lynching photographs set them in motion conceptually and physically, recovering the "antinomy" that Leigh Raiford sees embedded in the archive of lynching images.[81] In Richard Wright and Edwin Rosskam's Farm Security Administration photo-essay *Twelve Million Black Voices* (1941), for instance, photography is deployed as a mechanism for invalidating white visions of African Americans. Structured, as Nadell notes, around a "disjunction between what is seen and what is real," Wright's history of African American life approaches what he calls the "outward guise" and "garb" of blackness as a "charming, idyllic, romantic" image, which is starkly at odds with the "picture" in which African Americans live.[82] Included in the photo-essay is a lynching photograph in which twelve white men surround the bloodied body of a murdered black man (Figure 2.6). The stern expressions of the white men indicate their belief that they are acting in the service of justice and good order, but this is severely undercut by Wright's text: "Our bodies will be swung by ropes from the limbs of trees, will be shot at and mutilated."[83]

The initial publication of "Song of the Son" in the *Crisis* makes *Cane* proximate to a revisionist use of photography with which its own portraits of lynched bodies bear remarkable similarities. As in the reappropriated lynching photographs, Toomer visualizes the lynched body as an uncanny eclipse, to draw again from "Becky," which is unavoidably partial in its ideological disclosures. These partial disclosures, and the prejudices that color them, are signified through bodies and spaces that are as gap-ridden as *Cane* itself. Especially in the first part of the text, the possessive pronoun "her" is recruited in a nomenclature of categorization, by which women are apprehended as a series of discrete bodily parts: "her skin," "her hair," "her cheeks," and so on. Commensurate with the narrative drive toward holding down women's intractable bodies, this classificatory impulse is established via "Face" and "Portrait in Georgia" as a chronicle of the fragmenting aggressions of the Southern racial and social order. Toomer's blazon poems brutally recast the categorizing of female bodies as not so much pinning those bodies down, but as pinning them up—to a tree.

In much the same way as the increasingly explicit death scenes across "Karintha" through "November Cotton Flower" understand the damages of the narrative "I" as correlative to the violence of these scenes, the progression of more and more concrete depictions of lynched bodies from "Face" and "Song of the Son" to "Portrait in Georgia" divulges something like Hortense Spillers's "hieroglyphics of the flesh," which transcribe the captivity of the black female body to a fetishizing, destructive gaze.[84] The dashes that structure "Portrait in Georgia" emphasize the metaphoric freight of the analogues found for each body part within the highly conventionalized form of the blazon; the analogues are presented as addendums, attachments to and encroachments upon the body. Moreover, the lucidity of the similes—eyes balled into fagots, lips mangled into scars or welts—makes them work double-time, both describing and inscribing the deformation of the woman's body. The female body is established as a sight and a site, an icon of destruction and an open battleground caught between "old scars" and "new blisters."

Fig 2.6 Unknown photographer, Farmers around a lynched black man in Royston, Georgia, ca. 1935–1940. © Keystone-France/Gamma-Keystone. Image courtesy of Getty Images

In the scarifying of the body and the page, "Portrait in Georgia" collapses the pulling-apart of bodies into the pulling-apart of diction. The apertures that circumscribe and fracture the subjects and poetics of Toomer's blazon poems draw attention to the operations of the narrative frame in *Cane* more generally, interpreting the elisions and openings that cleave the composite text as signs of distress, as ruptures, rips, or tears. The paradigmatic spaces in *Cane* are monuments toward the text's aesthetic of interstices, enacting a play of contrasts between interiors and exteriors, and between light and darkness. The age-worn architecture of Halsey's workshop in "Kabnis" is structured around peripheries that are thresholds, inlets inviting entry and passage. The plaster on the walls has "fallen away in great chunks," leaving exposed "grayed and cobwebbed" laths. The split, disintegrating skin of the building expands the sense of the workshop as a contingent, precarious edifice: the sole "break-water for the rain and sunshine which otherwise would have free entry into the main floor" is a "sort of loft," a space that only approximately conforms to its purpose. The space is a network of lacunae that, thrown with light through a window "with as many panes as broken as whole," produces an undulating visual rhythm that is consistent with other descriptions of light in *Cane* (*C*, 134). Dispersed or diffuse in its effects, light in the text is constantly refracted or filtered through surfaces and objects. In the text piece "Theater" in the second section of *Cane*, for example, the "soft glow" of the Howard Theater "rushes to and compacts about, the shaft of light," which "streaks" from a high window, bifurcating the face of John: "One half his face is orange in it. One half his face is in shadow." The stage lights, too, offer up a "soft" illumination, "as if they shine through clear pink fingers" (67).

An image-cousin of the open web that defines Halsey's workshop, these splayed, translucent fingers also recall the strange description, in "Esther," of Esther's mind as "a pink meshbag filled with baby toes." This image appears in the same passage in which Esther's veins are configured as a fire-swept, shack-lined street. Esther's response to this psychological convergence of body and town is to seek solitude in a new enclosure: she closes up the store, "seeks her own room, and locks the door" (34). As Esther comes to contain a whole street of houses, and moves to contain herself in a house, the open weave of the pink-mesh bag comes to reflect a larger problem around the limits of bodies and things in Toomer's text. *Cane* might be the kind of book that contains an eerie collection of baby toes and other body parts, but it does so just barely.

Implicitly referring to the formal fragmentations of *Cane*, this operative tension between insides and outsides suggests how the text's framing devices graph the "logic of borders" that also defines the lynching scenario.[85] Trudier Harris has shown that, from the years of Reconstruction onward, the destruction of black bodies through lynching worked "to keep Blacks contained politically and socially" by promising punishment "for the slightest offense or the least deviation from acceptable lines of action."[86] The lynching scene represented "the most extreme deterritorialization of the body and its subjective boundaries," as Robyn Wiegman writes, "guarantee[ing] the white mob's privilege of physical and psychic penetration" and "definitional authority over social space."[87] In *Cane*, this logic of borders is most cogently illustrated by Fern's body, the surfaces of which are membranes of doubleness: volatile and fixed, open and sealed. The bodily penetration implied in the narrator's doing "something" to Fern in the canebrake exposes her skin as subject to intrusions at the very same moment that it is excruciatingly affirmed as an inviolable encasement, "tortured with something it could not let out." Fern's pressurized, protuberant body functions as the obverse expression of a radical indeterminacy between body and world that has already been established in this text piece and throughout the first part of *Cane*. Fern's eyes, which are so "strange" in their unreceptiveness to the advances of the men of the town, are, paradoxically, the "common delta" to which the "mobile rivers" of the Southern landscape flow (*C*, 21). The flooding of Fern's body transforms her into what Mikhail Bakhtin defines as the grotesque "body of carnival" that is "not separated from the world by clearly defined boundaries" but is instead "blended with the world."[88] Where the uncanny limits of the female body are registered in "Karintha" and "Becky" in its smoky scattering, and in "Face" and "Portrait in Georgia" in its weeping and splintering, in "Fern" the female body embanks whole landscapes.

Each of these grotesque mergers of world and body refer to the lynching ritual. Fern's burning torment of skin-as-cage reverberates through the "ash" and "flame" of "Portrait in Georgia" and the description of Tom Burwell's death in the final text piece of *Cane*'s first part: "Stench of burning flesh soaked the air. Tom's eyes popped. His head settled downward. The mob yelled" (*C*, 48). In the third part of *Cane*, these figurations are replicated in Kabnis's reaction to an actual threat of lynching. "You northern nigger, its time fer y t leave. Git along now," reads the message on a paper-wrapped rock thrown through Kabnis's window, and he is "squeezed" with a fear that "[c]aves him in. As a violent external pressure would, fear flows inside him. It fills him up. He bloats. He saves himself from bursting by dashing wildly from the room" (124). Bloating, burst blood vessels, bulging eyes: these are the bodily effects of lynching.

But like the NAACP's use of lynching photographs, *Cane* destabilizes the violent acts of containment that border these grotesque bodies by introducing an ambiguity around who, exactly, is their subject—or their object. In "Conversion," the poem that precedes "Portrait in Georgia," a drunken "African Guardian of Souls" yields, with a "Hosanna" and an "Amen," to the "new words and a weak palabra/Of a white-faced sardonic god" (*C*, 37). "Conversion" weighs in on "Portrait in Georgia," its white-faced deity and black-faced disciple prefiguring the slippage between white–black ash–flesh in which the latter poem lingers. It foregrounds the series of transmutations that make the woman's body, already caught up in an entwining of figural and literal meanings, into a playground for the combination of body and world, life and death, black and white—and female and male. Indeed, although I have been referring to the figure in "Portrait in Georgia" as a woman, the poem obfuscates its gender. Traditional readings of this poem explain its sequence of conversions as translations of the sight of a woman into the experience of a man. According to Richard Eldridge, it is "an image of a lynching scene" inaugurated by the forbidden desire of the black man for a white woman. "Each physical attraction brings the man closer to the consummation of death instead of love," Eldridge writes. "The braid of hair is really the lyncher's rope; the eyes kindle not only his passion but the fagots that set him on fire."[89] However, as Jeff Webb points out, the poem's imagining of the destruction of a male body must also be the destruction of the female body it figures as literal, with the result that the poem "argues for a basic equivalence between the social forces that would transform him into ashes and the linguistic or literary forces that transform her into metaphors."[90] In this sense, the black man who covets the white woman is not the only phantom haunting this poem. The lynching photograph, as Shawn Michelle Smith notes, is as much a "spectacle of whiteness" as of blackness, crowding into its frame black bodies with their white victimizers and audience.[91] The strategy of the Crisis was to bring this spectacle of whiteness into focus, and in "Portrait in Georgia," likewise, the white men and women by whose hands the "lyncher's rope" is interwoven into the hair of the white–black body also stand behind—and in—that body.

Thus, in the first instance, Toomer's blazon poems exploit the conceptual equivocality and sublimated violence of the blazon tradition in order to confer visibility upon trauma, elucidating Sliwinski's painfully limited labor of photographic spectatorship. They summon up expressive resources to bridge the divide between self and other according to which the experience of physical pain is, as Elaine Scarry writes, an "invisible geography" housed in the remote space of "the interior of someone else's body."[92] In "Face," as Doyle notes, this invisible geography is mapped through the body's "fusion with natural phenomena": streams, ripples, mist.[93] In "Portrait in Georgia," the principle of likeness that marries the body's "braided" and "coiled" hair with the rope taps the "expressive potential of the sign of the weapon" to expose the body's experience of physical violence.[94] In the second instance, and in Beckman's terms, by their silence Toomer's images of the lynched body yield troubling excesses. In drawing attention to the overlooked and unseen trauma of these bodies, they establish around all of Cane's damaged "hers" the "climate of mourning" that Patricia Yaeger associates with the Southern grotesque—both recovering black bodies from the symbolic periphery and making provision of "a forum where the established order can be redoubled, troubled, made palpable."[95] Toomer's lynched bodies figure their oppressors and torturers, catching them, as Martin Luther King Jr. said of police brutality in the Civil Rights era, "as a fugitive from a penitentiary is often caught—in gigantic circling spotlights . . . imprisoned in a luminous glare revealing the naked truth to the whole world."[96]

Posing the Black Body

What naked truth is illumined in *Cane*? In short, the untruths of naked skin. As "black flesh is burned in order to make a white body," Walter Benn Michaels notes in his reading of "Portrait in Georgia," Toomer transforms "a narrative of the attempt to preserve racial difference" through lynching into "a narrative of the origins of racial difference, a narrative in which white bodies are depicted as the consequence of violence against black bodies."[97] In an excellent new analysis of the same poem, Jay Watson regards it as a "double exposure" that exploits the irony at the heart of lynching ideology in the late nineteenth and early twentieth centuries. "Portrait in Georgia" makes clear how the very "intimacies between white women and black men" that this ideology sought to prevent were its own precondition and production. Its structuring dashes are "the Jim Crow social order writ small," and as they fall away in the final, enjambed lines of the poem, the white female body and the black male body are brought together in "a final hybridity" that reveals their "mutually constitutive subject positions: his violated, tortured body establishes her whiteness and charges it with value, even as the vulnerability of her slim white frame functions as a tacit demand that his flesh be *blackened*."[98]

Through the synchronous obliteration of blackness into whiteness and life into death, "Portrait in Georgia" blazons the maligning of the black body in the production of the white body. But by the poem's refusal to differentiate between black flesh and the white ash it resembles under fire, it also takes aim at "the visible economy of race, an economy of [body] parts that enables the viewer to ascertain the subject's rightful place in a racial chain of being." These are Wiegman's remarks on the circumstance of passing, in which "the seeming veracity of flesh can fail to register itself" through the social scrutiny of the body.[99] Whereas the hybridic body of the mulatto, in Samira Kawash's words, "transgresses the boundedness of whiteness and blackness," the passing body opens up an "abyss" between the perception and the knowledge of blackness.[100] As in "Bona and Paul," where Paul the "nigger" is, indeterminately, a "harvest moon" and an "autumn leaf," the passing body puts "whiteness, blackness, and boundary—in short, the entire basis of social order—into question."[101] In making blackness refer to whiteness as it goes up in flames, *Cane*'s lynching images demonstrate the sheer illegibility of raced (and gendered) skins. Like Claude Cahun's photomontages of the serialized self in the same decade, they anticipate Judith Butler's concept of the "morphological imaginary" of the body, by which embodied social identities emerge as "a sedimented effect of a reiterative or ritual practice."[102]

A precursor to the post-racialist discourse that emerged in Toomer's later writing, the supra-racialist portraits of lynched bodies in *Cane* reflect his unwillingness, in this earlier period, "to take bodily materiality as a kind of precultural *tabula rasa*."[103] As Whalan has explained, Toomer's involvement with the physical culture movement in the 1910s and 1920s was fundamental to his developing awareness of the ritualized, mediated constitution of social identity—and hence its instability and manipulability. The physical culture movement was popularized in the United States by figures such as Bernarr Macfadden, who published his disciplines and techniques for developing a muscular physique—and an idealized masculinity—in his magazine *Physical Culture* and elsewhere. Establishing a "more materialized, externalized locus for gender identity," the practice of building the body "offered an agency that contradicted the commonplace determinism that equated the raced and sexed body with destiny."[104]

This agency depended on the movement's emphasis on masculinity as a specular phenomenon, a subjectivity "founded upon the *attainment* of the physical image."[105] The posed body of physical culture was invariably the photographed body. The pages of *Physical Culture* were filled with photographic images of idealized physiques, more often than not Macfadden's own. "Prof. B. Macfadden in Classical Poses (Weakness a Crime!)" is the promise and admonition of one of the magazine's headlines, announcing the latest installment in a seemingly endless series of halftone reproductions of parts of Macfadden's body (see, for instance, Figure 2.7).[106] Toomer kept scrapbooks of pictures of posed men culled from these kinds of publications—and he even once, at college, posed for a photograph after their fashion (Figure 2.8). For Richard Dyer, the practice and culture of bodybuilding is inherently racialized, the "sense of separation" evoked by the hard, tight surfaces of the built body providing a defense against mergers with bodies that are othered according to concepts of racial or gender difference. At the same time, however, the determinism that defines this thinking is undermined by the "triumph of mind over matter, of imagination over flesh" that these bodies literalize.[107] As Whalan notes, as a "system of masculinity" based on repeated display, the physical culture movement bore a liberatory potential "when appropriated by racial groups whose bodies had been overdetermined by white racist discourse."[108] Macfadden wanted his photographic portraiture to give definition, as he wrote in the *Encyclopedia of Physical Culture* in 1912, to "a race of normal, sound, healthy and vigorous individuals."[109] But his vision of normative white masculinity is disordered through the rationale of "corporeal transformability" that was supposed to secure it, because, as Ann Fabian has shown, the self he fashioned in photographs

Fig 2.7 Unknown photographer, Bernarr Macfadden, full-length portrait standing on pedestal, ca. 1893. © F. W. Guerin. Image courtesy of Library of Congress, Prints and Photographs Division, LC-USZ62-89850

is "a series of poses, but poses that, like his infinite replication of personal images, [point] to no single immutable point of origin."[110]

   As the lynching photograph both shored up and undermined the "specular assurance" of white supremacist authority, so the photographs that promoted the posed masculinity of the physical culture movement conditioned its revolutionary implications.[111] And, with its hard, bounded surface replicating that of the built body, the photograph and its ontology of visual doubt also underwrote the discourses that facilitated Toomer's revisioning of racial materiality. Entering into competition for the meaning of the black body, *Cane* works, as Raiford says of antilynching imagery, "to transcend the frames to which [African Americans] have been confined, to move beyond racial fixity."[112] Toomer's composite text makes visible the normally invisible operations of the frame in the image of the black body—and so "un-fixes," in Fanon's terminology, the gaze of the other.[113] It is in the instant when the photograph "yields its frame to interpretation [that

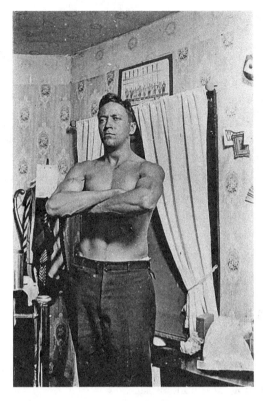

Fig 2.8 Unknown photographer, Jean Toomer at college, 1916. Image courtesy of the Jean Toomer Papers, James Weldon Johnson Collection, Beinecke Rare Book and Manuscript Library, Box 65, Folder 1491

it] opens up to critical scrutiny the restrictions on interpreting reality," as Butler writes in relation to the images of "torture in plain view, in front of the camera, even for the camera" at Abu Ghraib. In that moment, through "a disobedient act of seeing," the frame is exposed as a "mechanism of restriction."[114] As the movement between "Conversion" and "Portrait in Georgia" implicates the former's "white-faced sardonic god" in the alchemic transformations of the latter, *Cane* critiques the "hosannas" and "amens" that are the liturgy of white power. It underscores the weakness of its "weak palabra" and offers its own "new words" about its specular mechanisms of oppression (*C*, 37). These new words are, of course, new images, incorporating the icons, wounds, and souvenirs of lynching into a strategy of resistance. As *Cane*'s fragmentary, composite diction steals back flesh and body parts that have been made off with for brutally illegitimate ends, its mesh bag of black bodies registers the grievous damages of racialized violence, and, at end, the grievous damages of racialization itself.

A Theater of Overkill

Nested in the second part of *Cane*, "Her Lips Are Copper Wire" takes literally the writer Richard Aldington's claim that an Imagist poem must include phrases that give "a sudden shock of illumination."[115] In Toomer's poem, the consummation of the lover's desire for erotic connection with the beloved requires and constitutes her electric conversion. "[T]he main wires are insulate," and so the speaker commands the woman to release the flow of energy: "with your tongue remove the tape/and press your lips to mine/till they are incandescent" (*C*, 73). In figuring the pressed lips of the lover and the beloved as the touching of uninsulated wires, through which electric current flows and produces light, "Her Lips Are Copper Wire" models "the condition of photography's shock effect, its flare of immediacy," as David Trotter notes.[116] Yet here, as with the series of pictured women in the first part of Toomer's text, to be photographed is also to be burned. Karen Jackson Ford points out that there is a serious danger attendant in the poem's situating of electrical imagery in an urban scene in which "bright beads" of moisture cover the "yellow globes" of streetlights and the "corridors of billboards" are "dewy" (*C*, 73). "What would happen in this conjunction of moisture and electricity," Ford writes, "is not, in fact, incandescence but electrocution."[117] This light is a destructive, ruinous force, incinerating those it illuminates.

"Her Lips Are Copper Wire" recalibrates the transference and synthesis of "black flesh" with "white ash" in "Portrait in Georgia" through its yearning for the white-hot glow of incandescence—a word derived from the Latin *candescere*, meaning to become white.[118] The figurative and thematic link between the burning brightness of the woman's lips and the racial and physiological conversions thematized in "Portrait in Georgia" and "Conversion" is anchored in the text piece "Box Seat," which follows "Her Lips Are Copper Wire." Watching a burlesque performance at the Lincoln Theater, featuring boxing dwarfs, Dan Moore is overcome by a reverie in which he envisages himself rising from the "smoke and dust" of the collapsed theater with a "dynamo" in his right hand and, in his left hand, "a god's face that will flash white light from ebony." The god's face reworks the image of the "African Guardian of Souls" succumbing to a "white-faced sardonic god" in "Conversion." Dan's fantasy of "lightning" that "flashes" is pulled into the performative space of the Lincoln Theater, when its physical stimulus is revealed as the reflection of a mirror used by one of the performing dwarfs to single Dan out of the audience: "Some one's flashing. . . . Who in hell is flashing that mirror?" (*C*, 89). Manipulated by the dwarf, the mirrored stage lights produce Dan's black–white vision as they make him into an unwilling object of spectacle before the applauding house.

Sandwiched between "Theater" and "Box Seat," the streetscape of "Her Lips Are Copper Wire" comes to look like a theater, its incandescence aligned with the stage lights of the Howard Theater and the Lincoln Theater. The woman is pictured under the row of billboards as well as the "gleaming" yellow haze of the streetlamps—light that is refracted through the "soft" and "warm" lights that accompany the narrative climax of dreaming and illusion in "Theater." That the woman is on stage, at least metaphorically, is reinforced by the fourth stanza of the poem, where her words "play softly up and down/dewy corridors of billboards" (73). Marking a shift from second to third person, this stanza expands upon the "whispers" of the streetlamps in relation to, for instance, the vocal attentions of the audience when Dan Moore is flashed into sight.

Cane's growing interest in questions of performance and spectacle, across its second and third parts, is indexed not only by the settings of "Theater" and "Box Seat," but also by the shifting diction of the text, as the characters' thoughts are increasingly demarcated in and detached from the narrative schema of the text. Denoted in the form of dialogue in a play script, Dan's fantasy in "Box Seat," as well as the thoughts of John and Dorris in "Theater," are precursors to "Kabnis," a play script masquerading as a novella, or the other way around. Culminating in the final part of Toomer's text, this breaking-down of the *mise-en-page* extends the disassemblage of the portraits of lynched bodies in its first part. As the fragmented, listed structure of "Face" and "Portrait in Georgia" is revivified in the scripted format of "Theater," "Box Seat," and "Kabnis," the scenario of lynching becomes associated with the theater. During Kabnis's feverish night in the backyard, awed by the immediacy of Georgia and cowed by a nightmare of his own lynching beneath the courthouse tower, he rues his fate: "This loneliness, dumbness, awful, intangible oppression is enough to drive a man insane. Miles from nowhere. A speck on a Georgian hillside . . . an atom of dusk in agony on a hillside? That's a spectacle for you" (114). The notion of illegitimate sights established by the wordplay of "speck" and "spectacle" is elaborated, in the larger theater of "Kabnis," in the lynching stories that Professor Layman tells Kabnis. As Layman says, "Seen um shoot an cut a man t pieces who had died the night befo. Yassur. An they didnt stop when they found out he was dead—jus went on ahackin at him anyway" (121). He then shares the brutal story of Mame Lamkins:

> She was in the family-way, Mame Lamkins was. They killed her in th street, an some white man seeing th risin in her stomach as she lay there soppy in

her blood like any cow, took an ripped her belly open, an th kid fell out. It was living; but a nigger baby aint supposed t live. So he jabbed his knife in it an stuck it t a tree." (124)

Corroborating what Wiegman describes as the "performative qualities" of the lynching scene as a "refiguration of slavery's initial, dismembering scene,"[119] Layman portrays lynching as overkill, a hacking and ripping of bodies that not only mutilates the outside of the body but eviscerates its insides—in the case of Mame Lamkins, through a form of disembowelment. The movements of the lynch mob "ahacking" their dead victim are not operative but performative: they no longer kill him, but act out, overact, their killing of him. Likewise, central to the shock of the murders of Mame Lamkins and her child is their public exhibition, the one "soppy" on the street, the other "stuck" to a tree.

The story of Mame Lamkins and her baby is a close rewriting of the NAACP's account, in the 1919 publication *Thirty Years of Lynching in the United States, 1889–1918*, of the murder of the pregnant Mary Turner. This murder became "an archetypal instance of Southern barbarism" in the African American activist press.[120] Although lynching photographs conventionally worked to keep the actual violence out of the frame, depicting orderly mobs gathered soberly about their victims, the "visible excesses of mob violence" were eventually pressed into the service of the antilynching movement.[121] As Castronovo explains, the lynching scenario was "an aesthetic performance," evident in the *New York Times* coverage of a 1911 lynching in a Kentucky opera house, which described the "staging" of a "revenge play" or "melodrama" that drew to a close as "the lights were extinguished, the curtain lowered, and the mob then filed out."[122] Equally, the reappropriation of lynching photographs was, in Raiford's terms, "a performance, an attempt to affect public opinion and envision freedom through the specific dramaturgy, or staging, of black death."[123]

What first haunts Kabnis on that sleepless night is the "weird chill" of the songs borne on the "night winds" of Georgia:

White-man's land.
Niggers, sing.
Burn, bear black children
Till poor rivers bring
Rest, and sweet glory
In Camp Ground. (C, 111)

This is another song, like "Song of the Son," that sees lynched bodies. It pictures the "white-man's land" of *Cane* as a theater of death, in which black children are simultaneously born and burned. Alluded to in the second "sleep-song" Kabnis hears that night ("rock a-by baby . . . when the bough bends . . . cradle will fall . . . down will come baby" [113]), two nameless children drop from their mothers' wombs into death at opposite ends of Toomer's textual sequence. The corpses of Karintha and Mame Lamkins's offspring epitomize the broken black bodies that hang between life and death in *Cane*. They are the principal players in its dramaturgy of black birth as black death, which traces the origins of racialization in the burning of "black flesh" to "white ash." Patterned after the conceptual ambivalence and insurrectionary capacities of the photograph, Toomer's composite text restages the conventionalized spectacles of the white supremacist and patriarchal social order. However fleeting or obscure, Toomer's grotesque pictures of black bodies—whether dispersed or pierced, smoldering in ash or pinned to a tree—do not slip through the cracks and frames of his text. They linger in them.

3. Frozen in the Glassy, Bluestreaked Air

John Dos Passos's Photographic Metropolis

Near the end of John Dos Passos's *Manhattan Transfer* (1925), Ellen Thatcher meets her suitor, George Baldwin, at the Algonquin restaurant for dinner. When Baldwin asks her to marry him, Ellen begins to feel "a gradual icy coldness stealing through her like novocaine":

> It seemed as if she had set the photograph of herself in her own place, for-ever frozen into a single gesture . . . . Ellen felt herself sitting with her ankles crossed, rigid as a porcelain figure under her clothes, everything about her seemed to be growing hard and enamelled, the air bluestreaked with ciga-rettesmoke, was turning to glass.[1]

As Ellen's paralysis jams the diction of this passage into a stultified series of fragments, from "Ellen felt herself sitting" to "was turning to glass," Dos Passos conceives a setting of a female body as a photographic image that is consistent with the dramas of representation in *Three Lives* and *Cane*. The photographic-becoming of Ellen supplements other descriptions of her taut and impenetrable physical surfaces in *Manhattan Transfer*, especially in relation to the desirous approaches of the men of New York City. At another dinner, earlier in the novel, Ellen is, for her companion Jimmy Herf, a silent, still "porcelain figure under a bellglass" (272). Similarly, when at a high-society party, Ellen suddenly hears the voices of men "knotting about her," and she sits up from her armchair "cold white out of reach like a lighthouse. Men's hands crawl like bugs on the unbreakable glass. Men's looks blunder and flutter against it helpless as moths" (169).

Carol Shloss has drawn attention to the scene of Ellen's photographic freezing in arguing that Dos Passos derived a formal and conceptual model for his experimental, multilinear novel of New York from photography. In Shloss's view, the photograph serves as a symbol for the condition of anomie that plagues the characters in Dos Passos's early fiction and that is imaged in the "cumulative" or "collective picture" of *Manhattan Transfer*.[2] In making a rhetorical point about the novel's multiperspectivalist structure, Shloss follows a number of other scholars in compiling a long list of its minor characters. What this roster culled from the large population of *Manhattan Transfer* intimates is the listed formulation of Dos Passos's multilinear novel and its host of characters—not to mention its diction, as suggested by the fragmented expression that articulates the stiffening of Ellen's body at the Algonquin. It is not so much, as Shloss suggests, that the novel "leans toward" primary characters including Ellen Thatcher and away from secondary ones such as Ruth Prynne, the struggling theater actress, or Anna Cohen, the daughter of working-class Jewish immigrants.[3] Instead, the novel's construction of Ellen is capacitated by and refracted through Ruth's and Anna's serial appearances throughout the text. There is no doubt that Dos Passos's novel deploys the metaphor of the photograph, in Shloss's words, "as a 'skin,' a 'surface,' a reference to something absent, a fragment," in testifying to the subjective dangers of mere formalism in everyday life.[4] But it also, and more fully, shows its debt to photographic technologies in its essentially iterative mode of narration and characterization. By the novel's composite logic, both women's bodies and the modern city are rendered serially, accrued and assembled in sequence.

The performative aspect of the medicalized encounter in *Three Lives* and the dramaturgy of lynching in *Cane* is disclosed as the woman-in-series frustrates and subverts the viewing positions that constitute these scenes of social and political power. But in *Manhattan Transfer*, the serialized construction of the novel—and its women—relates specifically to its popular theatrical contexts. These contexts have been almost entirely overlooked in the scholarship, with the notable exception of Janet Galligani Casey's exploration of how Dos Passos's New York is organized around the "visual grammar of audience-stage relations" that "reproduces the male-female gaze dynamic of the culture at large."[5] In fact, as I argue in this chapter, Ellen Thatcher's narrative centrality in Dos Passos's composite text should be understood precisely in terms of her thespian career. Ellen is the star of a modern metropolis that is aligned with the world of the segmented spectacle of situations and set-pieces of the burlesque and vaudeville, which from the 1860s onward became increasingly associated with the variety-show format. The episodic form and aesthetic of *Manhattan Transfer* reference the syncopated series of theatrical scenes exemplified in New York City in the 1910s and the 1920s by Florenz Ziegfeld Jr.'s revue-style productions and embodied in the repetitive, rhythmic gestures of the famous chorus troupe that was their centerpiece.

To salvage the significant and distinctive theatrical contexts for Dos Passos's novel is also to salvage its photographic aspect. Photographic technologies were foundational to the style of Ziegfeld's revues and its chorines' performances and were also recruited in the apparatus of advertisement and celebrity that was subsidiary to Broadway theater in the early twentieth century. In attending to the photographic constitution of Dos Passos's narrative stage, I provide a new reading of what is routinely claimed to be the novel's consonance with the technologies of urban modernity. *Manhattan Transfer* emerges, unexpectedly, as an index for the body–machine complex in turn-of-the-century American culture. Spanning the 1890s through the 1920s, the novel represents the modern city and its persons as tabulated and archived: frozen in series by the control technologies of surveillance and statistics. In this sense, the depiction of Ellen Thatcher sitting "rigid as a porcelain figure under her clothes," as the Algonquin restaurant grows "hard and enamelled" around her, is the quintessence of her characterization in the modern city. It also emblematizes one of the most compelling narrative intrigues plotted through the multilinear text, namely, the close proximity and vast interchangeability of its narrated persons, as of bodies and their images.

Thus, although there are serious restrictions to the insurrectionary activity of the woman-in-series in *Manhattan Transfer*, Dos Passos finally implies the radical nondifference between Ellen Thatcher and the women who are her social and ethnic others—as well as how the photographic surface can serve simultaneously as a prison and a shield, an objectifying skin and a protective covering. The two previous chapters explored the subversive potential of female characters who are marked by the indices of social otherness, reclaiming the resistant and recalcitrant gaze of the nonwhite, non–middle-class woman in order to respond to one of feminism's "anekphrases," in Laura Wexler's terms: its "active and selective refusal" to consider racial and other categories of difference alongside and in its gendered analyses.[6] In the correlation between *Manhattan Transfer*'s fragmentary, additive narrative tactics and the mass entertainments of the late nineteenth and early twentieth centuries, and in the novel's broad critique of the patriarchal and white-centric specular economy of the modern metropolis, Dos Passos reveals relations of domination that are blind spots in feminist scholarship—not least the "internal dynamics of objectification within [feminism's] own ranks, woman over woman."[7]

A "Leg Show Dance" in a Skyscraper

On September 16, 1896, the *New York Times* reported that the infamous "Parisian beauty and singer" Anna Held (see Figure 3.1) had arrived in New York City to appear in the farce "A Parlor Match." According to the *Times*, Held's steamship ingress had been the source of much "rumor" and anticipation.[8] The gossipy chatter was encouraged by the theatrical entrepreneur Florenz Ziegfeld Jr., who spun the news that the Parisian performer took a daily dip in a bath of milk. Ziegfeld coordinated the delivery of large quantities of fresh milk with the arrival of

Fig 3.1 Aimé Dupont, Anna Held, full-length portrait, 1900. © Aimé Dupont. Image courtesy of Library of Congress, Prints and Photographs Division, LC-USZ62-22031

New York's reporters to Held's suite and then invited the reporters in for a glimpse of this latter-day Cleopatra enacting her luxurious, creamy ablutions.[9]

In a brown-cover notebook used by Dos Passos in the period 1919–1927, a scribbled reference to Held's off-Broadway debut is nested in a series of rough sketches of tumbling trapeze artists, ball-balancing seals, and top-hatted figures: "Anna Held in a Parlor Match at the Herald Sq. Theater."[10] Dos Passos was recalling this moment in theater, media, and pinup girl history and envisaging circus scenes around the same time as he was putting to paper the first sections of *Manhattan Transfer*. In the same brown notebook, he jotted down some thoughts preliminary to the drafting of the novel, including a sentence that would eventually appear in the first chapter of the novel with only small modification: "We'll call her Ellen after my mother said Mr. Thatcher with tears in his eyes on the arrival to the maternity hospital." The brown notebook also contains a list that reads like a *dramatis personæ*. Under the heading "Burlesque Play," Dos Passos lined up a series of stock characters including "The Footlight Queen," "The Jew," "The Bum," and "The Fairy." There is a comparable register of theatrical archetypes in another notebook he used in the early 1920s, which makes the connection to *Manhattan Transfer* explicit. In this second list, alongside references to "Chorus Girls" and an "Opening chorus—leg show dance," "The blonde Queen" is identified as "Nevada Jones," a character who performs vaudeville routines in the 1925 novel.[11]

Dos Passos's notebooks land us simultaneously in the Herald Square Theater with Held in "A Parlor Match" and on the elaborate, multilevel stage of the Ziegfeld Follies, the renowned Broadway revues Ziegfeld went on to produce annually from 1907 through 1931. The penciled reference in the checkered notebook to "leg show" choreography unavoidably conjures the Follies girl, the most famous of all chorus girls. As Linda Mizejewski points out, Held's arrival in New York City was the pretext for the most successful publicity stunt of the era, and Held served, upon her milk-bathed unveiling, as the "immediate precursor" to the haughty-stepped, feather-headdressed Follies girl whom Ziegfeld sent down the ornate staircase a decade later (see Figure 3.2).[12] In alluding to Ziegfeld's revue-style productions off and on Broadway, Dos Passos's notebooks imply the measure of equivalence between Held and the Follies girl, as well as between the stages on which they respectively appeared.

Dos Passos had an avid interest in the theater. As early as 1920, he turned his hand to an experimental play script; in the same year as *Manhattan Transfer* was published, his play "The Garbage Man" premiered in Boston; and before the decade was through, he would be heavily involved in New York's revolutionary theater scene—not only writing plays but also painting sets and designing posters.[13]

Fig 3.2 Unknown photographer (White Studio), Showgirls in the feather number at the Ziegfeld Follies of 1925. © Billy Rose Theatre Division, New York Public Library for the Performing Arts

Traditionally marginalized in both literary scholarship and in theater history, Dos Passos's theatrical work has in recent years received a welcome new focus.[14] The relevance of his investment in the world of the theater to *Manhattan Transfer* is indicated quite straightforwardly by the fact that its central character is a successful Broadway actress. In fact, the iconography around Ellen Thatcher in the novel incorporates the theatrical spectacle of the Ziegfeld Follies. Amid Dos Passos's vast modern cityscape, one skyscraper becomes the "obsession" of Jimmy Herf, a failed newspaperman and once-lover of Ellen, in his lonely nocturnal wanderings:

> Faces of Follies girls, glorified by Ziegfeld, smile and beckon to him from the windows. Ellie in a gold dress, Ellie made of thin gold foil absolutely lifelike beckoning from every window. And he walks around blocks and blocks looking for the door of the humming tinselwindowed skyscraper, round blocks and blocks and still no door. (*MT*, 327)

The reference to the Follies is doubly inscribed, through two phrases that form a loosely rhyming couplet: *Fac-es of Foll-ies girls/glor-i-fied by Zieg-feld*. The insistent diction is appropriate to a spectacle of replication in which Ellen proliferates into a series of beckoning bodies. She is not simply a Follies girl but an entire chorus of them laid out in a glittering grid. She abides by the same rule of seriality that organized the Follies revues, four-hour-long variety shows that interspersed full-scale pageant scenes with comedy routines and musical numbers. The rhythmic, combinatory unfolding of the mixed programs, which derived their overall effects "from the incongruous confrontation of each bit with the other, the ongoing flow that forces each scene to give way to the next,"[15] was represented visually in key sheets produced from photographs taken at live rehearsals and performances (see, for instance, Figure 3.3). Insofar as this structure resembled the repetitious routines of their star attraction, the Follies girl, the Ziegfeld Follies operated as a kind of chorus troupe writ large.

As the Ellens-as-Follies-girls wave and smile at Jimmy below, their routine of small, standardized gestures recalls the *tableau vivant*, the Follies girls' most famous trick, and its tensile invocation of the organic with the inorganic. Ziegfeld's chorus girls were reduced to automata within spectacles of militaristic or machine

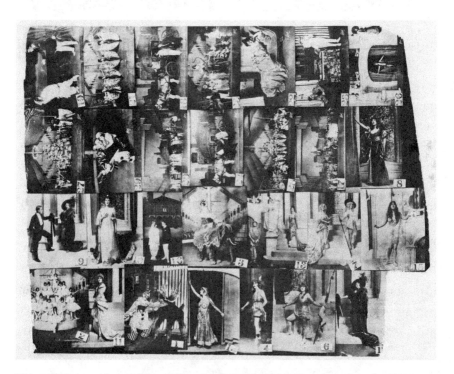

Fig 3.3 Unknown photographer (White Studio), Ziegfeld Follies of 1912 key sheet.
© Billy Rose Theatre Division, New York Public Library for the Performing Arts

aesthetics, corralled into geometric patterns and whirling tableaux modeled after rotating gearwheels and even, on occasion, made to act as machines such as telephone switchboards or dirigibles. Achieving an impression of propulsive dynamism out of the controlled, successive workings of its component parts, the conjoined and recursive sequence of gestures and movements that composed the Follies girls' skits produced the effect of collapsing body on body, segment into whole.[16] The Follies girl was thus poised, cool and gleaming, at the interface between the singular and the multiple, the personal and impersonal, and the animate and inanimate. Poised, indeed: the *tableau vivant* was essentially a balancing act between these oppositions, conflating female bodies with the extravagant *mise-en-scène* of Ziegfeld's revues. The visual thrill of these living pictures or living curtains was directly proportionate to their consummation of the paradoxical relation from which these grand tableaux derived their popular names. In *Manhattan Transfer*, the window-framed, beckoning bodies in the skyscraper function as a poetic variation on the *tableau vivant*'s embodied–disembodied equivocality: its demonstration of what Bill Brown calls the "indeterminate ontology" of objects and bodies that cannot be clearly distinguished.[17] The slippage, performed in and by the female body at the window, between the "glorified" Follies girl and the glittering mirage of Ellen, is compounded in the ontological incertitude of that body, which is at once "made of thin gold foil" and "absolutely lifelike." This description seems bent on undoing itself; if to be "lifelike" is to confirm, through simulation, the gap between life and its likeness, then the adverb *absolutely* undermines the guarantee it makes.

   Manhattan Transfer has been consistently understood as a novel patterned after the cinema rather than after the theater. Beginning at its first publication, readers like Sinclair Lewis discerned "the technique of the movie" in the novel's "flashes," "cut-backs," and "speed."[18] Subsequently, comments that Dos Passos made in the late 1960s attesting to the influence on his novel of Eisensteinian montage set the tone for scholarship that proposes formal continuities between the cinema and the novel's "kaleidoscopic" or "mosaic" form.[19] But as Michael Spindler and others have noted, Dos Passos's retrospective account of the development of his "montage" aesthetic was flawed. The author could not have seen Eisenstein's films before writing *Manhattan Transfer*, because they were not distributed in the United States until the late 1920s, and it is unlikely that he had read Eisenstein's film theory, as it did not appear in American journals before 1927.[20] Similarly, scholarly discussions of transmedia "crossfertilization," to use Claude-Edmonde Magny's term, in *Manhattan Transfer* often mobilize concepts of cinematic techniques and mechanisms fairly haphazardly or imprecisely, sometimes to the point of ahistoricity.[21]

The traces of New York's popular theater in the notebooks suggest other aesthetic, material, and sociological contexts for reading *Manhattan Transfer* than those that coalesce around 1920s cinema. As suggested by the prominence of theatrical settings in the second part of Toomer's *Cane*, set in Washington, the theater had by no means been supplanted by the cinema in the 1920s. To the contrary, this decade saw the peak of American theatrical production, with an average of 225 plays produced per year.[22] The fleeting, disjointed, striking amusements of the vaudeville stage along with those of the cinema were understood to rival and mirror the shocks and sensory intensities of modern urban life.[23] Moreover, and in keeping with one of the key insights of recent work on early cinema, namely the "instability" of its forms, institutions, spectatorial contexts, and visual pleasures, the uneven development of the cinema in the early part of the twentieth century in the United States was intimately caught up with the theater.[24] Early cinema occupied a shared exhibition context with the popular theater in the first decades of the century and inculcated, to some extent, its segmented arrangement. Ben Brewster has shown that even after the cinema moved from its first home, the vaudeville house, the format of the mixed show persisted to the end of the silent era and, in the big cities, much later. Programs at the nickelodeons, the small permanent theaters that were the crucial sites for the screening of short films across the United States after 1906, retained "the idea of the series of contrasting acts that dominated variety entertainment as a whole."[25]

Of the very few references to cinematic entertainments in *Manhattan Transfer*, the most significant is the nickelodeon, an exhibition site that was altogether old-fashioned by the time Dos Passos began drafting the novel in the early 1920s. The episode titled "Nickelodeon" begins with an epigraph that hangs on a nickel, the basic unit of currency in an economy of mass entertainment that runs on—or runs out of—technologies that are as ephemeral as the small coins they consume. "On Sixth Avenue on Fourteenth," we read, "there are still flyspecked stereopticons where for a nickel you can peep at yellowed yesterdays." In pairing the nickelodeon with the stereopticon, a slide projector dating from the mid-nineteenth century, *Manhattan Transfer* presages the interrelation between optical toys and the cinema that Jonathan Crary has conceptualized in terms of a modernized vision that overthrows perspectival realism for a destabilized, subjective organization of representation.[26] A variation on the stereoscope, a popular parlor device, the stereopticon forms compound images from the projections of two of more magic lanterns. Like other experiments in composite photography, its illusion is an assault on photographic referentiality and the unifications of the Cartesian scopic regime.[27] As with Crary's account of sensory immediacy through the modernization of vision, in which the forms and apparatuses of low, popular amusements and those of high-modernist art are entangled, Dos Passos's rendering of the stained stereopticon in the larger performative context of the modern city street—and through the disjunctive lexicon of the modernist found poem—accommodates the low-popular and the high-modern observer alike. As a result, it complicates conventional accounts of the novel's consonance with the rupturing, decentering aesthetic of visual nihilism and abstraction normally associated with elite modern art and cinema. A curbside travelogue unfolding as a series of fragmentary phrases, the epigraph's passage down Sixth Avenue presents the entertainments of New York's streets as serial and fleeting. Recording the "bruised notes" of foxtrots, waltzes, and blues numbers "limping" and "trailing" drunkenly out of New York dance halls, the epigraph makes the sonic residue of the dance halls' "gyrating tinsel memories" the (shinier) supplement to the stereopticon's "yellowed yesterdays." Not only is the stereopticon the "waste-basket of torn-up daydreams" with which the epigraph ends, but the city street is also a dumping ground for past, or, at best, passing, attractions (*MT*, 264).

Traveling by associative collocation, the "Nickelodeon" epigraph's principle of juxtaposition is consistent with the structural logic of Dos Passos's multilinear novel and the spatial design of the city in the novel. First, the epigraph's listed format repeats in miniature the accumulation of fragmentary and episodic prose blocks that comprise Dos Passos's novel. Second, and concomitantly, the journey of the epigraph down Sixth Avenue replicates the defining movements of pedestrians and vehicles in the striated space of Dos Passos's New York. In this street-tracked metropolis, on which wheels turn in unison and feet step in line, ranks of cars slither along roadways "with snaky flint of lights running in two smooth continuous streams" and people are "fed" into buildings "in two endless tapes through the revolving doors out into Broadway, in off Broadway" (153, 115). Jimmy Herf is agitated not merely by the perpetual revolutions of the revolving doors but also by the daily passage of "elbowing, shoving, shuffling" bodies ceaselessly traveling "into" and "in off" Broadway.

That the fragmentary narrative design of *Manhattan Transfer* is closely connected to, and constituent of, the contours of the modern metropolis it represents and configures is signaled by the fact that the novel originates with the kind of successive, linear movement that so disturbs Jimmy on Broadway. The "grinding out" of his life "like sausage meat" by the revolving doors is a version of the metaphoric transmutation of human bodies into foodstuffs that occurs in the opening vignette of the novel (115). *Manhattan Transfer* begins with an image of a crowd channeled and propelled in sequence, "press[ed] through the manuresmelling wooden tunnel of the ferryhouse, crushed and jostling like apples fed down a chute into a press" (15).

Scholars interested in decoding the structural logic of *Manhattan Transfer* have rarely extrapolated a spatial metaphor for the text from this initial, pressing movement, instead paying attention to the vortex, a different but related image pattern offered up by the novel through its depiction of a New York that drives its inhabitants "round and round in a squirrel cage" (202). It is not a coincidence that the dizzying momentum of the vortex obliquely mirrors the spinning film reel. Yet if we revisit Jimmy's dream of Ellen Thatcher amalgamated with the Follies girls—a move encouraged by the theatrical frame that shapes Dos Passos's notebooks— we encounter an emphatic demarcation of the city streetscape as a site for the kind of sequenced movement with which the novel opens. Ellen's sheer, shimmering multiplicity, mimed in her eternal beckoning and smiling on the latticed, glassy façade of the skyscraper, produces and corresponds to the relentless futility of Jimmy's retraced steps on the city street below. What this scene emphasizes is less the actual circularity of Jimmy's path than its repetitious circuitry. His steps "around blocks and blocks," "round blocks and blocks" are somewhat less round and round than they are over and over again—a point substantiated by the stammering repetition inscribed at the level of utterance in this passage. At the foot of the skyscraper, Jimmy succumbs to the torturously reiterative momentum that is proper to and standard in Dos Passos's tape-fed, apple-pressed metropolis.

In an essay that complicates the notion of *Manhattan Transfer*'s cinematic qualities, E. D. Lowry suggests that Dos Passos's method of narrative montage might register an adjustment to a public that had been schooled by the news media and vaudeville theater "to 'consume' an endless stream of events and sensations."[28] Lowry's "endless stream" is akin to Brewster's "idea of the series" in both theater and cinema in the early twentieth century. The lists of theater archetypes in the notebooks that lie behind the drafts of *Manhattan Transfer* affirm Lowry's intuition about the value of seeing Dos Passos's novel as a model of the stream of scenic spectacles represented in this period by Ziegfeld's theatrical productions, among other sensational entertainments. Structured by a still–moving juxtaposition of extended, languorous spectacle scenes with dynamic, energized variety numbers, the Follies revues contributed to the redefinition of spectatorial entertainments in modernism as, in Leo Charney's formulation, "a structure of peaks and valleys . . . composed from a chain of discrete moments traded off against slack moments."[29]

The streaming, streamlined movements in Dos Passos's metropolis refer openly to the vernacular theater forms and traditions with which *Manhattan Transfer* is invested. One epigraph begins, "Such afternoons the buses are crowded into line like elephants in a circusparade"; in another, titled "Went to the Animals' Fair," ranks of cars "flow in a long ribbon . . . towards the glow over the city that stands up incredibly into the night sky like the glow of a great lit tent, like the yellow tall bulk of a tentshow" (*MT*, 186, 199). Its streets lined with circus animals and the "torn-up daydreams" of New York's attractions, Dos Passos's Manhattan is a yellow-glowing "great lit tent"—and so is *Manhattan Transfer* as a whole. The novel's dreaming of the Follies reflects a larger collision among the reiterative, serial actions of the variety show or revue, the modern urban space, and the modern novel. Jimmy's march "around blocks and blocks" not only conveys the nonteleological tedium of his path but also shows the degree to which, in the block-by-block topography of its streets as in the "tinselwindowed" architecture of its high-rises, Dos Passos's New York—and the narrative that encodes it—is gridded with girls.

Character as Chorine

In the notebook in which Dos Passos remembered Anna Held, there is an unembellished catalogue of Ellen's sequenced evolution through *Manhattan Transfer*:

> Ellen Thatcher
> becomes
> Elaine Oglethorpe
> Helena Thatcher
> Helena Thatcher Herf[30]

Beneath this list, he gestured toward an idea that would grow into the main drama of the novel's opening episodes as well as into a symbolic intrigue that sets the structural and aesthetic terms for the text as a whole: "The birth of Ellen T in the maternity hospital—they mixed the babies up?" The splintering into multiplicity tabulated in the skyscraper of Jimmy's dream—and inscribed more matter-of-factly in the list of Ellen's successive iterations in Dos Passos's notebook—is augmented and vivified in the novel by the question, infinitely deferred, of Ellen's ancestry. At its opening, *Manhattan Transfer* worries over the hysterical cries of Ellen's mother, Susie, at the sight of the unlabeled baby girl who is brought to her: "It's not mine. It's not mine. Take it away. . . . That woman's stolen my baby" (*MT*, 18). The question of which baby is Susie's baby is an extension of other visual and ontological difficulties in this scene. A nurse carries a newborn child in a basket into a room with walls lined with other baskets; when she sets the basket down, the baby squirms "feebly like a knot of earthworms" (15). Even as the child is put in a basket-line series, the move from the singular to the plural effected by this simile posits her as a series. The knotty, writhing form embodies a number of vexed polarities similar to those that structured the Follies girls' performances: Is she an individual or a mass? a child or an animal? In the "opening chorus" of *Manhattan Transfer*, to borrow a phrase from Dos Passos's notebooks, the novel's main character takes her place as one of a chorus of girls.[31]

The presentation of Ellen as the Follies chorus troupe in the skyscraper does more than enmesh her in the same culture of gaudy spectacle as the Follies girls; it also relates her narrative function in *Manhattan Transfer* to the dazzling seriality and instability she shares, from birth, with those girls. Her centrality in the novel is parallel to her success on Broadway: she is the Follies girl par excellence, the archetypal figure in a battalion of girls whose celebrity counterintuitively rests on their anonymity. A model of stardom that requires rather than resists facelessness is consonant with the visual paradoxes of Dos Passos's metropolis, epitomized in the novel's opening scene of a hospital where difference is sameness and sameness is difference for babies and mothers alike. The antimonies corporealized in Ellen in these opening scenes are caught up with the recursive spatial design and activities of the city hospital ward, where rows of basket-kept babies replicate rows of bed-ridden new mothers. When Ed Thatcher nervously arrives at the maternity ward to visit his wife and newborn daughter, he finds "[r]ows of beds under bilious gaslight . . . faces fat, lean, yellow, white; that's her" (*MT*, 17). The drama of recognition in which he arrives at his wife's "white" countenance through a spectrum of strangers' faces is also one of misrecognition that regards mother like daughter—that is, as potentially indistinguishable from other women. So when Ed sees the row of babies and asks, "How do you tell them apart nurse?," the nurse's blithe reply summarizes the intrigue of endless substitutability that determines the activity of the row-lined hospital ward and of the novel in full: "Sometimes we cant" (18). Susie is distressed not only because the child she has been given may not be hers but also because it does not really matter one way or another.

Manhattan Transfer's opening scenes confirm the notion of Ellen's listed characterization specifically in relation to the striated, repetitive space of New York City. Through the strategies of juxtaposition and addition that organize both the novel and Ziegfeld's productions—each of which engages in practices of listing, of laying down in order—the opening vignette of the pressed, disembarking bodies is itself pressed into the scene of Ellen's birth. The stench of the "manuresmelling" ferry-house tunnel carries into the hospital, where the nurse carries the basket "at arm's length as if it were a bedpan"; the baby's body, like the channeled passageway through which bodies are fed into the modern metropolis, is soiled (15). The novel therefore initiates a relay between the modern urban space—the row-lined hospital, the chute-like ferry tunnel—and the body of this child, who is (and is not) Ellen. The hospital and the tunnel are presented as assemblages, as profoundly iterative.

The spatial metaphor of the sequence, in line with the revue structure of the Follies, prescribes an aesthetic and organizational framework for reading *Manhattan Transfer*. At the same time, it unveils Ellen as the nexus of a series of recastings and refigurations about which the narrative and the narrated city pivot. In this respect, as Dos Passos's characters amass in the crowded arena of the city street, they image the "masses," the overriding "political idea" and "aesthetic fantasy" associated with urban life, as Stefan Jonsson explains, from around the time of Held's New York debut.[32] A changeling child in a mixed-up maternity ward who grows up to be an inconstant wife in a churning metropolis, Ellen is reformed and reiterated in the novel by her suturing to other individuals through relations of interchangeability and transposition. Kathleen Komar's account of repetition as the primary structural principle of *Manhattan Transfer* effectively modifies the idea of the vortex toward a kinetic dynamism that is more relentlessly recurrent or sequential. For Komar, each of Dos Passos's characters "constantly retraces his own steps or those of another character."[33] When this observation is refracted through the image of the Follies-filled skyscraper and the circuitous footpath it imprints onto the street below, there appears a striking resemblance between the retraced steps of Dos Passos's characters and the precision dancing perfected on Broadway by the Follies girls. In its constant returning to Ellen above and beyond all other characters, *Manhattan Transfer* creates a dynamic of vacillation and exchange whereby the characters' steps follow Ellen's, by complement or contrast.

A number of scholars have identified a problem around the subjective status of the characters in *Manhattan Transfer*.[34] They seem, Joseph Warren Beach writes, to be "not quite *persons*" but rather "individuals made up of separate and unrelated moments."[35] For Cecelia Tichi, the novel features a "representative sampling" of standardized and interchangeable figures.[36] These descriptions can be refined with recourse to Siegfried Kracauer's concept of the chorus line's transmogrification of "individual girls" into the fractional components of "indissoluble girl clusters" in "The Mass Ornament," a 1927 essay, now famous, that is an especially nuanced example of the discourse of the masses in this period.[37] "The human figure enlisted in the mass ornament," claims Kracauer, "has begun the exodus from lush organic splendor and the constitution of individuality toward the realm of anonymity."[38] For Kracauer, as Jonsson points out, the mass ornament subordinates the human subject "under the reign of an abstract organization hidden from those who toil within it."[39] *Manhattan Transfer* dramatizes these organizational effects and subjects its readers to them. Harnessing the blank interstices that separate and bridge the episodes of the multilinear novel, Dos Passos habitually empties out and refills his characters through a technique of informational delay. By identifying characters only by subjective personal pronouns at the beginning of each new prose section, he recuperates their anonymity.[40] Anna Cohen, for instance, first appears in the novel as an unnamed woman caught in the arms of an unnamed man at the stoop of a tenement house. It is not until the woman has extricated herself from the man's embrace, run up four flights of stairs, and tiptoed into her room that she is called—rather, that she calls herself—by name: "Anna you've got to forget it or you wont sleep" (*MT*, 250).

As the characters enter and reenter the narrative as abstractions, half-remembered acquaintances passed on busy city streets, Dos Passos compounds the crises of identification in the novel's opening scenes. Depicting a "narrow island" metropolis where the "cramming" of "millionwindowed buildings" is replicated in the bodies "crammed" into subway cars, the novel works to composite the character of Ellen through accumulation and augmentation (23, 139). Anna's first appearance, near the beginning of the third part of the novel, is immediately followed by the scene in which Ellen and Jimmy return to New York City, after an absence of several years, with a baby in tow. "The baby with tiny shut purplish-pink face and fists lay asleep on the berth," the episode begins. "Ellen was leaning over a black leather suitcase. Jimmy Herf in his shirtsleeves was looking out of the porthole" (251). That the baby is unnamed is poignant, given that in the final scene of the novel's second section an unidentified woman visits a doctor for an abortion. When we join Ellen and Jimmy on the ferry, we do not yet know for certain that the woman in the doctor's clinic is Ellen; nor do we find out that Ellen and Jimmy are married until later in the ferry scene. Was the baby who was aborted the child of Ellen's now-deceased lover, Stan Emery, and, if not, is the baby on the ferry his or Jimmy's? The identity of the child on his or her first appearance is a mystery, as is Ellen's last appearance in the novel before this scene. The woman at the tenement house who turns out to be Anna is connected, at intervals, with the woman at the doctor's clinic who turns out to be Ellen and with the baby on the ferry who turns out to be Jimmy's. This triangulation of unidentified–identified bodies is further complicated by the fact that the baby with the "tiny shut pur-plishpink face" unequivocally recalls the baby with the "minute purple face" with which *Manhattan Transfer* begins (18). The child emerges as a repetition of Ellen herself.

This repetition unlocks an irony that configures the thematic and structural registers of *Manhattan Transfer*. Ellen is designated, according to her status as a woman-in-series conjoined to or substituted with the novel's other characters, as the matrix for an episodic, sequenced novel that begins with her beginnings. "You're so different, that's what it is about you," theater agent Harry Goldweiser says to her. "All these girls round New York here are just the same, they're monotonous." But Goldweiser's starry-eyed admiration for Ellen unravels in the scheme of *Manhattan Transfer*, as his belief in her unique allure slips neatly into a series of amorous declarations that stretches from John Oglethorpe to Jimmy Herf to George Baldwin (186). These men think Ellen is different from the rest of New York's women, but, as a star in the mode of the chorine, she distinguishes herself only to the degree that she does not distinguish herself.

When Baldwin, later in the novel, confides to Ellen that his life was "empty" and "hollow" before he met her, her nonplussed response discloses the almost-comical routineness of these encounters (336). The tedium of the romances undermines their testimony; it questions the idea of Ellen as personality, because Baldwin's passion is already rehearsed—not only by Goldweiser but also by himself. Immediately before their dinner-table conversation, Baldwin and Ellen run into Gus and Nellie McNiel, a woman with whom Baldwin had an affair years earlier. "Think of it I was crazy in love with her and now I cant remember what her first name was," he says to Ellen; "Funny isn't it?" (201). What is "funny" is the friction between this supposedly "crazy" attachment and Baldwin's amnesia, the relegation of Nellie to no more than the wife of Gus McNiel—her unnaming—making patently clear the fickleness of Baldwin's desires. What is also funny is that Baldwin cannot recall a name so similar to that of the woman who is her replacement and who is sitting directly across from him in the restaurant. The palindromic back-and-forth between Nellie and Ellen belies the slightness of the shift by which Ellen succeeds Nellie in Baldwin's affections.[41]

Ellen is situated in a series of wives that maps Baldwin's upward social mobility, even as she is remade as a series of wives through her own capriciousness and adultery—both of which plot the fragmentary unfolding of Dos Passos's multilinear novel. This irony is what makes so compelling the image, later in the novel, of a lonely Baldwin leafing through a cigar-store phonebook looking for Ellen under *H*: neither the *H* in Herf nor the *H* in Helena quite belongs to her (*MT*, 301). The textual traces of Ellen in the phonebook are a tabulated chronicle of her fabricated and refabricated identity and its intrinsic, even congenital, connection to her city. Recapitulating the splintering of her name into a listed amalgam through which Dos Passos charted the form of *Manhattan Transfer* in the drafts, the phonebook is another indexical record of the charged interaction and affinity among the unstable, serial Ellen; the reiterated, striated modern city; and the sequenced novel that narrates them both.

The Synthesis of Star and Sign

Toward the end of *Manhattan Transfer*, a "little roundfaced woman" called Mrs. Cunningham looks at a photograph of Mr. Jack Cunningham and his new bride embarking on their honeymoon in the rotogravure section of a newspaper: " 'Oh Jack you darling I love you just the same,' she said to the picture. Then she kissed it. . . . Then she stared in the face of the second Mrs Cunningham. 'Oh you,' she said and poked her finger through it" (293, 348). Two episodes earlier, James Merivale, the cousin of Jimmy Herf, sits at a gentleman's club with a couple of newspapers on his lap. He fantasizes about his own success reported on the pages of those papers: "Ten Million Dollar Success. . . . At the dinner of the American Bankers Association last night James Merivale, president of the Bank & Trust Company, spoke in answer to the toast 'Ten Years of Progressive Banking.' " Merivale's imagined speech is punctuated by the shutter mechanism of a press camera: "(flashlight photograph) . . . (flashlight photograph)" (345).

For Shloss, these instances manifest the collapse of the photographic process in Dos Passos's novel, which makes "everyone the photographer of himself, as if all of life were to be experienced through the viewfinder of a camera. There is no subject."[42] But they also corroborate the iterative form of this troubled subject— a subject split and sutured, her volatility brokered through her fungible relation to other narrative persons. In the first place, Mrs. Cunningham is still married to Jack Cunningham, and her odd, jealous confrontation not with her husband and his new wife but with their images in the newspaper figuratively extends the duplicity of the not-so-subtly named Cunningham, that is, a duplicity that produces duplication. When the first Mrs. Cunningham takes a stab at the second Mrs. Cunningham on the surface of the rotogravure section, *Manhattan Transfer* deploys the metaphor of the photograph to call attention to these doubled wives, with their matching marriage certificates, among the crowd of women in this composite city. James Merivale, too, is caught up with Cunningham's double-dealing— not least because the second Mrs. Cunningham is actually James's sister, Maisie. Earlier in the novel, Merivale discovers that he has bought a suit identical to that of his future brother-in-law, an accident that sets the terms for Merivale's projection of himself on the pages of the *Wall Street Journal*: he aspires to be seen and photographed as Jack Cunningham is, with Maisie on his arm. For Merivale, as for his sister Maisie, to be photographed is to be another's twin, to be caught wearing the same clothes, whether a pair of brown trousers or a wedding dress.

Couched in the final chapter of Dos Passos's novel—the same chapter in which Ellen succumbs to "the photograph of herself [set] in her own place, forever frozen into a single gesture"—these photographic encounters clarify the image of Ellen as a photograph as, specifically, a photograph in a newspaper. Whereas the Algonquin restaurant seems to turn "hard and enamelled" along with Ellen's body, the talking Baldwin appears to her like the "wooden face of a marionette [waggling] senselessly in front of her." As he leaves the hotel, Baldwin's stiff artificiality is collapsed into his status as, or his likeness to, a public—and therefore photographed—figure: he is "poised spry against the darkness in a tan felt hat and a light tan overcoat, smiling like some celebrity in the rotogravure section of a Sunday paper" (*MT*, 335–36).

Like some celebrity, or like Ellen Thatcher? She is, after all, the "certain charming young actress" who catches the attention of the gossipmongers at *Town Topics* magazine and whose affair with Stan Emery sets their "[m]alicious tongues" "wagging" earlier in the novel (182). As Janet Casey argues, *Manhattan Transfer* obsesses over Ellen's to-be-looked-at-ness, borrowing Laura Mulvey's classic phrase, in proportion to her function as an actress and a visual icon in Dos Passos's New York.[43] Ellen is the novel's most concise representation of a Foucauldian social dynamic "whereby women are contained through their very visibility, metaphorically 'disciplined' by male 'surveillance.' " Her intensely gendered position in the metropolis "ensures her cultural role as object of a (male) gaze regardless of venue."[44] Thus she registers as sinister the probing looks of those around her—from the "seagreedy eyes" of the sailors lounging in the park that "cling stickily to her neck, her thighs, her ankles" to the crowd at the Astor hotel whose "glances" are "like sticky tendrils of vines" catching at her as she walks past (*MT*, 129, 222). Reproducing the specular dynamic of the stage on which Ellen finds fame and material success, the thick, tendrilled atmosphere of New York's streets and spaces is, for her, "the air of unmitigated publicity, publicity as a condition, as a doom, from which there could be no appeal," which Henry James describes in *The American Scene* (1904–1905).[45] And *Manhattan Transfer*'s air of publicity—which is at the Algonquin "bluestreaked" and glassy—is substantially photographic. Prior to heading to the Astor, at a restaurant in the company of Harry Goldweiser, his sister, and another acquaintance, Ellen experiences an effect of estrangement and disassociation from the dinner party: "She sat looking at a picture of two women and two men eating at a table in a high paneled room under a shivering crystal chandelier" (*MT*, 222). Similarly, after Ellen aborts Stan's child at the end of the novel's second part, she "watches" herself as she hails a cab, inspecting "the tilt of her leather hat, the powder, the rosed cheeks, the crimson lips that are a mask on her face." The complete image is of a "wooden Indian, painted, with a hand raised at the street corner" (243). Approaching herself as we approach Dos Passos's characters, anonymized by his technique of informational delay, Ellen is one who is seen and pictured by others, snapped by press photographers at every restaurant and on every street corner.

When in 1933 Marilyn Miller and Clifton Webb sang on a Broadway stage, "On the avenue, fifth avenue, the photographers will snap us / And you'll find that you're in the rotogravure," Irving Berlin's lyrics acknowledged the already close, reciprocal relationship between the theater and the Sunday papers.[46] Produced as early as 1860, photographs of stage performers and entertainers were increasingly central to their commercial success, especially as the development of cheaper photolithography and printing processes in the final decade of the nineteenth century enabled popular theater journals such as New York's *Play-goer* to incorporate photographs of stage productions and of leading actors.[47] As Abigail Solomon-Godeau notes, the "rise of camera culture" in the second half of the nineteenth century and into the twentieth was inseparable from the "expanded conception of celebrity, with its auxiliary discourses of fashion and publicity" in this period.[48] Photographic postcards featuring stage personalities and other performers, like lynching photographs in the South and elsewhere, sold in their millions in the early twentieth century. They permitted a voyeuristic reformulation of a "public concept of personality," in Lawrence Senelick's words, that hinged upon the collection of "seraglios of paper images"—or, in Elizabeth Anne McCauley's coyer phrase, "portable objects of private devotion."[49]

Dos Passos gestures toward this phenomenon in *Manhattan Transfer*, when the bootlegger Congo Jake pulls out a newspaper-wrapped package of "postalcards," including one of "an Arab dancing girl. Nom d'une vache they got slippery bellybuttons" (*MT*, 105). As implied by Congo's appreciation of the woman's "slippery" form, photographs of performers and actors in this period tend to emphasize their bodies, in sharp distinction to the portraits of other famous figures, such as public dignitaries, with their focus on the expressive heads of their subjects.[50] Reflecting the function of the photographic theatrical portrait as an extension of the theatrical pose, this preoccupation with the body also betrays the way in which the bodies of actors and dancers served as erotic icons and fetish objects in this period, as is amply demonstrated by the 1896 scene of Anna Held in her milky bathtub—as well as in the famous collage of legs belonging to opera and ballet stars, produced in the 1860s by the studio of André-Adolphe-Eugène Disdéri, the inventor of the *carte de visite* (Figure 3.4). Passed around and (man)handled, theater postcards fetishized the female figure through what Mulvey terms "the cult of the female star"—not to mention the "spell of personality" Walter Benjamin discerns, in the 1930s, in the "separable, transportable" photographic and cinematographic images of film stars.[51]

Across *Manhattan Transfer*, the narrative of Ellen's life dramatizes the "feeling of strangeness" that Benjamin ascribes to the actor who, in "facing" the camera, is conscious of also facing the public. Taking her cues on the city stage, Ellen stands at the precipice of the aura's "shriveling" demise, for which the film industry—as well as the theatrical one, given its investment in photography as a technology of publicity—attempts to compensate through the "artificial build-up of 'personality' outside the studio."[52] In light of this, as well as the rapid expansion of advertising in the 1920s and 1930s documented by Roland Marchand and others, the apparition of the chorus troupe of Ellens in the windows of the skyscraper allegorizes Ellen's transformation into a series of advertisements on the façades of city buildings.[53] The skyscraper in *Manhattan Transfer*, as Paula Geyh suggests, is "an embodiment of the city's alluring consumerist discourse and a signifier of (also commodified) sexual desire."[54] The Follies girl was increasingly identified with the fashion model and the mannequin of city department store windows, appearing at various times in the 1910s and 1920s as a (reembodied) mannequin modeling high-end fashions. Ziegfeld's revues came to emulate the specular modality of the display window, which reflected, as Rachel Bowlby says, "an idealized image of the woman . . . who stands before it, in the form of the model she could buy or become."[55] The association of the female performer with consumable pleasures ran deep: theater journals had been sourcing fashion and beauty tips from actresses for almost a decade by the time the Follies girls began sharing their advice in newspapers and magazines in the 1910s.[56] Moreover, the development of card photography, and later of photography in newspapers, magazines, and billboard advertisements, constituted a disturbance to the "static domesticity" of the daguerreotype, sending images of female performers out onto public streets.[57] Participating in the same social field that, in *Cane* and *Three Lives*, relegates the running Karintha and the wandering Melanctha to the margins of their respective towns, the movements of women on the modern city street were firmly equated with prostitution. As early as the 1860s, Charles Baudelaire asserted a degree of equivalence between the actress and the courtesan as "creature[s] of show" and "object[s] of public pleasure."[58] They are both, as Solomon-Godeau points out, defined in relation to the commodity: the body of the prostitute as a joining of "seller and commodity"; the female performer "as a type of circulating goods."[59]

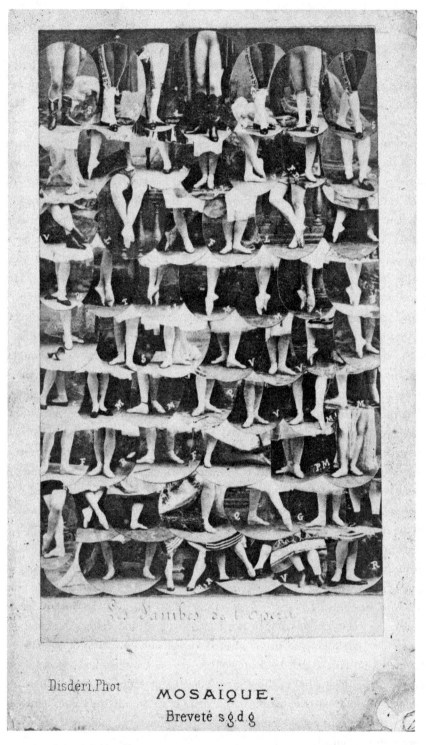

Fig 3.4 André-Adolphe-Eugène Disdéri, *Les jambes de l'opera* [*The Legs of the Opera*], ca. 1862. Image courtesy of J. Paul Getty Museum, Los Angeles

Ellen, too, is displayed as a commodity on the streets of New York. She acknowledges as much when she overhears a line of conversation on a subway car—"But she's made the biggest hit ever been made on Broadway"—and applies to herself the advertising slogan it repeats: "Greatest Hit on Broadway" (*MT*, 144). The "gold foil" Ellen is strung up on theater billboards, like the Follies girls on Broadway and at Coney Island (see Figure 3.5), and like her most important literary precursor in the relay of thespian social climbers in America's big cities, Theodore Dreiser's Carrie Meeber. As Ellen hails Jimmy from the skyscraper, Dos Passos recapitulates the scene from *Sister Carrie* (1900) in which Carrie's picture on a "pretty poster showing her as the Quaker Maid, demure and dainty" haunts George Hurstwood as he drifts, jobless and despondent, about New York City.[60]

Star and sign are compacted in a series of scenes in *Manhattan Transfer* featuring the stock market broker Joe Harland. Sitting, dejected, at a bench at the Battery, Harland stares at the sunset "like at a picture in a dentist's waiting room" (*MT*, 136–37). An old man at a nearby bench, holding the theater section of the newspaper in his hands, repeats, "Aint it a croime? Aint it a croime?" The man's speech is the tired, tiresome locution of a city where sunsets look like cheap pictures and where pictures of women in newspapers are nowhere near cheap enough. "Them young actresses all dressed naked like that. . . . Why can't they let you alone," the old man

Fig 3.5 Reginald Marsh, Crowd gathered in front of Parisian Follies Girl Show at Coney Island, ca. 1938. Image courtesy of Museum of the City of New York/Art Resource, New York

asks Harland. "If you aint got no work and you aint got no money, what's the good of em I say?" (137). Later in the novel, Harland drops a newspaper on the street and Jimmy Herf picks it up for him:

> A face made out of modulated brown blurs gave [Jimmy] a twinge as if something had touched a nerve in a tooth. No it wasn't, she doesn't look like that, yes TALENTED YOUNG ACTRESS SCORES HIT IN THE ZINNIA GIRL . . . .
>
> "Thanks, don't bother, I found it there," said Harland. Jimmy dropped the paper; she fell face down. (225–26)

These two passages reveal Jimmy's Follies dream as a variation on the beckoning torments of the pictured, commodified women in the theater section, eliding the difference between Ellen the woman and Ellen the picture of "modulated brown blurs" as "she" lands "face down." Dos Passos replays the moment from *Sister Carrie* when, beneath the "incandescent fire" of Carrie's name in electric lights on Broadway, Hurstwood confuses "a fine lithograph of Carrie, lifesize" on a gilt-framed posterboard for Carrie herself: "'That's you,' he said at last, addressing her. 'Wasn't good enough for you, was I?'"[61]

From James Merivale's and Mrs. Cunningham's negotiations with the signs of themselves and others, to the larger-scale negotiation of Ellen as a sign, *Manhattan Transfer* points up Bill Brown's indeterminate ontology of bodies and objects not primarily as an effect of the chorines' performances but as a generalized condition of the modern, photographed, metropolis. "Instructed by photographs," Susan Sontag writes in *On Photography*, "everyone is able to visualize . . . the geography of the body: for example, photographing a pregnant woman so that her body looks like a hillock, a hillock so that it looks like the body of a pregnant woman."[62] An especially striking example of this conceit is the series of female nudes produced by Edward Weston from the 1920s on. His nude studies, principally of Tina Modotti, his lover and collaborator for several years, and of his wife, Charis Wilson, emphasize form over personality, presenting the female body as a collection of sensuous but decontextualized body parts. "He was often fascinated by shapes that were not perfectly geometrical but were found in nature," notes Amy Conger, including "the back of a woman's torso that reminds many people of a pear, a nude that looks like a cloud, a cloud that looks like a nude, a bone, a rock, a pepper, a hill that looks like a woman's rear and vice versa."[63] In the continuities of shape and line in, for example, his photograph of Miriam Lerner's back and his still-life image of a bell pepper (Figures 3.6 and 3.7), Weston's work discloses the thingness of human beings and the humanness of things. (In 1931, a friend of Weston's referred to his still-life

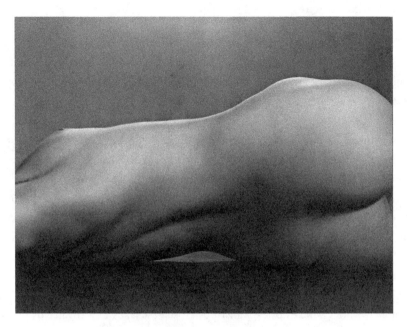

Fig 3.6 Edward Weston, Miriam Lerner, buttocks and back, 1925. © Center for Creative Photography, University of Arizona Foundation/Licensed by Viscopy, 2017. Image courtesy of J. Paul Getty Museum, Los Angeles, Gift of Melvin and Elaine Wolf

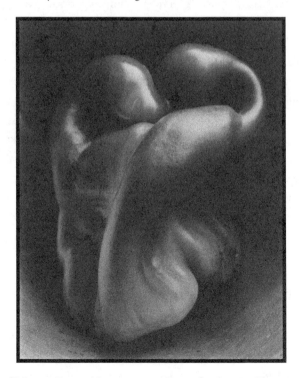

Fig 3.7 Edward Weston, Pepper No. 30, 1930. © Center for Creative Photography, University of Arizona Foundation/Licensed by Viscopy, 2017. Image courtesy of Art Resource, New York

image of a radish as "that naked, horseradish hussy." And, in 2003, when Conger asked participants at a conference on Weston's photography what they made of the eroticism of his nudes, one responded that they "found some of his vegetables sexier than his nudes."[64])

"Through an open window," we read early on in *Manhattan Transfer*, as Gus McNiel enters a saloon, "a streak of muddy sunlight caresses the rump of a naked lady who reclines calm as a hardboiled egg on a bed of spinach in a giltframed picture behind the bar" (*MT*, 51). Played up by the visual clarity of the metaphor of the "hardboiled egg on a bed of spinach," this moment at the bar makes tangible the correlation between pictured and consumed women in *Manhattan Transfer*. The lag between the appearance of the light-caressed "rump of a naked lady" and the "giltframed picture" that holds said lady's rump troubles the assumption of her nonrepresentational status. If Ellen Thatcher likewise amounts to a sequence of images in the theater section, a sequence of theater posters silently beckoning from New York's edifices of capitalist power, she partakes in a theater of realist representation that reticulates Philip Fisher's definition of the realist novel as a staging of the everyday as a "series of acts of exhibition" for public consumption, in which, as Amy Kaplan writes, "everyone is either a performer or a spectator, an inspector or a specimen."[65] In *Manhattan Transfer*, the narration of character is equivalent to Benjamin's "artificial build-up of 'personality' " through the machinations of celebrity in the age of mass production, and modern life is a series of fragmented appearances and gestures that are always evidence of that life's shriveled aura. Thus, the process by which Ellen is made photographic, posed across the novel as a reduction or devolution of her subjectivity, is also a distillation and revelation of its characterological terms. Gridded in the cells of the skyscraper and the episodic, multilinear novel, Ellen's photographic iconicity is shorthand for her status as a made object of narration, assembled out of textual fragments—from the smallest discursive indices of Dos Passos's prose style, to the echoes of *Sister Carrie*, to the traces of the two Mrs. Cunninghams and *Manhattan Transfer*'s other reiterated characters.

The Movements of the Machine

We cannot say that Dos Passos remembered Anna Held's New York appearance, because the year when Held first trod the boards of the Herald Square Theater was also the year of his birth. Spiraling out from this instance of impossible retrospection, *Manhattan Transfer* is attentive to a broad range of variously bygone technologies, emblematized by the nickelodeons and stereopticons on its city streets. Dos Passos's invocation of the decade of his birth in his notebook sits with his ambivalence toward the modern machine. "[C]raftsmanship is a damn fine thing, one of the few human functions a man can unstintingly admire," he wrote in 1929, in a *New Masses* review of Ernest Hemingway's *A Farewell to Arms*. "The drift of the Fordized world seems all against it."[66] In 1932, in the introduction to the Modern Library reprint of his 1921 novel *Three Soldiers*, he esteems writing that works "with speech straight and so dominat[es] the machine of production" over writing that "merely feeds the machine, like a girl in a sausage factory shoving hunks of meat into the hopper."[67]

It is ironic, given the persistent coding of Dos Passos as feminine in masculine high-modernist culture—as well as the fact that his writing has, Casey suggests, been elided in scholarly discussions of modernism for its failure "to conform to the masculine (or even misogynistic) bias of his time"—that he himself reflected a pejorative gendering of mass culture in his preference for "straight" writing—*straight* being a loaded term by any standard.[68] Notwithstanding his "paranoid" resistance to the "seductive lure" of mass culture, to borrow Andreas Huyssen's terms, Dos Passos is at other points far less rigorous in differentiating between sausage-pressing girls and the straight-and-narrow praxis of modern (masculine) writing.[69] In a 1935 essay, for instance, he considers the professional writer to be "a technician just as much as an electrical engineer is."[70]

Dos Passos's mixed attitudes toward modern machine culture serve to complicate conventional ascriptions of a machinic energy and structural force to his writing. Lisa Nanney offers the more-or-less representative view that *Manhattan Transfer* is "a product of the machine age," meaning both that the segmented pieces of its narration and the different parts of Dos Passos's cityscape, from characters to buildings to vehicles and so on, operate like "cogs" in "an active machine."[71] What remains unclear in these accounts is the function of this textual machine. In keeping with the productive resonance between the Follies revues and *Manhattan Transfer*, Dos Passos's engagement with machine culture in this novel is roughly compatible with the culture of the chorus line. By the 1920s, it was already commonplace to acknowledge how the precision dancing of chorus troupes emulated Henry Ford's semiautomatic production line. Kracauer's joke in "The Mass Ornament" about the chorines as the "products of American distraction factories" evokes the Follies girls' cold, impassive performances, which cultural critics associated with overmechanization virtually since the Follies girls' first staircase descent.[72] As an anonymous Broadway dance director told an "awed" and "depressed" Gilbert Gabriel, before the decade was up, "Our dance must evoke the dynamo, the axle worm, the crank-shaft, the clash of great, glinting metal rods in swiftly syncopating formation."[73]

In a 1931 essay, Kracauer claims that each time the chorus girls "[form] themselves into an undulating snake" they provide "a radiant illustration of the conveyor belt," and that the "mathematical precision" of their raised legs "joyfully" affirms "the progress of rationalization."[74] The correspondence he identifies between the choreography of the chorus and the workers' "hands in the factory" manifests the chorus and the factory's common technological basis in nineteenth-century chronophotographic experiments in physiology and human motion, pioneered by Étienne-Jules Marey and Eadweard Muybridge, among others.[75] What François Dagonet calls Marey's "passion for the trace," for uncovering the "jolts, rustlings, rhythms and continual tremors" of the body, was enlisted in the early twentieth-century regime of maximum productivity.[76] Drawing on motion studies into the labor of industrial workers, especially by Frank and Lillian Gilbreth in the United States, the industrial efficiency movement associated with Frederick Winslow Taylor sought the refinement of the individual movement into its "essential" or "minimum" form in an "economy of gesture" that was intended to permit the synchronization and streamlining of group activity in the workshop or plant. Repeating aspects of "fragmentation and fusion" familiar from Marey's chronophotographs, as Felicia McCarren notes, the minimum gesture in twentieth-century machine culture was produced through, and in response to, the "picture-making process" of the end of the previous century.[77] By the same token, the movements of the chorus line—those "demonstrations of mathematics" homologous to the assembly line—refer in their kinetic geometry to photography's interruption, isolation, and capture of human movement.[78] The Follies girls owe a silent debt to, for instance, Marey's single-plate chronophotograph of a white-uniformed male subject jumping from a standing-still position, taken around 1882, in which the man's airborne, multiplying legs form a prototype for their coordinated kicking (see Figures 3.8 and 3.9).

Although Kracauer discerned in the chorines' movements an affirmation of the "aesthetic reflex" of the *ratio* to which the capitalist system aspires, McCarren argues that forms of modern dance that internalize "the machine into the body" through streamlined gestures and group synchronicity often "imply a critique of technology" as they encode the logic of scientific management on the "ostentatiously non-productive" site of the stage. "The chorus line," McCarren explains, "diffuses and disperses the energy condensed in the movement for efficiency even as it brings the assembly line onstage."[79] Likewise, Dos Passos's "leg show dance" in a skyscraper brings machine aesthetics onto the narrative stage in order to ironize and destabilize it. Specifically, in its mergers of bodies and things, *Manhattan*

Fig 3.8 Étienne-Jules Marey, Fixed-plate chronophotograph of a jump from a standing-still position, ca. 1882. Image courtesy of Collège de France Archives

Fig 3.9 Unknown photographer (White Studio), Scene from the Ziegfeld Follies of 1924. © Billy Rose Theatre Division, New York Public Library for the Performing Arts

Transfer configures the mapping of the "vague and shifting" boundary lines between "the inert and the animate" that Thorstein Veblen traced in the machine culture of turn-of-the-century America.[80] The reiterative construction of Ellen across the novel represents and enacts the processes by which, in Mark Seltzer's account of the body–machine complex in the late nineteenth and early twentieth centuries, individuals are converted into numbers, cases, and visual displays through the collusion of "the visible and the calculable" through the technologies and practices of surveillance and statistics.[81] For Seltzer, who is drawing on Foucault, the primary achievement of Taylorism is the devising of "a system of supervision by representation" that replicates physical work processes on paper, collapsing the distinction between "production and processing," the body and the machine.[82] Taylorism provides an idiom of rationalization that posits the subjects of work processes as listed formulations—formulations very much like those with which the writing of *Manhattan Transfer* began, as well as those that delineate Ellen in the novel as a contested site for repetitive processes of naming and renaming.

Counting blocks in a taxi on her way to meet Baldwin at the Algonquin, Ellen thinks, "It must have been to keep from going crazy people invented numbers . . . . Probably that's what old Peter Stuyvesant thought, or whoever laid the city out in numbers." It is of utmost significance that her foundational myth of the city is conditioned by her "jangled nerves" at the prospect of becoming yet another version of herself through marriage to Baldwin. The "cold and emotionless" numbers that rationalize the cityscape—like the industrial factory under the supervisory mechanisms of Taylorist management—are equated with, even made equivalent to, Ellen's itemizing and fracturing through the machinations of divorce and remarriage that form her into *Manhattan Transfer*'s preeminent other woman (*MT*, 334). The scene visually tropes the modern industrial factory as it navigates, block by block, the distance Ellen has traveled from an unlabeled child to an insistently and repeatedly labeled woman: Thatcher, Oglethorpe, Herf, Baldwin.

Apprehending Ellen as a Taylorized body, a functionary of a body–machine complex that emerged at the time of her birth, illuminates how *Manhattan Transfer* stages the replacement of physical mechanisms with representational ones: the subordination of bodies to numbers, of the animate to the inert. In another taxicab, earlier in the novel, the luckless stage actress Ruth Prynne worriedly counts the coins in her purse while watching "the figures flickering on the taximeter" (264). Coming from a doctor's office where she is receiving treatment for an ailing throat, Ruth is haunted by thoughts of her diagnosis as she travels, a little later, on a subway car: "Cancer, he said. She looked up and down the car at the joggling faces opposite her. Of all those people one of them must have it. FOUR OUT OF

EVERY FIVE GET .... Silly, that's not cancer." Looking at the "green faces in the dingy light, under the sourcolored advertisements. FOUR OUT OF EVERY FIVE .... A trainload of jiggling corpses" (266), she experiences her body as an object abstracted and rationalized by statistical knowledge.[83] Lined with advertisements for laxatives, the subway car becomes a vessel for human waste, the deathly substitution of the statistic for the body.

This substitution anticipates Guy Debord's society of the spectacle, arising after "all that was once directly lived has become mere representation" and "assert[ing] that all human life, which is to say all social life, is mere appearance."[84] In Dos Passos's novel, the triumph of the Taylorist machine is also the triumph of the windowpanes of skyscrapers and taxicabs—and of their image-twin, the mirror. Like the department store mannequin, emulated on stage by the Follies girl, Ellen becomes a prop for the "thrilled iconography of standardized persons and things" that accompanied "the invention of a culture of numbers, models, and statistics."[85] When Ellen alights from the taxi and joins Baldwin at the Algonquin, she apprehends the "smart probing glances" of the people around her like "the sense of a mirror" (*MT*, 330). In the ladies' room of the restaurant, "Ellen stayed a long time looking in the mirror .... She kept winding up a hypothetical dollself and setting it in various positions. Tiny gestures ensued, acted out on various model stages. Suddenly she turned away from the mirror with a shrug of her toowhite shoulders and hurried to the dining room" (334). As David Seed notes, Ellen internalizes "the role of a male director" even as she becomes the "ornament" of stage direction.[86] Just as the skyscraper windows encase the ever-waving Ellens, the bathroom mirror before which Ellen performs her pageant of "tiny gestures" replicates the supervisory apparatus shared by the Follies stage, the industrial factory, and the modern city. Like a Follies girl, like a factory worker, Ellen becomes a machine as she is gazed at: an "intricate machine of sawtooth steel," as she is described earlier in the novel, of tiny, reiterated, economic gestures (*MT*, 209).

Whether the anatomical focus is the hands of the worker or the legs of the chorine, in factory and theater the pursuit of coordinated movement is controverted—and pathologized—by the fragmenting activity requisite to it. Demanding the worker–dancer's de-individuation and, as Isabelle Stengers suggests, the enslavement of the body in space and time, Taylorism's institutionalization of the smallest gestures of chronophotography replicates the reifying mechanisms of the photographic apparatus.[87] For Christian Metz, the link between photography and death evoked by Barthes in *Camera Lucida* includes the "immediacy" and "definitiveness" of the snapshot as an "instantaneous abduction of the object out of the world into another world, into another kind of time." The off-frame of the photograph enters into the commemorative order of the absent lack associated with the fetish: "Photography is a cut inside the referent, it cuts off a piece of it, a fragment, a part object, for a long immobile travel of no return."[88] Metz's description of the photograph as "a cut inside the referent" that also "cuts" up the referent highlights the violence of the snapshot's activity of abduction, its spatiotemporal disembodiment and displacement. This, as with the blazoned bodies in *Cane*, is a visual appropriation that lacerates.

Choreographed, abstracted, and fragmented, the female bodies in *Manhattan Transfer* also bear the wounds of photography's serial cuts. They are the moving targets of the kind of physical disciplines that circumscribe the industrial factory and the popular stage. "Look at the swell dame," Joe O'Keeffe tells Joe Harland as they sit together on a bench in Madison Square Garden. "Look at the way she walks. Aint she peacherino? That's the way I like 'em, all slick an frilly with their lips made up" (*MT*, 191). Immediately before running into Harland, O'Keeffe notices two girls sheltering themselves from the rain under a newspaper: "He snatched blue of their eyes, a glint of lips and teeth as he passed" (190). Turned into a listed series of component parts, of snatched visions of eyes, lips, gait, and attire, women's bodies enact the injuries of surveillance and control in the modern metropolis. Incorporated, simultaneously, in a listed series of female bodies through the episodic reiterations of the multilinear text, these bodies also register as traumatic the formal fragmentation of the novel. *Manhattan Transfer* is an extended meditation of the violence of containment through representation, brokered by the segmenting and framing of the narrative into parts within parts. The piecemeal bodies, like the piecemeal text, evince the disassembling excruciations of the listed sequence.

When Ellen returns to Baldwin's dinner table, the small movements of the dollself subside into complete stasis. She is now a sight rather than a subject, not merely the doll of her ladies' room vision but the sheer, slick vision itself, framed in and as glass. Her surrender to this glassy containment is of the same order as—and permits—the comfort she finds in the "cold and emotionless" numbers that terrify Ruth. For Michel de Certeau, walking in the metropolis subverts, disrupts, and evades the panoptic geometry of the "planned and readable city." De Certeau describes a "chorus of idle footsteps" that "are myriad, but do not compose a series. They cannot be counted because each unit has a qualitative character . . . . Their swarming mass is an innumerable collection of singularities."[89] But this kind of walking, which thrives in "lapses of visibility," is categorically not the chorus in which Ellen belongs.[90] In becoming a photograph, she becomes immured in the "graphical trails" de Certeau condemns as the reductive transcription of kinetic motion "into points that draw a totalizing and reversible line" on route surveys or maps—one of the "minor instrumentalities" that manages Foucault's disciplinary society.[91] Not unseen but seen, not organic but mechanical, not mobile but immobile, Ellen the photograph is fixed in and as her transcription, an extension and radicalization of the image of the Ellen as the Follies girls whose ceaseless beckoning synchs with the circuitous route of Jimmy's city walking. Docked and reduced to a "point" on de Certeau's "totalizing and reversible line," Ellen becomes a unit of calculation and computation, the abstract afterimage of her own monitored rationalization.

She therefore bears out Kracauer's description of the reduction of moving people, whether traveling or dancing, to "mere spatio-temporal points" under the conditions of technological modernity.[92] It is not in walking but in traveling by taxicab that Ellen capitulates to the statistical grid of the city—in a vehicle that, even in releasing the body spatially and temporally, is recruited in "the parallel yet paradoxical effort to regulate that mobility, to channel attention and structure the subject's potentially anarchic participation" in city life, as Charney suggests.[93] Her mechanized movement along the taxi routes is visible from the aerial view of New York—the view depicted in the stereocard of downtown Manhattan in 1925 (Figure 3.10)—which de Certeau conceptualizes as an "immense texturology" that is pure representation, "an optical artifact" analogous to the facsimiles of urban planners and cartographers.[94] "To be lifted to the summit of the World Trade Center is to be lifted out of the city's grasp," he wrote in the 1980s, in an "elevation" that transfigures the viewer "into a voyeur. It puts him at a distance. It transforms the bewitching world by which one was 'possessed' into a text that lies before one's eyes. It allows one to read it, to be a solar Eye, looking down like a god."[95] Modeling the camera, this "solar Eye" arrests the "agitation" of the city streets into a seeable, readable text. More than fifty years earlier, Kracauer spoke in a similar way about chorus-line choreography, likening the mass ornament to "aerial photographs of landscapes and cities" that do not "emerge out of the interior of the given conditions, but rather [appear] above them." In Manhattan Transfer, Ellen and the women in series with her are scrutinized and constituted from just this top-down, photographic view. They participate in the "construction" of the "stage setting" of New York without ever grasping it "in its totality."[96]

Women in Glass Windows

In its realist effects, as Peter Buse notes, photography may "supersede even glass as the transparent medium par excellence, so rarely do we look at it instead of through it onto the content it reveals."[97] As Dos Passos's critique of the psychosocial domination

Fig 3.10 Unknown photographer, Stereo card of downtown Manhattan skyline, New York City, ca. 1925. © JT Vintage. Image courtesy of Art Resource, New York

of the gaze in the machine city is embodied—more accurately, embalmed—in the figure of Ellen, grinding to a still-moving halt on the sequenced space of the metropolis, it inspires this rare modality of sight. Her "hard and enamelled" surfaces—like those of the city observed from above—are an infrastructure of vision, revealing its gendered, racialist, and nativist architecture. That Ellen herself reinforces this architecture is unveiled in the final chapter of *Manhattan Transfer*, which opens the curtains on a woman whose body is publically envisioned and celebrated in accordance with pejorative typologies of gender, ethnicity, race, and class. Yet, at the same time, by its composite form and characterization, the novel suggests the subversive potential of the other (and othered) serialized women in the metropolis—who, unlike Ellen, model de Certeau's "chorus of idle footsteps" in the city's "lapses of visibility." Hence, whereas for Ellen the photograph is foremost an imprisoning structure, Dos Passos's composite writing—like *Three Lives* and *Cane*—reveals and breaks open this structure, denaturalizing habitual fictions of social difference and schematizing limited forms of release, for the woman-in-series, from the tyranny of fetishization, objectification, and destruction.

When Ellen, in the final moments of *Manhattan Transfer*, is frozen in a photographic pose under the smoky Algonquin air, she concretizes her connection with the Statue of Liberty, developed throughout the novel. First glimpsed by Ed Thatcher as he sits with a young Ellen on a bench at the Battery, standing "vague as a sleepwalker among the curling smoke," the statue also catches the eye of a young Jimmy a few pages later (*MT*, 65). Jimmy's childish description of the "tall green woman in a dressing gown standing on an island holding up her hand" prefigures the serial appearances of Ellen dressed in various shades of green throughout the novel: "a goldgreen dress," "a gown of nilegreen silk," a "metalgreen evening dress" (71, 145, 169, 237). In these outfits, Ellen feels like "a stiff castiron figure" or "cold out of reach like a lighthouse" (237, 145). The statue that stands over and symbolizes New York is brought most fully into the orbit of Ellen's serialized construction when Ellen is put on a pedestal at Madame Soubrine's dress shop. "This is the last time I have a dress like this, I'm sick of wearing blue and green," Ellen complains to the Madame, who mutters while she fiddles with the hem of the "pale green" gown: "Perfect Greek simplicity, wellgirded like Diana . . . the ultimate restraint of an Annette Kellerman, holding up the lamp of liberty, the wise virgin." Looking at herself in the reflection of the "tall pierglass," Ellen thinks, "She's right . . . I am getting a hard look" (353).

The reference to Annette Kellerman cements the affiliation of New York's lamp-lifting synecdoche and the standardization and commodification of the white female body in the modern city. An Australian diving champion, vaudeville star, and cinema actress, Kellerman's books and mail-order pamphlets on the ideal female physique appealed to women in this period in much the same way as Bernarr Macfadden's physical culture publications appealed to men.[98] By incorporating in the novel Kellerman's brand of "ultimate restraint," which was underwritten by racialist and nativist discourses of beautiful or "superior" physiques in the early twentieth century, Dos Passos lends new consequence to the images of Ellen "cold white out of reach" in New York's crowded dining halls and of the Elliedoll's "toowhite" shoulders.[99] Bringing out Ellen's dress, Madame Soubrine shrills, "Vous la femme la plus belle de New Yorrk" (*MT*, 353). Recalling the billboard slogans that interpellate Ellen throughout the novel ("Greatest hit on Broadway"), Madame Soubrine's rhapsody of virginal, restrained femininity veers back to an earlier scene in the novel, in which Mrs. Culveteer, Ed Thatcher's neighbor, praises Ellen's "strength of character and deep Christian living" and her ability to "withstand the temptations of stage life nowadays." "Mrs Oglethorpe," Mrs. Culveteer tells Ellen—who is, in fact, leaving John Oglethorpe for Stan Emery—"you've no idea how closely we follow your career, in the Sunday papers and all. . . . It's inspiring to think of a young girl and wife coming so sweet and unspoiled through all of that" (184). Ellen's wellgirded purity, as much as the public fiction of her sweet and unspoiled life, is another false vision in another encasing mirror.

The dress-shop scene emphasizes Ellen's studied whiteness and disengagement from her social others, which conditions her attitude toward a young man in a "foreignlooking cap" selling flowers on the street outside the shop:

> Through the smell of arbutus she caught for a second the unwashed smell of his body, the smell of immigrants, of Ellis Island, of crowded tenements. Under all the nickelplated, goldplated streets enameled with May, uneasily

she could feel the huddling smell, spreading in dark slow crouching masses
like corruption oozing from broken sewers, like a mob. (352)

Ellen, who enters the shop in order to escape the "crouching" and "oozing" immigrant "mob," is consistently described as "clean, cool, smooth, and creamy . . . in
contrast to the hot, sweaty, often gritty streets," as Susan Keller notes. This "costume of elite femininity protects her; it is a shield of cosmetics and expensive
clothes that keeps her separate from other people."[100] This, too, was the costume of
the Follies girl, who was promoted in the 1910s and 1920s as an "authentic body"
that was " 'select' and true to American 'types' " and so demarcated from "its more
threatening Others."[101] As Mizejewski argues, the insistently anglicized and hetero-
sexualized body of the Ziegfeld girl served as a prominent site for the negotiation
of fears surrounding European immigration into the United States and the migra-
tion of African American populations from the southern states into the North in
this period. She modeled racial "purity."[102]

Whether Follies girl, mannequin, picture postcard, or billboard, whether porcelain or copper and steel, the "most beautiful girl" in Dos Passos's metropolis is
always getting a hard—and chalk-white—look. But at end, *Manhattan Transfer*
broaches Ellen's bourgeois privilege by bringing her, unwillingly, into contact with
the working-class Anna Cohen. In the final chapter, Anna lies on an iron bed with
her lover, Dick, in a small shoebox-shaped room that faces onto Broadway. The
window shade is broken, and the piercing glow of electric lights patterns the ceil-
ing with changing colors. "Oh Dick I wish you'd fix that shade, those lights give me
the willies," says Anna. "The lights are alright Anna," he replies; "it's like bein in a
theater" (*MT*, 346). This is a theater of infidelity, an affair under lights, with Anna
as the other woman—to Dick's wife, and to Ellen. Inverting the spectacle of the
waving Ellens in the windows of Jimmy's dream, we join Anna on the other side
of the windowpane, witnessing her discomfort at being seen on Broadway. This
move asserts the difference between the chorus girl as a "type" of factory worker
and the actual factory worker. One in a line of "bowed heads auburn, blond, black,
brown" in a "long low room with long tables down the middle," Anna's work as a
scab seamstress positions her within a markedly more concrete version of the lists
of characters found in the Dos Passos archives (311).

In the novel's climactic scene, Anna and Ellen are framed as mirror images of
one another, situated on either side of the dress shop's "tall pierglass." While in the
front Ellen gazes critically at her "hard look" in the mirror, Anna is busy sewing
out in the back. When a fire starts in a pile of tulle near Anna and she is severely
injured in the blaze, the narration proposes a complex identification between her

and Ellen. At the smell of singed fabric, Ellen enters into the back of the shop, moving through the glass door and down a corridor to where "something moaning" is pulled "out of the charred goods." Ellen sees "an arm in shreds, a seared black red face, a horrible naked head." Out on the street, she "tries to puzzle out why she is so moved; it is as if some part of her were going to be wrapped in bandages, carried away on a stretcher" (355).

It is crucial to note that Ellen identifies with Anna only once she is broken, horrifically, into a series of fragmentary remains. According to Leslie Fiedler, the sight of the damaged or freakish body is always to some degree erotic, arousing "a temptation to go beyond looking to *knowing* in the full carnal sense the ultimate other." This is, at base, "a dream of breaking the last taboo against miscegenation."[103] Up until this point in the novel, Ellen exemplifies the transparency of whiteness, that is, whiteness as a form of social power and dominance secured by its "seeming not to be anything in particular." When "whiteness qua whiteness does come into focus," Richard Dyer observes, "it is often revealed as emptiness, absence, denial or even a kind of death."[104] In this sense, Ellen's photographic-becoming sits on a continuum with her disgust at the "unwashed smell" of the bodies that "overcrowd" the New York tenements. It represents her retreat into the "unmarked" category of whiteness (and of class privilege).

Where the working-class, nonwhite women-in-series in *Cane* and *Three Lives* disappear under the hegemonic power of—and in resistance to—racialist and nativist taxonomies of thought, Ellen disappears even as she reinforces and is socially shielded by those taxonomies. Even so, when Ellen looks at the disfigured Anna at the end of *Manhattan Transfer*, the erotic charge that passes between the two women seems to be generated by their similarity rather than their difference to one another—undercutting Ellen's derogatory stance toward Anna and other immigrant and working-class subjects. By her itemized attention to the arm, face, and head of the "something" amid the "charred goods," along with her troubling sense that "some part of her" is being carried off in bandages, Ellen apprehends Anna as she herself is apprehended in the novel: not as a whole body but as an assemblage of body parts, hovering between someone and something. To be "moved" by the violent tragedy of a stranger is not really remarkable, and the lack of sympathy Ellen betrays in her bewilderment at her reaction suggests that she is puzzling out something other than Anna's fate. Stopped in her city-crossing tracks because she feels the bandaged fragments of Anna to be "some part of her," Ellen recognizes, in the spectacle of the body-in-series, her own status as a part-object, a cut fragment associated with the photographic incision of the real.

Ellen finally, briefly, intuits the way in which all of New York's women are grafted damagingly in series with her, reduced to stations on the same statistical charts.

She not only puts together the thematic, structural, and aesthetic puzzle of Dos Passos's composite text, but also perceives her own whiteness and its function as a powerfully operative fiction in the panoptic order of the metropolis. In a groundbreaking 2001 essay, "The Mirage of an Unmarked Whiteness," Ruth Frankenberg critiques the theory of whiteness as abstract and invisible—a theory she helped to conceptualize—as "a white delusion." Asking to whom, exactly, whiteness is invisible, Frankenberg argues for "the simultaneity of whites' visibility for some," especially those who are not white, "and the tenaciousness of their capacity to disappear, discursively, for others," especially those who are.[105] Whiteness is "in a continual state of being dressed and undressed, of marking and cloaking."[106] However momentary and partial, Ellen's cognizance of her commonality with and nondifference from Anna is coextensive with an awareness of her own manifest whiteness and, as follows, her complicity in a violently discriminatory social order. At Madame Soubrine's, the fitting of pale green gowns is metaphorically hemmed to the dressing and undressing, the cloaking and uncloaking, of whiteness.

After Ellen pulls herself away from the scene of her own dispersed and disjointed subjectivity, she travels through the city by taxi to meet Baldwin at the Algonquin one last time. During this retracked trip, Ellen's thoughts whir "like a busted mechanical toy," exposing the other women Ellen might be, or the other women it does not matter that she is not. She thinks:

> Suppose I'd been horribly burned, like that girl, disfigured for life. . . . Suppose I'd gone with that young man with the ugly necktie who tried to pick me up . . . riding uptown and then down again on the bus, with his knee pressing my knee and his arm round my waist, a little heavy petting in a doorway. . . . There are lives to be lived if only you didn't care. (*MT*, 356)

Anna is the spectral figure behind these lives, explicitly in Ellen's reference to her tragic disfigurement and implicitly in Ellen's recapitulation of Anna's first entrance in the novel on the tenement doorstep in Bouy's fondling arms. Her life is the raw narrative material for a number of roles Ellen might adopt, much as she would parts in a Broadway play.

And, in the end, it is Anna who serves most fully as the novel's locus of subversive female power. Even though Ellen's taxi-riding body is locked into the city's grid, women's feet, as Paula Rabinowitz argues, signify unevenly in relation to "freedom and constraint—at once powerful symbols of mobility and icons of and for desire."[107] The period in which Dos Passos is writing is that in which Gabrielle "Coco" Chanel modeled and monetized an unprecedented physical, economic, and imaginative freedom for flappers to "dance, walk, and ride" in public spaces.[108]

In this light, the scene of Anna's disfigurement suggests the potential power of women's footwork in the modern city. This is the description of Anna in the fire:

> The white tulle shines too bright. Red hands clutch suddenly out of the tulle, she cant fight off the red tulle all round her biting into her, coiled about her head. The skylight's blackened with swirling smoke. The room's full of smoke and screaming. Anna is on her feet whirling round fighting with her hands the burning tulle all round her. (*MT*, 355)

In a sophisticated analysis of this passage, Paul Petrovic interprets Anna's "whirling" in the flames, and under the cover of the smoke, as a kind of dance that symbolizes a fight for autonomy. Across *Manhattan Transfer*, Anna exhibits a "growing resistance to the forces that would confine her, and even though she last appears only as an object of Ellen's meditation on the fire, that meditation prophesies the way horrific scarring may bring Anna economic power and free her from the male gaze." Her disfigurement, according to Petrovic, closes off "the normal 'decent' life of a woman of her ethnicity and class" and opens up "a chance to capitalize on her body in a way that reverses existing power relations."[109] Of course, it could just as easily reproduce her body as an object of spectacle, subject to what Rosemarie Garland-Thompson calls the "illicit looking" initiated by the public designation of the bodies of people with physical disabilities as both "to-be-be looked-at and not-to-be-looked at."[110] Still, as the shining whiteness of the tulle is consumed by the black smoke, Anna's frenetic, painful, appearing and disappearing dance offers an alternative form of movement to the automatized movement of Ellen.

In her account of the mechanization of the female body in managerial discourse in the early twentieth century, Katherine Stubbs discusses a short story by the trade unionist Gertrude Barnum, published in a labor publication in the 1910s. In the story, a young factory worker, Edna, bemoans the susceptibility of her fellow workers to the manipulations of their managers. As she says, "anyone can pull a string and make 'em spin round and round." But when Edna attends a union meeting, the narrator notes that the union women, by contrast, "cannot be wound up by a little key of flattery and made to go contentedly round and round like wax figures twelve hours a day." To Edna's protest that the women at her factory are "a collection of wax works," the union president responds, "All you have to do is wire them for electricity, keep up the current, and make the connection."[111] As Stubbs points out, Barnum appropriates the discourse of female mechanization in the early twentieth century, a "rhetorical construction of women as analogous to machines [that] seemed to make possible the supervision, manipulation, and control of women throughout the economic sphere."[112] Her story suggests that the sheer "artificiality of the version of embodiment" applied to women can "become the means of staging a resistance that was simultaneously symbolic and concrete." Energizing and animating the factory mannequins, Barnum envisions a new form of mechanical body that is

> capable of electrification: a factory floor crowded with agitated women, all of whom share in a powerful common relay. In this scenario, "getting wired" is equivalent to forging dynamic connections to other women .... This final vision is in a sense the schematization of a technologically enabled counter-public sphere, the promotion or plugging of a new female collectivity.[113]

In *Manhattan Transfer*, the possibility of female solidarity between Anna and Ellen follows a different current of energy, or at least is ignited through a different kind of burning, as the "red hands" of the fire fought by Anna's hands become the "some part" of Ellen "wrapped in bandages, carried away on a stretcher." This possibility is extinguished in the last moments of Dos Passos's novel, as Ellen purposefully forgets the revelation of her intimate, terrible connection with Anna and the rest of New York's other women: "When the taxi stops and the tall doorman opens the door," she "steps out with dancing pointed girlish steps, pays, and turns, her cheeks a little flushed, her eyes sparkling with the glinting seablue night of deep streets, into the revolving doors" (*MT*, 356–57). With this pretty series of gestures, the Elliedoll responds to her final curtain call as the star of the Follies and of the glistening, night-washed "deep streets" of New York—which, in *Manhattan Transfer*, is exactly the same thing. She surrenders to Barnum's pulled strings, "wound up" and spun "round and round" in the endless revolutions of the Algonquin's "shining soundless" glass doors. She shakes off the "sudden pang of something forgotten"—the gesture of inclusion in Anna's "fighting" hands—and "advanc[es] smiling towards two gray men in black with white shirtfronts getting to their feet, smiling, holding out their hands" (357). She is welcomed back into the panoptic order of the modern city. But, in preserving the difference between these "gray" hands and Anna's burned and blackened ones, Dos Passos leaves us in little doubt of the damages of his photographic metropolis, nor of the psychosocial poverty of its frozen star attraction.

4. Torn, Burned, and Yet Dancing

F. Scott Fitzgerald's Hollywood Writing

"The consciousness of rupture," writes Susan Stanford Friedman, introducing a collection of psychoanalytically oriented essays on James Joyce, "may well be a defining characteristic of modernity, but this psychic reality could itself represent the repression rather than the abandonment of what came before."[1] For Friedman, the texts of Joyce and others are sites for what Freud called "working through" the "repetition compulsion" to "remembering."[2] Modernist writing is delicately and insistently encoded with psychodynamic processes of repression and return, the perpetual revisitation of an unresolved past event as is manifest by, for instance, the paratactical formulations in Stein's *Three Lives*, as they parallel James Snead's notion of the "cut," a sudden break that drags against forward motion and teleological formations of history.[3] The oscillations of concealment and revelation that define the grammar and the decoding mechanisms of Freud's dream work are shadowed in the repetitive movements of the woman-in-series in and out of sight, in and through the gaps and intervals of modernist writing. Indeed, one of the metaphors Freud uses to describe his psychoanalytic method is the peeling back of the layers of the palimpsest—an interpretative work that I model by parsing the composite logic of *Three Lives, Cane,* and *Manhattan Transfer* alongside the visual syntax and epistemological instability of serial or composite photography.

This final chapter addresses aspects of modernism's composite textuality that remain submerged in the preceding chapters, by considering it in a different guise and a different context. In her discussion of Joyce, Friedman adapts Freud's analysis of serial or "consecutive" dreams—which are "often based on common ground and must accordingly be interpreted in connection with one another"—in reading *A Portrait of the Artist as a Young Man* (1916) in relation to the posthumously published *Stephen Hero* (1944), along with the extant draft material around those texts.[4] Comprising "distinct parts of a larger composite 'text' whose parts are like the imperfectly erased layers of a palimpsest," each of these texts is an alternative but not hierarchized variant in a textual "chain" that is layered with the evidence of the displacement, condensation, or revision of the dream-work.[5] This evidence, Friedman says, can be investigated through acts of intertextual "superimposition."[6] In documenting the repeated return of the serialized woman across texts by four major modernist authors, by theoretically superimposing their female characters, my approach is similar to Friedman's—albeit widening its scope beyond the work of a particular author. Yet it is also true that the woman-in-series materializes in other writing by the authors I discuss. In Dos Passos's work, to take one example, the characterological relay that conjoins Ellen Thatcher with Anna Cohen, Nellie McNiel, and Ruth Prynne in *Manhattan Transfer* extends to Ellen's near-namesakes in the *U.S.A.* trilogy (1930–1936): Eleanor Stoddard and Eveline Hutchins. These women, whose friendship is a structural axis of the trilogy, are Ellen's rough contemporaries, setting up shop in New York in the same historical moment as her star begins to rise, and heading off to Paris, just like her, as Red Cross nurses at the outbreak of war in 1914. Eleanor, like Ellen, is "cool and white and collected," a social climber and master of reinvention determined to escape the "stockyard stench" of her working-class upbringing; Eveline shares Ellen's barely concealed anxiety and listless disappointment with New York's endless stream of social gatherings and romances.[7] Ziegfeld and his Follies feature in *U.S.A.* too: in *Nineteen-Nineteen*, Eveline attends the 1914 Follies revue in Chicago, and in *The Big Money*, Ziegfeld himself plucks Margo Dowling out of obscurity and puts her into the front row of the chorus. As the glass-hardened, smoke-covered Ellen is reconfigured as Margo, who appears at the end of the trilogy as "a porcelain doll" enveloped in a "dizzy swirl of cigarettesmoke," she emerges as one of the "ghosts of platinum girls" haunting *U.S.A.* at its denouement.[8]

In turning to F. Scott Fitzgerald's late work, specifically his writing in, of, and for Hollywood in the year before his death in December 1940, I extend my argument about the proximity of the woman-in-series to sequenced photography and the Fordist production line, theorized in the previous chapter in relation to the format of the variety show and the choreography of chorus girls. In doing so, however, I deal with the mode of composite textuality identified by Friedman. This chapter examines the two major writing projects Fitzgerald undertook in 1939 and 1940: the screenplay "Cosmopolitan," an adaptation of Fitzgerald's 1931 short story "Babylon Revisited," and *The Last Tycoon*, a novel, never finished, set in studio-era Hollywood.[9] Whether by the generic imperatives of institutionalized textual production in Hollywood, or the randomized contingencies of historical chance, Fitzgerald's screenplay and unfinished novel are fragmentary and palimpsestic. They are aligned, however unintentionally, with metatextual high-modernist works that "flaunt their bodies and invite the stares of their readers," in Michael Kaufman's words, "show[ing] their printed bodies for what they are: print and paper."[10] Precursory, contingent, relatively unbounded, Fitzgerald's Hollywood writing lays bare—and lays bare in—its textual skins.

Like the Hollywood backlot, which looks to Cecelia Brady, the narrator in *The Last Tycoon*, "like the torn picture books of childhood, like fragments of stories dancing in an open fire" (*LT*, 25), Fitzgerald's Hollywood writings are unstable textual sites that quiver and sway with layered and potential significations: torn, burned, and yet dancing. Where Friedman suggests that draft manuscripts and notes might aid in the interpretation of repressed material, which "erupt[s] into the gaps of the later text" in a textual chain, these eruptions occur unevenly and transversely in Fitzgerald's Hollywood work.[11] As a textual sequence, which also implicates the *Saturday Evening Post* story "Babylon Revisited," "Cosmopolitan" and *The Last Tycoon* recalibrate the trope of the woman-in-series in concert with the "generalized logic of substitution, citationality, and seriality" that Jani Scandura identifies as constituent of Hollywood film production.[12] Personifying this logic of production and consumption, the characters of Victoria Wales, in the screenplay, and Kathleen Moore, in the novel, manifest Hollywood celebrity in the 1930s as a mediating and specifically photographing discourse, which captivates and thrills not so much by its scarcity as by its standardizing "proliferation and promiscuity."[13] Fitzgerald's Hollywood produces a chain of stand-ins and body doubles that redoubles—and troubles—the iconographic syntax of stardom that it is supposed to sanction: a string of gleaming glamour shots, a series of lingering close-ups.

"Cosmopolitan" and *The Last Tycoon* show the reiterative logic of studio-era Hollywood to be derived from the basic seriality of the photogrammatic track. As Laura Mulvey and other scholars in the still–moving field have argued, classical narrative film, somewhat like avant-garde cinema, counterbalances and fuses optical movement and narrative dynamics with moments of standstill.[14] As this still–moving dialectic shapes the specular logic of the star system in the studio era and maps the "optically unthought of the moving image," that is, the "jagged seriality" of the photogrammatic track, it also underwrites the "flack and static of an increasingly 'technologized' literary technique" in modernism.[15] In Garrett Stewart's evocative terms, all of the composite literary texts I have examined in terms of serial photography simultaneously reflect the "oscillating materiality of the cinematic mirage" as they "[vibrate] with the undulant undoing of continuous signification."[16] But Fitzgerald's Hollywood texts, thematically grooved by the "flitting litter" of discrete images that is modernist writing's filmic affiliate, much more directly intimate the tracings of the photogram.[17]

This chapter conceives the writing that emerges under the conditions of the "genius of the system" of hierarchical, interdependent, mechanized Hollywood studio production as a markedly literal instantiation of Stewart's technologized inscription.[18] On *The Last Tycoon*'s backlot of fire-spun, fragmented stories, Kathleen Moore embodies the condition and the limit of Hollywood presence: she is the subject and the sign of the filmic cut. Emerging in her first (dis)appearance in the novel as the image of Monroe Stahr's dead wife, the movie star Minna Davis, Kathleen stands for the concealment and disclosure of the photogram's stillness through the technical strategies of continuity editing and acousmatic synchronization in Hollywood film. The filmic allegory is elaborated in "Cosmopolitan," which openly positions the child, Victoria Wales, as the double of her dead mother, Helen. In connection to *The Last Tycoon*, Fitzgerald's screenplay represents a strategic form of revision similar to Richard Moreland's concept of "revisionary repetition," which, in William Faulkner's writing, carves open a "critical space" in which sociopolitical structures are reconfigured and silenced voices are heard.[19] Just as reading *Three Lives*, *Cane*, and *Manhattan Transfer* as composite texts establishes new figurations of female subjectivity that allow for expressions of resistance to the dominant visual and representational order of modernity, reading Fitzgerald's screenplay with *The Last Tycoon*—as mutually referring shadow texts—uncovers the subversive tactics enacted by Helen Wales through her absent presence in the former text. In Freudian thought, the return of the repressed is the return of the mother, the inexplicable, untranscribable female other. In "Cosmopolitan," the dead mother remains unseen and unheard—but she is afforded a symbolic form of agency in her invisibility and her silence.

The written texts at the borderlands of Hollywood cinema are, as Karen Beckman notes, "site[s] of excess" in which we "glimpse the eruption of the film's repressed material."[20] This repressed material includes the seductive inducements of stillness and the hyperbolic discourses of femininity in classical Hollywood cinema, as well as the technological and textual bodies that are most fully masked in and by it: the industrial apparatus of film production and the praxis of screenwriting. In composite, *The Last Tycoon* and "Cosmopolitan" reveal this writing praxis as interdependent, socially embedded, and institutionally circumscribed. The collaborative or corporate author—the author in composite—is a repressed figure in all literary production, not to mention scholarly production. She languishes in the corners of cultural history, called up only occasionally in, for instance, the category-defying declaration of the avant-garde writer and artist Claude Cahun: "My lover will not be the subject of my drama; s/he will be my collaborator."[21] But the composite author is less completely hidden in studio-era Hollywood, and so less easily ignored. As Fitzgerald's Hollywood writing attests, this repressed figure, with its shadowy, supplementary bodies, is an apparition that ghosts—as it writes—the woman-in-series.

Writing (on) the Studio Lot

According to the film producer Monroe Stahr in *The Last Tycoon*, there are no "good writers out here" in Hollywood, only those who will "accept the system and stay decently sober" (*LT*, 57–58). Stahr's "system" is a dreaming of the Hollywood dream factory in the studio era, a fictional repetition of the rationalized production procedures at Metro-Goldwyn-Mayer (MGM) in the early 1930s. It functions by a principle of replication and substitution, consigning "good writers" and their work to the overflowing wastebaskets of planned obsolescence. As Stahr explains, "we have all sorts of people—disappointed poets, one-hit playwrights, college girls—we put them on an idea in pairs and if it slows down we put two more writers working behind them. I've had as many as three pairs working independently on the same idea" (58). Stahr's secret puppetry is visualized when the novelist George Boxley enters Stahr's office "with the air of being violently dragged though no one apparently had a hand on him" and is forced into a chair by "two invisible attendants." These are the active poltergeists of what Boxley calls the "conspiracy" of writerly collaboration as a mechanism of institutional control (31). They are at home in a Hollywood that Cecelia Brady accepts "with the resignation of a ghost assigned to a haunted house" (3)—a gothic metaphor that, as Michael Nowlin points out, involves "a discordant recognition that something is amiss" in this dream factory.[22]

The aggression of Boxley's invisible attendants is at odds with Stahr's courteous tone, which the producer uses again, later in the novel, when meeting with a husband-and-wife writing team. Looking at the wife "as if he could read her handwriting through the typescript," Stahr bemoans the system he devised, call-ing it "a shame . . . gross, commercial, to be deplored" (*LT*, 58). In moments when Stahr's paternalistic air masks his ruthless business acumen, Fitzgerald satirizes the Hollywood studio's treatment of the screenwriters holed up at the back of the lot in "a row of iron maidens left over from silent days and still resounding the full moans of cloistered hacks and bums" (100). Yet in the confrontation staged between the novelist, Boxley, and the Hollywood scenarist and studio boss, Stahr—thinly veiled stand-ins for English writer Aldous Huxley and MGM pro-ducer Irving Thalberg, respectively—the latter comes out on top. Improvising a mystery out of a match-lit stove, a pretty stenographer, and a pair of black gloves, Stahr demonstrates to Boxley that the art of "making pictures" is more than men "always duelling and falling down wells . . . wearing strained facial expressions and talking incredible and unnatural dialogue" (31–32). As Boxley is swept up by Stahr's narrated scene, *The Last Tycoon* exhibits a fascination with, and respect for, the techniques of Hollywood storytelling. When the ghostly escorts finally seem to release Boxley, the episode does not dramatize the author's regrettable capitulation to Hollywood's demands but, instead, a general acceptance of those demands and the artistic sensibility they support.

Fitzgerald's feelings toward Hollywood were as mixed as Dos Passos's were toward the modern machine. In his notes for *The Last Tycoon*, Fitzgerald defended the "private grammar" of the moving pictures against the dismissive attitudes of those in the East whose interests reach only to "the pretensions, the extravagances and vulgarities" of Hollywood.[23] In May 1940, he wrote to his wife, Zelda, that "the standard of writing from the best movies, like [Alfred Hitchcock's] *Rebecca*, is, believe it or not, much higher at present than that in the commercial magazines."[24] The previous winter, he lauded the cinema as "the greatest of all human medi-ums of communication" in a letter to his daughter Scottie.[25] But although in these remarks and in *The Last Tycoon* he seems, like Cecelia Brady, "obstinately unhor-rified" by Hollywood's spooks and schemes (*LT*, 3), in the essays collected in *The Crack-Up* just a few years earlier, in 1936, Fitzgerald describes himself as "haunted" by the cinema. Writing during a period of professional and personal disappoint-ment, he claims to have realized that

> the novel, which at my maturity was the strongest and supplest medium
> for conveying thought and emotion from one human being to another, was
> becoming subordinated to a mechanical and communal art that, whether
> in the hands of Hollywood merchants or Russian idealists, was capable of
> reflecting only the tritest thought, the most obvious emotion. It was an art
> in which words were subordinate to images, where personality was worn

down to the inevitable low gear of collaboration. . . . [T]here was a ran-
kling indignity . . . in seeing the power of the written word subordinated to
another power, a more glittering, a grosser power.[26]

This Fitzgerald, grieving his "maturity" as a writer in the face of the "gross" and
"glittering" juggernaut of Hollywood and avant-garde cinema, was memorialized
in the description of him in an interview with the *New York Post*'s Michel Mok that
same year: "His trembling hands, his twitching face with its pitiful expression of a
cruelly beaten child."[27]

The image of Fitzgerald beaten and bullied by the Hollywood machine was
to stick. When he died of heart failure in his bed in the last weeks of 1940, he
seemed, to his friend and posthumous editor Edmund Wilson, another casualty of
Hollywood's "already appalling record of talent depraved and wasted."[28] For many
scholars, in turn, Fitzgerald is the exemplary victim in "the Hollywood vampire
story," an enduring mythology that demonizes Hollywood as "a malevolent entity
that feeds on the brains of artists."[29] Yet Fitzgerald's *Ledger* makes clear the willful
duplicity of his view of himself as a novelist who occasionally churned out short
stories for popular slicks like *Collier's* and the *Saturday Evening Post* and film treat-
ments and script work for MGM. Apart from a brief period following the success
of his first novel, *This Side of Paradise* (1920), earnings from Fitzgerald's novels
never met his expenses; the lion's share of his income in the 1920s was derived
from the publication of short stories, and as early as December 1920, he was dividing his time between writing novels and writing for the movies.[30] Fitzgerald might
well have believed that the work he was doing in Hollywood after 1937 was, as he
wrote to Scottie, "the last tired effort of a man who once did something finer."[31] But
he was always a commercial writer, and he had one foot in Hollywood long before
he went West in 1937 as a contract screenwriter with MGM.[32]

Since the 1950s, and increasingly over the last thirty or so years, scholars have
interpreted the stylistic and perspectival effects of Fitzgerald's novels with reference
to the cinema, apprehending (and performing) the transformation of Fitzgerald's
"pen [into] a camera, moving, describing, and recording cinematically," to quote
from a recent study.[33] Accounts of Fitzgerald's cinematic writing notably exclude
his actual screenwriting, which remains understudied as a result of structural
oppositions that inhere in discussions of his work: the serious versus the ephemeral, the high versus the low, the word versus the image, and the individual artist
versus the machine of interdependent mass production—or, in Fitzgerald's words
in *The Crack-Up* essay, personality ground under the low gear of collaboration.
These oppositions mark out the same gendered terrain as Dos Passos's pejorative

attitude toward writers who "merely [feed] the machine, like a girl in a sausage factory shoving hunks of meat into the hopper."[34] In the same year that Fitzgerald moved to Hollywood, writers who headed West for work were snubbed by the New York theater critic George Jean Nathan, who, writing for *Scribner's Magazine*, saw them succumbing to "Hollywood harlotry."[35]

To be sure, Fitzgerald's ambition, as he headed to Hollywood in 1937, was to "fight the rest [of the writers] tooth and nail until, in fact or in effect, I'm alone on the picture."[36] Hence Fitzgerald's hero in *The Last Tycoon* is a fictionalized homage to Irving Thalberg, the Hollywood producer who positioned himself most effectively between "capitalization and production, between conception and execution" at MGM from the mid-1920s into the 1930s.[37] Monroe Stahr, who professes himself to be the "unity" of the studio system (*LT*, 58), its very syntax, is a prototype of what would come to be known as the auteur, the autonomous artist–director imagined to transcend the overdetermined regiments of collaboration and commercialization in studio-era Hollywood. As Jonathan Veitch notes, it is through this romantic male figure, who stage manages the "enchanted distorted" dance of children's stories on the "fairyland" backlot (*LT*, 25), that *The Last Tycoon* recoups the "dense, shifting network of discourse and convention" that constitutes the classical Hollywood medium "under the debatable category of authorship."[38]

The irony of Fitzgerald's mystification of Hollywood processes through his representation of Stahr is that it reinforces the "myth of solitary genius" that, codified in auteur theory and beyond, contributed to the historical devaluation of the screenwriter and the denigration of the screenplay.[39] As Matthew Bruccoli notes, Fitzgerald's main problem in Hollywood was that he did not "work well with collaborators."[40] He quarreled with Marcel de Sano on the script for *Red-Headed Woman* in 1931, as well as with E. E. Paramore and Joseph Mankiewicz while working on *Three Comrades* in 1937 and 1938. Fitzgerald's antipathy toward Hollywood's interdependent procedures prefigures the scholarly anxiety around the "corrupting" influence of his collaborating partners. Even Winston Wheeler Dixon, who seeks to incorporate Fitzgerald's screenwriting in his larger corpus, counters the idea of the writer as a "compromised automaton" by dismissing the contributions of his Hollywood collaborators, claiming that they cheapened his artistic "vision."[41]

The screenplay, then, is the salient sign and object of studio-era Hollywood as a place in which, as Richard Fine writes, the "profession of authorship . . . was under attack"—and, certainly, in transition.[42] As a rule, as Jack Stillinger points out, the authorship of films is practically "unassignable." Shaped by large numbers of agents in production histories riddled with conflicts of interest and intent, films are also capital-intensive products, subject to the vicissitudes of the mass audience in the form of preview audiences, censors, film reviewers, and so on.[43] Moreover, the corporate studio itself, as Jerome Christensen argues, bears not only a stylistic stamp but also an "individualized speech" that determines the "objectives and meanings" of its products.[44] Given that the majority of films in classical Hollywood are also adaptations of "original" written texts, the writing of a screenplay was a collaborative, institutionalized encounter that was multiplied profusely along its thick chain of production. When Fitzgerald was brought onto the working script for *Gone with the Wind* in early 1939, at least a dozen screenwriters had already gone before him; his job was polishing and "patching," excising small details, trimming individual lines, and restoring dialogue lifted directly from Margaret Mitchell's novel.[45] Fitzgerald's penciled insertions and deletions to *Gone with the Wind*, a script that was already a many-layered palimpsest, represent his Hollywood writing at its most fractional and indistinct. But the problems in accrediting authorship to this script imply the difficulties posed by the screenplay in general, as it constellates into an array of drafts and versions through the serial, partial, and variously opaque operations of numerous writers and other agents.

Textual Intermittence

A multiform and indeterminate textual object, evolving through diffuse processes, manifesting in varied material and commercial configurations, and continuously affected by the motivated entanglements of its readers, the screenplay substantiates recent approaches to textual editing such as Jerome McGann's "theory of versions" and John Bryant's notion of the "fluid text."[46] As Steven Price notes, the multivalence of the screenplay, which has led to its marginalization in the scholarship of literature and film, is lately accepted in literary studies "as a general condition of all texts." The screenplay is a functional archetype in efforts to reveal "the concealed practices that have aided [literary studies] in defining itself in opposition to the non-literary."[47]

Fitzgerald's Hollywood writing, in particular, occasions the reappraisal of low and high cultural forms as contiguous to one another—even implying an effect of "alikeness," in Leo Bersani's terms, between the cultural artifacts and discourses of popular film and literary modernism.[48] It also foregrounds what Foucault describes as the "coming into being of the notion of 'author' [as] the privileged moment of individualization in the history of ideas, knowledge, literature, philosophy, and the sciences."[49] The conceit of individualization is unraveled not only in Fitzgerald's screenwriting, but in the unfinished *The Last Tycoon*. This text—which is really a "collocation of materials," as Philip Cohen notes—necessitates the collaboration of other agents in institutionalized directives and exigencies, in this case of scholarly book publishing.[50] Yet the editorial debates that encircle the novel are defined by a preoccupation with the solitary author and the singular, authoritative text. Fitzgerald left behind working drafts that amount to about two-thirds of a new novel, as well as five different outline charts and more than 200 pages of notes.[51] The draft material, encompassing seventeen of the projected thirty episodes of the novel, was edited for publication in 1941 by Edmund Wilson, who also appended a detailed synopsis of the episodes that remained unwritten. Convinced that the first edition "disguises the gestational nature of Fitzgerald's drafts and conveys the impression of a more nearly finished work," Matthew Bruccoli released a substantially revised edition of the book in the early 1990s. Working to expurgate the marks borne on the text by Wilson's "heavy" hand—or, rather, the marks of Fitzgerald's "process of development and refinement" erased by that hand—Bruccoli constructs a single text out of the extant documents that seeks to approximate, as closely as possible, Fitzgerald's last-known intentions.[52]

Even in affirming Fitzgerald's (incoherent) writing process, Bruccoli's edition exemplifies the (coherent) eclectic orientation toward the single author and the primary, clear reading text associated with the Greg–Bowers editorial tradition. "*Fitzgerald's prose,*" Bruccoli writes in the preface to the new edition, "*has not been rewritten.*"[53] This strident, defensive comment indicates the moralized hazards that the work of the editor is seen to carry: most critically, the disfigurement and vulgarization of the authorial text. These hazards also condition Milton Stern's strange formulation of the posthumously published unfinished work as a collaboration not between the author and the editor per se but between the author and "the exercise of taste, instinct, care, and knowledge of the editor." Stern's philosophy of editorial "taste" is "amorphous": "It is a vibration of mutual identity . . . . It is a fine sense of what the author sounds like. It is a non-egotistical, sympathetic presentiment of what the author would want and of what is more important than the corrective facts."[54]

Stern's editor shuttles between a dynamic identification by which the "ego" and "sympathies" of the editor are displaced by those of the lost author and the reanimation of that author's lifeless body through a revitalizing ventriloquy that speaks out its choked, inchoate, uncorrected desires. This is a remarkably close figuration of Kathleen Moore, the doppelgänger of Monroe Stahr's dead wife in *The Last Tycoon*. Like Kathleen, Stern's imagined editor is the ghostly afterimage and double of the author, too close and yet not close enough to the original. It is, as we will see, Kathleen's voice that distinguishes her from Minna Davis; similarly, in unfinished texts, to get up close and personal with the author is to slip unseamlessly into the place of the other, never exactly dubbing the authorial voice. Reaching toward an absent body made paradoxically present upon the asperate, irregular surface of the manuscript, the eclectic editor's substitutionary mode of reading and writing is always frustrated and diverted.

For Steve McCaffery, the fragmentary textual trace is "the mark of an absence previously present."[55] It is a "derivative presence" that, like the photograph for Barthes, presents "death in the future" in the face of she who will, inevitably, suffer the "defeat of Time" and become *what has been*.[56] As Bryant suggests in his thesis on textual "fluidity," the absence of the author is apparent on the pages of draft manuscripts not as "an undifferentiated blank," but as "layerings of absence" in the vacillations and competitions of its revisions.[57] In its pathologized self-effacement, Stern's and Bruccoli's editorial philosophy reacts against, and compensates for, the tensile operations of presence and absence that collect on the incomplete manuscript like dust—dust being, as Carolyn Steedman says, the material shorthand for the "ceaseless making and unmaking" of the world, "the impossibility of things disappearing, or going away, or being gone."[58] The archive's trace evidence of imperishability is constituent of the pursuit of the lost Fitzgerald, which cannot help but be both elegiac and erotic in its practices of elicit reading, its scrutiny of "something that was not intended for your eyes."[59] (The testimony of Fitzgerald's partner, Sheilah Graham, was that "Scott intended to rewrite the first part [of *The Last Tycoon*] entirely—he wouldn't want it seen as it is."[60])

Dancing like Cecelia's backlot of fragmentary stories, *The Last Tycoon* and "Cosmopolitan" are imbricated with a Barthesian erotics of reading in which the fragmentary glimpse is the foci of desire. As Barthes asks in *The Pleasure of the Text*, "Is not the most erotic portion of a body *where the garment gapes*?" What seduces is "the intermittence of skin flashing between two articles of clothing . . . the staging of an appearance-as-disappearance."[61] The naked flesh of Fitzgerald's Hollywood texts appears in flashes, as the texts move back and forth between absence and presence, fragment and whole. Fitzgerald's scattered, dusty remains in the drafts, notes, and ephemera are fetishized fragments that produce and reproduce desire for the absent author—and the absent complete text—whose lack they signify.[62] Existing liminally in "an ambiguous space of imaginary plenitude" and excess, the textual fragment is an "undecidable textuality" such as that described by Jacques Derrida and Jean Baudrillard in their respective discussions of the aphoristic mode. It is, as Sean Braune writes, the "remaining trace of a larger writing that exists as an imaginary supplement . . . as pure potential in a sort of libidinous energy catalyzing in the mind of the reader and critic."[63]

Editorial, analytic, or otherwise, any engagement with Fitzgerald's unfinished novel is conducted in the symbolic gaps around it as a fragment and a totality, a text at once inside and outside of its symbolic and material boundaries. And, if the unfinished text engenders a peculiar "agendic force" in readers and literary scholars, so too does the screenplay, which shares its precursory and intermediary functions.[64] As Ted Nannicelli and others have pointed out, the interaction of the industrial document of the screenplay with the whole and complete film has been central to its rejection as a work of art and an object of scholarly inquiry.[65] The screenplay is the shadowy double of the film, "seemingly physically separate and yet operating as a second, parallel form that can never wholly be repressed."[66] But in its paucity and difficulty, it initiates, as Pier Paolo Pasolini argues, an "intense" and creative exercise of readerly engagement that seeks "a 'visual' completeness which it does not have, but at which it hints." The reader of the screenplay—much like the collaborators with whom Fitzgerald worked in Hollywood, or the editors who worked "with" Fitzgerald after his death—is charged with decoding its "desire for form": "a void" made legible in the "coarseness and incompleteness" of its terse, connotative language and its fragmentary, episodic—indeed, aphoristic—script.[67]

"There never was a good biography of a good novelist," wrote Fitzgerald in a notebook in the early 1930s. "There couldn't be. He's too many people if he's any good."[68] This assertion, in a modified form, finds its way into Cecelia Brady's more sardonic mouth in *The Last Tycoon*: "Writers aren't people exactly. Or, if they're any good, they're a whole *lot* of people trying so hard to be one person. It's like actors, who try so pathetically not to look in mirrors. Who lean *back*ward trying— only to see their faces in the reflecting chandeliers" (*LT*, 12). In the first instance, the notion of the writer as "a whole *lot* of people trying so hard to be one person" refers reflexively to Fitzgerald's method of combinatory or additive characteriza- tion. Speaking of the manuscript drafts of *The Great Gatsby* in 1924, Fitzgerald admitted that Jay Gatsby was "blurred and patchy" because he was an "amalgam" who "started as one man I knew and then changed into myself."[69] Some fifteen years later, Fitzgerald found an industrial metaphor for this method in relation to *The Last Tycoon*, describing the "early character-planting phase" of writing as a process of "welding together hundreds of stray impressions and incidents to form the fabric of entire personalities."[70] In the second instance, the "too many" writer who cannot be summed up in the whole or complete texts of biography, let alone contained in her own skin, illustrates the problem of authorship in Hollywood. No "good" writer is only one writer, and this is especially true in the studios' mirror-encrusted halls, where writers and actors are made into versions of themselves and others by the many-angled refractions of their images. Hollywood's permeable conglomerates of citational bodies make it entirely appropriate that Cecelia's description of writers on the studio lot as a "whole *lot* of people" is a voice thrown from the writer's notebook. In Fitzgerald's Hollywood, one's words—and one's image—are almost those of another: not-quite-verbatim utterances that measure the distance between the novelist who is "too many people if he's any good" and the writer who is "a whole *lot* of people trying so hard to be one person."

The "condition" of mass production, Stahr tells Boxley late in *The Last Tycoon*, "is that we have to take people's own favorite folklore and dress it up and give it back to them" (*LT*, 106–107). Boxley then pitches an idea for a picture that demonstrates that he is becoming "a real picture man": "Let each character see himself in the other's place . . . . The policeman is about to arrest the thief when he sees that the thief actually has his face. I mean show it that way. You could almost call the thing 'Put Yourself in My Place'" (108). Turning on the intrigue of interchangeability, the imagined acts of Hollywood writing in *The Last Tycoon* replicate their own system of production, the condition of repetition with a difference, of folklore in a new costume. This effect is compounded in the unfinished novel, as the spaces between Hollywood's serialized bodies and stories adjoin the capacious gaps of the aphoristic fragment–text. In delving into these gaps—which are also, metaphorically, the intervals between photograms along the track of classical film—we uncover in Hollywood's visual realm a vexation of subject and object familiar from the composite modernist writing of Stein, Toomer, and Dos Passos.

Repetition With a Difference

In the collisions between its narrative world and its material fragmentations as an unfinished text, *The Last Tycoon* is a "writing of the disaster," in Maurice Blanchot's formulation, in which absence and presence, lack and excess, fragment and whole condense and interchange.[71] Gorging "an open wound in the seascape" upon a rock promontory past Santa Monica, Stahr's half-built beach house is a poignant symbol for his doomed, "incomplete" life (*LT*, 81)—in the scheme of the novel's projected narrative, in which he was to die in an airplane crash, and in the scheme of the unfinished text itself. The scaffolded fuselage also reads as a memorial to Fitzgerald, whose premature death heightens the tragedy of Stahr's (and *The Last Tycoon*'s) never-realized end, and vice versa. Repeatedly, uncannily, the thematic preoccupations of *The Last Tycoon* interlock with its aleatory, fluid form.

As Mitchell Breitwieser notes, the novel's plot is organized around "the opening of divisions within what had seemed to be secure wholes," from the professional tensions in the Hollywood studio to the "inner fractures" riven by Stahr's desire for the woman who is and is not his dead wife.[72] When Stahr and Kathleen drive back to Hollywood from the unfinished beach house, they feel themselves to be "different people." "Four times they had driven along the shore road today, each time a different pair," we read. "He asked her to sit close in the car and she did but they did not seem close because for that you have to seem to be growing closer. Nothing stands still" (*LT*, 95). Split into various iterations of themselves, Stahr and Kathleen embody Fitzgerald's accumulative mode of characterization in the flux and chance of writing. Never standing still and yet not growing closer, their moving stasis in the car weds their changeability, their serialized constitution, to the contingencies of textual composition. The characters are as incompletely wrought as Stahr's beachside house: some rooms fully furnished and contained; others bare and unadorned under the star-punctured sky.

What scholars have appreciated as a deep connection between *The Last Tycoon*'s episodic, scenic structure and "spoken, rapid, and staccato" language, on the one hand, and the narrative exposition of the Hollywood screenplay, on the other, is at least to some degree a function of the text's unfinished state.[73] Dixon holds that the novel's epigrammatic, notational style "inherently requires visualization" and transforms its reader into "a camera" as well as the "director" of that camera's movement, made to confer Pasolini's visual completeness on the novel.[74] But just how terse and episodic *The Last Tycoon* would have remained through the process of drafting, revision, and editing is, and will always be, an open question. Still, when Fitzgerald states in his notebook that he wants to achieve, in Stahr's unfinished house, the "odd effect of the place like a set," he intuits the compatibility between abortive discursive and physical structures and Hollywood's processes and products.[75] An extension of the movie set, filled with studio props and conceived by Stahr as "a nice place to read scripts" (*LT*, 82), the unfinished house returns us to the studio where such scripts are written and filmed in piecemeal, layered chunks, according to serialized work processes that mimic the rapid progress of film's twenty-four frames-per-second. In his personal projection room at the end of each day at the studio lot, Stahr spends his hours passing judgment on a parade of film runs from the comfort of an "overstuffed chair" that, in its hyperbolic corpulence, is an apt throne for the master of a celluloid world on repeat (52). Described in terms that recall the "fragments of stories dancing in an open fire" in the backlot, the lengths of film are "dreams [hanging] in fragments at the far end of the room," either relegated to the discard pile or elevated to "be dreamed in crowds" (56). A troop of French Canadians pushes their canoes up a rapid; the director calls "Cut," and the actors relax and laugh together as the rushing water in the studio tank stops flowing. Over and over, the upriver illusion slackens and breaks, generating a stop–start tedium that traces and reiterates the terms of Hollywood spectacle. The river is a flow that halts, a simulation of movement produced in and through the stillness that structures the scenic series of takes in the backlot and on the photogrammatic track.

"And then," we are told after the fragmentary dream of the French Canadians evaporates in Stahr's projection room, "two men met endlessly in a door, recognized each other and went on. They did it wrong. Again they met, they started, they went on" (56). Tracking a relentless meeting and parting of bodies, the funny inertia of these impassive phrases is coextensive with Fitzgerald's representation of Hollywood as a magical zone in which everything is converted into a routine: a place where things, and bodies, always happen more than once. This cinematic poetics of light-hearted futility had already found an icon in the comic, dislocative body of Charlie Chaplin in his early gestural films, which embraced the "sin of repetition," as André Bazin once wrote.[76] Chaplin recounts that, when he met Gertrude Stein at a dinner party in Beverly Hills during her 1934 lecture tour of the United States, she expressed her admiration for his work by pitching a film idea to him: "She would like to see me in a movie just walking up the street and turning a corner, then another corner, and another."[77] Intersecting with the "endless" meeting of the two men in Fitzgerald's rushes, Stein's cinema dream of Chaplin forever circling the block suggests the degree to which an antimimetic, elliptical impulse normally associated with the avant-garde is embedded in the production of classical film.

Developed in lectures and essays in the 1930s, Stein's concept of cinematic insistence applies to both experimental and narrative film. In a lecture given during the 1934 tour, "Portraits and Repetition," she compares her attempts to write in a "continuous present" to the operations of film:

> [I]t was like a cinema picture made up of succession and each moment having its own emphasis and its own existence and so there was the moving and the existence of each moment . . . . I of course did not think of [the insistent style] in terms of the cinema, in fact I doubt whether at that time I had ever seen a cinema but, I cannot repeat this too often, everyone is of one's period and this our period was undoubtedly the period of the cinema and series production.[78]

As Ellen Berry notes, Stein's insistent writing is analogous to the discrete photo-grams that form "a series of fluid continuously present moments that gradually build toward an image." A rotational, repetitive style at home "inside the cam-era," it is "a prose equivalent of unsutured cinema—cinema with the seams show-ing rather than cinema as seamless narrative."[79] It is for this reason that Julian Murphet has questioned whether Stein is referring to cinema proper or to chrono-photography, as the "revolving shutter mechanism" of her sentences break down movement into immobile parts.[80]

Stein's series production is a neat shorthand for the accumulation and linkage of photogrammatic indices that is a condition of all film. The popular narrative films made during the period when Stein was touring the United States, in par-ticular, participated in a late modernist economy of "ever-changing sameness," as Scandura notes. The mature Hollywood studio system and the star system adju-vant to it presupposed and produced an "audience sophisticated enough to make infinite distinctions between infinitely substitutable images and narratives." This mass audience was weaned on cycle or serial films that, in repeating conventional plots, narrative conceits, or actor pairings, were "distinguishable by a singularity that could be read only against the frame of repetition."[81] As this ever-changing sameness produced piles of props, costumes, and set pieces—such as the jutting assortment of discarded staircases photographed by Edward Weston on the MGM backlot in 1939 or 1940 (Figure 4.1)—Hollywood audiences became accustomed to seeing Bette Davis walk down the exact same staircase in three different Warner Brothers pictures. Hollywood's mass audience was, then, adroit at performing the "successive," forgetful acts of attention that, for Stein, gauge the cinema's "inevi-table beginning of beginning again and again and again."[82] The "principle" of the cinema, Stein wrote in a 1935 essay, is that "each picture is just infinitesimally dif-ferent from the one before," initiating a productive ambiguity over the term "pic-ture," which could refer to a whole film or an individual filmic frame.[83] Although in 1934 Stein doubted she had "ever seen a cinema," her observation in the 1940 memoir *Paris France* that the "characteristic thing of the twentieth century" is "the idea of production in series, that one thing should be like every other thing, and that it should all be made alike and quantities of them" pertains to the serialized production and consumption of studio-era Hollywood as a late modern offshoot of Taylorist efficiency and Fordist mass production.[84]

As Mark Goble has argued, after the unexpected popular success of *The Autobiography of Alice B. Toklas* in 1932, Stein self-consciously positioned her writ-ing, with its "palpable difficulty and opacity and aspiration to materiality," in a "cinematic" world defined as such "for all the ways in which it permits Stein herself

Fig 4.1   Edward Weston, MGM storage lot, ca. 1939–1940. © Center for Creative Photography, University of Arizona Foundation/Licensed by Viscopy, 2017. Image courtesy of Art Resource, New York

to register the effects of stardom and celebrity."[85] Stein's imagined Chaplin film demonstrates the function of Chaplin's repetitive movements in visualizing, in Michael North's words, "the whole process of copying, without which the movies are unimaginable," and so pointing up "the inherent instability of every object and person in a film."[86] A couple of years after she met Chaplin in Hollywood, Stein elaborated the trope of repetition as a destabilizing reproduction by writing him—or, more exactly, "A man who looks like Charlie Chaplin"—into *A Play Called Not and Now*.[87] As a host of characters who look like celebrities stand around looking at one another, the 1936 play trades in and off the names of stars as public commodities—a variation on one of the central intrigues of *The Autobiography of Alice B. Toklas*, namely, the dazzling proliferation of more-or-less famous "somebodies" brought by "everybody" within the thickly convivial "metropolitan sociality" of the atelier at 27 rue de Fleurus.[88] In the context of her comments about the cinema in "Portraits and Repetition" and elsewhere, the play and the quasi-autobiography suggest that Stein's awareness of the aesthetic of interstices forged in the serialized movement from photogram to photogram in cinema, and from film to film in 1930s movie theaters, extends to the mediation of film stars' bodies on screen and off.

Sitting with Stahr in the beach house in *The Last Tycoon*, Kathleen wonders at what point their sleeping together "was settled," when "nothing in the world could keep it from happening." Her words have "an experienced ring" that Stahr finds attractive: "In his mood which was passionately to repeat yet not recapitulate the past it was right that it should be that way" (*LT*, 89). As Stahr repeats yet does not recapitulate the past by sleeping with a woman who is the spitting image of his dead wife, he and Kathleen are enrolled in one another's sexual histories; by accepting his place in the series of men that presumably comprise Kathleen's "experience," Stahr mirrors Kathleen's position as a woman after Minna Davis. Just before this exchange, the pair discuss the feeling of intimate distance that will follow them on the drive back to Hollywood later that night. Stahr says that he feels "very close" to Kathleen, and he is "full of such tender love for her that he held her tightly till a stitch tore in her dress." But to Kathleen, Stahr seems "far away"; she asks him, "Don't you always think—hope that you'll be one person and then find you're still two?" (88). Sexual union is here a figure for disunion. Like the tight embrace that tears Kathleen's dress, rending a Barthesian gap of fetishized desire, its intimacy registers and ensures the couple's fragmentation into series.

From Film Star to Glamour Shot

The inescapable seriality of a romance stimulated by a passion to repeat yet not recapitulate—and, especially, of the woman who is the object of this passion—allegorizes the repetition with a difference that structures every level of Hollywood text-making and consumption. These are the reiterative significations of Stein's series production, from backlot to filmstrip, and from film star to glamour shot. *The Last Tycoon* makes a joke of Kathleen's status as a woman-in-series, not least in the jarring effect of Stahr's claim that Kathleen is "the most attractive woman I've met since I don't know when" (94)—a patent lie, because even Kathleen knows that he is initially attracted to her because of her resemblance to Minna. When Kathleen and Stahr first meet, she is trespassing on the backlot with a friend. The next day, Stahr's efforts to track down the woman who is "[n]ot Minna and yet Minna" result in a telephone call with a woman he believes is her (59). But the woman who returns Stahr's call is not the woman who is not Minna: Stahr has accidentally contacted Kathleen's friend, Edna.

A series of different versions of herself along the beach road, Kathleen is also sutured in series with Minna, Edna, and the narrator, Cecelia Brady, whose own desire for Stahr puts her in a relation of competition with all three women. This procession of women parading for Stahr and about Kathleen recalls Stein's description, in the voice of Toklas in *The Autobiography of Alice B. Toklas*, of sitting and talking with "all all the wives" associated with the litany of "geniuses, near geniuses and might be geniuses" who "unroll, an endless vista through the years" at the Paris salon.[89] The fleeting appearances of these wives in the atelier's social panorama function, as Goble suggests, in line with the cameo appearance in Hollywood film, which "refers to celebrity in both the dubious aggregate and the splendid particular, to celebrity as both a product of the assembly line and incandescent personality."[90] Like the "endless variety" of famous visitors swirling in and out of the revolving door of Stein and Toklas's salon, the "all all the wives" in Fitzgerald's Hollywood "vista" activate a relay of presence and absence that structures the phenomenology of Hollywood stardom and the pleasures of cinematic spectatorship in the studio era.[91] This was nowhere more obvious than at MGM, "the studio of stars" fictionalized in *The Last Tycoon*, where profitability was derived from a "managerial capacity" to multiply stars on the screen. MGM "consolidat[ed] a studio monopoly on uniqueness" as the "star studio" of "taste" and "quality."[92]

The varied practices of body doubling, which included the use of substitutes for lighting checks, photo-doubling for long shots or inserts, and stunt work, evolved in tandem with the standardization of the film industry in the 1920s and the 1930s. As Ann Chisholm explains, the body double was crucial to the schematics of the Hollywood star system and the specular logic of classical film.[93] In the mutual masquerade of the star and her double, both are displaced, made interchangeable and replaceable—suspended, in Goble's terms, between the splendid particular and the dubious aggregate. "A beautifully acted scene thrown away," says Stahr angrily after viewing one of the film runs in the projection room. "It wasn't centered. The camera was set up so it caught the beautiful top of Claudette [Colbert]'s head all the time she was talking. . . . Tell Tim he could have saved wear and tear by using her stand-in" (*LT*, 53). An instrument of efficiency, militating against the waste of wear and tear, the stand-in is associated with Kathleen's substituting and substitutable body through the episodic progress of the unfinished text. Stahr's phone conversation with Edna—who stands in for Kathleen as Kathleen stands in for the film star Minna Davis—immediately follows Stahr's viewing of the rushes and his description of the studio's "system" for managing "disappointed poets, one-hit playwrights, college girls." Before he answers the phone, Stahr considers the possibility that the woman he saw in the backlot might be "an actress who had got herself up to look like Minna as he had once had a young actress made up like Claudette Colbert and photographed her from the same angles" (58).

In the vicinity of Claudette Colbert and the nameless stand-ins who are the function and guarantee of her celebrity, Kathleen is enfolded into the culture of endless rewriting and repetition on the studio lot, "dressed up" as Minna in line with Stahr's repurposing of the mass audience's "favorite folklore." Boxley's "Put Yourself in My Place" summarizes the institutional effects of filmic substitution hidden in the plain sight of the camera, such that the thief does not actually have the face of the policeman who arrests him but rather is filmed as if he does: "I mean show it that way," Boxley clarifies. Kathleen comes into being in *The Last Tycoon* in what amounts to a spectacle of rebirth.[94] After an earthquake that Cecelia describes as "some nightmare attempt to attach our navel cords again and jerk us back to the womb of creation," Kathleen is delivered to Stahr on an "impromptu river" caused by burst water mains on the backlot (*LT*, 23, 26). Bearing "the face of his dead wife, identical even to the expression," Kathleen's "warm and glowing" body returns Stahr to Minna's funeral: "the still sour room, the muffled glide of the limousine hearse, the falling concealing flowers" (26). As Kathleen emerges as the stand-in who replaces the star, Minna's death is cast as a metaphor for the disappearance of the latter that structures the appearance of the former.

A supplementary presence summoned up by the studio's managerial directives, Kathleen in her watery (re)incarnation partakes of the same intermittence as *The Last Tycoon*, offering up fragmentary traces and glimpses of a larger textuality that remains absent: the whole projected film and the whole projected star. She is a "site of excess" that surfaces Hollywood's "repressed material," from the photographic border-texts of the complete film to the editorial cut in the film.[95] Before the earthquake, Cecelia describes the office of her father, studio executive Bradogue Brady, the walls of which are adorned with a series of pictures including "a signed photograph of Minna Davis, Stahr's dead wife, and photos of other studio celebrities" (*LT*, 22). In this, Minna's first appearance in the novel, Cecelia's deadpan description of the dead woman modulates the pathos of the framed image, which equivocates between two mediated signs of loss: Minna's face is embalmed in a photographic stillness that is lacerated and intensified by the scribbled mark of her autographing hand. This palimpsest of Barthes's "death in the future" in the past understands celebrity as an evacuation of personhood in the guise of personality, much like Ellen's anonymous stardom in Dos Passos's photographic metropolis. Minna's autograph presents stardom as, in Judith Brown's terms, "a ghostly and empty space . . . that frames an impossible desire" for the celebrity's image, which remains "resistant" to its fans even as it appears "almost close enough to touch."[96] Meant to give proof of proximity to the star, the star's signature actually maps the unbridgeable distance between the star and those who are not the star.

As the soft, painterly focus of early Hollywood photography gave way to the stylized, high-contrast norms of "Rembrandt lighting" in the 1920s, the glamour shot became central to the "elaborate machine of image-building" of film celebrity.[97] By the height of its popularity, midway through the following decade, it was considered to be a more important technology for the dissemination of the star's image than the films in which she appeared. The glamour shot emblematizes the photographic constitution of Hollywood stardom as metaphor, mythology, and material condition. Starlight travels thousands of light years "in a flash," as Eduardo Cadava writes, and is "an illumination in which the present bears within it the most distant past and where the distant past suddenly traverses the present moment . . . . Like the photograph that presents what is no longer there, starlight names the trace of the celestial body that has long since vanished. The star is always a kind of ruin."[98] Participating in an economy of ruined images—or images "in crisis," as Régis Durand would say—the Hollywood star is always disappearing along with the photograph's "sudden vanishing of the present tense, splitting into the contradiction of being simultaneously too late and too early."[99] Like the circulation of the photograph, the promulgation of the star entails a discursive, physical, and spatiotemporal survival that makes a mockery of the death of the subject that it foreshadows and foregrounds.[100]

The glamour shot not only literalizes the fact of Hollywood appearance as a form of photographic disappearance but concretizes it, stylistically, by its invocation of photographic stillness as a form of death. Photographers working in studio-era Hollywood produced images that expressly register the "taut intimacy between *thingness* and *personality*," the "oscillation between portrait and still life," that is associated with the pleasures of photography in general, as we saw in the confusion between hardboiled eggs and naked women in Dos Passos's photographic metropolis, as well as between Edward Weston's sexy vegetables and unsexy nudes.[101] The brilliant illumination of the glamour shot sculpts skins into smooth, flawless surfaces and suspends bodies in static perfection. It offers "a machine aesthetic in the guise of a human," as Stuart Ewen puts it.[102] The most famous example of this effect is the hyperbolic intensity of Greta Garbo's face as described by Barthes: a "face-object" that represents "a kind of absolute state of the flesh, which could be neither reached nor renounced" (see, for instance, Figure 4.2).[103]

Fig 4.2 Unknown photographer, Production portrait of Greta Garbo, *Anna Christie* (MGM, 1930). © HIP. Image courtesy of Art Resource, New York

Preceded in the sequence of the unfinished text by the photograph of the actually vanished Hollywood star, Kathleen's body hovers between life and death under the glare of artificial lights. Before the open door of her home, Stahr is confronted with a "face and form and smile against the light from inside. It was Minna's face—the skin with its peculiar radiance as it phosphorus had touched it . . . that had fascinated a generation" (*LT*, 64). In Garbo's glamour shots, as Brown suggests, personality lives and dies "in the lunar quality of her skin, the glow that erased the human detail and staged the tremendous and ethereal vitality of her eyes."[104] Framed by the door, bathed in light, the erasure of Kathleen's face in the phosphorescent glow of Minna's face parodies the effect of the glamour shot that hangs in Brady's office.

On their first date, too, Stahr "judges" Kathleen "as he would a shot in a picture" (*LT*, 80). As unclear as Stein's "each picture is just infinitesimally different from the one before," this judgment of Kathleen invokes both the glamour shot and the extended close-up, a technique of narrative deceleration in classical film that, as Steven Jacobs notes, betrays the exhibitionism of the star system and "unmistakably refers to the numerous publicity pictures that made the actor's or actress's face already famous."[105] The close-up is a disruptive force in classical narrative film, making legible the discontinuity between shots that is the paradoxical precondition of its homogeneous space. Continuity editing is hewed by what Mary Ann Doane calls a "spatial violence of editing and framing" that it emphatically denies; it represents "a magical sleight of hand," in Beckman's words, "creating a smooth whole out of violently extracted bits and pieces."[106] As Doane argues, this technical conceit sustains the coherence of the filmic diegesis by working against "the recognizable although imprecise differences between close-up, medium shot and long shot" and the disquieting effect of disproportionality entailed in the movement between shots. But, in spite of these efforts, variations of scale allow "for perturbation, dissonances within the structuration of space [that] are by-products, barely contained and unenvisaged effects" of narrative film.[107]

In *The Last Tycoon*, the scene in which Kathleen and Edna are carried down the backlot's impromptu river offers a remarkably close analogy for one of the formal techniques for displacing the threat of the close-up in early cinema: the translation of the problem of size into the problem of distance, by tethering the gradual shifts from long or medium shot to close-up to the movements of a character toward the camera. "Say—look there!" says Stahr's colleague, Robby,

> On top of a huge head of the god Siva, two women were floating down the
> current . . . . The two refugees had found sanctuary along a scroll of curls on

its bald forehead and seemed at first glance to be sightseers on an interesting bus-ride through the scene of the flood.

"Will you look at that, Monroe!" said Robby. "Look at those dames!"

Dragging their legs through sudden bogs they made their way to the
bank of the stream. Now they could see the women looking a little scared
but brightening at the prospect of rescue.

Robby's repeated admonishments for Stahr to "look" at the two women demarcate the transitions of scale in this scene, as the "sightseers" come into view, "a
little scared but brightening." The scene culminates in the shocking revelation of
Minna's face in close-up: "Smiling faintly at [Stahr] from not four feet away was
the face of his dead wife . . . . Across the four feet of moonlight the eyes he knew
looked back at him, a curl blew a little on a familiar forehead, the smile lingered
changed a little according to pattern, the lips parted—the same" (*LT*, 26).

Kathleen is given as a glamour shot and in close-up, both of which emulate
the stasis of the photogram that is repressed in the totalizing flow of classical film.
As *The Last Tycoon* harks back to a technique of early cinema that sought to allay
the anxieties of filmgoers over the disturbing effects of the close-up, Stahr's shock
at the return of his vanished wife comes to mirror other kinds of shock in cinema history. As Susan Stewart argues, the miniature is "a diminutive, and thereby
manipulable, version of experience, a version which is domesticated and protected
from contamination," but the gigantic, which envelopes and encloses us, can be
known only "partially." The first is "contained"; the second is a "container."[108] From
its earliest incarnation as a form of attraction—which, in Tom Gunning's formulation, works to "rupture a self-enclosed fictional world"—the close-up unsettled
cinema audiences by its fragmentation of the human form and its grotesque mon-
umentality.[109] Fitzgerald satirizes the experience of the domination and violation
of the mimetic body in the exhibition sites of early cinema through the "huge head
of the god Siva," an enormous object that gauges the trauma of scale disguised
as distance. A makeshift "sanctuary" and bus-like vessel—that is, after Stewart, a
container—the gigantism of the disembodied head miniaturizes the forms of the
women perched "along a scroll of curls." At the same time, it serves as a carica-
tural precursor for the headshot of Kathleen-as-Minna. When the "curls" on the
huge head become the "curl" on Kathleen's "familiar forehead," the scene augments
the unnatural swelling of Kathleen's size affected by her gradual movement into
Stahr's sight. The head of the idol—as much as the head of Kathleen, who represents another kind of idolatry—is a travesty of the celebrity pictured up close or
glamourized.

Yet another instance of standing-in and place-changing in *The Last Tycoon*, the relation between the idol and Kathleen preserves the disorientations that troubled the first spectators of cinema and that reflect the "dialectic of the real and the unreal . . . the body and disembodiment" that accompanied cinema's larger-than-life visions.[110] In early film, humans and objects are "equally pictures, photographs," as Béla Balázs writes. "In significance, intensity, and value men [*sic*] and things were thus brought on to the same plane."[111] When Robby exclaims "Look at those dames!," *The Last Tycoon* bids us to look at Hollywood cinema as the spectators of the earlier cinema of attractions looked, seeing the close-up for what it is: a huge picture.

In soliciting a reflexive form of spectatorship on the Hollywood backlot—akin to Raymond Bellour's *spectator pensif*, whose contemplation suspends the normal temporal operations of film—*The Last Tycoon* understands the disruption of the studio by the accident of the flood as homologous to the disruption to narrative cinema by the close-up.[112] The introduction of sound and the institutionalization of classical film transformed the style of film sets, such that the Hollywood backlot in the studio era contained a variety of "permeable and fragmentary material sites that could be sutured cinematically into a coherent and closed visual statement." This included the construction of multiple, scaled versions of the "same" set for big-budget pictures.[113] The water in Fitzgerald's backlot, which floods "around the Station" and into "the Jungle and the City Corner," tracks its rivers and "sudden bogs" in the gaps between the sets that are effaced by the camera and in post-production editing. Channeling the lot, the flood reveals the repeated fragmentations of the Hollywood set—discrete edifices in serial formation, which, mediated through filming and editing processes, replicate the logic of progression from long shot to close-up within the studio's wider logic of repetition and citation. This is only emphasized by the fact that the head of Siva, the cogent symbol for the apprehension of narrative film constituted in and as a massive, projected picture, is "unloosed from a set of Burma" (*LT*, 26)—cut, that is, from the whole of the set.

On the flooded backlot, Stahr's reverie of Minna's funeral is broken with the sound of a "voice . . . that was not Minna's voice": " 'We're sorry,' said the voice. 'We followed a truck in through a gate' " (27). The body double in cinema is not meant to speak, and so "the" voice of Kathleen is, for Stahr, disembodied and mechanized. Film is a dualistic technology that "necessarily makes an incision or cut between the body and the voice," as Michel Chion writes, but US cinema is obsessed with the successful "embodiment" or "nailing-down" of the voice through vocal synchronization.[114] Sound narrative film crafts a "myth of origins," in Rick Altman's words, through the displacement of our attention from the technological or industrial source of sound by the pointing of the camera not to the loudspeaker but to the speaker whose lips move on screen.[115] This collusion of sound and image—a stratagem of absence in service of narrative continuity and unity that parallels that of the star and the body double—is disrupted by the unfamiliar timbre of Kathleen's voice. Refusing to be a silent substitute, upsetting the relation of subject to object, Kathleen initiates a mismatch of body and voice that ruptures the wholeness of the star's presence before Stahr—and, concomitantly, the wholeness of the narrative film. The voice that is not Minna's voice is a presence that should be absent, which signals, in turn, an absence that is not present. Like the glamour shot and the close-up, Kathleen's voice opens a gap in the world of *The Last Tycoon*, revealing the seamed mechanics of Hollywood presence.

When Stein first saw her "speaking body on screen" in a 1930s newsreel, the experience greatly upset her. Writing in 1935, she described the "slightly mixed-up feeling" that the "talking picture" gave her: "imagine what is that compared to never having heard anybody's voice speaking while a picture is doing something, and that voice and that person is yourself."[116] She returned to this event in *Everybody's Autobiography* (1937): "I saw myself almost as large and moving around and talking I did not like particularly the talking, it gave me a very funny feeling and I did not like that funny feeling."[117] Besides the representational dispossession and sheer scale of her body on screen, what seems especially troubling to Stein is the "speaking" of her "voice" alongside the "picture [of her body] doing something." Susan McCabe suggests that Stein's discomfort "emerged from seeing herself as a whole animate body, a reproduction that did not match her sense of dislocated corporeality."[118] Or, perhaps, the opposite is true: Stein's experience of the cinematic as discordant or dislocating reflects the unseamlessness of its synchronization of "that voice" and that body. Perhaps Stein was struck by the question that Altman sees begged in all sound—where did that come from?—and by the enigmatic rerouting of that question from apparatus to diegesis through vocal synchronization.[119]

Perhaps, in other words, she heard a voice that did not quite match her own, a repetition with a difference, like Kathleen's voice as it establishes her as Minna's irrepressible double, the Derridean "dangerous supplement" in Fitzgerald's Hollywood.[120] In doubling Minna, Kathleen also doubles the apparatus of the camera—one of many bulky technological bodies that crowd the studio set (see Figure 4.3)—and the film reel, standing in for the repetitive images of the star and the cuts that delineate and suture those images. Minna Davis is the minimum, and Kathleen Moore the more, of classical cinema, showing its excesses in and as its serialized lack.

Fig 4.3 Milton Gold, Production shot from *Suez* (Twentieth-Century Fox, 1939) featuring Loretta Young. © Twentieth Century-Fox Film Corporation. Image courtesy of Photofest

"'We're sorry,' said the voice. 'We followed a truck in through a gate.'" These words break the smooth surface of Stahr's Hollywood romance. By Kathleen's difference from Minna, Breitwieser observes, *The Last Tycoon* relinquishes "the supposition that Stahr's second love is the first beloved *redivivus*." As Stahr embraces a repetitive but not recapitulative second love, Fitzgerald accommodates a desire that splits the carefully constructed façade of his romantic hero—a desire that "crack[s] Stahr open, rather than up."[121] *The Last Tycoon* thus implies how the culture and technology of Hollywood, which allegedly cracked Fitzgerald up, can and does produce an affective engagement akin to what Eisenstein called the ecstatic pathos of film, literally *ex stasis*, to "be beside oneself."[122] Or, as Boxley would say, to be put in someone else's place. As the fragmentations of the unfinished novel offer a repetition with a difference of Hollywood series production, *The Last Tycoon* puts us in something else's place, positioning us inside the camera of Stein's unsutured cinema of insistence. And, as Kathleen's reiterative, supplementary body hypostatizes film's photogrammatic and acousmatic tracks, it also resuscitates what Altman identifies as the second casualty of vocal synchronization: "the scandalous fact that sound films begin as language—the screenwriter's—and not as pure image."[123] This is all the more apparent in "Cosmopolitan," a screenplay that is an index for the written track that narrative cinema hides from sight as quickly as it displaces and disremembers the photogram on screen.

Repetition With Another Difference

"There are no second acts in American lives," wrote Fitzgerald in the notes for *The Last Tycoon*.[124] For Breitwieser, Monroe Stahr "culminates and closes" an age that begins with US president Andrew Jackson, whose mansion Stahr visits near the beginning of *The Last Tycoon*, and Fitzgerald's Hollywood represents "the geographical terminal beach for the series of longings that began with Dutch sailors staring at Long Island" at the close of *The Great Gatsby*.[125] But the death of Stahr in a plane crash never made it beyond the realm of working notes and novel outlines—and, even in that realm, the proposed ending of the novel incorporates an event of symbolic progeniture that lengthens the lineage of the "last" tycoon. A trio of children was to come upon the wreckage and rifle the possessions of the dead bodies of Stahr and his two companions. As Fitzgerald wrote to Kenneth Littauer at *Collier's* magazine, "[t]he possessions which the children find, symbolically determine their attitude toward their act of theft," with the boy who finds Stahr's briefcase being the one who "saves and redeems all three by going to a local judge and making a full confession."[126] From the vacuum that is the unwritten ending of Fitzgerald's text, the novel's already-developed motif of serialized bodies is stressed by the child's shadowing of the dead Stahr. Hollywood might be a terminus, but it is one in which one does not so much terminate as repeat.

A lack that signifies a whole, a whole that signifies a lack, the return of Minna as Kathleen gestures toward other forms of return in Fitzgerald's Hollywood writing. Following the termination of his contract with MGM in January 1939, Fitzgerald freelanced on a number of scripts for several different studios and began drafting and seeking an advance for *The Last Tycoon*.[127] In the first weeks of 1940, independent producer Lester Cowan invited Fitzgerald to lunch to discuss the adaptation to the screen of Fitzgerald's story, "Babylon Revisited." By the end of January, Fitzgerald's new agent, William Dozier, had negotiated a deal with Cowan, and Fitzgerald sold the screen rights to the story for a thousand dollars.[128] From March to August, Fitzgerald worked steadily on the screenplay, which he titled "Cosmopolitan," sometimes with Cowan's help. Both men intended it to be a Shirley Temple vehicle, and Fitzgerald at one point met with Temple and her mother, Gertrude.

Although Fitzgerald always remained hopeful that "Cosmopolitan" would be produced, it reached the cinema screen only in a severely altered form: in the 1954 MGM romance, *The Last Time I Saw Paris*, starring Elizabeth Taylor and based on a script by Julius and Philip Epstein with Richard Brooks.[129] In adapting his own short story, Fitzgerald has been said to be "unique among modern writers whose work has been 'savaged' by Hollywood in that he did it all by himself in cold blood and while sober."[130] Drawn from what is considered to be one of Fitzgerald's best short pieces, "Cosmopolitan" is seen to exemplify the unhappy lesson learned by Charlie Wales in the story, who "suddenly realize[s] the meaning of the word 'dissipate' . . . to make nothing from something."[131] The screenplay is almost always dismissed as a melodramatic, predictable, and clunky capitulation to the demands of Hollywood merchants and the formulae of Hollywood bathos. Like Charlie, who wishes he could "jump back a whole generation" to regain the simple pleasures of life before his surrender to the decadent mores of Paris in the roaring twenties, Fitzgerald scholars have wished they could turn back the clock to the time before the tragic, evocative "Babylon Revisited" became a Hollywood farce.

In spite of its flaws, "Cosmopolitan" does not so much dissipate the earlier story as recalibrate and intensify Charlie's dream of the past in it—a dream that strains toward the past's return in the present, in a reincarnated, same-but-different body. In "Babylon Revisited," Charlie repeats Gatsby's quest for the lost woman in seeking to regain custody of his daughter, Honoria, three years after the death of his wife, Helen. That his longing for his daughter is imbricated with his deeper longing for his wife is indicated by his fantasy of communion with Helen "in the white, soft light that steals upon half sleep near morning": "she was in a swing in a white dress, and swinging faster and faster all the time, so that at the end he could not hear clearly all that she said." This infantile image of Helen implies Honoria's substitutionary value for her father. When Honoria, like her swinging mother, slips from his grasp at the end of the story, Charlie's belief that "Helen wouldn't have wanted him to be so alone" phrases the child's custody as a form of companionship that partially redresses the loss of his wife.[132]

Repeating this theme with a difference, "Cosmopolitan" demonstrates the importance of reading Fitzgerald's writing as a "textual chain" that must, in Friedman's terms, be analytically "superimposed." Fitzgerald's strategic reformulation resembles Faulkner's "revisionary repetition," a refitting of plots, episodes, and characters across a range of textual modes—including the Hollywood screenplay— that "repeats some structured event, in order somehow to alter that structure and its continuing power." Rather than compulsively repeating familiar structures of thought as a charm against unfamiliar ones, Richard Moreland explains, revisionary repetition "works to inscribe marks of change, specificity, and difference within and around that structure."[133] It amplifies voices that have been silenced, including those of black people and women, which testify to "the fact that modernism's supposedly universal consciousness was a consciousness predominantly middle class, white, and male."[134] Likewise, the textual chain of "Cosmopolitan" and *The Last Tycoon* listens out for the repressed voice of the female other in classical film. If Fitzgerald's screenplay finally returns to the repressed labor of the screenwriter, it cannot help but emphasize the stronghold of the classed, racialized, and gendered figure of the solitary author and the fiction of the singular text over the modernist consciousness—and our consciousness of modernism.

On reading *The Great Gatsby* in 1925, Stein told Fitzgerald, "This is as good a book [as *This Side of Paradise*] and different and older and that is what one does, one does not get better but different and older and that is always a pleasure."[135] Almost ten years later, Fitzgerald wrote in an essay in the *Saturday Evening Post*, "Mostly, we authors repeat ourselves. . . . [We] tell our two or three stories—each time in a new disguise—maybe ten times, maybe a hundred, as long as people will listen."[136] Just as difference is pleasure for Stein, in Fitzgerald's writing the new disguise matters—as it does for Stahr, in his "dressed up" romances and in his film productions. In the introduction to the published version of "Cosmopolitan," which carries the title *Babylon Revisited: The Screenplay*, Budd Schulberg describes the enormous liberty Fitzgerald took in revising "Babylon Revisited," retaining the story's principal characters but revising central plot points along with its broad narrative trajectory. This, Schulberg notes, is unusual among writers, who are more often than not "stubbornly faithful to their original creations."[137] Fitzgerald's writings across divergent media oscillate back and forth by effects of reflection, augmentation, and intercession—a textual interference that is especially busy in relation to the thematic preoccupation with reiterated female bodies. The opening scenes of "Cosmopolitan" feature Victoria, the little girl Honoria with a new name, attempting to board a train at a Paris station. At the ticket booth and on the train platform, a "COLUMN OF LITTLE ORPHANS about Victoria's age" led by two nuns obstruct Victoria's attempt to abscond from Paris, where she has been living in the custody of her aunt and uncle (*BR*, 20). Victoria is caught up visually with the two-by-two row of children who repeatedly block her path, foreshadowing the familial drama of "Cosmopolitan" and evoking Shirley Temple's repeated appearances as a child orphan, including the role of Shirley Black in *Bright Eyes* (1934). This comic scene also leads into the intrigue around Victoria's falsified identity as the train crosses over into Switzerland. Victoria avoids the inquiries of a Swiss official searching for "a little runaway American girl" by feigning her membership in the "brood of Near-Eastern children" traveling with their mother (30, 25). The mother's "huge passport" "contains photographs not only of the three children with her but, apparently, of about six others besides." When the entire family begins to speak excitedly in a foreign language, Victoria evades the scrutiny of the guard by pretending to "jabber, too, in a language exactly like theirs" (32).

As Victoria claims the photographic image of another by a racialized deceit of the voice, this scene of impersonation introduces the trope of substitutionary role-play that, in the screenplay, shapes Victoria's relationship with her father Charles. Victoria's jettisoning of her own identity as a "little runaway American girl" is supplemented by the lively pantomimes and games of appropriation in which she engages with her father. The following sequence of "Cosmopolitan" initiates the screenplay's contrapuntal narrative structure, transitioning with a dissolve from the compartment of the train to the pier where the Wales family is departing for France some months earlier. On the pier, Charles pretends to have only just met Victoria. He introduces himself by name with a tip of his hat, and Victoria, "playing up," responds in turn:

> They pause in their walk and shake hands.
> WALES   Married or single?
> VICTORIA   No, not married—single.
> [. . .]
> WALES   (indicating the doll in her arms.)
>   But I see you have a child, Madam.
> Victoria looks at her doll, almost with surprise. (38)

A variation on a passage from "Babylon Revisited," this conversation articulates in strikingly different ways in the screenplay. When Victoria remarks, "I'm behind the times for my age. I'm obsolescent," Charles replies, "The word is *adolescent*—and you're *not*—yet—thank heaven!" (39). Victoria is "obsolescent" and yet not quite "adolescent," and the wordplay she instigates by her misuse of the former term saddles her eleven-year-old body with a chronologic and generational volatility that is only heightened when, in the next scene, she is handed a baby to mind while its British nurse fixes its carriage.

The child who is both behind and before her times—another Temple trope—Victoria is positioned across "Cosmopolitan" as her mother's substitute. Even while the troubled Helen Wales languishes in her darkened room on the ship, Victoria's passionate desire to "please" her father, "to be a companion to him," and "to be interesting to him" as they walk together on the ship, amounts to a kind of seduction, an attempt to usurp her mother in her father's affections (56, 57). Victoria's sense of her own coming-of-age, evident again when she reprimands her father by telling him she has "gotten too old for [his] brand of joke" (57), is marshaled toward her status as her mother's double—if not actually making her mother obsolescent, then at least taking her place once she is obsolescent.

After Helen's suicide at sea, Victoria says to her father, "I like you better than anybody—and you like me better than anybody, don't you—now Mother's dead?" This statement, and Charles's response to it, is virtually identical to those given in "Babylon Revisited." As Charles replies in "Cosmopolitan," "Of course, I do. But you won't always like me best, honey. You'll grow up and meet somebody your own age and go marry him, and forget you ever had a father" (130). In the screenplay, much more than in the story, what inheres in these lines is not the temporariness of Victoria's devotion to her father but, rather, the potential for that devotion to rival that of a wife—implicit in Charles's alignment of the daughter's marriage with the forgetting of the father, the first love. This is because in "Cosmopolitan," unlike in "Babylon Revisited," Victoria constantly reminds her father—as well as her Aunt Marion—of her dead mother. As Charles says of Victoria, "If she turns her head sideways, it's *her* head; if she turns her face sideways, it's *her* face; if she turns her chin, it's *her* chin" (97). By instating this measure of similitude between Victoria and Helen, "Cosmopolitan" figures its father–daughter relationship in accordance with the same logic of Hollywood substitutability that informs *The Last Tycoon*. Like Kathleen's relation to Minna in the unfinished novel, Victoria is the image of her dead mother, who is never to appear on screen. The closest we get to Helen is the door to her suite on the ship, cautiously opened by Victoria in the same hour that Helen is to go to her death:

> VICTORIA   The Doctor's coming, Mother.
> As if someone beckoned her inside, she goes in.
> INT. CABIN—SHOOTING TOWARD THE DOOR—showing Victoria
> with her back against the door.
> VICTORIA   I hope you feel better.
> (pause; she gets no answer.
> *We hear a match struck*). (61)

Moving from the outside to the inside of the cabin, the camerawork extends the abstraction of the silent someone who seems to bid Victoria to enter the suite. Evading the gaze of the camera altogether, as well as her actualization in the form of spoken dialogue in the screenplay, Helen is more fully invisible and inaudible than her earlier incarnation in "Babylon Revisited," that white-clad ghost who "swing[s] faster and faster all the time, so that at the end [Charles] could not hear clearly all that she said."[138] Thus the repeated claims about Victoria's resemblance to her mother lead us to look to the child to discern a likeness to a woman we have never seen—a woman who is decisively not an image and yet is now, like Minna, nothing more than an image. "Darling, do you ever think of your mother?" says Charles to Victoria later on. "I don't want you to ever forget her. Have you got a picture of her?" (*BR*, 129). But Victoria's own face is this picture, an apparition of her mother's never-apparent appearance.

As Victoria's masquerade of her mother makes wifeliness into a drama of reinscription, "Cosmopolitan" revisits the theme of incest central to Fitzgerald's 1934 novel, *Tender is the Night*. This is nowhere more obvious than in the sickly and not a little disturbing poem that Victoria composes for her father on his birthday:

> Be my wife in the strife for life
> In the hustle and bustle of everyday life,
> Be my wife, be my wife,
> Be my teeny weeny darling little wife,
> Be my little, little, little wife. (152)

In *Tender is the Night*, as Michael North points out, the actual incest that precipitates Nicole Diver's illness is replayed in the relationship between her husband, Dick, and the film star Rosemary Hoyt, summed up blithely in the title of the film that has earned Rosemary international fame: *Daddy's Girl*. For North, Dick's attraction to younger women reflects the "ingrown and repetitive nature" of the film medium, which "infantilizes its audience" by fostering "an appetite for repetition, for the pure experience of mediation itself." But where *Tender is the Night* expresses anxiety over the camera's "compulsive" and "constricting" repetition,[139] the revisionary repetition of "Cosmopolitan" admits and exceeds those functions. Speaking for her father in her poem, Victoria's description of herself as a miniaturized replacement for her dead mother proposes a circuitous form of self-identification that shows her up as a charm of and against the reiterative machinations of classical Hollywood film. Drawing on Claude Lévi-Strauss's discussion of the reduction of scale entailed in representation as enlarging "our power over a homologue of the [represented] thing," Goble theorizes the cameo appearance in classical film as "an eminently small phenomenon of celebrity [that] trades on a mode of identification that remains somewhat removed from the totalizing engrossment in narrative."[140] Victoria's smallness operates in a different but commensurate way—and not only because she is represents a role for, and so a type of, the prototypical child star. In delivering her little poem into the telephone receiver, Victoria is holding the line open for her father as he hurriedly makes stock market deals in the hotel suite. Her announcement of her own status as a picture of her mother is couched in what Bellour calls a "moment of inaction" or a "slump" of attention in classical cinema—a "dull or semi-dull" moment that serves to "maintain a certain slack in its regime of fiction to avoid the risk of abstraction, or, simply, a certain absurdity, worst of all: the absurdity of diegetic improbability."[141]

Thus Fitzgerald's screenplay parodies film's slack moments when Victoria asks the exasperated caller on the line, "Are you still there?" (*BR*, 152). With her ear to the receiver of the telephone as to the narrative of the screenplay, stalling both, Victoria stands for the photogrammatic and acousmatic discontinuities requisite, with Bellour's dead moments, to the cinema's continuity of perception. And, as she asserts herself as her mother's stand-in, she reveals the centrality of the representational code of the feminine to the cinema's continuity of narrative. A figure of excess, whose surplus is paradoxically manifest in a vigorous smallness, the "little, little, little wife" in "Cosmopolitan" embodies what Doane calls the "hyperbolizing [of] the accoutrements of femininity," which works to deny "the production of femininity as closeness, of presence-to-itself" by rending a gap between female characters and their gendered performances.[142] The screenplay underscores the subterfuge of Hollywood's imaging of the feminine through the charade of Victoria's impersonation of her unimaged mother—a performative act that seeks to conceal her mother's death, contriving a presence that is absent and a closeness that is distant. The gap between Helen and Victoria comes to parallel the gap between Helen and her representation. Had Helen moved into the cinema's gendered sights before her death, the screenplay suggests, her image would only ever have been a mask of the same kind as that assumed by her daughter.

Wild Sounds Off Screen

The nonappearance of Helen and her hyperbolic reappearance in the "teeny weeny" body of her daughter infixes an act of resistance in Fitzgerald's screenplay. Entering into the tradition of the vanishing woman who destabilizes the spectacle of female objecthood, Helen is never pictured and yet returns to the picture of "Cosmopolitan" in the image of her daughter; she evades her appearance and resists her disappearance. At once, the woman beyond the limits of the camera in Fitzgerald's screenplay is also the woman behind those limits, as Helen's relegation to the off-screen of "Cosmopolitan" entails her symbolic assumption of the role of director or cameraperson. Even as she persistently refuses her own visualization in the earlier scene at her room on the ship, she anchors the perspective of the camera, which remains angled toward Victoria at the doorway. Helen's control over her nonimage—and her attendant gaze on her reimage, Victoria—is illustrated in the destruction of Victoria's handheld camera, which the child carries with her on the ship. After disembarking into a gathering crowd of reporters, a distraught Victoria accidentally drops her camera onto the dock: "CLOSE SHOT—THE CAMERA—crushed under the weight of the truck. No one sees" (BR, 75). A token of Helen's death, the crushed camera also signifies Helen's refusal to be captured by the film camera, her circumvention of the subject–object relations of classical film.

Although Victoria seems to deflect attention away from her mother to herself, the specular directionality of the screenplay can be conceived the other way around: the mother deflects attention to the daughter by simultaneously evacuating and filling the screen of the text. "Meanwhile, the photographers have snapped Victoria, who covers her eyes with both knuckles after the flash of the bulb," read the directions in the scene of Victoria's disembarkation from the ship (69). Entrapped and assaulted by the press cameras, moments before her own camera is lost and destroyed, Victoria is made into a visual object as her mother disembodies the technological body of the camera apparatus. "Portraying moving lips on the screen convinces us that the individual thus portrayed—and not the loudspeaker—has spoken the words we have heard," as Altman writes. The image of moving lips "disguises the source of the words," obfuscating the mechanical and writerly origins of sound film by locking together the discrete material phenomena of the photogrammatic and acousmatic tracks.[143] Helen frustrates both of these tracks, revealing the break between image and sound as between body and image.

Bar the sound of the struck match from inside the suite, the only sound that comes from the unseen Helen—or seems to come from her—is a "wild shriek" that communicates the event of her suicide:

> A DARK SKY FILLED WITH SEA GULLS
> The sudden sound of a wild shriek—which breaks down after a moment, into the cry of the gulls as they swoop in a great flock down toward the water. Through their cries we hear the ship's bell signaling for the engines to stop.
> MEDIUM SHOT—STERN OF THE SHIP
> Ship receding from the camera as the awful sounds gradually die out.
> FADE OUT. (BR, 64)

It remains unclear whether the wild shriek comes from Helen; it might be the shocked reaction of those who discover her body. At any rate, we can hardly recognize a voice we have never heard. The untraceable, intractable quality of the voice is accentuated as it intermingles with nonhuman sounds, "break[ing] down . . . into the cry of the gulls" and the tolling bell of the ship—sounds that the screenplay tethers to visual origins by the images of the birds and the ship.

Not in spite of but because of its sonic dispersal and visual diversion, the wild shriek is Helen's inarticulate swan song, as she bows out, by her suicide, of the Wales family and the world of the screenplay alike. It is a first and final word that bears testament to her death as an evasion of what Kaja Silverman terms the "surveillance system" of classical film, which stridently locates "the male voice at the point of apparent textual origin, while establishing the diegetic containment of the female voice."[144] The success of this system depends on the complementary effects of its visual and auditory modes:

> To permit a female character to be seen without being heard would be to activate the hermeneutic and cultural codes which define woman as "enigma," inaccessible to definitive male interpretation. To allow her to be heard without being seen would be even more dangerous, since it would disrupt the specular regime upon which dominant cinema relies; it would put her beyond the reach of the male gaze (which stands for the cultural "camera") and release her voice from the signifying obligations which that gaze enforces.

In consequence, Silverman suggests, feminist filmmakers have troubled the identification of the image of the female star through the separation of body from voice, "jettisoning synchronization, symmetry, and simultaneity in favor of dissonance and dislocation."[145] The wild shriek in "Cosmopolitan" carries the dangers that Silverman associates with the woman who is heard without being seen, even as it communicates the vanishing of a woman who has never really appeared and who does not really vanish. Neither contained in nor distinguished from the sounds of the birds and the bells, the shriek is a ventriloquized voice, thrown from the outside to the inside—and the inside to the outside—of the screenplay: from Helen's visible–invisible location beyond the signifying obligations of the male gaze. The unseen woman's "awful sounds" wrench the narrative diegesis, stopping the ship and, as it recedes from the view of the camera, making it disappear.

A salient repetition of Esther's disintegration of the Southern town in Toomer's *Cane*, this tearing of the "safe place of the story" inhabited by classical cinema, in Stephen Heath's terms, is deepened through the perspectival experiments in Fitzgerald's screenplay.[146] As Dixon has noted, about half of the shots in "Cosmopolitan" are designated to be filmed from the perspective of Victoria, and these point-of-view sequences deviate significantly from the third-person narrative voice in "Babylon Revisited."[147] The discontinuity between what is seen and what is heard serves Fitzgerald's "attempt to tell a story from a child's point of view *without* sentimentality," as the author wrote in a note appended to the last revised typescript of the screenplay.[148] For example, when Charles and Victoria enter the ship's dining salon, Victoria is intrigued by the display table, especially "a sailing ship that the chef has carved out of ice" that waves "a little French flag at the stern" (*BR*, 52, 54). As we hear Charles talk stocks with the ship's captain, the camera "COMES DOWN AND REMAINS at Victoria's level" (54).

The "over the shot" directives in "Cosmopolitan" allow for voices that are heard from beyond the cinema screen in such a way as to query, again, the anchorage of sound to sight that hinges narrative film. Sound travels more flexibly than light, producing "the illusion of 'hearing around corners' that which we cannot see around corners." Whereas sight is identified with proximity and presence, sound carries "the tension of the unknown" and is therefore "the ideal method of introducing the invisible, the mysterious, the supernatural."[149] Shifting back and forth between Victoria's level and the standpoint of the adult spectator, the screenplay's split perspective incorporates sounds from around the corner of the field in frame that serve to trouble its narrative contiguity. Alongside Helen's wild voice, the sounds carried from the off-screen of the screenplay signify the phenomenon of fading or aphanisis that Jacques Lacan associates with the entrance of the subject into language. "I identify myself in language," he writes, "but only by losing myself in it like an object."[150] Moving between the viewpoint of the child and of the adult, entwining the appearance of one and the disappearance of the other, "Cosmopolitan" associates the voice with absence as well as—or instead of—presence.

In this way, the screenplay belies the claim of narrative cinema to fix and deliver the "real" sounds that emanate from its unified, anthropomorphic bodies, staging the subjective "division between meaning and materiality"—between the social body and the biological body—which the voice situates.[151] In indicating that we are to see one thing and hear another, the "over the shot" directives repeat verbatim the trope initiated with the "voice . . . that was not Minna's voice" in *The Last Tycoon*. Just as Kathleen's voice shocks Stahr, and us, out of Hollywood's smoothly synchronized dreams, the shifts in and out of Victoria's perspective in "Cosmopolitan" admit the dislocative processes by which those dreams come to flickering life on the cinema screen. The miniature form of the ice-carved sailing ship in the dining room that catches Victoria's eye and the eye of the camera corresponds to the smallness of the little girl's point of view—and, of course, Victoria's role as Helen's diminutive double. The tiny ship on a ship tropes the serial, scaled sets of studio-era Hollywood, emblematizing the cinematic play of scale with reference to a different social practice of miniaturization.

The Filmic (T)Race of the Screenwriter

Framed in the tiny view of "Cosmopolitan," the sequence in the dining salon mounts a "scenographic joke"—a phrase Garrett Stewart uses to describe the technological satire in the famous scene of Charlie Chaplin's "orphic recuperation" amid the turning cogwheels of an industrial machine in *Modern Times* (1936). "As if sprocket by sprocket, rocketed forward as spun image as well as stunned agent, Charlie's mechanistic reduction becomes the very picture of cinema's picturation, an icon of frame advance in heavy-industrial disguise," Stewart writes. "Flattened out and rolled over in instantaneously layered succession, the world's most famous screen image becomes, in short, his own photogram: raw material of all specular awe" (see Figure 4.4).[152] Fitzgerald's screenplay models the raw material of film, but it does so through the successive mechanisms of a different kind of modern machine. "This lady is not well," asserts a stewardess on the ship, gossiping in French with a colleague about Helen early in "Cosmopolitan." "I heard her say Monsieur was like a stock ticker, and she dreamed that she kept pulling the little strip of paper out of his mouth. Pulling and pulling and pulling, and no end" (*BR*, 50). As the "pulling and pulling" of the "little strip" is echoed in the convulsive "clack-clack-clack" of the ticker tape machine throughout the screenplay (56), "Cosmopolitan" establishes a metaphorical confluence between the stock market ticker tape and the sprocketed film image.

But is this really Helen's nightmare, or is it Fitzgerald's dream? Relaying as hearsay the vision of Charles as a ticker tape machine, the maid is unaware that Victoria, who is in earshot, understands French. Disturbed to realize that Victoria has overheard the conversation, the maid asks her, "You won't repeat this, a petite demoiselle like you?" (50). In earshot of the demoiselle whose petiteness establishes her as a figure for the cinema's repetitions and rescalings, the maid's gossipy utterance also speaks the unspeakable in film: its underlying filmic track. Yet the messages transmitted on the ticker tape consist of readable text—the alphabetical and numerical symbols that replaced the dots and dashes of Morse code emitted by the telegraph machine. Given this, along with the fact that the thin paper strip

Fig 4.4 Charlie Chaplin as a factory worker in *Modern Times* (1936). © United Artists.
Image courtesy of Photofest

runs through Charles's body and out of his mouth, the image of the ticker tape machine more fully symbolizes the on-paper acts of composition that constitute the hidden written track of cinema. The writing spooled from the body of the typewriter is also spooled from the body of the screenwriter.

Thus Fitzgerald visualizes his own Hollywood praxis, much as *Modern Times* figures the manipulation of the photogrammatic track by a human agent. Tooled out of the machine through reverse-action footage of his tooling into the machine, Chaplin's escape is identical to his descent; this "tricking of the image track" neutralizes the danger of the machine that threatens to crush and dismember his body.[153] It represents the victory of the comedic routine of the human body over the routinized machine of film, as well as of the movie director over his apparatus. "Cosmopolitan," similarly, is a writing of filmic marks that shows filmic marks as writing. In September 1940, Fitzgerald reported to Zelda that "the Shirley Temple script is looking up again and is my great hope for attaining some real status out here as a movie man and not a novelist."[154] His high hopes for the screenplay no doubt related to his satisfaction in adapting his own fiction, and in doing so alone. As he had told Zelda a week earlier, "They've let a certain writer here direct his own pictures. . . . If I had that chance I would attain my real goal in coming here in the first place."[155] As I noted earlier, Fitzgerald's desire to exceed the norms of studio authorship reflects the dismissive attitudes toward collaboration that have historically buried his screenwriting. But "Cosmopolitan" works in specific ways to exhume that writing. The ticker tape stream replicates nothing so much as the stream of scenes and list of lines that comprise the screenplay, emphasized by the alphabeticized and numbered organization of its script ("Sequence A" comprising shots 1 to 41, "Sequence B" comprising shots 42 to 111, and so on). Objects and props that are to accumulate in a single shot or set are given in the screenplay as successive catalogues: the family on the train in the opening sequence of "Cosmopolitan" leaves behind an assemblage of "debris" including "orange rinds, banana skins, waxed paper," and Charles at his first appearance stuffs his coat pockets "full of tickets, passports, baggage checks, etc." (*BR*, 33, 36). So, too, are montage sequences: when Charles first realizes that Helen is missing, a close-up of his "very distraught" face is to be superimposed with the images of other faces "all speaking to him"—an effect denoted in an orderly series on the page:

VOICES

Not here, Mr. Wales.
Not there, Mr. Wales.
Not in her room.
Not in the bar, Mr. Wales.
Not in there, Mr. Wales. (64)

In fact, the written word and its auxiliary textual forms are made to carry a heavy narrative load across the screenplay, which contains a large number of directives for close-up shots of telegrams, handwritten letters, newspapers—and, of course, lengths of ticker tape. More often than not, these textual objects are carried by hands disembodied by the camera, such as in the scene when Charles signs over his guardianship of Victoria to her aunt: "As the SCENE LIGHTENS, we are looking at a SHEAF OF PAPERS held in a pair of masculine hands. A page is turned and the reading continues" (103). Not only lingering on acts of reading, the screenplay also asks its projected audience to perform such acts by using overlaid images of newspaper headlines to communicate essential plot points, from the stock market crash to Helen's suicide. Reflecting the trope of spinning newspapers associated with early 1930s "B" movies and film noir—a trope that was, by the time

Fitzgerald was writing "Cosmopolitan," already out of fashion and increasingly an object of parody—the reliance on the written textual object might also be understood as hangovers from Fitzgerald's literary work, indications of his imperfect grasp of the dictums for Hollywood scenarios he jotted down in the notes for *The Last Tycoon*: "ACTION IS CHARACTER"; "Always begin with a mannerism."[156] In any case, the effect of the textual objects incorporated in "Cosmopolitan" is to mirror the writing that is "Cosmopolitan." The death of Helen, the wife of a prominent businessman, precedes her diminution into a series of notational fragments: a sensational headline in a newspaper—"AMERICAN MILLIONAIRE'S WIFE LEAPS TO DEATH!"—and a label on a piece of luggage belonging to "HELEN WALES, NEW YORK" (*BR*, 66, 90). The second of these, given to appear as an insert, vexes the illusion of filmic continuity and emphasizes the impossibility of locating Helen inside or outside the text. "HELEN WALES" is no longer in or from "NEW YORK," and the tag insert remediates her absence in the screenplay in relation to the equivocal location of Fitzgerald's screenplay itself: inside and outside of classical film and its study.

Working double-time, in composite, as a textual fragment of Helen and the screenplay, the luggage tag is a fetish object that elicits desire for the male, white, solitary author. As the vanishing woman of "Cosmopolitan" is co-opted as a figure for the vanishing screenwriter, we confront in Fitzgerald's Hollywood writing the limits of its resistance to the gendered containments of classical Hollywood. But we also confront another set of limits: those that delineate, in Moreland's words, modernism's "supposedly universal consciousness," contoured, as it is, by notions of racial, gender, and class difference, and upheld by the (also racialized, gendered, and classed) myth of the solitary genius and the stable, singular text. Embedded in the masculinist field of literary modernism, the woman-in-series repeatedly disrupts what we might call the continuity mode of modernist writing, which occludes the recalcitrant, running-off female figures that are symbolically central to it. In and out of the sights of modernist writing—and of modernist studies—the woman-in-series reconfigures silence as speech, absence as presence, and objects as also, vacillatingly, subjects. As the shrill "clack-clack-clack" that is the sonic (t) race of the ticker tape machine punctures the continuity of the cinema machine, the woman-in-series makes herself heard at the very moment that she seems to be silenced. She appears at the very moment that she seems to disappear. And, in the process, she dredges up other repressed figures—not least the composite authors, and composite scholars, of literary modernism.

Coda

Shared Hallucinations

In 1938, the photographer Walker Evans exhibited 100 of his photographs at the Museum of Modern Art in New York City. Culled from more than ten years of photographic experiment and reflection, the exhibition was the first one-person show by a photographer hosted by the museum. In the book that accompanied the exhibition, featuring eighty-seven of the images on display and titled *American Photographs*, the writer and art critic Lincoln Kirstein esteemed Evans's "surgical" photographic method, by which the "facts of our homes and times" are captured and communicated as a series of "unrelieved, bare-faced, revelatory" visions.[1] Evans, he asserts, is a "visual doctor," whose task is "to fix and to show the whole aspect of our society, the sober portrait of its stratifications, their backgrounds and embattled contrasts."[2] The photographs "are arranged to be seen in their given sequence. . . . They are not extremely easy to look at. They repel an easy glance. They are so full of facts they have to be inspected with more care than quickness. The physiognomy of a nation is laid on your table."[3]

Kirstein depicts the characteristic Evans: the unmannered documentary photographer facing his subjects directly, transparently, innocently, the straightness of his gaze equated with the static regularity of his head-on angle of view and his use of stark but unobtrusive frontal lighting. This picture of Evans was encouraged by the photographer himself, especially in later life; in a 1971 interview, he stressed that the only real difference between his "documentary style" and a "literal document" such as "a police photograph of a murder scene" was its relative use value: "a document has use, whereas art is really useless."[4] Yet Kirstein's remarks about the sequenced structure and meditative ethos of *American Photographs* suggest how Evans's physiognomy of the American nation—like actual physiognomic photography—reveals the stratifications of society and, at once, the stratifications of its own representational schema. Because each photograph in Evans's sequence is positioned on the recto page, with the verso side left blank but for the relevant plate number, Kirstein's "given sequence" is also, as he writes elsewhere in the essay, an accumulating "pile" of prints laid next to and on top of one another.[5] In this sense, *American Photographs* is a kind of optical toy. The play of the photobook encompasses its conceptual unfolding, as we leaf through the pages to discover what Alan Trachtenberg calls the "texture of relations" wrought in its "continuities, doublings, reversals, climaxes, and resolutions"—though this is not its only operation.[6] To turn over its bound, foliated sheets, one by one, is to model the decomposition of its visual effects: to rifle through its overlaid images as an infrastructure of vision, alongside that of Stein's bridged Bridgepoint, Toomer's wounded Georgia, Dos Passos's gridded New York City, and Fitzgerald's unsmooth, unseamless Hollywood. To move through *American Photographs*, in other words, is to actuate the palimpsestic, piecemeal structure of the photographic sequence, approaching an effect similar to that of Francis Galton when he metaphorically decomposited his composite portraits by reimagining them as statistical tables. Indeed, Kirstein seems uncannily to recall Galton's standardizing generalizations when he suggests that the "power" of Evans's national physiognomy consists in his "so detail[ing] the effect of circumstances on familiar specimens that the single face, the single house, the single street, strikes with the strength of overwhelming numbers, the terrible cumulative force of thousands of faces, houses and streets."[7]

In spite of Evans's retrospective avowal of his work as transcendently aesthetic and apolitical, *American Photographs* is positioned ambiguously in relation to the vast and hierarchized photographic archive of the panoptic state. Allan Sekula suggests that toward the end of his life, Evans, having been "transformed into the senior figure of modernist genius," seemed to be unable to "recognize the combative and antiarchival stance" of his earlier work. For Sekula, *American Photographs* exemplifies the way in which photographic images do not "necessarily play into the hands of the police" and can, in fact, bear "the polyphonic testimony of the oppressed and exploited."[8] To be sure, the first image in Evans's photographic sequence, "License Photo Studio, New York," is positioned at the interface between the archival and the antiarchival (Figure C.1). These modes are signified through the competing forms of discourse that mark up the signage on the exterior of the

Fig C.1 Walker Evans, "License Photo Studio, New York, 1934." © Walker Evans Archive, Metropolitan Museum of Art. Image courtesy of Art Resource, New York

photographic studio. Whereas the advertisements for "Notary Public" and license photographs establish the building as a site of the intrusion of instrumental and bureaucratic imperatives in everyday life, the graffiti framing those advertisements ironizes and delimits these imperatives. Scratched twice into the side of the building, the solicitation "Come up and see me sometime" freights the darkened studio with the suggestion of clandestine and illicit encounters. The photograph turns on the possibility of the revision and circumvention of law and order—as in *Cane*, in which the image of the black Madonna on the courthouse wall interrogates the dictates of white supremacy and gives the black woman the "living patterns" to reorganize them.

Evans's opening photograph is the first in a triptych of images that explicitly introduces "the theme of the image" that is expanded throughout the photographic sequence so as to emphasize "the constructive role of the camera."[9] More specifically, *American Photographs* reflects a keen awareness of the Surrealistic impulse of all photography, its ceaseless production of Sontag's particalized, fungible, homologous "notes on reality," which enact a perspectival leveling of bodies and objects, of persons and representations.[10] One particularly arresting image included in the first part of *American Photographs* ironically recasts the notion of Evans's "bare-faced" aesthetic through the head-on angling of the camera—one of the stylistic aspects often considered central to his straightness—via what Elza Adamowicz identifies as the "exploded space" of the head in Surrealism.[11] In "Torn Movie Poster," as in other images depicting found objects across Evans's sequence, the camera angle serves to eliminate deep space in the frame (Figure C.2). This, combined with the removal of the foreground and the lateral ground through the close cropping of the image, puts the flat surface of the movie poster on the same plane of reference as the surface of the photograph itself. The image implies a measure of equivalence between the couple on the movie poster it pictures and, for instance, the portrait positioned over the page, of the "Alabama Cotton Tenant Farmer," the woman known as Annie Mae Gudger, who features in *Let Us Now Praise Famous Men* (1941), the experimental documentary work on which Evans collaborated with James Agee (see Figure C.3).

Conferring mystery on the original poster image by extricating it from its spatial, geographical, and commercial contexts, Evans's activity of framing does not so much deprive the poster of dramatic substance as redirect it, transposing the question of what so terrifies the woman into a metatextual key. What seems to capture the woman's wide-eyed gaze is the photographic frame itself, the clean expanse of white space that contains and faces her on the recto and verso pages, respectively: Judith Butler's forcible frames in the guise of an austere, minimalist poetics of negation. Depicting a woman who is already playing a role—whose pose of white femininity is, like Ellen Thatcher or Minna Davis, as well rehearsed and hyperbolic as her stance of panicked victimhood in the poster—Evans's image is at pains to disclose its own status as an image. Both scared and scarred, the woman's apparent vulnerability to the damages of the photographic frame and the Hollywood typology of the innocent female victim is ingrained in the marred, corrugated surface of the poster. The rippled creases on the faces of the couple,

Fig C.2   Walker Evans, "Torn Movie Poster, 1930." © Walker Evans Archive, Metropolitan Museum of Art. Image courtesy of Art Resource, New York

Fig C.3 Page spread, Walker Evans, *American Photographs* (New York: Eakins Press, 1966), featuring "Alabama Cotton Tenant Farmer Wife, 1936." © Walker Evans Archive, Metropolitan Museum of Art. Image courtesy of Art Resource, New York

which resemble both falling tears and lacerations, supplement the large rip in the poster that slashes open the woman's forehead. Because the surface of the poster and the surface of the image are collapsed into one another, these textual traces of dilapidation symbolize the wounds of representation itself. The deep gorge in the woman's face produces a Surrealist convulsion of the real, as Rosalind Krauss would say after André Breton. Its chaotic, foliated rips and tears are the signs of signification.

The weathered surface of the poster also registers the woman's emplacement as an image in series with other images, cordoned off from and yet sutured to the Alabama farmer's wife. *American Photographs* has already established the modern world as a "STUDIO" as vast as the capitalized sign in "Penny Picture Display, Savannah" is overbearing (Figure C.4). In this image, the second in the photographic sequence, the plainspoken vernacular of commercial portraiture—modified by Evans's clean and planar aesthetic—interprets the (white) human image as pure form. The arrangement of flat, regularized icons is requisite to the schematizing of the human image as a prop of the modern trade in photographs, involving Evans along with the Savannah portraitist. The version of "Penny Picture Display" included in *American Photographs* is tightly cropped, cutting off the entire top row of portraits, as well as those that line the bottom, right, and left edges of the image. This cropping suggests the centrifugal force of the grid, which appears as one section of a potentially infinite matrix of image blocks. As the image is made continuous with the world beyond the photographic frame, Evans gives us Félix

Fig C.4 Walker Evans, "Penny Picture Display, Savannah, 1936." © Walker Evans Archive, Metropolitan Museum of Art. Image courtesy of Art Resource, New York

Nadar's photographopolis or Siegfried Kracauer's blizzard of photographs. He depicts a relentless mapping of image onto world, a subsuming of world as image, which is presaged by the submission of the photographic subjects to the norms of the modern portrait session and the promotion of the studio's capitalistic activity.

"Torn Movie Poster," in sequence, concisely illustrates the discursive, historical processes by which subjectivities are constituted: the "facialization machines" that, as Gilles Deleuze and Félix Guattari explain, channel singularity, polyvocality, and indeterminacy into regularized social faces in accordance with the disciplinary apparatus of the modern state.[12] If Evans's photographic physiognomy implies that the modern United States is a vast facialization machine, mass-producing racial, social, and gendered identities, it also implies that the automated mechanisms that secure that nation's face are subject to disruption, recalibration, or reverse engineering. Certainly the exposure of the undersurface of the movie poster could be seen to show up the enduring solidity and overriding power of the edifices of social control.[13] But the wall on which the poster hangs does not quite appear in the dense visual zone of the gash, such that the revelation of the paper-thin shards that comprise the poster—and the photograph itself—evokes the basic, ineluctable shallowness of the image. This superficiality, this physical and ideological meagerness or lack, entails the image's susceptibility to defacement. If we reenvision "Torn Movie Poster" in line with the defaced signage of the legitimate–illegitimate photographic site with which American Photographs begins, the woman's forehead appears to be not merely broken into, violently attacked, but, more fully, breaking open. The monochrome mess of the rip is an explosive emanation, a silent eruption from within the woman that evinces her resistance to the enframing matrix of the physiognomy of the United States. In a world that, as Kracauer says, has taken on a photographic face, Evans's image portrays less the woman's passive objectification than her activity of re-facialization, or, rather, un-facialization.

In this self-destructive, defiant move, the woman bursts and shatters herself partially out of sight. Provoking a radical transvaluation of deathly absence as a form of lively presence—as well as of the photograph's aphasiac obfuscations and ambiguities as the locus of its ethical possibilities—she emblematizes the subversive power of the woman-in-series in the composite modernist writing of the early twentieth century. The woman-in-series bids us enter into the "*shared* hallucination" that is initiated, for Barthes, by the "bizarre medium" of photography.[14] Caught up "crazily" in the love and pity "stirred by Photography," cradling "what is dead, what is going to die," Barthes writes, "my eyes were touched with a kind of painful and delicious intensity, as if I were suddenly experiencing the effects of a strange drug."[15] Touching eyes, enfolding bodies, the photograph's *la vérité folle* also reaches into literary modernism, as both generate moments of suspension in the social and political order of modernity—entering into the intimate, communal space of the in-between, the interval, where the mergers and inversions of subjects and objects are staged. This propinquity and reciprocity of image and word is itself a kind of shared hallucination, inducing a vivid dream of a female figure exploded and exploding, burned and dancing, an object of loss and of ghostly returns.

Notes

Introduction

1. Francis Galton, *Inquiries into Human Faculty and Its Development* (London: J. M. Dent and Sons, 1907), 10.

2. Francis Galton, "Composite Portraits, Made by Combining Those of Many Different Persons Into a Single Resultant Figure," *Journal of the Anthropological Institute* 8 (1879): 132–33.

3. Galton, *Inquiries*, 233.

4. Ronald R. Thomas, *Detective Fiction and the Rise of Forensic Science* (Cambridge: Cambridge University Press, 1999), 240.

5. Joel Smith, "More Than One: Sources of Serialism," in *More Than One: Photographs in Sequence*, ed. Smith (Princeton, NJ: Princeton University Art Museum, 2008), 10.

6. Gertrude Stein, *Three Lives* (New York: Penguin, 2000), 124.

7. Steve McCaffery, *Prior to Meaning: The Protosemantic and Poetics* (Evanston, IL: Northwestern University Press, 2001), 207; Maurice Blanchot, "The Song of the Sirens: The Experience of Proust," in *The Book to Come*, trans. Charlotte Mandell (Stanford, CA: Stanford University Press, 2003), 14.

8. Roland Barthes, *Camera Lucida: Reflections on Photography*, trans. Richard Howard (London: Vintage, 2000), 96. Recent discussions of photography exhibit a measure of frustration with Barthes's approach to photography, as well as that of Susan Sontag and Walter Benjamin, the two other major theorists of the medium. The scholarly pushback is especially emphatic in James Elkins's critiques of Barthes, recently in *What Photography Is* (New York and London: Routledge, 2011). In a 2013 essay, however, Karen Beckman calls for attempts to "speak differently" with Barthes about photography. Following Beckman, this book does not turn away from *Camera Lucida*—nor the work of Sontag or Benjamin—but instead applies Barthes's observation that the photograph stages "a desperate resistance to any reductive system." See Beckman, "Nothing to Say: The War on Terror and the Mad Photography of Roland Barthes," in *On Writing With Photography*, ed. Beckman and Liliane Weissberg (Minneapolis and London: University of Minnesota Press, 2013), 297–330; Barthes, *Camera Lucida*, 8.

9. On the problem of these limits, see Anne E. Fernald, "Women's Fiction, New Modernist Studies, and Feminism," *MFS Modern Fiction Studies* 59.2 (2013): 229–40; and Michael Bibby, "The Disinterested and Fine: New Negro Renaissance Poetry and the Racial Formation of Modernist Studies," *Modernism/modernity* 20.3 (2013): 485–501.

10. Samira Kawash, *Dislocating the Color Line: Identity, Hybridity, and Singularity in African-American Literature* (Stanford, CA: Stanford University Press, 1997), 213.

11. Mary Ann Doane, "Film and the Masquerade: Theorizing the Female Spectator," *Screen* 23.3–4 (1982): 81. Theories of female masquerade were first developed in Joan Rivière's 1929 essay "Womanliness as a Masquerade," reproduced in *Formations of Fantasy*, ed. Victor Burgin, James Donald, and Cora Kaplan (London: Methuen, 1986), 35–44; and in Luce Irigaray, *This Sex Which Is Not One*, trans. Catherine Porter (Ithaca, NY: Cornell University Press, 1985).

12. Elizabeth Abel, "Skin, Flesh, and the Affective Wrinkles of Civil Rights Photography," in *Feeling Photography*, ed. Elspeth H. Brown and Thy Phu (Durham, NC, and London: Duke University Press, 2014), 99.

13. Karen Beckman, *Vanishing Women: Magic, Film, and Feminism* (Durham, NC, and London: Duke University Press, 2003), 158. Other studies pursuing a similar line of thought include Avery F. Gordon, *Ghostly Matters: Haunting and the Sociological Imagination* (Minneapolis: University of Minnesota Press, 1997); Peggy Phelan, *Unmarked: The Politics of Performance* (London and New York: Routledge, 1993); Terry Castle, *The Apparitional Lesbian: Female Homosexuality and Modern Culture* (New York: Columbia University Press, 1993); and Patricia White, *Uninvited: Classical Hollywood Cinema and Lesbian Responsibility* (Bloomington: Indiana University Press, 1993).

14. Anne Anlin Cheng, *Second Skin: Josephine Baker and the Modern Surface* (Oxford: Oxford University Press, 2011), 121.

15. Régis Durand, "How to See (Photographically)," in *Fugitive Images: From Photography to Video*, ed. Patrice Petro (Bloomington: Indiana University Press, 1995), 147.

16. Michel Foucault, "Nietzsche, Genealogy, History," in *The Foucault Reader*, ed. Paul Rabinow (New York: Pantheon, 1984), 82.

17. "Messy contingency" is Allan Sekula's term in "The Body and the Archive," *October* 39 (Winter 1986): 52–53.

18. David Campany, *Photography and Cinema* (London: Reaktion Books, 2008), 13.

19. See Nancy Armstrong, *Fiction in the Age of Photography: The Legacy of British Realism* (Cambridge, MA: Harvard University Press, 1999). Other studies connecting photography to nineteenth-century writing include Daniel A. Novak, *Realism, Photography, and Nineteenth- Century Fiction* (Cambridge: Cambridge University Press, 2008); Miles Orvell, *The Real Thing: Imitation and Authenticity in American Culture, 1880–1940* (Chapel Hill: University of North Carolina Press, 1989); and Susan S. Williams, *Confounding Images: Photography and Portraiture in Antebellum American Fiction* (Philadelphia: University of Philadelphia Press, 1997).

20. Michael North, *Camera Works: Photography and the Twentieth-Century Word* (Oxford: Oxford University Press, 2005), 25.

21. See Karen Jacobs, *The Eye's Mind: Literary Modernism and Visual Culture* (Ithaca, NY: Cornell University Press, 2001); Martin Jay, *Downcast Eyes: The Denigration of Vision in Twentieth-Century French Thought* (Berkeley: University of California Press, 1993); and

Jay, "Photo-Unrealism: The Contribution of the Camera to the Crisis of Ocularcentrism," in *Vision and Textuality*, ed. Stephen Melville and Bill Readings (Durham, NC: Duke University Press, 1995), 344–62.

22. Edgar Allan Poe, "The Daguerreotype," in *Classic Essays on Photography*, ed. Alan Trachtenberg (New Haven, CT: Leete's Island Books, 1980), 38.

23. Bertolt Brecht, "The Threepenny Lawsuit" (1932), cited in Walter Benjamin, *The Arcades Project*, trans. Howard Eiland and Kevin McLaughlin (Cambridge, MA: Harvard University Press, 1999), 687.

24. Jacobs, *Eye's Mind*, 18–19.

25. Ibid., 8.

26. Mark Seltzer, *Bodies and Machines* (New York and London: Routledge, 1992), 115; Barthes, *Camera Lucida*, 4.

27. Susan Sontag, *On Photography* (London: Penguin, 2008), 111, 100.

28. Aaron Scharf, *Art and Photography* (London: Allen Lane, 1983), 211. Benjamin's comments on the "optical unconscious" are in "The Work of Art in the Age of Mechanical Reproduction," in *Illuminations: Essays and Reflections*, ed. Hannah Arendt and trans. Harry Zohn (New York: Schocken Books, 2007), 217–52.

29. Jean-Louis Comolli, "Machines of the Visible," in *The Cinematic Apparatus*, ed. Teresa de Lauretis and Stephen Heath (New York: St. Martin's Press, 1980), 123.

30. North, *Camera Works*, 11.

31. Novak, *Realism*, 5–6.

32. Stuart Burrows, *A Familiar Strangeness: American Fiction and the Language of Photography, 1839–1945* (Athens, GA, and London: University of Georgia Press, 2008), 11. *Familiar Strangeness* is one of a number of studies that, in attending to the intersections of photography and modernist writing, emulate or expand the scope of Carol Shloss's *In Visible Light: Photography and the American Writer: 1840–1940* (New York: Oxford University Press, 1987). These include Joseph R. Millichap, *The Language of Vision: Photography and Southern Literature in the 1930s and After* (Baton Rouge: Louisiana State University Press, 2016); Sara Blair, *Harlem Crossroads: Black Writers and the Photograph in the Twentieth Century* (Princeton, NJ: Princeton University Press, 2007); and Paul Hansom, ed., *Literary Modernism and Photography* (Westport, CT, and London: Praeger, 2002).

33. Jacobs, *Eye's Mind*, 19.

34. The "photography effect" is Jonathan Crary's term in *Techniques of the Observer: On Vision and Modernity in the Nineteenth Century* (Cambridge, MA: MIT Press, 1990), 13. Given this approach to the relationship of photography and modernist writing, I engage in limited and selective ways with photographic theory and history. Overall, too, I am less interested in modernist writers' attitudes toward photography and their remarks on its influence (or otherwise) on their practice, than in the disclosures of photographic allegory in their writing and the cultural training of photography in the reading of their work.

35. Burrows, *Familiar Strangeness*, 11.

36. This book also responds to Burrows's conspicuous silence about the gendered aspect of this photographic twinning—evident even in his careful reading of Janie Crawford's photographic crisis of self-recognition in Hurston's 1937 novel *Their Eyes Were Watching God*.

37. Garrett Stewart's *Between Film and Screen: Modernism's Photo Synthesis* (Chicago: University of Chicago Press, 1999) is the only sustained attempt to date to trace the implications of the still–moving field for literary modernism. His sense of the equivalence between the photogram and the lexical phonogram is foundational to my argument, as I subsequently discuss, but the interest of his study is in a generalized theory of modernist inscription rather than in the close reading of individual literary texts per se.

38. There has been a proliferation of such titles over the last decade or so. See especially Laurent Guido and Olivier Lugon, eds., *Between Still and Moving Images* (New Barnet, UK: John Libbey, 2012); Eivind Røssaak, ed., *Between Stillness and Motion: Film, Photography, Algorithms* (Amsterdam: Amsterdam University Press, 2011); Karen Beckman and Jean Ma, eds., *Still Moving: Between Cinema and Photography* (Durham, NC: Duke University Press, 2008); and Laura Mulvey, *Death 24x a Second: Stillness and the Moving Image* (London: Reaktion Books, 2006).

39. George Baker, "Photography's Expanded Field," in *Still Moving*, ed. Beckman and Ma, 179.

40. Roland Barthes, "The Third Meaning: Research Notes on Some Eisenstein Stills," in *Image-Music-Text*, trans. Stephen Heath (London: Fontana, 1977), 66–67.

41. Barthes, *Camera Lucida*, 27.

42. Baker, "Photography's Expanded Field," 179.

43. Campany, *Photography and Cinema*, 18.

44. See Anne McCauley, *Industrial Madness: Commercial Photography in Paris, 1848–1871* (New Haven, CT, and London: Yale University Press, 1994).

45. As Christopher Pinney notes, the spatial distribution achieved through the compositional activities of anthropologists is different from Galton's method of superimposition. Nevertheless, their projects of photographic generalization seek similarly essentialized conclusions about race and class. See Pinney, *Photography and Anthropology* (London: Reaktion Books, 2011), 86.

46. Galton, "Composite Portraits," 140.

47. Sekula, "Body," 54. This taxonomical principle shapes the frontispiece to Galton's *Inquiries into Human Faculties and Its Development* (1883), which features eight sets of composites as an integrated, cohesive ensemble under the title "Specimens of Composite Portraiture." This gridded assemblage mirrors the eugenicist family albums Galton designed in this same period, which promoted a standardized method for collating "biological histories" and divining "the mental and bodily faculties of [a family's] children." See Francis Galton, *Record of Family Faculties* (London: Macmillan, 1884), 5, 1.

48. Orvell, *Real Thing*, 78.

49. Smith, "More Than One," 9, 14, 9.

50. See Friedrich Kittler, *Discourse Networks 1800/1900* (Stanford, CA: Stanford University Press, 1990). The forms of serialized photography I mention here are derived from Smith, "More Than One," 14–28. The essays in Smith's edited collection, *More Than One*, are exemplary of new work on serial photography; see also Andrew Roth, ed., *The Open Book: A History of the Photographic Book from 1978 to the Present* (Göteborg, Sweden: Hasselblad Center, 2004); Martin Parr and Gerry Badger, *The Photobook: A History*, 2 vols. (London: Phaidon, 2004, 2006); and Carol M. Armstrong, *Scenes in a Library: Reading the Photograph in the Book, 1843–1875* (Cambridge, MA: MIT Press, 1998).

51. László Moholy-Nagy, "From Pigment to Light," in *Photography in Print: Writings from 1816 to the Present*, ed. Vicki Goldberg (Albuquerque: University of New Mexico Press, 1988), 348.

52. László Moholy-Nagy, *Painting, Photography, Film*, trans. Janet Seligman (London: Lund Humphries, 1987), 40, 23.

53. For a detailed reading of Moholy-Nagy's photographic sequence, see Pepper Stetler, "'The New Visual Literature': László Moholy-Nagy's *Painting, Photography, Film*," *Grey Room* 32 (Summer 2008): 88–113.

54. Félix Nadar, "*La première épreuve de photographie aérostatique*," in *Quand j'étais photographe* (Paris: Seuil, 1994), 104; Eduardo Cadava, "Nadar's Photographopolis," intro. to *When I Was a Photographer*, by Félix Nadar, trans. Cadava and Liana Theodoratou (Cambridge, MA: MIT Press, 2015), xii.

55. Siegfried Kracauer, "Photography," in *The Mass Ornament: Weimar Essays*, trans., ed., and intro. Thomas Y. Levin (Cambridge, MA: Harvard University Press, 1995), 58, 59.

56. Although less prominent than Atget's and Sander's hugely influential projects, a host of women photographers also experimented with serialized imagery in the late nineteenth and early twentieth centuries. See, for instance, Julia Margaret Cameron's posed, soft-focus photographic illustrations of historical and literary scenes in the 1860s and 1870s, as well as her practice, like many other women in the Victoria era, of organizing her work into photographic albums; Gertrude Käsebier's various photographic cycles, including the motherhood cycle (1890s–1910s) and her famous portraits of the Sioux (1898); and Berenice Abbott's transposition of Atget's Parisian project to New York City (1935–1939), along with other photographic projects funded through New Deal initiatives during the Depression, principally that of Dorothea Lange.

57. Leaflet insert accompanying *Antlitz der Zeit*, in possession of Gunther Sander; cited in Ulrich Keller, "Conceptual and Stylistic Aspects of the Portraits," in *August Sander: Citizens of the Twentieth Century: Portrait Photographs 1892–1952*, ed. Gunther Sander, trans. Linda Keller (Cambridge, MA: MIT Press, 1989), 23. Although Sander's photographic atlas was not published during his lifetime, his plans for its arrangement are preserved in this leaflet as well as in the annotated typescript draft of the "ground plan" he devised in 1924, which is reproduced in *August Sander*, 36–37.

58. August Sander, letter to Peter Abelen, January 16, 1951; cited in ibid., 36.

59. Minor White, cited in James Baker Hall, *Minor White: Rites and Passages: His Photographs Accompanied by Excerpts From His Diaries and Letters* (New York: Aperture, 1978), 12.

60. Theodor Adorno, *Negative Dialectics*, trans. E. B. Ashton (New York: Continuum, 1987), 13.

61. Blake Stimson, *The Pivot of the World: Photography and Its Nation* (Cambridge, MA: The MIT Press, 2006), 37, 33.

62. Ibid., 37–38.

63. See Rosalind Krauss, "Sculpture in the Expanded Field," in *The Originality of the Avant-Garde and Other Modernist Myths* (Cambridge, MA: MIT Press, 1985), 276–90, and Baker, "Photography's Expanded Field," 177–81.

64. Emily Dickinson, *Selected Letters*, ed. Thomas H. Johnson (Cambridge, MA: Harvard University Press, 1986), 39.

65. My reading of the dash follows Deidre Fagan, "Emily Dickinson's Unutterable Word," *Emily Dickinson Journal* 14.2 (2005): 70.

66. Siegfried Kracauer, *Theory of Film: The Redemption of Physical Reality*, intro. Miriam Bratu Hansen (Princeton, NJ: Princeton University Press, 1997), 46–59.

67. Miriam Bratu Hansen, Introduction to Kracauer, *Theory of Film*, vii–xlv, xxv.

68. Keller, "Conceptual," 37.

69. Marta Braun, "Muybridge's Scientific Fictions," *Studies in Visual Communication* 10.3 (1984): 4–5.

70. Mary Ann Doane, *The Emergence of Cinematic Time: Modernity, Contingency, the Archive* (Cambridge, MA: Harvard University Press, 2002), 60.

71. Linda Williams, *Hard Core: Power, Pleasure, and the "Frenzy of the Visible"* (Berkeley: University of California Press, 1989), 41.

72. This line of argument follows Shawn Michelle Smith, *At the Edge of Sight: Photography and the Unseen* (Durham, NC, and London: Duke University Press, 2013), 81–82.

73. Elizabeth Abel, *Signs of the Times: The Visual Politics of Jim Crow* (Berkeley: University of California Press, 2010), 79.

74. Pierre Bourdieu, *The Field of Cultural Production: Essays on Art and Literature* (Cambridge: Polity Press, 1993), 32, 33.

75. Karen Beckman and Jean Ma, Introduction to *Still Moving*, 6.

76. Bernard Chardère, *Le roman des Lumières* (Paris: Gallimard, 1995), cited in Tom Gunning, "New Thresholds of Vision: Instantaneous Photography and the Early Cinema of Lumière," in *Impossible Presence: Surface and Screen in the Photogenic Era*, ed. Terry Smith (Sydney: Power Publications, 2001), 95. For a historical account of this public display, see Laurent Mannoni, *The Great Art of Light and Shadow: Archaeology of the Cinema*, intro. Tom Gunning (Exeter, UK: Exeter University Press, 2000), 425.

77. See Henri Bergson, *Creative Evolution*, trans. Arthur Mitchell (New York: Henry Holt and Company, 1911).

78. Stewart, *Between Film and Screen*, 266, 262.

79. Ibid., 23, 6.

80. Ibid., 6.

81. This is a rich and diverse field of inquiry, but its most important works are Claude-Edmonde Magny, *The Age of the American Novel: The Film Aesthetic of Fiction Between the Two Wars*, trans. Eleanor Hochman (New York: Ungar, 1972); Alan Spiegel, *Fiction and the Camera Eye: Visual Consciousness in Film and the Modern Novel* (Charlottesville: University Press of Virginia, 1976); P. Adams Sitney, *Modernist Montage: The Obscurity of Vision and Cinema and Literature* (New York: Columbia University Press, 1990); Susan McCabe, *Cinematic Modernism* (Cambridge: Cambridge University Press, 2005); and David Seed, *Cinematic Fictions* (Liverpool, UK: Liverpool University Press, 2009).

82. See Sara Danius, *The Senses of Modernism: Technology, Perception, and Aesthetics* (Ithaca, NY, and London: Cornell University Press, 2002); Andreas Huyssen, "Mass Culture as Woman: Modernism's Other," in *After the Great Divide: Modernism, Mass Culture, Postmodernism* (Bloomington and Indianapolis: Indiana University Press, 1986), 53.

83. Tom Gunning first articulated his concept of the "cinema of attractions" in "The Cinema of Attractions: Early Film, Its Spectator and the Avant-Garde," *Wide Angle* 8.3–4 (1986): 63–70.

84. This accords with David Trotter's historicized scrutiny of theories of modernist writing that make quick recourse to Eisenstein and his compeers, which supplies a first

response to the disordered chronologies of transmedia reciprocity by circling back to cinema as medium vis-à-vis its commitment to representational "neutrality" over narrative art in its first decade. Where Trotter catches sight of fantasies around the cinema's "indifferent automatism," my backward glance takes in something different: the camera's problematic relation to the real. See Trotter, *Cinema and Modernism* (Malden, MA: Blackwell, 2007).

85. Stewart, *Between Film and Screen*, 7, 8.

86. John Dos Passos, *Manhattan Transfer* (London: Penguin, 2000), 335.

87. Sontag, *On Photography*, 68.

88. Rosalind Krauss, "Photography in the Service of Surrealism," in *L'Amour fou: Photography and Surrealism*, by Rosalind Krauss and Jane Livingstone (New York: Abbeville, 1985), 35, 31.

89. Jean Toomer, *Cane* (New York: Liveright, 2011), 18.

90. Ibid., 38.

91. Susan Stanford Friedman, "(Self)Censorship and the Making of Joyce's Modernism," in *Joyce: The Return of the Repressed*, ed. Friedman (Ithaca, NY, and London: Cornell University Press, 1993), 22.

92. Stewart, *Between Film and Screen*, 7.

93. Jani Scandura, *Down in the Dumps: Place, Modernity, American Depression* (Durham, NC: Duke University Press, 2008), 220.

94. Richard C. Moreland, *Faulkner and Modernism: Rereading and Rewriting* (Madison: University of Wisconsin Press, 1989), 20–21.

95. Walter Benjamin, "N [Theoretics of Knowledge; Theory of Progress]," *Philosophical Forum* 15.1–2 (1983–1984): 5–6.

96. Scandura, *Down in the Dumps*, 27.

97. Karen Beckman and Liliane Weissberg, Introduction to *On Writing With Photography*, ed. Beckman and Weissberg, xii.

98. Sontag, *On Photography*, 22–23, 112.

99. Elkins, *What Photography Is*, 20, 28; Smith, *At the Edge*, 6–8.

100. W. J. T. Mitchell, "Showing Seeing: A Critique of Visual Culture," in *What Do Pictures Want? The Lives and Loves of Images* (Chicago: University of Chicago Press, 2005), 336–56; Elspeth H. Introduction to Brown and Phu, *Feeling Photography*, ed. Brown and Phu, 19.

101. Julia Kristeva, "Psychoanalysis and the Polis," in *The Kristeva Reader*, ed. Toril Moi (New York: Columbia University Press, 1986), 308.

102. Barthes, *Camera Lucida*, 113, 115, 117.

103. Smith, *At the Edge*, 37. Smith is well aware of the racialized and gendered "training" of Barthes's *Camera Lucida*; for her, it is photography's "mad" embrace that might "release Barthes from the limitations of his own racial and sexual problematics." See *At the Edge*, 23–38.

104. See Margaret Olin, *Touching Photographs* (Chicago and London: University of Chicago Press, 2012).

105. Barthes, *Camera Lucida*, 21.

106. Ibid., 82.

Chapter 1

1. Gertrude Stein, *Three Lives* (New York: Penguin, 1990), 3. All further references are to this edition and are given parenthetically in the text as *TL*.

2. Lisi Schoenbach, "'Peaceful and Exciting': Habit, Shock, and Gertrude Stein's Pragmatic Modernism," *Modernism/modernity* 11.2 (2004): 240.

3. Gertrude Stein, *The Autobiography of Alice B. Toklas* (London: Zephyr Books, 1947), 62.

4. Sonia Saldívar-Hull, "Wrestling Your Ally: Stein, Racism, and Feminist Critical Practice," in *Women's Writing in Exile*, ed. Mary Lynn Broe and Angela Ingram (Chapel Hill: University of North Carolina Press, 1989), 193.

5. Rebecca Emily Berne, "Regionalism, Modernism, and the American Short Story Cycle" (PhD diss., Yale University, 2007), 72.

6. Gertrude Stein, *The Making of Americans* (Normal, IL: Dalkey Archive Press, 1995), 349, 386.

7. Fredric Jameson, *Postmodernism, or, The Cultural Logic of Late Capitalism* (Durham, NC: Duke University Press, 1991), 25.

8. Sianne Ngai, *Ugly Feelings* (Cambridge, MA: Harvard University Press, 2005), 288, 263.

9. Mary Wilson, *The Labors of Modernism: Domesticity, Servants, and Authorship in Modernist Fiction* (Farnham, Surrey, and Burlington, VT: Ashgate, 2013), 62.

10. See Berne, "Regionalism," 48–80.

11. Nancy Glazener, "Dialogic Subversion: Bakhtin, the Novel and Gertrude Stein," in *Bakhtin and Cultural Theory*, ed. Ken Hirschkop and David Shepherd (Manchester, UK: Manchester University Press, 2001), 172.

12. See Marianne DeKoven, *Rich and Strange: Gender, History, Modernism* (Princeton, NJ: Princeton University Press, 1991), 68–69. These last oppositions are DeKoven's, although I revise her claim that race in *Three Lives* is "a highly ambiguous force" that contributes to the text's "generic indeterminacy . . . rather than to any racist or antiracist, conservative or subversive, thematic configuration." In working through the political dimensions of *Three Lives*, I follow several powerful critiques of white feminist accounts of Stein's modernist experimentation that abridge these dimensions, namely Saldívar-Hull, "Wrestling Your Ally," 181–98; Milton A. Cohen, "Black Brutes and Mulatto Saints: The Racial Hierarchy of Stein's 'Melanctha,'" *Black America Literature Forum* 18.3 (1984): 119–21; and Karin Cope, "'Moral Deviancy' and Contemporary Feminism: The Judgment of Gertrude Stein," in *Feminism Beside Itself*, ed. Diane Elam and Robyn Wiegman (New York: Routledge, 1995), 155–78.

13. Rosalind Krauss, "Photography in the Service of Surrealism," in *L'Amour fou: Photography and Surrealism*, by Rosalind Krauss and Jane Livingstone (New York: Abbeville Press, 1985), 28, 31.

14. Siegfried Kracauer, *Theory of Film: The Redemption of Physical Reality*, intro. Miriam Bratu Hansen (Princeton, NJ: Princeton University Press, 1997), 46–59.

15. See Douglas Mao and Rebecca L. Walkowitz, "Modernisms Bad and New," intro. to *Bad Modernisms*, ed. Mao and Walkowitz (Durham, NC, and London: Duke University Press, 2006), 1–18, and "The New Modernist Studies," *PMLA* 123.3 (2008): 737–48.

16. Emily Dickinson, *Selected Letters*, ed. Thomas H. Johnson (Cambridge, MA: Harvard University Press, 1986), 39; Houston A. Baker and Dana D. Nelson, "Violence, the Body and 'The South,'" *American Literature* 73.2 (2001): 232.

17. Stein, *Autobiography*, 42–43.

18. This approach shapes many of the major studies of Stein's early writing, including Richard Bridgman, *Gertrude Stein in Pieces* (New York: Oxford University Press, 1971);

Wendy Steiner, *Exact Resemblance to Exact Resemblance: The Literary Portraiture of Gertrude Stein* (New Haven, CT: Yale University Press, 1978); Marjorie Perloff, *The Poetics of Indeterminacy: Rimbaud to Cage* (Princeton, NJ: Princeton University Press, 1981); Jayne L. Walker, *The Making of a Modernist: Gertrude Stein from* Three Lives *to* Tender Buttons (Amherst: University of Massachusetts Press, 1984); and Lisa Ruddick, *Reading Gertrude Stein: Body, Text, Gnosis* (Ithaca, NY: Cornell University Press, 1990).

19. Philip Heldrich, "Connecting Surfaces: Gertrude Stein's *Three Lives*, Cubism, and the Metonymy of the Short Story Cycle," *Studies in Short Fiction* 34 (1997): 428; Gertrude Stein, "A Transatlantic Interview, 1946," in *A Primer for the Gradual Understanding of Gertrude Stein*, ed. Robert Bartlett Hass (Los Angeles: Black Sparrow, 1971), 15–35.

20. Or it could be that this kind of looking has not been clear-sighted enough. As Marjorie Perloff suggests, the comparison between Stein's writing and Cubist art has often hinged on notions of abstract art that fail to appreciate the "peculiar tension between conventional symbols . . . and stylized images of reality" in Cubist painting. Perloff's understanding of Cubism as poised "between reference and compositional game" is a painterly interpretative model for Stein's writing that corresponds with my own photographic one; see Perloff, *Poetics*, 70–72. It is worth noting, too, that Cubism has important debts to photographic technologies, most often acknowledged in discussions of Marcel Duchamp's *Nude Descending a Staircase* (1912) as it relates to the chronophotographic studies of Étienne-Jules Marey.

21. John Whittier-Ferguson, "Stein in Time: History, Manuscripts, and Memory," *Modernism/modernity* 6.1 (1999): 116.

22. Review of *Three Lives*, by Gertrude Stein, Pittsburg *Post*, January 17, 1910, in Gertrude Stein and Alice B. Toklas Papers 1837–1961, Clipping Book, 1909–1914, Series I: Writings of Gertrude Stein, Box 77, Folder 1408, Yale Collection of American Literature, Beinecke Rare Book and Manuscript Library, Yale University, New Haven, CT. All of the reviews I cite in this chapter are found in this clipping book.

23. Review of *Three Lives*, by Gertrude Stein, Rochester New York *Post Express*, December 24, 1909.

24. "A Three-Fold Character Study," review of *Three Lives*, by Gertrude Stein, *Washington Herald*, December 12, 1909.

25. Review of *Three Lives*, by Gertrude Stein, unidentified newspaper, Boston Massachusetts Transcripts, January 29, 1910.

26. Maria Damon, "Writing, Social Science, and Ethnicity in Gertrude Stein and Certain Others," in *Modernism, Inc.: Body, Memory, Capital*, ed. Jani Scandura and Michael Thurston (New York: New York University Press, 2001), 143. On Stein's "minority discourse," see Damon's earlier essay, "Gertrude Stein's Doggerel 'Yiddish': Women, Dogs, and Jews," in *The Dark End of the Street: Margins in American Vanguard Poetry* (Minneapolis, MN: University of Minnesota Press, 1993), 202–35.

27. Review of *Three Lives*, by Gertrude Stein, *Jewish Comment*, ca. 1909. That this review was published in a Jewish newspaper complicates, but also underscores, my point about the eugenicist freight of this discourse. This is especially true in light of Galton's efforts to uncover a Jewish type through his technique of composite portraiture; in his view, the composites of Jews offered the strongest proof of the veracity of racial typologies.

28. The first two quotations are from "An Extraordinary Book," review of *Three Lives*, by Gertrude Stein, *Springfield Union*, August 14, 1910; the last two are from *Jewish Comment*, ca. 1909.

29. "Notable Piece of Realism," review of *Three Lives*, by Gertrude Stein, *Boston Evening Globe*, December 18, 1909.

30. On Riis's contribution to these discourses, see Luc Sante, Introduction to *How the Other Half Lives: Studies Among the Tenements of New York*, by Jacob Riis (New York and London: Penguin, 1997), ix–xxv; Bonnie Yochelson and Daniel Czitrom, *Rediscovering Jacob Riis: Exposure Journalism and Photography in Turn-of-the-Century New York* (New York: New Press, 2007), xiii–xx; and Maren Stange, *Symbols of Ideal Life: Social Documentary Photography in America, 1890–1950* (New York: Cambridge University Press, 1989), 1–46.

31. This follows Elspeth H. Brown and Thy Phu, Introduction to *Feeling Photography*, ed. Brown and Phu (Durham, NC, and London: Duke University Press, 2014), 12–13.

32. Review of *Three Lives*, by Gertrude Stein, *The Nation*, January 20, 1910, and *New York Evening Post*, January 22, 1910.

33. Roland Barthes, *Camera Lucida: Reflections on Photography*, trans. Richard Howard (London: Vintage, 2000), 80–81.

34. Shawn Michelle Smith, *At the Edge of Sight: Photography and the Unseen* (Durham, NC, and London: Duke University Press, 2013), 29–30.

35. Frantz Fanon, *Black Skin, White Masks*, trans. Charles Markmann (New York: Grove Press, 1967), 112.

36. "Unconventional Tales," review of *Three Lives*, by Gertrude Stein, *Boston Morning Herald*, January 8, 1910.

37. Georgiana Goddard King, "A Review of Two Worlds: Gertrude Stein," *International*, June 1913, 158.

38. King, "Two Worlds," 157.

39. Fanon, *Black Skins*, 111–12; Barthes, *Camera Lucida*, 80.

40. King, "Two Worlds," 157.

41. Alfred Stieglitz, "Editorial," in *Camera Work: The Complete Illustrations, 1903–1917* (Cologne, Germany: Taschen, 1997), 660–61.

42. Ulla Haselstein, "Gertrude Stein's Portraits of Matisse and Picasso," *New Literary History* 34.4 (2003): 732.

43. See Silvan Tomkins, *Affect, Imagery, Consciousness*, 4 vols. (New York: Springer, 1963–1992).

44. Anne Anlin Cheng, *Second Skin: Josephine Baker and the Modern Surface* (Oxford: Oxford University Press, 2011), 111.

45. Krauss, "Photography," 35, 28.

46. Ibid., 35, 31. Krauss derives the notion of "convulsive beauty" from André Breton, *L'amour fou* (Paris: Gallimard, 1937).

47. Jonathan Levin, "'Entering the Modern Composition': Gertrude Stein and the Patterns of Modernism," in *Rereading the New: A Backward Glance at Modernism*, ed. Kevin J. H. Dettmar (Ann Arbor: University of Michigan Press, 1992), 159.

48. Michael North, *The Dialect of Modernism: Race, Language, and Twentieth-Century Literature* (New York: Oxford University Press, 1994), 73.

49. Gertrude Stein, *Paris France* (London: B. T. Batsford, 1940), 59.

50. Schoenbach, "'Peaceful,'" 240. Stein's comments about "civilization" in 1940 also raise the specter of her pro-Fascist associations during the Second World War, in the light of

which Amy Feinstein has called for new approaches to Stein's Jewish identity. See Feinstein's introduction to a paper Stein wrote while a student at Radcliffe College, "The Modern Jew Who Has Given Up the Faith of His Fathers Can Reasonably and Consistently Believe in Isolation," *PMLA* 116.2 (2001): 416–18.

51. Stein, *Paris France*, 1–2.

52. Schoenbach, " 'Peaceful,' " 245.

53. Susan Sontag, *On Photography* (London: Penguin, 2002), 68.

54. Gertrude Stein, "Composition as Explanation," in *Selected Writings of Gertrude Stein*, ed. and intro. Carl Van Vechten (New York: Vintage, 1972), 517.

55. Gertrude Stein, *Picasso* (New York: Dover, 1938), 21, 49.

56. Gertrude Stein, "Lecture II," in *Narration: Four Lectures* (Chicago: University of Chicago Press, 2010), 19–27.

57. Susan Stanford Friedman, "Definitional Excursions: The Meanings of Modern/ Modernity/Modernism," *Modernism/modernity* 8.3 (2001): 494–95.

58. Stein, "Lecture II," 19.

59. Stein, "Composition," 522.

60. Laura Doyle, "The Flat, the Round, and Gertrude Stein: Race and the Shape of Modern(ist) History," *Modernism/modernity* 7.2 (2000): 264.

61. Wilson, *Labors*, 77.

62. Sontag, *On Photography*, 75.

63. David Lomas, *The Haunted Self: Surrealism, Psychoanalysis, Subjectivity* (New Haven, CT, and London: Yale University Press, 2000), 53–54.

64. Krauss, "Photography," 28.

65. Ibid., 19.

66. Ibid., 28, 40.

67. Louis Aragon and André Breton, "Le Cinquantenaire de l'hystérie, 1878–1928," *La révolution surréaliste* 11 (March 15, 1928): 20–22, in *What Is Surrealism? Selected Writings*, ed. Franklin Rosemount (New York: Monad Press, 1978), 320–21.

68. Susan Rubin Suleiman, *Subversive Intent: Gender, Politics, and the Avant-Garde* (Cambridge, MA, and London: Harvard University Press, 1990), 103.

69. Tom Gunning, "In Your Face: Physiognomy, Photography, and the Gnostic Mission of Early Film," *Modernism/modernity* 4.1 (1997): 13–15.

70. Lomas, *Haunted Self*, 53, 56. See also Jean Baudrillard, *Seduction*, trans. Brian Singer (New York: St. Martin's Press, 1990).

71. Allen S. Weiss, *The Aesthetics of Excess* (Albany: State University of New York Press, 1989), 94.

72. Mark Niemeyer, for instance, holds to the possibility of Jeff's "full" explanation of Melanctha's behavior in "Hysteria and the Normal Unconscious: Dual Natures in Gertrude Stein's 'Melanctha,'" *Journal of American Studies* 28 (1994): 77–90.

73. Krauss, "Photography," 28.

74. Claude Cahun, *Disavowals, or, Cancelled Confessions*, trans. Susan de Muth, ed. and intro. Jennifer Mundy (Cambridge, MA: MIT Press, 2007), 1; Katharine Conley, *Surrealist Ghostliness* (Lincoln: University of Nebraska Press, 2013), 64.

75. Elizabeth Wright, *Speaking Desires Can Be Dangerous: The Poetics of the Unconscious* (Cambridge: Polity Press, 1999), 275; André Breton, "Manifesto of Surrealism," in *Manifestoes*

of Surrealism, trans. Richard Seaver and Helen R. Lane (Ann Arbor: University of Michigan Press, 2007), 9. Cahun was committed to Breton's Surrealist project, but her work sits uneasily between Surrealism and Symbolism. As Jennifer Mundy notes, Cahun was drawn not to exploring the unconscious but instead to "her conscious mind, with all its contradictory impulses and equivocal emotions." Mundy, Introduction to *Disavowals*, by Cahun, xvii.

76. Claude Cahun, *Aveux non avenus*, in *Écrits*, ed. François Leperlier (Paris: Jean-Michel Place, 2002), 335; Cahun, *Disavowals*, 127.

77. Cahun, *Aveux non avenus*, 118; Cahun, *Disavowals*, 103. For a larger discussion of *Aveux non avenus* as a reaction against the conservative sexual politics of the post–World War I period, see Jennifer L. Shaw, *Reading Claude Cahun's* Disavowals (Surrey, UK: Ashgate, 2013), 105–36.

78. Mundy, Introduction, xiv.

79. Cahun, *Disavowals*, 1, 204.

80. Shaw, *Reading*, 19.

81. For other readings of this image, see Honor Lassalle and Abigail Solomon-Godeau, "Surrealist Confession: Claude Cahun's Photomontages," *Afterimage* 19 (March 1992): 11–12, and Shaw, *Reading*, 152–60.

82. Karen Beckman, "Nothing to Say: The War on Terror and the Mad Photography of Roland Barthes," in *On Writing with Photography*, ed. Beckman and Liliane Weissberg (Minneapolis and London: University of Minnesota Press, 2013), 300.

83. Daylanne K. English, *Unnatural Selections: Eugenics in American Modernism and the Harlem Renaissance* (Chapel Hill: University of North Carolina Press, 2004), 113.

84. Sontag, *On Photography*, 14, 15.

85. Barthes, *Camera Lucida*, 14.

86. Aldon Lynn Nielsen, *Reading Race: White American Poets and the Racial Discourse in the Twentieth Century* (Athens: University of Georgia Press, 1988), 28.

87. Karen Beckman, *Vanishing Women: Magic, Film, and Feminism* (Durham, NC, and London: Duke University Press, 2003), 7.

88. Ibid., 158.

89. Glazener, "Dialogic Subversion," 169–70.

90. Walker, *Making of a Modernist*, 27.

91. Glazener, "Dialogic Subversion," 172.

92. North, *Dialect of Modernism*, 61, 70. Corinne E. Blackmer makes a similar argument in "African Masks and the Arts of Passing in Gertrude Stein's 'Melanctha' and Nella Larsen's *Passing*," *Journal of the History of Sexuality* 4.2 (1993): 230–63.

93. François Leperlier, *Claude Cahun: L'écart et la metamorphose* (Paris: Jean-Michel Place, 1992), 111.

94. Dawn Ades, "Surrealism, Male-Female," in *Surrealism: Desire Unbounded*, ed. Jennifer Mundy (Princeton, NJ: Princeton University Press, 2001), 194.

95. I cite Félix Nadar, whose description of Balzac's notion of photographic spectrality draws on a conversation he had with the novelist; see Nadar, *When I Was a Photographer*, trans. Eduardo Cadava and Liana Theodoratou (Cambridge, MA: MIT Press, 2015), 4.

96. Ibid., 3.

97. Cahun, *Disavowals*, 1.

98. See Mary Ann Doane, "Film and the Masquerade: Theorizing the Female Spectator," *Screen* 23.3–4 (1982): 81–82.

99. Victoria Rosner, *Modernism and the Architecture of Private Life* (New York: Columbia University Press, 2005), 68.

100. Janice L. Doane, *Silence and Narrative: The Early Novels of Gertrude Stein* (Westport, CT, and London: Greenwood, 1986), 54.

101. Elaine Scarry, *The Body in Pain: The Making and Unmaking of the World* (New York: Oxford University Press, 1985), 19, 7, 6.

102. Martha Stoddard Holmes and Tod Chambers, "Thinking Through Pain," *Literature and Medicine* 24.1 (2005): 133; Susannah B. Mintz, *Hurt and Pain: Literature and the Suffering Body* (London: Bloomsberg, 2013), 2, 7.

103. Michel Foucault, "The Ethics for the Concern of Self as a Practice of Freedom," in *The Final Foucault*, trans. J. D. Gauthier, ed. James Bernauer and David Rasmussen (Cambridge, MA: MIT Press, 1988), 13, 12.

104. Lois McNay, *Foucault and Feminism: Power, Gender and the Self* (Cambridge and Malden, MA: Polity Press, 2013), 173.

105. Lennard J. Davis, *Bending Over Backwards: Disability, Dismodernism, and Other Difficult Positions* (New York: New York University Press, 2002), 98, 100.

106. Ibid., 99.

107. James A. Snead, "Repetition as a Figure of Black Culture," in *Black Literature and Literary Theory*, ed. Henry Louis Gates Jr. (New York: Methuen, 1984), 67.

108. This follows Jennifer L. Fleissner, who considers *Three Lives* in relation to the "cut" and Freud's *Wiederholungszwang* in *Women, Compulsion, Modernity: The Moment of American Naturalism* (Chicago and London: University of Chicago Press, 2004), 258–66.

109. Karen Beckman and Jean Ma, Introduction to *Still Moving: Between Cinema and Photography*, ed. Beckman and Ma (Durham, NC: Duke University Press, 2008), 15.

110. Cathy Caruth, *Unclaimed Experience: Trauma, Narrative, and History* (Baltimore: Johns Hopkins University Press, 1996), 100. Caruth refers to Jacques Lacan, *Four Fundamental Concepts*, 29–41, and Sigmund Freud, *The Interpretation of Dreams*, trans. James Strachey (New York: Avon, 1965), 548.

111. Caruth, *Unclaimed Experience*, 105.

112. Friedman, "Definitional Excursions," 495.

113. Doane, *Silence and Narrative*, 54; Walker, *Making of a Modernist*, 23.

114. Barthes, *Camera Lucida*, 113, 117.

Chapter 2

1. George Hutchinson, "Jean Toomer and American Racial Discourse," *Texas Studies in Literature and Language* 35.2 (1993): 244.

2. Jean Toomer, "A New Race in America" (1931), in *A Jean Toomer Reader: Selected Unpublished Writings*, ed. Frederik L. Rusch (New York: Oxford University Press, 1993), 105.

3. Jean Toomer, *Cane* (New York: Liveright, 2011), 17. All further references are to this edition and are given parenthetically in the text as *C*.

4. Alice Walker, "The Divided Life of Jean Toomer," *New York Times Book Review*, July 13, 1980, 16.

5. Sara Blair, *Harlem Crossroads: Black Writers and the Photograph in the Twentieth Century* (Princeton, NC: Princeton University Press, 2007), xx.

6. Apart from Blair's *Harlem Crossroads*, studies that explore the relationship between writing and images in the Harlem Renaissance include Caroline Goeser, *Picturing the New*

Negro: Harlem Renaissance Print Culture and Modern Black Identity (Lawrence: University Press of Kansas, 2007); Anne Carroll, *Word, Image, and the New Negro: Representation and Identity in the Harlem Renaissance* (Bloomington: Indiana University Press, 2005); and Martha Jane Nadell, *Enter the New Negroes: Images of Race in American Culture* (Cambridge: Cambridge University Press, 2004).

7. Katherine Henninger, *Ordering the Façade: Photography and Contemporary Southern Women's Writing* (Chapel Hill: University of North Carolina Press, 2007) 16.

8. Susan Stanford Friedman, "Definitional Excursions: The Meanings of Modern/ Modernity/Modernism," *Modernism/modernity* 8.3 (2001): 508.

9. Laura Doyle, "The Flat, the Round, and Gertrude Stein: Race and the Shape of Modern(ist) History," *Modernism/modernity* 7.2 (2000): 262–63, 269.

10. Michael North, *The Dialect of Modernism: Race, Language, and Twentieth-Century Literature* (New York: Oxford University Press, 1994), 64; Ann Anlin Cheng, *Second Skin: Josephine Baker and the Modern Surface* (Oxford: Oxford University Press, 2011), 166.

11. North, *Dialect of Modernism*, 162.

12. Jean Toomer, letter to Waldo Frank, December 12, 1922, in *Jean Toomer Reader*, 26. Toomer's original grammar and syntax are preserved here.

13. Bernard Bell, *The Contemporary African American Novel: Its Folk Roots and Modern Literary Branches* (Amherst: University of Massachusetts Press, 2004), 108.

14. J. Gerald Kennedy, "Toward a Poetics of the Short Story Cycle," *Journal of the Short Story in English* 11 (1988): 11.

15. Michael Awkward, *Negotiating Difference: Race, Gender, and the Politics of Positionality* (Chicago: University of Chicago Press, 1995), 23–42.

16. Jean Toomer, "The *Cane* Years," in *The Wayward and the Seeking: A Collection of Writings by Jean Toomer*, ed. Darwin T. Turner (Washington, DC: Howard University Press, 1980), 123.

17. Robert H. Brinkmeyer Jr., "Wasted Talent, Wasted Art: The Literary Career of Jean Toomer," *The Southern Quarterly* 20.1 (1981): 83–84.

18. Cynthia Earl Kerman and Richard Eldridge, *The Lives of Jean Toomer: A Hunger for Wholeness* (Baton Rouge: Louisiana State University Press, 1987), xiii.

19. Jean Toomer, *Book X*, Second Draft, Jean Toomer Papers, Yale Collection of American Literature, Beinecke Rare Book and Manuscript Library, Yale University (hereafter cited as Jean Toomer Papers); cited in Mark Whalan, "'Taking Myself in Hand': Jean Toomer and Physical Culture," *Modernism/Modernity* 10.4 (2003): 598.

20. Whalan, "Taking Myself in Hand," 598.

21. Kerman and Eldridge, *Lives of Jean Toomer*, xiii.

22. Cherene Sherrard-Johnson, *Portraits of the New Negro Woman: Visual and Literary Culture in the Harlem Renaissance* (New Brunswick, NJ: Rutgers University Press, 2007), 17.

23. Nellie McKay, *Jean Toomer, Artist: A Study of His Literary Life and Work, 1894–1936* (Chapel Hill: University of North Carolina Press, 1984), 5.

24. Robert B. Jones, *Jean Toomer and the Prison-House of Thought: A Phenomenology of the Spirit* (Amherst: University of Massachusetts Press, 1993), 49, 51–58.

25. Jean Toomer, letter to John McClure, June 30, 1922, Jean Toomer Papers; cited in Charles Scruggs, "The Photographic Print, the Literary Negative: Alfred Stieglitz and Jean

Toomer," *Arizona Quarterly: A Journal of American Literature, Culture, and Theory* 53.1 (1997): 80.

26. Scruggs, "Photographic Print," 80. For other scholarship that acknowledges how Toomer disrupts the notion of coherent racial identities by straddling various identifications, see J. Martin Favor, *Authentic Blackness: The Folk in the New Negro Renaissance* (Durham, NC: Duke University Press, 1999), 53–80, and Hutchinson, "American Racial Discourse," 226–50, as well as his "Identity in Motion: Placing *Cane*," in *Jean Toomer and the Harlem Renaissance*, ed. Geneviève Fabre and Michel Feith (New Brunswick, NJ: Rutgers University Press, 2001), 38–56.

27. Sherwood Anderson to Jean Toomer, 1922, Jean Toomer Collection, Fisk University Archives, Nashville, TN (hereafter cited as Jean Toomer Collection); cited in Darwin T. Turner, "An Intersection of Paths: Correspondence Between Jean Toomer and Sherwood Anderson," in *Jean Toomer: A Critical Evaluation*, ed. Therman O'Daniel (Washington, DC: Howard University Press, 1988), 99.

28. Jean Toomer, letter to Sherwood Anderson, December 18, 1922, Jean Toomer Collection; cited in Mark Helbling, "Sherwood Anderson and Jean Toomer," in *Jean Toomer: A Critical Evaluation*, 116.

29. Alain Locke, "The New Negro," in *The New Negro*, ed. Locke (New York: Atheneum, 1992), xxvii.

30. Jean Toomer, letter to Sherwood Anderson, December 22, 1922, Jean Toomer Collection; cited in Turner, "Intersection of Paths," 102.

31. Sherwood Anderson, letter to Gertrude Stein, March, 1924, in *Sherwood Anderson/ Gertrude Stein: Correspondence and Personal Essays*, ed. Ray Lewis White (Chapel Hill: University of North Carolina Press, 1972), 37.

32. Jean Toomer, letter to Waldo Frank, ca. summer 1923, Jean Toomer Collection; cited in Helbling, "Sherwood Anderson," 114.

33. Charles Scruggs and Lee VanDemarr, *Jean Toomer and the Terrors of American History* (Philadelphia: University of Pennsylvania Press, 1998), 146, 155.

34. Jean Toomer, letter to Alfred Stieglitz, January 10, 1924, Jean Toomer Papers; cited in Martha Jane Nadell, "Race and the Visual Arts in the Works of Jean Toomer and Georgia O'Keeffe," in *Toomer and the Harlem Renaissance*, ed. Fabre and Feith, 155.

35. Jean Toomer, letter to Alfred Stieglitz, January 10, 1924, Jean Toomer Papers; cited in Nadell, "Race and the Visual Arts," 157.

36. Cheng, *Second Skin*, 13.

37. Jean Toomer, letter to Alfred Stieglitz, May 2, 1924, Jean Toomer Papers; cited in Nadell, "Race and the Visual Arts," 153.

38. Jean Toomer, letter to Alfred Stieglitz, August 4, 1925, in *Jean Toomer Reader*, 281.

39. See, for instance, Frederick L. Rusch, "Form, Function, and Creative Tension in *Cane*: Jean Toomer and the Need for the Avant-Garde," *MELUS* 17.4 (1991–1992): 24–25; and Bowie Duncan, "Jean Toomer's *Cane*: A Modern Black Oracle," *CLA Journal* 15 (1972): 223–33.

40. Jean Toomer, letter to Georgia O'Keeffe, January 13, 1924, in *Jean Toomer Reader*, 280–81.

41. Nadell, "Race and the Visual Arts," 151.

42. Toomer, "The *Cane* Years," 126.

43. Walter Benn Michaels, *Our America: Nativism, Modernism, and Pluralism* (Durham, NC: Duke University Press, 1995), 63.

44. Jean Toomer, "Notes for Novel," Jean Toomer Papers; cited in Mark Whalan, *Race, Manhood, and Modernism: The Short Story Cycles of Sherwood Anderson and Jean Toomer* (Knoxville: University of Tennessee Press, 2007), 185–86.

45. Walter Benjamin, "The Work of Art in the Age of Mechanical Reproduction," in *Illuminations: Essays and Reflections*, ed. Harrah Arendt, trans. Harry Zohn (New York: Schocken Books, 2007), 237, 223.

46. Laura Doyle, *Bordering on the Body: The Racial Matrix of Modern Fiction and Culture* (New York: Oxford University Press, 1994), 97.

47. Not only is the exhibition of *L'arrivée d'un train en gare de La Ciotat* erroneously dated to 1895—it took place in January 1896—but the story of the audience's hysterical reaction at its first screening is likely, as Tom Gunning suggests, to be apocryphal; see Gunning, "An Aesthetic of Astonishment: Early Film and the (In)Credulous Spectator," *Art and Text* 34 (Spring 1989): 31–45.

48. Lynne Kirby, *Parallel Tracks: The Railroad Car and Silent Cinema* (Durham, NC: Duke University Press, 1997), 44–45. On the cinema's mobilized gaze, see Anne Friedberg, *Window Shopping: Cinema and the Postmodern* (Berkeley: University of California Press, 1993).

49. That Stieglitz's composite portrait shares its name with Galton's photographic experiments implies the unexpected similarities between the two. One of the variations Stieglitz imagined on his portraiture project, according to O'Keeffe, was of a "photographic diary" of a single individual from birth until death—a project that recalls Galton's assemblage of composite images of individuals "taken at different times, perhaps even years apart." See O'Keeffe, Introduction to *Georgia O'Keeffe, A Portrait*, by Alfred Stieglitz (New York: Metropolitan Museum of Art, 1978), and Galton, "Composite Portraits, Made by Combining Those of Many Different Persons Into a Single Resultant Figure," *Journal of the Anthropological Institute* viii (1879): 140.

50. Anne Middleton Wagner, *Three Artists (Three Women): Modernism and the Art of Hesse, Krasner, and O'Keeffe* (Berkeley: University of California Press, 1996), 88.

51. Marcia Brennan, *Painting Gender, Constructing Theory: The Alfred Stieglitz Circle and American Formalist Aesthetics* (Cambridge, MA: MIT Press, 2001), 83.

52. O'Keeffe, Introduction, 81.

53. Brennan, *Painting Gender*, 82–83.

54. Sally Bishop Shigley, "Recalcitrant, Revered, and Reviled: Women in Jean Toomer's Short Story Cycle, *Cane*," *Short Story* 9.1 (2001): 89, 93.

55. Ibid., 91.

56. Jay Watson, *Reading for the Body: The Recalcitrant Materiality of Southern Fiction, 1893–1985* (Athens: University of Georgia Press, 2012), 8.

57. Catherine Gunther Kodat, "To 'Flash White Light from Ebony': The Problem of Modernism in Jean Toomer's *Cane*," *Twentieth Century Literature* 46.1 (2000): 8.

58. Janet M. Whyde, "Mediating Forms: Narrating the Body in Jean Toomer's *Cane*," *Southern Literary Journal* 26.1 (1993): 46.

59. Whalan, *Race*, 202, 33.

60. Rachel Farebrother, "'Adventuring Through the Pieces of a Still Unorganized Mosaic': Reading Jean Toomer's Collage Aesthetic in *Cane*," *Journal of American Studies* 40.3 (2006): 512.

61. bell hooks, *Black Looks: Race and Representation* (Boston: South End Press, 1992), 116.

62. Susan Sontag, *On Photography* (London: Penguin, 2008), 11, 14–15.

63. Elizabeth Alexander, *The Black Interior* (Saint Paul, MN: Graywolf, 2004), 177.

64. Blair, *Harlem Crossroads*, 13.

65. Susan Sontag, *Regarding the Pain of Others* (New York: Farrar, Straus and Giroux, 2003), 24.

66. Sontag, *On Photography*, 22; Sontag, *Regarding the Pain*, 83.

67. Judith Butler, "Torture and the Ethics of Photography: Thinking with Sontag," in *Frames of War: When is Life Grievable?* (London: Verso, 2009), 67–70.

68. Sontag, *Regarding the Pain*, 1.

69. Sharon Sliwinski, "A Painful Labor: Photography and Responsibility," in *Representations of Pain in Art and Visual Culture*, ed. Maria Pia Di Bella and James Elkins (New York and London: Routledge, 2013), 68–69.

70. Roland Barthes, *Camera Lucida: Reflections on Photography*, trans. Richard Howard (London: Vintage, 2000), 117; Butler, "Torture," 100.

71. Karen Beckman, "Nothing to Say: The War on Terror and the Mad Photography of Roland Barthes," in *On Writing With Photography*, ed. Beckman and Liliane Weissberg (Minneapolis and London: University of Minnesota Press, 2013), 317.

72. Tom Gunning, "Tracing the Individual Body: Photography, Detectives, and Early Cinema," in *Cinema and the Invention of Modern Life*, ed. Leo Charney and Vanessa R. Schwartz (Berkeley: University of California Press, 1995), 18, 19.

73. bell hooks, "In Our Glory: Photography and Black Life," in *Art on My Mind: Visual Politics* (New York: New Press, 1995), 61, 60.

74. See Jean Toomer, "Song of the Son," *The Crisis: A Record of the Darker Races* 23.6 (1922): 261, http://www.modjourn.org/render.php?id=1297796255203127&view=mjp_object. *Cane*'s prebook history remains understudied. In one of the only articles to address this history, Eurie Dahn interprets the publication of "Song of the Son" in the *Crisis* as evidence of Toomer's initial interest "in reaching a black, politically engaged, and elite readership." See Dahn, "*Cane* in the Magazines: Race, Form, and Global Periodical Networks," *The Journal of Modern Periodical Studies* 3.2 (2012): 127–30.

75. Russ Castronovo, "Beauty Along the Color Line: Lynching, Aesthetics, and the 'Crisis,'" *PMLA* 121.5 (2006): 1443.

76. Jessie Redmon Fauset, "Brawley's 'Social History of the American Negro,'" review of *A Social History of the American Negro*, by Benjamin Brawley, *Crisis*, 260.

77. This follows Doyle, *Bordering on the Body*, 86.

78. Nancy J. Vickers, "Members Only: Marot's Anatomical Blazons," in *The Body in Parts: Fantasies of Corporeality in Early Modern Europe*, ed. David Hillman and Carla Mazzio (New York: Routledge, 1997), 16, 19. In fact, as Jonathan Sawday explains, the blazon developed alongside the scientific practice of anatomical dissection, such that its metaphoric intrusions into human bodies are entwined with actual intrusions. See Sawday, *The Body Emblazoned: Dissection and the Human Body in Renaissance Culture* (London: Routledge, 1995), 183–229.

79. Amy Louise Wood, *Lynching and Spectacle: Witnessing Racial Violence in America, 1890–1940* (Chapel Hill: University of Carolina Press, 2009) 76, 98.

80. Ibid., 199.

81. Leigh Raiford, "Lynching, Visuality, and the Un/Making of Blackness," *Nka: Journal of Contemporary African Art* 20 (Fall 2006): 24.

82. Nadell, *Enter the New Negroes*, 119; Richard Wright, *Twelve Million Black Voices: A Folk History of the Negro in the United States* (New York: Viking, 1941), 11, 35.

83. Ibid., 43.

84. Hortense J. Spillers, "Mama's Baby, Papa's Maybe: An American Grammar Book," in *The Black Feminist Reader*, ed. Joy James and T. Denean Sharpley-Whiting (Boston: Wiley-Blackwell, 2000), 61.

85. Robyn Wiegman, *American Anatomies: Theorizing Race and Gender* (Durham, NC: Duke University Press, 1995), 81.

86. Trudier Harris, *Exorcising Blackness: Historical and Literary Lynching and Burning Rituals* (Bloomington: Indiana University Press, 1984), 19.

87. Wiegman, *American Anatomies*, 94–95.

88. Mikhail Bakhtin, *Rabelais and His World*, trans. Helene Iswolsky (Cambridge, MA: MIT Press, 1968), 27.

89. Richard Eldridge, "The Unifying Image in Part One of Jean Toomer's *Cane*," in *Jean Toomer: A Critical Evaluation*, ed. Therman O'Daniel (Washington, DC: Howard University Press, 1988), 234.

90. Jeff Webb, "Literature and Lynching: Identity in Jean Toomer's *Cane*," *ELH* 67.1 (2000): 211.

91. Shawn Michelle Smith, *Photography on the Color Line: W. E. B. Du Bois, Race, and Visual Culture* (Durham, NC, and London: Duke University Press, 2004), 118.

92. Elaine Scarry, *The Body in Pain: The Making and Unmaking of the World* (New York: Oxford University Press, 1985), 3–4.

93. Doyle, *Bordering on the Body*, 86.

94. Scarry, *Body in Pain*, 17.

95. Patricia Yaeger, *Dirt and Desire: Reconstructing Southern Women's Writing, 1930–1990* (Chicago: University of Chicago Press, 2000), 81, 224.

96. Martin Luther King Jr., *Why We Can't Wait* (New York: Harper and Row, 1964), 30.

97. Michaels, *Our America*, 61–62.

98. Watson, *Reading for the Body*, 4, 7, 5. In a line of thought that accords with my emphasis on the revisionist and recuperative functions of African American photography, Watson goes on to suggest that the disappearance of the black body in "Portrait in Georgia" might not denote its "eradication by rope and fagot" but, by contrast, "a lynching averted." Ibid., 9.

99. Wiegman, *American Anatomies*, 21.

100. Samira Kawash, *Dislocating the Color Line: Identity, Hybridity, and Singularity in African-American Literature* (Stanford, CA: Stanford University Press, 1997), 131, 125.

101. Ibid., 131.

102. Judith Butler, *Bodies That Matter: On the Discursive Limits of "Sex"* (London and New York: Routledge, 1993), 9, 10.

103. Whalan, *Race*, 187.

104. Ibid., 175, 32.

105. Ibid., 32.

106. See Ann Fabian, "Making a Commodity of Truth: Speculations on the Career of Bernarr Macfadden," *American Literary History* 5.1 (1993): 51–76.

107. Richard Dyer, *White* (London: Routledge, 1997), 152–53.

108. Whalan, *Race,* 178–80.

109. Bernarr Macfadden, *Encyclopedia of Physical Culture* (New York: Physical Culture Publishing, 1912), 2416.

110. Whalan, *Race,* 178; Fabian, "Making a Commodity," 58.

111. Wiegman, *American Anatomies,* 94–95.

112. Raiford, "Lynching," 26.

113. I allude here to Fanon's description of the experience of the "crushing objecthood" of the racial identification enforced by others: "the glances of the other fixed me, in the sense in which a chemical solution is fixed by a dye." See Fanon, *Black Skin, White Masks,* trans. Charles Markmann (New York: Grove Press, 1967), 109.

114. Butler, "Torture," 71–72, 84.

115. Richard Aldington, "The Art of Poetry," *Dial* 69 (1920): 170; cited in North, *Dialect of Modernism,* 171.

116. David Trotter, *Literature in the First Media Age: Britain Between the Wars* (Cambridge, MA: Harvard University Press, 2013), 24.

117. Karen Jackson Ford, *Split-Gut Song: Jean Toomer and the Poetics of Modernity* (Tuscaloosa: University of Alabama Press, 2005), 82–84, 85.

118. Trotter notes this in *Literature,* 24–25.

119. Wiegman, *American Anatomies,* 91.

120. Barbara Foley, "'In the Land of Cotton': Economics and Violence in Jean Toomer's *Cane,*" *African American Review* 32.2 (1998): 191.

121. Wood, *Lynching and Spectacle,* 86–88, 183.

122. Castronovo, "Beauty Along the Color Line," 1451; the newspaper report is "Lynched on Stage; Shots Came from Pit," *New York Times,* April 21, 1911, 1.

123. Raiford, "Lynching," 29.

Chapter 3

1. John Dos Passos, *Manhattan Transfer* (London: Penguin, 2000), 335. All further references are to this edition and are given parenthetically in the text as *MT.*

2. Carol Shloss, *In Visible Light: Photography and the American Writer, 1840–1940* (Oxford: Oxford University Press, 1987), 148, 146.

3. Ibid., 145.

4. Ibid., 148.

5. Janet Galligani Casey, *Dos Passos and the Ideology of the Feminine* (Cambridge: Cambridge University Press, 1998), 115.

6. Laura Wexler, *Tender Violence: Domestic Visions in an Age of U.S. Imperialism* (Chapel Hill: University of North Carolina Press, 2000), 58.

7. Ibid., 59.

8. "Mlle. Anna Held Arrives: Naïve Talk of the Parisian Beauty and $1,500-a-Week Singer," *New York Times,* September 16, 1896, http://timesmachine.nytimes.com/timesmachine/1896/09/16/104113257.html.

9. My account follows Linda Mizejewski, *Ziegfeld Girl: Image and Icon in Culture and Cinema* (Durham, NC, and London: Duke University Press, 1999), 41.

10. John Dos Passos, "Brown Cover Notebook—Notes, Verse," John Dos Passos Papers, Series III: Personal, Box 126, Sleeve 12, Albert and Shirley Small Special Collections Library, University of Virginia, Charlottesville.

11. John Dos Passos, "Black Checkered Notebook—Notes, Verse, Sketches," John Dos Passos Papers, Series III: Personal, Box 126, Sleeve 11, Albert and Shirley Small Special Collections Library, University of Virginia, Charlottesville.

12. Mizejewski, *Ziegfeld Girl*, 41.

13. But note that Dos Passos's attitude toward the theatre was quite ambivalent during this period, as evidenced by the 1925 essay, "Is the 'Realistic' Theatre Obsolete?" in *The Major Nonfictional Prose*, ed. Donald Pizer (Detroit, MI: Wayne State University Press, 1988), 75–78.

14. See Thomas Fahy, "Planes, Trains, and Automobiles: Technology and the Suburban Nightmare in the Plays of John Dos Passos," in *Staging Modern American Life: Popular Culture in the Experimental Theatre of Millay, Cummings, and Dos Passos* (New York: Palgrave Macmillan, 2011), 85–131; and Kevin Trumpeter, "Furnishing Modernist Fiction: The Aesthetics of Refuse," *Modernism/modernity* 20.2 (2013): 307–26.

15. I am repurposing Dana Polan's remarks, which she makes in relation to postwar musical films and contemporary interview television shows; see "Brief Encounters: Mass Culture and the Evacuation of Sense," in *Studies in Entertainment: Critical Approaches to Mass Culture*, ed. Tania Modleski (Bloomington and Indianapolis: Indiana University Press, 1986), 182.

16. This description follows Joel Dinerstein, *Swinging the Machine: Modernity, Technology, and African American Culture Between the World Wars* (Amherst and Boston: University of Massachusetts Press, 2003), 191–97.

17. Bill Brown, *A Sense of Things: The Object Matter of American Literature* (Chicago and London: University of Chicago Press, 2003), 137.

18. Sinclair Lewis, "Manhattan at Last!," review of *Manhattan Transfer*, by John Dos Passos, *Saturday Review*, December 5, 1925, 361, http://www.unz.org/Pub/SaturdayRev-1925dec05-00361.

19. Dos Passos stated in 1968, "At the time I did [*Manhattan Transfer*] I'm not sure whether I had seen Eisenstein's films. The idea of montage had an influence on the development of this sort of writing. I may have seen [*Battleship*] *Potemkin*." Dos Passos, *Major Nonfictional Prose*, 247.

20. See Michael Spindler, "John Dos Passos and the Visual Arts," *Journal of American Studies* 15.3 (1981): 391–405. There are examples of avant-garde montage films that were made in the United States in this period, most significantly Paul Strand and Charles Sheeler's *Manhatta* (1921). Gretchen Foster finds continuities between *Manhatta* and *Manhattan Transfer* and points to the possibility that Dos Passos saw this film. Yet Juan Suárez has cautioned against overstating the similarities between European films of that time and *Manhatta*; the former are augmented by an "aggressive despair" that is absent from the latter's "Whitmanian celebration [of the] modern material world." See Foster, "John Dos Passos's Use of Film Technique in *Manhattan Transfer* and *The 42nd Parallel*," *Literature/Film Quarterly* 14.3 (1986): 189; and Suárez, "City Space, Technology, Popular Culture: The Modernism of Paul Strand and Charles Sheeler's *Manhatta*," *Journal of American Studies* 36.1 (2002): 96.

21. Claude-Edmonde Magny, *The Age of the American Novel: The Film Aesthetic of Fiction Between the Two Wars*, trans. Eleanor Hochman (New York: Ungar, 1972), 22. Arguments that make recourse to D. W. Griffith's *The Birth of a Nation* (1915), the montage film Dos Passos most likely did see before writing *Manhattan Transfer*, fail to observe the clear discrepancy

between Griffith's purposes and those of his Soviet peers. Critical narratives about the montage technique of Dos Passos make more historical sense when applied to his writing after his personal encounters with the Russian filmmakers during a 1928 trip to the Soviet Union. As David Seed suggests, Dos Passos's meeting with Eisenstein intensified his pursuit of "cinematic" goals. See Seed, *Cinematic Fictions* (Liverpool, UK: Liverpool University Press, 2009), 137–45. For an especially insightful account of how the *U.S.A.* trilogy, begun in 1929, invites comparisons with Soviet techniques, see Shloss, *In Visible Light*, 149–75.

22. Ann Douglas, *Terrible Honesty: Mongrel Manhattan in the 1920s* (New York: Farrar, Straus, and Giroux, 1995), 60.

23. Ben Singer, "Modernity, Hyperstimulus, and the Rise of Popular Sensationalism," in *Cinema and the Invention of Modern Life*, ed. Leo Charney and Vanessa R. Schwartz (Berkeley: University of California Press, 1995), 90–92.

24. Charlie Keil and Shelley Stamp, Introduction to *American Cinema's Transitional Era: Audiences, Institutions, Practices*, ed. Keil and Stamp (Berkeley: University of California Press, 2004), 11.

25. Ben Brewster, "Periodization of Early Cinema," in *American Cinema's Transitional Era*, ed. Keil and Stamp, 71.

26. See Jonathan Crary, *Techniques of the Observer: On Vision and Modernity in the Nineteenth Century* (Cambridge, MA: MIT Press, 1990).

27. On the historical connection between Galton's composite portraits and the stereoscope, see Carlo Ginsburg, "Family Resemblances and Family Trees: Two Cognitive Metaphors," *Critical Inquiry* 30.3 (2004): 537–56.

28. E. D. Lowry, "The Lively Art of *Manhattan Transfer*," *PMLA* 84.6 (1969): 1629–30.

29. Leo Charney, *Empty Moments: Cinema, Modernity, and Drift* (Durham, NC, and London: Duke University Press, 1998), 75. Amy Koritz offers a wider discussion of rhythms of repetition and fragmentation in 1920s theatre in *Culture Makers: Urban Performance and Literature in the 1920s* (Urbana and Chicago: University of Illinois Press, 2009), 19–38.

30. There is an almost identical list inscribed on the inside cover of the notebook in which Dos Passos drafted the first episodes of Ellen's story circa 1924. See John Dos Passos, "Ellen Thatcher—Chap I / Protochapter I," John Dos Passos Papers, Series II: Writings, Box 58, Binder 2, Albert and Shirley Small Special Collections Library, University of Virginia, Charlottesville.

31. Dos Passos, "Black Checkered Notebook."

32. Stefan Jonsson, *Crowds and Democracy: The Idea and Image of the Masses from Revolution to Fascism* (New York: Columbia University Press, 2013), 7. The idea of the masses is also thematized through Dos Passos's characteristic narrative idiom of merged words—for example, "manuresmelling."

33. Kathleen L. Komar, *Pattern and Chaos: Multilinear Novels by Dos Passos, Döblin, Faulkner, and Koeppen* (Columbia, SC: Camden House, 1983), 17–18.

34. This is also true for Dos Passos's 1921 novel, *Three Soldiers*, in which the members of a community of AWOL soldiers in France during World War I are denoted not by their names but by their physical and ethnic characteristics. Similarly, the characters in the narrative sections of *U.S.A.* have regularly been considered lifeless in comparison with the figures in the historical biographical sections of the trilogy.

35. Joseph Warren Beach, "*Manhattan Transfer*: Collectivism and Abstract Composition," in *Dos Passos, the Critics, and the Writer's Intentions*, ed. Allen Belkind (Carbondale: Southern Illinois University Press, 1971), 57, 63–64.

36. Cecelia Tichi, *Shifting Gears: Technology, Literature, Culture in Modernist America* (Chapel Hill and London: University of North Carolina Press, 1987), 198. There is a limit to the extent to which the characters form a representative sample. In line with the studied whiteness of the Follies girls, people of color are largely excluded from *Manhattan Transfer*, as John Carlos Rowe notes in "John Dos Passos's Imaginary City in *Manhattan Transfer*," in *Afterlives of Modernism: Liberalism, Transnationalism, and Political Critique* (Hanover, NH: Dartmouth College Press, 2011), 69–70.

37. Siegfried Kracauer, "The Mass Ornament," in *The Mass Ornament: Weimar Essays*, ed. and trans. Thomas Y. Levin (Cambridge, MA: Harvard University Press, 1995), 76.

38. Ibid., 83.

39. Jonsson, *Crowds and Democracy*, 156.

40. Seed notes that we often "register a continuity of action but a change of character," making it "sometimes slightly unclear who is doing what in the novel" and so allowing Dos Passos to dramatize "overlaps in his characters' fortunes." See Seed, *Cinematic Fictions*, 134.

41. Baldwin knows Ellen as Elaine, but the aural echo nevertheless rings out for the reader, because Ellen is the name used consistently by the narrator.

42. Shloss, *In Visible Light*, 148.

43. It is pertinent to note that Laura Mulvey acknowledges Ziegfeld's contribution to entrenching the woman "displayed as sexual object" as the *leitmotif* of erotic spectacle, in "Visual Pleasure and Narrative Cinema," in *Visual and Other Pleasures* (New York: Palgrave Macmillan, 2009), 19.

44. Casey, *Dos Passos*, 116, 115.

45. Henry James, *The American Scene* (London: Penguin, 1994), 11.

46. The song is "Easter Parade," and it debuted on Broadway in the 1933 revue "As Thousands Cheer."

47. This account follows David Mayer, "The Actress as Photographic Icon: From Early Photography to Early Film," in *The Cambridge Companion to the Actress*, ed. Maggie B. Gale and John Stokes (Cambridge: Cambridge University Press, 2007), 74–94.

48. Abigail Solomon-Godeau, "Legs of the Countess," *October* 39 (Winter 1986): 68–69.

49. Lawrence Senelick, "Eroticism in Early Theatrical Photography," *Theatre History Studies* 11 (1991): 1, 8; Elizabeth Anne McCauley, *A. A. E. Disdéri and the Carte de Visite Portrait Photograph* (New Haven, CT, and London: Yale University Press, 1985), 111.

50. Senelick, "Eroticism," 2.

51. Mulvey, "Visual Pleasure," 22; Walter Benjamin, "The Work of Art in the Age of Mechanical Reproduction," in *Illuminations*, ed. and intro. Hannah Arendt (New York: Schocken Books, 2007), 230–31.

52. Benjamin, "Work of Art," 230–31.

53. See Roland Marchand, *Advertising the American Dream: Making Way for Modernity, 1920–1940* (Berkeley: University of California Press, 1985), xxxi–xxii.

54. Paula E. Geyh, "From Cities of Things to Cities of Signs: Urban Spaces and Urban Subjects in *Sister Carrie* and *Manhattan Transfer*," *Twentieth Century Literature* 52.4 (2006): 433–34.

55. Rachel Bowlby, *Just Looking: Consumer Culture in Dreiser, Gissing, and Zola* (New York: Methuen, 1985), 32. On the Follies girl as mannequin and model, see Mizejewski, *Ziegfeld Girl*, 89–103.

56. Mizejewski, *Ziegfeld Girl*, 99; Mayer, "Actress as Photographic Icon," 90.

57. Senelick, "Eroticism," 1.

58. Charles Baudelaire, "The Painter of Modern Life," in *Baudelaire: Selected Writings on Art and Artists*, trans. P. E. Charvet (Cambridge: Cambridge University Press, 1981), 431.

59. Solomon-Godeau, "Legs of the Countess," 68.

60. Theodore Dreiser, *Sister Carrie* (Oxford: Oxford University Press, 1999), 419.

61. Ibid., 451.

62. Susan Sontag, *On Photography* (London: Penguin, 2008), 100.

63. Amy Conger, Introduction to *Edward Weston: The Form of the Nude* (London: Phaidon, 2005), 13.

64. See Nancy Newhall, ed., *The Daybooks of Edward Weston*, vol. 1 (Millerton, NY: Aperture 1961), 231, and Conger, Introduction, 12.

65. Philip Fisher, "Appearing and Disappearing in Public: Social Space in Late Nineteenth-Century Literature and Culture," in *Reconstructing American Literary History*, ed. Sacvan Bercovitch (Cambridge, MA: Harvard University Press, 1986), 177; Amy Kaplan, *The Social Construction of American Realism* (Chicago and London: University of Chicago Press, 1988), 7.

66. John Dos Passos, Review of *A Farewell to Arms*, by Ernest Hemingway, in *Major Nonfictional Prose*, 122.

67. John Dos Passos, Introduction to *Three Soldiers*, in *Major Nonfictional Prose*, 147–48.

68. The consignment of Dos Passos to the margins of modernist studies—in spite of his participation in a high-modernist aesthetic of technologized innovation that remains a structural principle in accounts of modernist writing—leads Linda Wagner to question whether we are somehow "embarrassed by" or "at odds, critically" with his work. In addressing this issue, Casey points to the alignment of the author with a "pejorative effeminacy" and to the "threat" posed by his writing as it "[appropriates] the feminine as a site for radicalist challenges." See Linda W. Wagner, "Dos Passos: Some Directions in the Criticism," *Resources for American Literary Study* 13 (August 1983): 204; Casey, *Dos Passos*, 4.

69. Andreas Huyssen, "Mass Culture as Woman: Modernism's Other," in *After the Great Divide: Modernism, Mass Culture, Postmodernism* (Bloomington and Indianapolis: Indiana University Press, 1986), 53, 55.

70. John Dos Passos, "The Writer as Technician," in *Major Nonfictional Prose*, 169. Tichi takes up the figure of the engineer as a model for Dos Passos's work, arguing that the engineer's "efficient, functional, component-part designs" provided a key example for writing that emulated the functional integration of the machine; see Tichi, *Shifting Gears*, 98.

71. Lisa Nanney, *John Dos Passos* (Chapel Hill: University of North Carolina, 1998), 156–57. Alfred Kazin was perhaps the first to describe Dos Passos's writing in these terms, referring to him in 1943 as "the first of the 'technological' novelists" in *On Native Grounds: An Interpretation of Modern American Prose Literature* (London: Jonathan Cape, 1943), 344.

72. Kracauer, "Mass Ornament," 75.

73. Gilbert W. Gabriel, "Taps!—A Requiem," *Vanity Fair*, August 1929, 32; cited in Dinerstein, *Swinging the Machine*, 196. See also Edmund Wilson's description of the "peculiar frigidity and purity" of the Follies girls, in *The American Earthquake: A Documentary of the Twenties and Thirties* (New York: Doubleday, 1958), 51.

74. Siegfried Kracauer, "Girls and Crisis," in *The Weimar Republic Sourcebook*, ed. Anton Kaes, Martin Jay, and Edward Dimendberg (Berkeley, California: University of California Press, 1994), 565.

75. Kracauer, "Mass Ornament," 79.

76. François Dagonet, *Étienne-Jules Marey: A Passion for the Trace*, trans. Robert Galeta with Jeanine Herman (New York: Zone, 1992), 12.

77. Felicia McCarren, *Dancing Machines: Choreographies of the Age of Mechanical Reproduction* (Stanford, CA: Stanford University Press, 2003), 132, 29.

78. Kracauer, "Mass Ornament," 75–76, 79. In fact, Kracauer discusses the fragmentation of the "whole" body that is concealed in the mass ornament's streamlined kineticism: "The Tiller Girls can no longer be reassembled into human beings after the fact. Their mass gymnastics are never performed by the fully preserved bodies, whose conditions defy rational understanding. Arms, thighs, and other segments are the smallest component parts of the composition." See ibid., 78.

79. McCarren, *Dancing Machines*, 130, 144.

80. Thorstein Veblen, *The Theory of the Leisure Class: An Economic Study of Institutions* (New York: Dover, 1994), 7, 8.

81. Mark Seltzer, *Bodies and Machines* (New York and London: Routledge, 1992), 100.

82. Ibid., 159.

83. Carey James Mickalites makes this point in "*Manhattan Transfer*, Spectacular Time, and the Outmoded," *Arizona Quarterly: A Journal of American Literature, Culture, and Theory* 67.4 (2011): 71–72.

84. Guy Debord, *Society of the Spectacle*, trans. Donald Nicholson-Smith (New York: Zone, 1995), 12. A number of scholars, including Mickalites and Geyh, have applied Debord's theory of the spectacle to *Manhattan Transfer*.

85. Seltzer, *Bodies and Machines*, 4, 5.

86. Seed, *Cinematic Fictions*, 133.

87. Isabelle Stengers, *Power and Invention: Situating Science*, trans. Paul Bains (Minneapolis: University of Minnesota Press, 1997), 38.

88. Christian Metz, "Photography and Fetish," *October* 34 (Autumn 1985): 84.

89. Michel de Certeau, *The Practice of Everyday Life* (Berkeley: University of California Press, 1984), 93, 97.

90. Ibid., 94.

91. Ibid., 97, 99; Michel Foucault, *Discipline and Punish: The Birth of the Prison*, trans. Alan Sheridan (New York: Vintage, 1995), 221. On the relevance of de Certeau's theory of walking to *Manhattan Transfer*, see Susan Keller's treatment of Ellen's nonsubversive tactics in "Compact Resistance: Public Powdering and *Flânerie* in the Modern City," *Women's Studies* 40 (2011): 306–307.

92. Siegfried Kracauer, "Travel and Dance," in *The Mass Ornament*, 71.

93. Charney, *Empty Moments*, 71.

94. de Certeau, *Practice of Everyday Life*, 92–93.

95. Ibid., 92.

96. Kracauer, "Mass Ornament," 77.

97. Peter Buse, "Stage Remains: Theatre Criticism and the Photographic Archive," *Journal of Dramatic Theory and Criticism* 12.1 (1997): 78.

98. On Kellerman's engagement with discourses of physical culture and ideal femininity, see Christine Schmidt, "Second Skin: Annette Kellerman, the Modern Swimsuit, and an
Australian Contribution to Global Fashion" (PhD diss., Queensland University of Technology,
2008), 160–64, 185–87, and Schmidt and Jinna Tay, "Undressing Kellerman, Uncovering
Broadhurst: The Modern Woman and 'Un-Australia,'" *Fashion Theory* 13.4 (2009): 490–92.

99. These discourses also underwrote the Taylorist notion of efficiency, which as
Suzanne Raitt has shown served as a crux not only for developments in the manufactur-
ing industry but in the projects of imperialism and eugenics. Linking low productivity
and "decadents, the unemployed, the 'inferior races,' and childless women" in the popular
imagination, the elimination of waste was taken up as a "moral crusade" and a measure of
racial and ethical superiority. See Raitt, "The Rhetoric of Efficiency in Early Modernism,"
Modernism/modernity 13.1 (2006): 836.

100. Keller, "Compact Resistance," 322.

101. Mizejewski, *Ziegfeld Girl*, 119–20.

102. Ibid., 110–11.

103. Leslie Fiedler, *Freaks: Myths and Images of the Secret Self* (New York: Simon and
Schuster, 1978), 137.

104. Richard Dyer, *White* (London: Routledge, 1997), 44, 45.

105. Ruth Frankenberg, "The Mirage of an Unmarked Whiteness," in *The Making and
Unmaking of Whiteness*, ed. Birgit Brander Rasmussen et al. (Durham, NC: Duke University
Press, 2001), 73, 81.

106. Ibid., 74.

107. Paula Rabinowitz, "Barbara Stanwyck's Anklet: The Other Shoe," in *Accessorizing
the Body: Habits of Being*, ed. Christini Giorcelli and Paula Rabinowitz (Minneapolis and
London: University of Minnesota Press, 2011), 185–208.

108. Martha Banta, "Coco, Zelda, Sara, Daisy, and Nicole: Accessories for New Ways of
Being a Woman," in *Accessorizing the Body*, ed. Giorcelli and Rabinowitz, 89.

109. Paul Petrovic, "'To Get to the Center': Recovering the Marginalized Woman in John
Dos Passos's *Manhattan Transfer*," *Studies in American Naturalism* 4.2 (2009): 152, 170.

110. Rosemarie Garland-Thompson, "The Politics of Staring: Visual Rhetorics of
Disability in Popular Photography," in *Disability Studies: Enabling the Humanities*, ed.
Garland-Thompson, Sharon L. Snyder, and Brenda Jo Brueggemann (New York: Modern
Language Association of America, 2002), 57.

111. Gertrude Barnum, "This Style: Six Twenty-Nine," in *Sealskin and Shoddy:
Working Women in American Labor Press Fiction, 1870–1920*, ed. Anne Schofield
(New York: Greenwood, 1988), 159–60.

112. Katherine Stubbs, "Mechanizing the Female: Discourse and Control in the Industrial
Economy," *differences: A Journal of Feminist Cultural Studies* 7.3 (1995): 141–42.

113. Ibid., 158–60.

Chapter 4

1. Susan Stanford Friedman, Introduction to *Joyce: The Return of the Repressed*, ed.
Friedman (Ithaca, NY, and London: Cornell University Press, 1993), 5.

2. Sigmund Freud, "Recollection, Repetition, and Working Through," in *Therapy and
Technique*, ed. Philip Rieff (New York: Collier Books, 1963), 157–66.

3. James A. Snead, "Repetition as a Figure of Black Culture," in *Black Literature and Literary Theory*, ed. Henry Louis Gates Jr. (New York: Methuen, 1984), 59–79.

4. Sigmund Freud, *The Interpretation of Dreams*, trans. James Strachey (New York: Avon, 1965), 563.

5. Susan Stanford Friedman, "(Self)Censorship and the Making of Joyce's Modernism," in *Joyce*, 22.

6. Ibid., 25–29.

7. John Dos Passos, *U.S.A.: The 42nd Parallel, Nineteen-Nineteen, The Big Money* (London: Lehmann, 1950), 584, 165.

8. Ibid., 1157, 1163.

9. The titles of both texts are a source of contention. The final typescript version of Fitzgerald's screenplay, revised on August 12, 1940, is titled "Cosmopolitan," but it was published under the title of *Babylon Revisited* in 1993. I retain Fitzgerald's title for the screenplay in this chapter, though I cite F. Scott Fitzgerald, *Babylon Revisited: The Screenplay*, intro. Budd Schulberg (New York: Carroll & Graf, 1993); all further references to this edition are given parenthetically in the text as *BR*. Although the unfinished novel was published as *The Last Tycoon* in 1941, the 1993 Cambridge edition, edited by Matthew J. Bruccoli, carried a new title: *The Love of the Last Tycoon*. I use the original title, agreeing with Milton Stern that the evidence of the holograph and typescript do not adequately support Bruccoli's change; see Stern, "On Editing Dead Modern Authors: Fitzgerald and *Trimalchio*," *The F. Scott Fitzgerald Society Newsletter* 10 (December 2000): 15, n.2. But, unless otherwise noted, I cite Bruccoli's edition, because of its special investment in the gestational nature of the unfinished novel: F. Scott Fitzgerald, *The Love of the Last Tycoon*, ed. Bruccoli (New York and London: Scribner, 2003); all further references to this edition are given parenthetically in the text as *LT*.

10. Michael Kaufman, *Textual Bodies: Modernism, Postmodernism, and Print* (Lewisberg, PA: Bucknell University Press, 1994), 14.

11. Friedman, "(Self)Censorship," 28.

12. Jani Scandura, *Down in the Dumps: Place, Modernity, American Depression* (Durham, NC, and London: Duke University Press, 2008), 220.

13. Mark Goble, *Beautiful Circuits: Modernism and the Mediated Life* (New York: Columbia University Press, 2010), 85.

14. See Laura Mulvey, "Visual Pleasure and Narrative Cinema," in *Visual and Other Pleasures* (New York: Palgrave Macmillan, 2009), 14–27, and *Death 24x a Second: Stillness and the Moving Image* (London: Reaktion Books, 2006), especially 67–84.

15. Garrett Stewart, *Between Film and Screen: Modernism's Photo Synthesis* (Chicago and London: University of Chicago Press, 1999), 7, 23, 266.

16. Ibid., 266.

17. Ibid., 23.

18. Thomas Schatz borrows the phrase "genius of the system" from André Bazin in *The Genius of the System: Hollywood Filmmaking in the Studio Era* (Minneapolis and London: University of Minnesota Press, 2010).

19. Richard C. Moreland, *Faulkner and Modernism: Rereading and Rewriting* (Madison: University of Wisconsin Press, 1989), 4–5, 20–21.

20. Karen Beckman, *Vanishing Women: Magic, Film, and Feminism* (Durham, NC, and London: Duke University Press, 2003), 134.

21. Claude Cahun, *Aveux non avenus*, in *Écrits*, ed. François Leperlier (Paris: Jean-Michel Place, 2002), 118; Claude Cahun, *Disavowals, or, Cancelled Confessions*, trans. Susan de Muth, ed. and intro. Jennifer Mundy (Cambridge, MA: MIT Press, 2007), 103.

22. Michael Nowlin, "'A Gentile's Tragedy': Bearing the Word About Hollywood in *The Love of the Last Tycoon*," *The F. Scott Fitzgerald Review* 2.1 (2003): 162.

23. F. Scott Fitzgerald, *The Last Tycoon*, ed. Edmund Wilson (London: Penguin, 2001), 191.

24. F. Scott Fitzgerald, letter to Zelda Fitzgerald, May 18, 1940, in *F. Scott Fitzgerald: A Life in Letters*, ed. Matthew J. Bruccoli and Judith S. Baughman (New York and London: Touchstone, 1994), 444.

25. F. Scott Fitzgerald, letter to Francis Scott Fitzgerald, winter 1919, in *Life in Letters*, 384.

26. F. Scott Fitzgerald, "Handle with Care," in *The Crack-Up*, ed. Edmund Wilson (New York: New Directions, 1945), 78.

27. Michel Mok, "The Other Side of Paradise, Scott Fitzgerald, 40, Engulfed in Despair," *New York Post*, September 25, 1936, in *F. Scott Fitzgerald in His Own Time: A Miscellany*, ed. Matthew J. Bruccoli and Jackson R. Bryer (Kent, OH: Kent State University Press, 1971), 294.

28. Edmund Wilson, *The Boys in the Back Room* (San Francisco: Colt, 1941), 56.

29. Tom Cerasulo, *Authors Out Here: Fitzgerald, West, Parker, and Schulberg* (Columbia, SC: University of South Carolina Press, 2010), 1. Cerasulo is an exception to the rule, approaching Fitzgerald's work in Hollywood as a site of negotiation with the "mechanical and communal art" he derided in *The Crack-Up*.

30. This follows Robert A. Martin, "Hollywood in Fitzgerald: After Paradise," in *The Short Stories of F. Scott Fitzgerald: New Approaches in Criticism*, ed. Jackson R. Bryer (Madison: University of Wisconsin Press, 1982), 128, 133. Fitzgerald's *Ledger*, from the period 1919–1938, is held in the Matthew J. and Arlyn Bruccoli Collection of F. Scott Fitzgerald, Digital Collections Department, University of South Carolina, 2013, http://library.sc.edu/digital/collections/fitzledger.html.

31. F. Scott Fitzgerald, letter to Francis Scott Fitzgerald, July 7, 1938, in *The Letters of F. Scott Fitzgerald*, ed. Andrew Turnbull (New York: Scribner's, 1963), 33.

32. In fact, Fitzgerald had already taken short trips to Hollywood in 1927 and 1931; during the first visit, he and Zelda did a screen test—an unsuccessful one—for a film adaptation of *This Side of Paradise*. In 1937, too, Fitzgerald seriously applied himself to the art and trade of screenwriting: in his first few months under contract at MGM, he watched dozens of the studio's films and compiled hundreds of file cards detailing their plot lines and conventions. See Tom Dardis, *Some Time in the Sun* (London: André Deutsch, 1976), 41.

33. Gautam Kundu, *Fitzgerald and the Influence of Film: The Language of Cinema in the Novels* (Jefferson, North Carolina and London: McFarland and Company, 2008), 29.

34. John Dos Passos, Introduction to *Three Soldiers*, in *The Major Nonfictional Prose*, ed. Donald Pizer (Detroit, MI: Wayne State University Press, 1988), 147–48.

35. George Jean Nathan, "Theater," *Scribner's Magazine* 102.5 (1937): 66; cited in Richard Fine, *West of Eden: Writers in Hollywood, 1928-1940* (Washington, DC, and London: Smithsonian Institution Press, 1993), 2.

36. F. Scott Fitzgerald, letter to Francis Scott Fitzgerald, July 1937, in *Life in Letters*, 331.

37. Schatz, *Genius of the System*, 47.

38. Jonathan Veitch, "Reading Hollywood," *Salmagundi* 126/127 (2000): 207.

39. Jack Stillinger, *Multiple Authorship and the Myth of Solitary Genius* (New York and Oxford: Oxford University Press, 1991).

40. Matthew J. Bruccoli, *Scott and Ernest: The Authority of Failure and the Authority of Success* (New York: Random House, 1978), 138.

41. Winston Wheeler Dixon, *The Cinematic Vision of F. Scott Fitzgerald* (Ann Arbor: University of Michigan Research Press, 1986), 4, 1. This view is seriously complicated by Fitzgerald's track record in Hollywood. Although he worked on six different film projects during his eighteen months under contract at MGM, Fitzgerald received screen credit for only one, *Three Comrades*. His other projects were *A Yank at Oxford, Infidelity, The Women, Madame Curie*, and *Marie Antoinette*. The first of these was a patching job; the last of these Fitzgerald worked on for only a few days. In the case of *Infidelity*, Fitzgerald was initially put on to the script alone, but the film's director, Hunt Stromberg, became frustrated with his slow progress and reallocated Fitzgerald to *The Women*, on which he was teamed first with Sidney Franklin, and then with Donald Ogden Stewart. But Stromberg remained unsatisfied with Fitzgerald's work, and reassigned him to collaborate with Franklin on *Madame Curie*. Fitzgerald was halfway through drafting this script when his contract was terminated. See Dardis, *Some Time*, 26–77.

42. Fine, *West of Eden*, 159.

43. Stillinger, *Multiple Authorship*, 174, 163.

44. Jerome Christensen, *America's Corporate Art: The Studio Authorship of Hollywood Motion Pictures* (Stanford, CA: Stanford University Press, 2012), 14, 13.

45. Fitzgerald describes the work on *Gone with the Wind* in a February 25, 1939, letter to Maxwell Perkins, in *Dear Scott/Dear Max: The Fitzgerald–Perkins Correspondence*, ed. John Kuehl and Jackson R. Bryer (New York: Scribner's, 1971), 255.

46. See Jerome McGann, *The Textual Condition* (Princeton, NJ: Princeton University Press, 1991), and John Bryant, *The Fluid Text: A Theory of Revision and Editing for Book and Screen* (Ann Arbor: University of Michigan Press, 2002).

47. Steven Price, *The Screenplay: Authorship, Theory and Criticism* (London: Palgrave Macmillan, 2010), 101.

48. Leo Bersani, "I Can Dream, Can't I?" *Critical Inquiry* 40.1 (2013): 30.

49. Michel Foucault, "What is an Author?" in *The Foucault Reader*, ed. Paul Rabinow (New York: Pantheon, 1984), 101.

50. Philip Cohen, "Is There a Text in This Discipline? Textual Scholarship and American Literary Studies," *American Literary History* 8.4 (1996): 737.

51. The manuscripts of *The Last Tycoon* are held in the F. Scott Fitzgerald Papers, Series 1: Writings, 1910–1989, Boxes 7a, 7b, 7c, and 8a, Department of Rare Books and Special Collections, Princeton University Library, Princeton, NJ, and are published as *F. Scott Fitzgerald Manuscripts V: The Last Tycoon: Manuscript and Revised Typescript for the First 17 Episodes, With the Author's Plans and Notes*, 3 vols., ed. Matthew J. Bruccoli (New York and London: Garland, 1990–1991).

52. Bruccoli, preface, vii, xiv, xiii.

53. Matthew J. Bruccoli, "A Note on the Title," in Fitzgerald, *Love of the Last Tycoon*, xx.

54. Stern, "On Editing," 10.

55. Steve McCaffery, *Prior to Meaning: The Protosemantic and Poetics* (Evanston, IL: Northwestern University Press, 2001), 207.

56. Roland Barthes, *Camera Lucida*, trans. Richard Howard (London: Vintage Books, 2000), 96.

57. Bryant, *Fluid Text*, 12.

58. Carolyn Steedman, *Dust* (Manchester, UK: Manchester University Press, 2001), 164. Editorial self-effacement has a long pedigree. Maxwell Perkins, Fitzgerald's editor and, indeed, one of the most influential editors of the modernist period, once pronounced that the editor should be a "little dwarf on the shoulder of a great general"—or, in a formulation that reveals more fully the gendered imperatives that distinguish authors from editors, a "handmaiden." See A. Scott Berg, *Max Perkins: Editor of Genius* (New York: Dutton, 1978), 123, 6. Stillinger discusses some of the pragmatic reasons for editorial self-effacement in *Multiple Authorship*, 150–55.

59. Steedman, *Dust*, 150.

60. Harold Ober, record of a telephone call with Sheilah Graham, cited in Dardis, *Some Time*, 76.

61. Roland Barthes, *The Pleasure of the Text*, trans. Richard Miller (New York: Hill and Wang, 1975), 9–10.

62. This follows Sean Braune, "How to Analyze Texts That Were Burned, Lost, Fragmented, or Never Written," *symplokē* 21.1–2 (2013): 239–55.

63. Ibid., 252, 248. Braune glosses Jacques Derrida, "Fifty-Two Aphorisms for a Foreword," in *Psyche: Inventions of the Other*, vol. 2, ed. Peggy Kamuf and Elizabeth Rottenberg (Stanford, CA: Stanford University Press, 2008), 117–26, and Jean Baudrillard, *Fragments: Conversations with François L'Yvonnet*, trans. Chris Turner (London: Routledge, 2004), 21–28.

64. Braune, "How to Analyze," 241.

65. The question of whether the screenplay can be considered a work of art is a live one. Against Noël Carroll's view, expounded, for example, in *The Philosophy of Motion Pictures* (London: Blackwell, 2008), Ted Nannicelli argues for the aesthetic value of the screenplay in *A Philosophy of the Screenplay* (New York: Routledge, 2013).

66. Price, *Screenplay*, 53.

67. Pier Paolo Pasolini, "The Screenplay as a 'Structure That Wants to be Another Structure,'" in *Heretical Empiricism*, ed. Louise K. Barnett, trans. Ben Lawton and Louise K. Barnett (Bloomington and Indianapolis: Indiana University Press, 1988), 189, 188.

68. F. Scott Fitzgerald, "Notebook," in *Crack-Up*, 177.

69. F. Scott Fitzgerald, letter to John Peale Bishop, ca. August 9, 1925, in *Life in Letters*, 126.

70. F. Scott Fitzgerald, letter to Zelda Fitzgerald, November 2, 1940, cited in Matthew J. Bruccoli, *The Last of the Novelists: F. Scott Fitzgerald and* The Last Tycoon (Carbondale: Southern Illinois University Press, 1977), 38.

71. Maurice Blanchot, *The Writing of the Disaster: L'écriture du désastre*, trans. Ann Smock (Lincoln: University of Nebraska Press, 1995), 33.

72. Mitchell Breitwieser, "Jazz Fractures: F. Scott Fitzgerald and Epochal Representation," *American Literary History* 12.3 (2000): 374, 375.

73. Sergio Perosa, *The Art of F. Scott Fitzgerald*, trans. Charles Matz (Ann Arbor: University of Michigan Press, 1965), 151.

74. Dixon, *Cinematic Vision*, 87.

75. F. Scott Fitzgerald, "Notes: Stahr and Kathleen," in *The Last Tycoon*, ed. Wilson, 182.

76. André Bazin, *What is Cinema?*, vol. 1, trans. Hugh Gray (Berkeley: University of California Press, 1974), 151.

77. Charles Chaplin, *My Autobiography* (New York: Simon and Shuster, 1964), 306–307.

78. Gertrude Stein, "Portraits and Repetition," in *Lectures in America*, ed. Wendy Steiner (London: Virago, 1998), 198, 177.

79. Ellen E. Berry, "Modernism/Mass Culture/Postmodernism: The Case of Gertrude Stein," in *Rereading the New: A Backward Glance at Modernism*, ed. Kevin J. H. Dettmar (Ann Arbor: University of Michigan Press, 1992), 174.

80. Julian Murphet, "Gertrude Stein's Machinery of Perception," in *Literature and Visual Technologies: Writing After Cinema*, ed. Murphet and Lydia Rainford (Hampshire, UK, and New York: Palgrave Macmillan, 2003), 77–78.

81. Scandura, *Down in the Dumps*, 221, 220.

82. Gertrude Stein, "Composition as Explanation," in *Selected Writings of Gertrude Stein*, ed. and intro. Carl Van Vechten (New York: Vintage, 1972), 518.

83. Gertrude Stein, "How Writing Is Written," in *How Writing Is Written: Volume II of the Previously Uncollected Writings of Gertrude Stein*, ed. Robert Bartlett Haas (Los Angeles: Black Sparrow Press, 1974), 158.

84. Gertrude Stein, *Paris France* (London: B. T. Batsford, 1940), 61.

85. Goble, *Beautiful Circuits*, 86, 89.

86. Michael North, *Reading 1922: A Return to the Scene of the Modern* (New York and Oxford: Oxford University Press, 1999), 171.

87. Gertrude Stein, *A Play Called Not and Now*, in *Last Operas and Plays*, ed. Carl Van Vechten (Baltimore: Johns Hopkins University Press, 1995), 422.

88. Gertrude Stein, *The Autobiography of Alice B. Toklas* (Stockholm and London: Zephyr Books, 1947), 50. "Metropolitan sociality" is Sara Blair's term in "Home Truths: Gertrude Stein, 27 Rue de Fleurus, and the Place of the Avant-Garde," *American Literary History* 12.3 (2000): 433.

89. Stein, *Autobiography*, 97.

90. Goble, *Beautiful Circuits*, 93.

91. Stein, *Autobiography*, 132, 97.

92. Christensen, *America's Corporate Art*, 4–5.

93. See Ann Chisholm, "Missing Persons and Bodies of Evidence," *Camera Obscura* 15.1 (2000): 123–43.

94. This follows Kermit W. Moyer, "Fitzgerald's Two Unfinished Novels: The Count and the Tycoon in Spenglerian Perspective," *Contemporary Literature* 15.2 (1974): 254.

95. Beckman, *Vanishing Women*, 135.

96. Judith Brown, *Glamour in Six Dimensions: Modernism and the Radiance of Form* (Ithaca, NY, and London: Cornell University Press, 2009), 103.

97. Richard Dyer, *Stars* (London: British Film Institute, 1998), 17.

98. Eduardo Cadava, *Words of Light: Theses on the Photography of History* (Princeton, NJ: Princeton University Press, 1997), 23–30.

99. Régis Durand, "How to See (Photographically)," in *Fugitive Images: From Photography to Video*, ed. Patrice Petro (Bloomington: Indiana University Press, 1995), 147; the second quote is from Thierry De Duve, "Time Exposure and Snapshot: The Photograph as Paradox," *October* 5 (Summer 1978): 121.

100. This follows Cadava, *Words of Light*, 13.

101. Ann Anlin Cheng, *Second Skin: Josephine Baker and the Modern Surface* (Oxford: Oxford University Press, 2011), 116. In reading Baker's studio photographs, Cheng

articulates a different quality of light to that emphasized by Richard Dyer, for whom Hollywood's pearlized lighting effects in Hollywood reflect ideals of white racial purity (see Richard Dyer, *White* [London: Routledge, 1997], 82–144, and *Heavenly Bodies: Film Stars and Society* [New York: St. Martin's, 1986], 19–66). For Cheng, the "hard sheen" of Baker's surfaces is somewhat aligned with the "shellacked beauty" of Garbo and other Hollywood celebrities. Given the rupturing effects of Kathleen's image, I see her bathed in this second kind of light, which provides evidence of female objectification and acts as a kind of protective "covering." See Cheng, *Second Skin*, 111–21.

102. Stuart Ewen, *All Consuming Images: The Politics of Style in Contemporary Culture* (New York: Basic Books, 1988), 89.

103. Roland Barthes, "The Face of Garbo," in *Mythologies* (New York: Hill and Wang, 1972), 56–57.

104. Brown, *Glamour*, 101.

105. Steven Jacobs, *Framing Pictures: Film and the Visual Arts* (Edinburgh: Edinburgh University Press, 2011), 139.

106. Mary Ann Doane, "Scale and the Negotiation of 'Real' and 'Unreal' Space in the Cinema," in *Realism and the Audiovisual Media*, ed. Lúcia Nagib and Cecília Mello (New York: Palgrave MacMillan, 2009), 71; Beckman, *Vanishing Women*, 135.

107. Doane, "Scale," 71, 77.

108. Susan Stewart, *On Longing: Narratives of the Miniature, the Gigantic, the Souvenir, the Collection* (Durham, NC: Duke University Press, 1993), 69, 71.

109. Tom Gunning, "The Cinema of Attractions: Early Film, Its Spectator and the Avant-Garde," *Wide Angle* 8.3–4 (1986): 65.

110. Doane, "Scale," 63–64.

111. Béla Balázs, *Theory of Film: Character and Growth of a New Art*, trans. Edith Bone (New York: Dover, 1970), 58.

112. See Raymond Bellour, "The Pensive Spectator," in *The Cinematic*, ed. David Campany (Cambridge, MA: MIT Press, 2007), 119–23.

113. Scandura, *Down in the Dumps*, 200–201.

114. Michel Chion, *The Voice in Cinema*, ed. and trans. Claudia Gorbman (New York: Columbia University Press, 1999), 125, 130.

115. Rick Altman, "Moving Lips: Cinema as Ventriloquism," *Yale French Studies* 60 (1980): 69.

116. Gertrude Stein, "I Came and Here I Am," in *How Writing is Written*, 68.

117. Gertrude Stein, *Everybody's Autobiography* (New York: Vintage, 1973), 288–89.

118. Susan McCabe, *Cinematic Modernism* (Cambridge: Cambridge University Press, 2005), 61.

119. Altman, "Moving Lips," 74.

120. See Jacques Derrida, " . . . That Dangerous Supplement," in *Of Grammatology*, trans. Gayatri Chakravorty Spivak (Baltimore: Johns Hopkins University Press, 1976), 141–64.

121. Breitwieser, "Jazz Fractures," 374, 375.

122. Sergei Eisenstein, *Nonindifferent Nature: Film and the Structure of Things*, trans. Herbert Marshal (Cambridge: Cambridge University Press, 1987), 27.

123. Altman, "Moving Lips," 69.

124. See Bruccoli, *Last of the Novelists*, 153.

125. Breitwieser, "Jazz Fractures," 373, 372.

126. F. Scott Fitzgerald, letter to Kenneth Littauer, September 29, 1939; cited in Bruccoli, *Last of the Novelists*, 29–30.

127. Specifically, and in order, from February to September 1939 Fitzgerald worked on *Winter Carnival* for United Artists, *Air Raid* for Paramount, *Open That Door* for Universal, *Everything Happens at Night* for Twentieth-Century Fox, and *Raffles* for Samuel Goldwyn.

128. This account follows Aaron Latham, *Crazy Sundays: F. Scott Fitzgerald in Hollywood* (London: Secker and Warburg, 1972), 238–40.

129. Even though the Epstein twins were initially hired by Cowan to rewrite the text of "Cosmopolitan," the 1954 film is more properly derived from "Babylon Revisited" than Fitzgerald's 1940 screenplay. The film only loosely follows the plot and characterization of either text, but it bears a far closer resemblance to Fitzgerald's story and includes key lines of dialogue from it that are absent in the screenplay.

130. Dardis, *Some Time*, 70.

131. F. Scott Fitzgerald, "Babylon Revisited," in *The Short Stories of F. Scott Fitzgerald: A New Collection*, ed. Matthew J. Bruccoli (New York: Scribner's, 1989), 620.

132. Ibid., 628, 633.

133. Moreland, *Faulkner and Modernism*, 4, 5.

134. Ibid., 20–21.

135. Gertrude Stein, letter to F. Scott Fitzgerald, May 22, 1925, in Fitzgerald, *Crack-Up*, 308.

136. F. Scott Fitzgerald, "One Hundred False Starts," in *Afternoon of an Author: A Selection of Uncollected Stories and Essays* (New York: Scribner, 1957), 132.

137. Budd Schulberg, Introduction to *Babylon Revisited: The Screenplay*, by F. Scott Fitzgerald (New York: Carroll & Graf, 1993), 12–13.

138. Fitzgerald, "Babylon Revisited," 628.

139. Michael North, *Camera Works: Photography and the Twentieth-Century Word* (Oxford: Oxford University Press, 2005), 135, 140.

140. Claude Lévi-Strauss, *The Savage Mind* (Chicago: University of Chicago Press, 1966), 23–24; Goble, *Beautiful Circuits*, 91.

141. Raymond Bellour, "Hitchcock, The Enunciator," trans. Bertrand Augst and Hilary Radner, *Camera Obscura* 2 (Fall 1977): 83.

142. Mary Ann Doane, *Femmes Fatales* (New York: Routledge, 1991), 25–26.

143. Altman, "Moving Lips," 69–70.

144. Kaja Silverman, *The Acoustic Mirror: The Female Voice in Psychoanalysis and Cinema* (Bloomington and Indianapolis: Indiana University Press, 1988), 164, 45.

145. Ibid., 164, 165.

146. Stephen Heath, *Questions of Cinema* (Bloomington: Indiana University Press, 1981), 55.

147. Dixon, *Cinematic Vision*, 65.

148. F. Scott Fitzgerald, Author's Note to "Cosmopolitan" ("Babylon Revisited"), in F. Scott Fitzgerald Papers, Series 1: Writings, 1910–1989, Moving Picture Scripts, Box 30b, Department of Rare Books and Special Collections, Princeton University Library, Princeton, NJ.

149. Altman, "Moving Lips," 73, 74.

150. Jacques Lacan, "Function and Field of Speech and Language in Psychoanalysis," in *Écrits: A Selection*, trans. Alan Sheridan (New York: Norton, 1977), 86.

151. Silverman, *Acoustic Mirror*, 43–44.

152. Stewart, *Between Film and Screen*, 306–307.

153. Ibid., 308–309.

154. F. Scott Fitzgerald, letter to Zelda Fitzgerald, September 21, 1940, in *Letters*, 124–25.

155. F. Scott Fitzgerald, letter to Zelda Fitzgerald, September 14, 1940, in *Life in Letters*, 464.

156. Fitzgerald, *The Last Tycoon*, ed. Wilson, 193, 196.

CODA

1. Lincoln Kirstein, "Photographs of America: Walker Evans," in *American Photographs*, by Walker Evans (New York: Museum of Modern Art, 1988), 194, 198.

2. Ibid., 199, 194.

3. Ibid., 200.

4. Leslie Katz, "Interview with Walker Evans," *Art in America* 59.2 (1971): 87.

5. Kirstein, "Photographs," 198.

6. Alan Trachtenberg, *Reading American Photographs: Images as History, Mathew Brady to Walker Evans* (New York: Hill and Wang, 1989), 259.

7. Kirstein, "Photographs," 199.

8. Allan Sekula, "The Body and the Archive," *October* 39 (Winter 1986): 64, 59. In recent years, scholars have begun to recognize the abstract and self-reflexive elements of Evans's photography—which are obscured by conventional understandings of his documentary style—as well as his contributions to avant-garde art practice in the 1930s. See Jeff Allred, *American Modernism and Depression Documentary* (Oxford: Oxford University Press, 2010), 111–16; and Hugh Davis, "'Syncopations of Chance': *Let Us Now Praise Famous Men* as Surrealist Ethnography," in *The Making of James Agee* (Knoxville: University of Tennessee Press, 2008), 105–98.

9. Trachtenberg, *Reading*, 260.

10. Susan Sontag, *On Photography* (London: Penguin, 2008), 111.

11. Elza Adamowicz, "Monsters in Surrealism: Hunting the Human-Headed Bombyx," in *Modernism and the European Unconscious*, ed. Peter Collier and Judy Davies (Cambridge: Polity Press, 1990), 297.

12. See Gilles Deleuze and Félix Guattari, *A Thousand Plateaus: Capitalism and Schizophrenia*, trans. Brian Massumi (Minneapolis: University of Minnesota Press, 1987), 167–91.

13. This is the argument James Goodwin makes about "Minstrel Showbill, 1936," an image in *American Photographs* that is similar to "Torn Movie Poster," in *Modern American Grotesque: Literature and Photography* (Columbus: Ohio State University Press, 2009), 36–37.

14. Roland Barthes, *Camera Lucida: Reflections on Photography*, trans. Richard Howard (London: Vintage, 2000), 115.

15. Ibid., 116–17.

Works Cited

Abel, Elizabeth, *Signs of the Times: The Visual Politics of Jim Crow* (Berkeley: University of California Press, 2010).

Abel, Elizabeth, "Skin, Flesh, and the Affective Wrinkles of Civil Rights Photography," in *Feeling Photography*, ed. Elspeth H. Brown and Thy Phu (Durham, NC, and London: Duke University Press, 2014), 93–123.

Adamowicz, Elza, "Monsters in Surrealism: Hunting the Human-Headed Bombyx," in *Modernism and the European Unconscious*, ed. Peter Collier and Judy Davies (Cambridge, UK: Polity Press, 1990), 283–302.

Ades, Dawn, "Surrealism, Male-Female," in *Surrealism: Desire Unbounded*, ed. Jennifer Mundy (Princeton, NJ: Princeton University Press, 2001), 171–202.

Adorno, Theodor, *Negative Dialectics*, trans. E. B. Ashton (New York: Continuum, 1987).

Aldington, Richard, "The Art of Poetry," *Dial* 69 (1920): 166–80.

Alexander, Elizabeth, *The Black Interior* (Saint Paul, MN: Graywolf, 2004).

Allred, Jeff, *American Modernism and Depression Documentary* (Oxford: Oxford University Press, 2010).

Altman, Rick, "Moving Lips: Cinema as Ventriloquism," *Yale French Studies* 60 (1980): 67–79.

Aragon, Louis, and André Breton, "Le cinquantenaire de l'hystérie, 1878–1928," *La révolution surréaliste* 11, March 15, 1928, in *What is Surrealism? Selected Writings*, ed. Franklin Rosemount (New York: Monad Press, 1978), 20–22.

Armstrong, Carol M., *Scenes in a Library: Reading the Photograph in the Book, 1843–1875* (Cambridge, MA: MIT Press, 1998).

Armstrong, Nancy, *Fiction in the Age of Photography: The Legacy of British Realism* (Cambridge, MA: Harvard University Press, 1999).

Awkward, Michael, *Negotiating Difference: Race, Gender, and the Politics of Positionality* (Chicago: University of Chicago Press, 1995).

Baker, George, "Photography's Expanded Field," in *Still Moving: Between Cinema and Photography*, ed. Karen Beckman and Jean Ma (Durham, NC: Duke University Press, 2008), 175–88.

Baker, Houston A. Jr., and Dana D. Nelson, "Violence, the Body and 'The South,'" *American Literature* 73.2 (2001): 231–44.

Bakhtin, Mikhail, *Rabelais and His World*, trans. Helene Iswolsky (Cambridge, MA: MIT Press, 1968).

Balázs, Béla, *Theory of Film: Character and Growth of a New Art*, trans. Edith Bone (New York: Dover, 1970).

Banta, Martha, "Coco, Zelda, Sara, Daisy, and Nicole: Accessories for New Ways of Being a Woman," in *Accessorizing the Body: Habits of Being*, ed. Christini Giorcelli and Paula Rabinowitz (Minneapolis and London: University of Minnesota Press, 2011), 82–107.

Barnum, Gertrude, "This Style: Six Twenty-Nine," in *Sealskin and Shoddy: Working Women in American Labor Press Fiction, 1870–1920*, ed. Anne Schofield (New York: Greenwood, 1988), 159–60.

Barthes, Roland, "The Face of Garbo," in *Mythologies*, trans. John Cape (New York: Hill and Wang, 1972), 56–57.

Barthes, Roland, *The Pleasure of the Text*, trans. Richard Miller (New York: Hill and Wang, 1975).

Barthes, Roland, "The Third Meaning: Research Notes on Some Eisenstein Stills," in *Image-Music-Text*, trans. Stephen Heath (London: Fontana, 1977), 52–69.

Barthes, Roland, *Camera Lucida: Reflections on Photography*, trans. Richard Howard (London: Vintage, 2000).

Baudelaire, Charles, "The Painter of Modern Life," in *Baudelaire: Selected Writings on Art and Artists*, trans. P. E. Charvet (Cambridge: Cambridge University Press, 1981), 390–436.

Baudrillard, Jean, *Seduction*, trans. Brian Singer (New York: St. Martin's Press, 1990).

Baudrillard, Jean, *Fragments: Conversations with François L'Yvonnet*, trans. Chris Turner (London: Routledge, 2004).

Bazin, André, *What is Cinema?*, vol. 1, trans. Hugh Gray (Berkeley: University of California Press, 1974).

Beach, Joseph Warren, "*Manhattan Transfer*: Collectivism and Abstract Composition," in *Dos Passos, the Critics, and the Writer's Intentions*, ed. Allen Belkind (Carbondale: Southern Illinois University Press, 1971), 54–69.

Beckman, Karen, *Vanishing Women: Magic, Film, and Feminism* (Durham, NC, and London: Duke University Press, 2003).

Beckman, Karen, "Nothing to Say: The War on Terror and the Mad Photography of Roland Barthes," in *On Writing With Photography*, ed. Karen Beckman and Liliane Weissberg (Minneapolis and London: University of Minnesota Press, 2013), 297–330.

Beckman, Karen, and Jean Ma, Introduction to *Still Moving: Between Cinema and Photography*, ed. Beckman and Ma (Durham, NC: Duke University Press, 2008), 1–22.

Beckman, Karen, and Jean Ma, eds., *Still Moving: Between Cinema and Photography* (Durham, NC: Duke University Press, 2008).

Beckman, Karen, and Liliane Weissberg, Introduction to *On Writing With Photography*, ed. Beckman and Weissberg (Minneapolis and London: University of Minnesota Press, 2013), ix–xvii.

Beckman, Karen, and Liliane Weissberg, eds., *On Writing With Photography* (Minneapolis and London: University of Minnesota Press, 2013).

Bell, Bernard, *The Contemporary African American Novel: Its Folk Roots and Modern Literary Branches* (Amherst: University of Massachusetts Press, 2004).

Bellour, Raymond, "Hitchcock, The Enunciator," trans. Bertrand Augst and Hilary Radner, *Camera Obscura* 2 (Fall 1977): 67–92.

Bellour, Raymond, "The Pensive Spectator," in *The Cinematic*, ed. David Campany (Cambridge, MA: MIT Press, 2007), 119–23.

Benjamin, Walter, *The Arcades Project*, ed. Rolf Tiedemann, trans. Howard Eiland and Kevin McLaughlin (Cambridge, MA Harvard University Press, 1999).

Benjamin, Walter, "N [Theoretics of Knowledge; Theory of Progress]," *Philosophical Forum* 15.1–2 (1983–1984): 1–40.

Benjamin, Walter, "The Work of Art in the Age of Mechanical Reproduction," in *Illuminations: Essays and Reflections*, ed. and intro. Harrah Arendt, trans. Harry Zohn (New York: Schocken Books, 2007), 217–52.

Berg, A. Scott, *Max Perkins: Editor of Genius* (New York: Dutton, 1978).

Bergson, Henri, *Creative Evolution*, trans. Arthur Mitchell (New York: Henry Holt and Company, 1911).

Berne, Rebecca Emily, "Regionalism, Modernism, and the American Short Story Cycle" (PhD diss., Yale University, 2007).

Berry, Ellen E., "Modernism/Mass Culture/Postmodernism: The Case of Gertrude Stein," in *Rereading the New: A Backward Glance at Modernism*, ed. Kevin J. H. Dettmar (Ann Arbor: University of Michigan Press, 1992), 167–90.

Bersani, Leo, "I Can Dream, Can't I?," *Critical Inquiry* 40.1 (2013): 25–39.

Bibby, Michael, "The Disinterested and Fine: New Negro Renaissance Poetry and the Racial Formation of Modernist Studies," *Modernism/modernity* 20.3 (2013): 485–501.

Blackmer, Corinne E., "African Masks and the Arts of Passing in Gertrude Stein's 'Melanctha' and Nella Larsen's *Passing*," *Journal of the History of Sexuality* 4.2 (1993): 230–63.

Blair, Sara, "Home Truths: Gertrude Stein, 27 Rue de Fleurus, and the Place of the Avant-Garde," *American Literary History* 12.3 (2000): 417–37.

Blair, Sara, *Harlem Crossroads: Black Writers and the Photograph in the Twentieth Century* (Princeton, NJ: Princeton University Press, 2007).

Blanchot, Maurice, *The Writing of the Disaster: L'écriture du désastre*, trans. Ann Smock (Lincoln: University of Nebraska Press, 1995).

Blanchot, Maurice, "The Song of the Sirens: The Experience of Proust," in *The Book to Come*, trans. Charlotte Mandell (Stanford, CA: Stanford University Press, 2003), 11–25.

Bourdieu, Pierre, *The Field of Cultural Production: Essays on Art and Literature* (Cambridge, UK: Polity Press, 1993).

Bowlby, Rachel, *Just Looking: Consumer Culture in Dreiser, Gissing, and Zola* (New York: Methuen, 1985).

Braun, Marta, "Muybridge's Scientific Fictions," *Studies in Visual Communication* 10.3 (1984): 2–21.

Braune, Sean, "How to Analyze Texts That Were Burned, Lost, Fragmented, or Never Written," *symplokē* 21.1–2 (2013): 239–55.

Breitwieser, Mitchell, "Jazz Fractures: F. Scott Fitzgerald and Epochal Representation," *American Literary History* 12.3 (2000): 359–81.

Brennan, Marcia, *Painting Gender, Constructing Theory: The Alfred Stieglitz Circle and American Formalist Aesthetics* (Cambridge, MA: MIT Press, 2001).

Breton, André, *L'Amour fou* (Paris: Gallimard, 1937).

Breton, André, "Manifesto of Surrealism," in *Manifestoes of Surrealism*, trans. Richard Seaver and Helen R. Lane (Ann Arbor: University of Michigan Press, 2007), 1–47.

Brewster, Ben, "Periodization of Early Cinema," in *American Cinema's Transitional Era: Audiences, Institutions, Practices*, ed. Charlie Keil and Shelley Stamp (Berkeley: University of California Press, 2004), 66–75.

Bridgman, Richard, *Gertrude Stein in Pieces* (New York: Oxford University Press, 1971).

Brinkmeyer, Robert H. Jr., "Wasted Talent, Wasted Art: The Literary Career of Jean Toomer," *The Southern Quarterly* 20.1 (1981): 75–84.

Brown, Bill, *A Sense of Things: The Object Matter of American Literature* (Chicago and London: University of Chicago Press, 2003).

Brown, Elspeth H., and Thy Phu, eds., *Feeling Photography* (Durham, NC, and London: Duke University Press, 2014).

Brown, Elspeth H., and Thy Phu, Introduction to *Feeling Photography*, ed. Brown and Phu (Durham, NC, and London: Duke University Press, 2014), 1–25.

Brown, Judith, *Glamour in Six Dimensions: Modernism and the Radiance of Form* (Ithaca, NY, and London: Cornell University Press, 2009).

Bruccoli, Matthew J., *The Last of the Novelists: F. Scott Fitzgerald and* The Last Tycoon (Carbondale: Southern Illinois University Press, 1977).

Bruccoli, Matthew J., *Scott and Ernest: The Authority of Failure and the Authority of Success* (New York: Random House, 1978).

Bruccoli, Matthew J., and Jackson R. Bryer, eds., *F. Scott Fitzgerald in His Own Time: A Miscellany* (Kent, OH: Kent State University Press, 1971).

Bryant, John, *The Fluid Text: A Theory of Revision and Editing for Book and Screen* (Ann Arbor: University of Michigan Press, 2002).

Burrows, Stuart, *A Familiar Strangeness: American Fiction and the Language of Photography, 1839–1945* (Athens and London: University of Georgia Press, 2008).

Buse, Peter, "Stage Remains: Theater Criticism and the Photographic Archive," *Journal of Dramatic Theory and Criticism* 12.1 (1997): 77–96.

Butler, Judith, *Bodies That Matter: On the Discursive Limits of "Sex"* (New York: Routledge, 1993).

Butler, Judith, "Torture and the Ethics of Photography: Thinking With Sontag," in *Frames of War: When is Life Grievable?* (London: Verso, 2009), 63–100.

Cadava, Eduardo, *Words of Light: Theses on the Photography of History* (Princeton, NJ: Princeton University Press, 1997).

Cadava, Eduardo, "Nadar's Photographopolis," introduction to *When I Was a Photographer*, by Félix Nadar, trans. Cadava and Liana Theodoratou (Cambridge, MA: MIT Press, 2015), ix–xlviii.

Cahun, Claude, *Aveux non avenus*, in *Écrits*, ed. François Leperlier (Paris: Jean-Michel Place, 2002).

Cahun, Claude, *Disavowals, or, Cancelled Confessions*, trans. Susan de Muth, ed. and intro. Jennifer Mundy (Cambridge, MA: MIT Press, 2007).

Campany, David, *Photography and Cinema* (London: Reaktion Books, 2008).

Carroll, Anne Elizabeth, *Word, Image, and the New Negro: Representation and Identity in the Harlem Renaissance* (Bloomington: Indiana University Press, 2005).

Carroll, Noël, *The Philosophy of Motion Pictures* (London: Blackwell, 2008).

Caruth, Cathy, *Unclaimed Experience: Trauma, Narrative, and History* (Baltimore: Johns Hopkins University Press, 1996).

Casey, Janet Galligani, *Dos Passos and the Ideology of the Feminine* (Cambridge: Cambridge University Press, 1998).

Castle, Terry, *The Apparitional Lesbian: Female Homosexuality and Modern Culture* (New York: Columbia University Press, 1993).

Castronovo, Russ, "Beauty Along the Color Line: Lynching, Aesthetics, and the 'Crisis,'" *PMLA* 121.5 (2006): 1443–59.

Cerasulo, Tom, *Authors Out Here: Fitzgerald, West, Parker, and Schulberg* (Columbia: University of South Carolina Press, 2010).

Chaplin, Charles, *My Autobiography* (New York: Simon and Shuster, 1964).

Chardère, Bernard, *Le roman des Lumières* (Paris: Gallimard, 1995).

Charney, Leo, *Empty Moments: Cinema, Modernity, and Drift* (Durham, NC, and London: Duke University Press, 1998).

Cheng, Anne Anlin, *Second Skin: Josephine Baker and the Modern Surface* (Oxford: Oxford University Press, 2011).

Chion, Michel, *The Voice in Cinema*, ed. and trans. Claudia Gorbman (New York: Columbia University Press, 1999).

Chisholm, Ann, "Missing Persons and Bodies of Evidence," *Camera Obscura* 15.1 (2000): 123–61.

Christensen, Jerome, *America's Corporate Art: The Studio Authorship of Hollywood Motion Pictures* (Stanford, CA: Stanford University Press, 2012).

Cohen, Milton A., "Black Brutes and Mulatto Saints: The Racial Hierarchy of Stein's 'Melanctha,'" *Black America Literature Forum* 18.3 (1984): 119–21.

Cohen, Philip, "Is There a Text in This Discipline? Textual Scholarship and American Literary Studies," *American Literary History* 8.4 (1996): 728–44.

Comolli, Jean-Louis, "Machines of the Visible," in *The Cinematic Apparatus*, ed. Teresa de Lauretis and Stephen Heath (New York: St. Martin's Press, 1980), 121–42.

Conger, Amy, *Edward Weston: The Form of the Nude* (London: Phaidon, 2005).

Conley, Katharine, *Surrealist Ghostliness* (Lincoln: University of Nebraska Press, 2013).

Cope, Karin, "'Moral Deviancy' and Contemporary Feminism: The Judgment of Gertrude Stein," in *Feminism Beside Itself*, ed. Diane Elam and Robyn Wiegman (New York: Routledge, 1995), 155–78.

Crary, Jonathan, *Techniques of the Observer: On Vision and Modernity in the Nineteenth Century* (Cambridge, MA: MIT Press, 1990).

Dagonet, François, *Étienne-Jules Marey: A Passion for the Trace*, trans. Robert Galeta with Jeanine Herman (New York: Zone, 1992).

Dahn, Eurie, "*Cane* in the Magazines: Race, Form, and Global Periodical Networks," *The Journal of Modern Periodical Studies* 3.2 (2012): 119–35.

Damon, Maria, "Gertrude Stein's Doggerel 'Yiddish': Women, Dogs, and Jews," in *The Dark End of the Street: Margins in American Vanguard Poetry* (Minneapolis: University of Minnesota Press, 1993), 202–35.

Damon, Maria, "Writing, Social Science, and Ethnicity in Gertrude Stein and Certain Others," in *Modernism, Inc.: Body, Memory, Capital*, ed. Jani Scandura and Michael Thurston (New York: New York University Press, 2001), 133–50.

Danius, Sara, *The Senses of Modernism: Technology, Perception, and Aesthetics* (Ithaca, NY, and London: Cornell University Press, 2002).

Dardis, Tom, *Some Time in the Sun* (London: André Deutsch, 1976).

Davis, Hugh, "'Syncopations of Chance': *Let Us Now Praise Famous Men* as Surrealist Ethnography," in *The Making of James Agee* (Knoxville: University of Tennessee Press, 2008), 105–98.

Davis, Lennard J., *Bending Over Backwards: Disability, Dismodernism, and Other Difficult Positions* (New York: New York University Press, 2002).

de Certeau, Michel, *The Practice of Everyday Life* (Berkeley: University of California Press, 1984).

De Duve, Thierry, "Time Exposure and Snapshot: The Photograph as Paradox," *October* 5 (Summer 1978): 111–25.

Debord, Guy, *Society of the Spectacle*, trans. Donald Nicholson-Smith (New York: Zone, 1995).

DeKoven, Marianne, *Rich and Strange: Gender, History, Modernism* (Princeton, NJ: Princeton University Press, 1991).

Deleuze, Gilles, and Félix Guattari, *A Thousand Plateaus: Capitalism and Schizophrenia*, trans. Brian Massumi (Minneapolis: University of Minnesota Press, 1987).

Derrida, Jacques, " . . . That Dangerous Supplement," in *Of Grammatology*, trans. Gayatri Chakravorty Spivak (Baltimore: Johns Hopkins University Press, 1976), 141–64.

Derrida, Jacques, "Fifty-Two Aphorisms for a Foreword," in *Psyche: Inventions of the Other*, vol. 2, ed. Peggy Kamuf and Elizabeth Rottenberg (Stanford, CA: Stanford University Press, 2008), 117–26.

Dickinson, Emily, *Selected Letters*, ed. Thomas H. Johnson (Cambridge, MA: Harvard University Press, 1986).

Dinerstein, Joel, *Swinging the Machine: Modernity, Technology, and African American Culture Between the World Wars* (Amherst and Boston: University of Massachusetts Press, 2003).

Dixon, Wheeler Winston, *The Cinematic Vision of F. Scott Fitzgerald* (Ann Arbor: University of Michigan Research Press, 1986).

Doane, Janice L., *Silence and Narrative: The Early Novels of Gertrude Stein* (Westport, CT, and London: Greenwood, 1986).

Doane, Mary Ann, "Film and the Masquerade: Theorizing the Female Spectator," *Screen* 23.3–4 (1982): 74–87.

Doane, Mary Ann, *Femmes Fatales* (New York: Routledge, 1991).

Doane, Mary Ann, *The Emergence of Cinematic Time: Modernity, Contingency, the Archive* (Cambridge, MA: Harvard University Press, 2002).

Doane, Mary Ann, "Scale and the Negotiation of 'Real' and 'Unreal' Space in the Cinema," in *Realism and the Audiovisual Media*, ed. Lúcia Nagib and Cecília Mello (New York: Palgrave Macmillan, 2009), 63–81.

Dos Passos, John, "Black checkered notebook–Notes, Verse, Sketches," manuscript, n.p., John Dos Passos Papers, Series III: Personal, Box 126: Diaries and Notebooks, Notebooks 1919–1927 n.d., Sleeve 11. Albert and Shirley Small Special Collections Library, University of Virginia, Charlottesville.

Dos Passos, John, "Brown cover notebook–Notes, Verse," manuscript, n.p., John Dos Passos Papers, Series III: Personal, Box 126: Diaries and Notebooks, Notebooks 1919–1927 n.d., Sleeve 12. Albert and Shirley Small Special Collections Library, University of Virginia, Charlottesville.

Dos Passos, John, "Ellen Thatcher–Chap I/Protochapter I," manuscript, n.p., John Dos Passos Papers, Series II: Writings, Box 58: Binders, Binder 2. Albert and Shirley Small Special Collections Library, University of Virginia, Charlottesville.

Dos Passos, John, *U.S.A.: The 42nd Parallel, Nineteen-Nineteen, The Big Money* (London: Lehmann, 1950).

Dos Passos, John, "*A Farewell to Arms*," review of *A Farewell to Arms*, by Ernest Hemingway, in *The Major Nonfictional Prose*, ed. Donald Pizer (Detroit, MI: Wayne State University Press, 1988), 122.

Dos Passos, John, Introduction to *Three Soldiers*, in *The Major Nonfictional Prose*, ed. Donald Pizer (Detroit, MI: Wayne State University Press, 1988), 147–48.

Dos Passos, John, "Is the 'Realistic' Theater Obsolete?," in *The Major Nonfictional Prose*, ed. Donald Pizer (Detroit, MI: Wayne State University Press, 1988), 75–78.

Dos Passos, John, *The Major Nonfictional Prose*, ed. Donald Pizer (Detroit, MI: Wayne State University Press, 1988).

Dos Passos, John, "The Writer as Technician," in *The Major Nonfictional Prose*, ed. Donald Pizer (Detroit, MI: Wayne State University Press, 1988), 169–72.

Dos Passos, John, *Three Soldiers* (New York: Penguin, 1997).

Dos Passos, John, *Manhattan Transfer* (London: Penguin, 2000).

Douglas, Ann, *Terrible Honesty: Mongrel Manhattan in the 1920s* (New York: Farrar, Straus and Giroux, 1995).

Doyle, Laura, *Bordering on the Body: The Racial Matrix of Modern Fiction and Culture* (New York: Oxford University Press, 1994).

Doyle, Laura, "The Flat, the Round, and Gertrude Stein: Race and the Shape of Modern(ist) History," *Modernism/modernity* 7.2 (2000): 249–71.

Dreiser, Theodore, *Sister Carrie* (Oxford: Oxford University Press, 1999).

Duncan, Bowie, "Jean Toomer's *Cane*: A Modern Black Oracle," *CLA Journal* 15 (1972): 223–33.

Durand, Régis, "How to See (Photographically)," in *Fugitive Images: From Photography to Video*, ed. Patrice Petro (Bloomington: Indiana University Press, 1995), 141–51.

Dyer, Richard, *Heavenly Bodies: Film Stars and Society* (New York: St. Martin's Press, 1986).

Dyer, Richard, *White* (London: Routledge, 1997).

Dyer, Richard, *Stars* (London: British Film Institute, 1998).

Eisenstein, Sergei, *Nonindifferent Nature: Film and the Structure of Things*, trans. Herbert Marshal (Cambridge: Cambridge University Press, 1987).

Eldridge, Richard, "The Unifying Image in Part One of Jean Toomer's *Cane*," in *Jean Toomer: A Critical Evaluation*, ed. Therman O'Daniel (Washington, DC: Howard University Press, 1988), 213–36.

Elkins, James, *What Photography Is* (New York and London: Routledge, 2011).

English, Daylanne K., *Unnatural Selections: Eugenics in American Modernism and the Harlem Renaissance* (Chapel Hill: University of North Carolina Press, 2004).

Evans, Walker, *American Photographs* (New York: Museum of Modern Art, 1988).

Ewen, Stuart, *All Consuming Images: The Politics of Style in Contemporary Culture* (New York: Basic Books, 1988).

Fabian, Ann, "Making a Commodity of Truth: Speculations on the Career of Bernarr Macfadden," *American Literary History* 5.1 (1993): 51–76.

Fagan, Deidre, "Emily Dickinson's Unutterable Word," *Emily Dickinson Journal* 14.2 (2005): 70–75.

Fahy, Thomas, "Planes, Trains, and Automobiles: Technology and the Suburban Nightmare in the Plays of John Dos Passos," in *Staging Modern American Life: Popular Culture in the Experimental Theater of Millay, Cummings, and Dos Passos* (New York: Palgrave Macmillan, 2011), 85–131.

Fanon, Frantz, *Black Skin, White Masks*, trans. Charles Markmann (New York: Grove Press, 1967).

Farebrother, Rachel, "Adventuring Through the Pieces of a Still Unorganized Mosaic: Reading Jean Toomer's Collage Aesthetic in *Cane*," *Journal of American Studies* 40.3 (2006): 503–21.

Fauset, Jessie Redmon, "Brawley's 'Social History of the American Negro,'" review of *A Social History of the American Negro*, by Benjamin Brawley, *The Crisis: A Record of the Darker Races* 23.6 (1922): 260. Accessed at http://www.modjourn.org/render.php?id=12 97796255203127&view=mjp_object.

Favor, J. Martin, *Authentic Blackness: The Folk in the New Negro Renaissance* (Durham, NC: Duke University Press, 1999).

Fernald, Anne E., "Women's Fiction, New Modernist Studies, and Feminism," *MFS Modern Fiction Studies* 59.2 (2013): 229–40.

Fiedler, Leslie, *Freaks: Myths and Images of the Secret Self* (New York: Simon and Schuster, 1978).

Fine, Richard, *West of Eden: Writers in Hollywood, 1928–1940* (Washington and London: Smithsonian Institution Press, 1993).

Fisher, Philip, "Appearing and Disappearing in Public: Social Space in Late Nineteenth-Century Literature and Culture," in *Reconstructing American Literary History*, ed. Sacvan Bercovitch (Cambridge, MA: Harvard University Press, 1986), 157–74.

Fitzgerald, F. Scott, "Cosmopolitan" ("Babylon Revisited"), typescript with author's corrections, August 12, 1940, F. Scott Fitzgerald Papers, Series 1: Writings, 1897–1944, Moving Picture Scripts, Box 30b, Department of Rare Books and Special Collections, Princeton University, Princeton, NJ.

Fitzgerald, F. Scott, *The Last Tycoon*, autograph and typewritten manuscripts, F. Scott Fitzgerald Papers, Series 1: Writings, 1910–1989, Boxes 7a, 7b, 7c, and 8a, Department of Rare Books and Special Collections, Princeton University Library, Princeton, NJ.

Fitzgerald, F. Scott, *The Crack-Up*, ed. Edmund Wilson (New York: New Directions, 1945).

Fitzgerald, F. Scott, "One Hundred False Starts," in *Afternoon of an Author: A Selection of Uncollected Stories and Essays*, intro. Arthur Mizener, 127–36. (New York: Scribner's, 1957), 127–36.

Fitzgerald, F. Scott, *The Letters of F. Scott Fitzgerald*, ed. Andrew Turnbull (New York: Scribner's, 1963).

Fitzgerald, F. Scott, "Babylon Revisited," in *The Short Stories of F. Scott Fitzgerald: A New Collection*, ed. and with a preface by Matthew J. Bruccoli (New York: Scribner's, 1989), 616–33.

Fitzgerald, F. Scott, *F. Scott Fitzgerald Manuscripts V: The Last Tycoon: Manuscript and Revised Typescript for the First 17 Episodes, With the Author's Plans and Notes*, 3 vols., ed. Matthew J. Bruccoli. (New York and London: Garland, 1990–1991).

Fitzgerald, F. Scott, *Babylon Revisited: The Screenplay*, intro. Budd Schulberg (New York: Carroll & Graf, 1993).

Fitzgerald, F. Scott, *F. Scott Fitzgerald: A Life in Letters*, ed. Matthew J. Bruccoli and Judith S. Baughman (New York and London: Touchstone, 1994).

Fitzgerald, F. Scott, *The Last Tycoon*, ed. and with a foreword by Edmund Wilson (London: Penguin Classics, 2001).

Fitzgerald, F. Scott, *The Love of the Last Tycoon*, ed. and with a preface and notes by Matthew J. Bruccoli (New York and London: Scribner's, 2003).

Fitzgerald, F. Scott, *F. Scott Fitzgerald's Ledger, 1919-1938*, Matthew J. and Arlyn Bruccoli Collection of F. Scott Fitzgerald, Digital Collections Department, University of South Carolina, 2013. Accessed at http://library.sc.edu/digital/collections/fitzledger.html.

Fleissner, Jennifer L., *Women, Compulsion, Modernity: The Moment of American Naturalism* (Chicago and London: University of Chicago Press, 2004).

Foley, Barbara, "'In the Land of Cotton': Economics and Violence in Jean Toomer's *Cane*," *African American Review* 32.2 (1998): 181-98.

Ford, Karen Jackson, *Split-Gut Song: Jean Toomer and the Poetics of Modernity* (Tuscaloosa: University of Alabama Press, 2005).

Foster, Gretchen, "John Dos Passos's Use of Film Technique in *Manhattan Transfer* and *The 42nd Parallel*," *Literature/Film Quarterly* 14.3 (1986): 189-94.

Foucault, Michel, "Nietzsche, Genealogy, History," in *The Foucault Reader*, ed. Paul Rabinow (New York: Pantheon, 1984), 76-100.

Foucault, Michel, "What is an Author?," in *The Foucault Reader*, ed. Paul Rabinow (New York: Pantheon, 1984), 101-20.

Foucault, Michel, "The Ethics for the Concern of Self as a Practice of Freedom," in *The Final Foucault*, ed. James Bernauer and David Rasmussen and trans. J. D. Gauthier (Cambridge, MA: MIT Press, 1988), 1-20.

Foucault, Michel, *Discipline and Punish: The Birth of the Prison*, trans. Alan Sheridan (New York: Vintage, 1995).

Frankenberg, Ruth, "The Mirage of an Unmarked Whiteness," in *The Making and Unmaking of Whiteness*, ed. Birgit Brander Rasmussen, Eric Klinenberg, Irene J. Nexica, and Matt Wray (Durham, NC: Duke University Press, 2001), 72-96.

Freud, Sigmund, "Recollection, Repetition, and Working Through," in *Therapy and Technique*, ed. Philip Rieff (New York: Collier, 1963), 157-66.

Freud, Sigmund, *The Interpretation of Dreams*, trans. James Strachey (New York: Avon, 1965).

Friedberg, Anne, *Window Shopping: Cinema and the Postmodern* (Berkeley: University of California Press, 1993).

Friedman, Susan Stanford, Introduction to *Joyce: The Return of the Repressed*, ed. Friedman (Ithaca, NY, and London: Cornell University Press, 1993), 1-20.

Friedman, Susan Stanford, "(Self)Censorship and the Making of Joyce's Modernism," in *Joyce: The Return of the Repressed*, ed. Friedman (Ithaca, NY, and London: Cornell University Press, 1993), 21-57.

Friedman, Susan Stanford, "Definitional Excursions: The Meanings of Modern/Modernity/ Modernism," *Modernism/modernity* 8.3 (2001): 493-513.

Gabriel, Gilbert W., "Taps!—A Requiem," *Vanity Fair*, August 1929, 32.

Galton, Francis, "Composite Portraits, Made by Combining Those of Many Different Persons Into a Single Resultant Figure," *Journal of the Anthropological Institute* 8 (1879): 132–44.

Galton, Francis, *Record of Family Faculties* (London: Macmillan, 1884).

Galton, Francis, *Inquiries into Human Faculty and Its Development* (London: J. M. Dent and Sons, 1907).

Garland-Thompson, Rosemarie, "The Politics of Staring: Visual Rhetorics of Disability in Popular Photography," in *Disability Studies: Enabling the Humanities*, ed. Sharon L. Snyder, Brenda Jo Brueggemann, and Rosemarie Garland-Thompson (New York: Modern Language Association of America, 2002), 56–75.

Geyh, Paula E., "From Cities of Things to Cities of Signs: Urban Spaces and Urban Subjects in *Sister Carrie* and *Manhattan Transfer*," *Twentieth-Century Literature* 52.4 (2006): 413–42.

Ginsburg, Carlo, "Family Resemblances and Family Trees: Two Cognitive Metaphors," *Critical Inquiry* 30.3 (2004): 537–56.

Glazener, Nancy, "Dialogic Subversion: Bakhtin, the Novel and Gertrude Stein," in *Bakhtin and Cultural Theory*, ed. Ken Hirschkop and David Shepherd (Manchester, UK: Manchester University Press, 2001), 155–76.

Goble, Mark, *Beautiful Circuits: Modernism and the Mediated Life* (New York: Columbia University Press, 2010).

Goeser, Caroline, *Picturing the New Negro: Harlem Renaissance Print Culture and Modern Black Identity* (Lawrence: University Press of Kansas, 2007).

Goodwin, James, *Modern American Grotesque: Literature and Photography* (Columbus: Ohio State University Press, 2009).

Gordon, Avery F., *Ghostly Matters: Haunting and the Sociological Imagination* (Minneapolis: University of Minnesota Press, 1997).

Guido, Laurent, and Olivier Lugon, eds., *Between Still and Moving Images* (New Barnet, UK: Libbey, 2012).

Gunning, Tom, "The Cinema of Attractions: Early Film, Its Spectator and the Avant-Garde," *Wide Angle* 8.3–4 (1986): 63–70.

Gunning, Tom, "An Aesthetic of Astonishment: Early Film and the (In)Credulous Spectator," *Art and Text* 34 (Spring 1989): 31–45.

Gunning, Tom, "Tracing the Individual Body: Photography, Detectives, and Early Cinema," in *Cinema and the Invention of Modern Life*, ed. Leo Charney and Vanessa R. Schwartz (Berkeley: University of California Press, 1995), 15–45.

Gunning, Tom, "In Your Face: Physiognomy, Photography, and the Gnostic Mission of Early Film," *Modernism/modernity* 4.1 (1997): 1–29.

Gunning, Tom, "New Thresholds of Vision: Instantaneous Photography and the Early Cinema of Lumière," in *Impossible Presence: Surface and Screen in the Photogenic Era*, ed. Terry Smith (Sydney: Power Publications, 2001), 71–100.

Hall, James Baker, *Minor White: Rites and Passages: His Photographs Accompanied by Excerpts from his Diaries and Letters* (New York: Aperture, 1978).

Hansen, Miriam Bratu, Introduction to *Theory of Film: The Redemption of Physical Reality*, by Siegfried Kracauer (Princeton, NJ: Princeton University Press, 1997), vii–xlv.

Hansom, Paul, ed., *Literary Modernism and Photography* (Westport, CT, and London: Praeger, 2002).

Harris, Trudier, *Exorcising Blackness: Historical and Literary Lynching and Burning Rituals* (Bloomington: Indiana University Press, 1984).

Haselstein, Ulla, "Gertrude Stein's Portraits of Matisse and Picasso," *New Literary History* 34.4 (2003): 723–43.

Heath, Stephen, *Questions of Cinema* (Bloomington: Indiana University Press, 1981).

Helbling, Mark, "Sherwood Anderson and Jean Toomer," in *Jean Toomer: A Critical Evaluation*, ed. Therman O'Daniel (Washington, DC: Howard University Press, 1988), 111–20.

Heldrich, Philip, "Connecting Surfaces: Gertrude Stein's *Three Lives*, Cubism, and the Metonymy of the Short Story Cycle," *Studies in Short Fiction* 34 (1997): 427–39.

Henninger, Katherine, *Ordering the Façade: Photography and Contemporary Southern Women's Writing* (Chapel Hill: University of North Carolina Press, 2007).

Holmes, Martha Stoddard, and Tod Chambers, "Thinking Through Pain," *Literature and Medicine* 24.1 (2005): 127–41.

hooks, bell, *Black Looks: Race and Representation* (Boston: South End Press, 1992).

hooks, bell, "In Our Glory: Photography and Black Life," in *Art on My Mind: Visual Politics* (New York: New Press, 1995), 54–64.

Hurston, Zora Neale, *Their Eyes Were Watching God* (London: Virago, 1986).

Hutchinson, George, "Jean Toomer and American Racial Discourse," *Texas Studies in Literature and Language* 35.2 (1993): 226–50.

Hutchinson, George, "Identity in Motion: Placing *Cane*," in *Jean Toomer and the Harlem Renaissance*, ed. Geneviève Fabre and Michel Feith (New Brunswick, NJ: Rutgers University Press, 2001), 38–56.

Huyssen, Andreas, "Mass Culture as Woman: Modernism's Other," in *After the Great Divide: Modernism, Mass Culture, Postmodernism* (Bloomington and Indianapolis: Indiana University Press, 1986), 44–64.

Irigaray, Luce, *This Sex Which Is Not One*, trans. Catherine Porter (Ithaca, NY: Cornell University Press, 1985).

Jacobs, Karen, *The Eye's Mind: Literary Modernism and Visual Culture* (Ithaca, NY: Cornell University Press, 2001).

Jacobs, Steven, *Framing Pictures: Film and the Visual Arts* (Edinburgh: Edinburgh University Press, 2011).

James, Henry, *The American Scene* (London: Penguin, 1994).

Jameson, Fredric, *Postmodernism, or, The Cultural Logic of Late Capitalism* (Durham, NC: Duke University Press, 1991).

Jay, Martin, *Downcast Eyes: The Denigration of Vision in Twentieth-Century French Thought* (Berkeley: University of California Press, 1993).

Jay, Martin, "Photo-Unrealism: The Contribution of the Camera to the Crisis of Ocularcentrism," in *Vision and Textuality*, ed. Stephen Melville and Bill Readings (Durham, NC: Duke University Press, 1995), 344–62.

Jones, Robert B., *Jean Toomer and the Prison-House of Thought: A Phenomenology of the Spirit* (Amherst: University of Massachusetts Press, 1993).

Jonsson, Stefan, *Crowds and Democracy: The Idea and Image of the Masses From Revolution to Fascism* (New York: Columbia University Press, 2013).

Kaplan, Amy, *The Social Construction of American Realism* (Chicago: University of Chicago Press, 1988).

Katz, Leslie, "Interview with Walker Evans," *Art in America* 59.2 (1971): 82–89.

Kaufman, Michael, *Textual Bodies: Modernism, Postmodernism, and Print* (Lewisberg, PA: Bucknell University Press, 1994).

Kawash, Samira, *Dislocating the Color Line: Identity, Hybridity, and Singularity in African-American Literature* (Stanford, CA: Stanford University Press, 1997).

Kazin, Alfred, *On Native Grounds: An Interpretation of Modern American Prose Literature* (London: Jonathan Cape, 1943).

Keil, Charlie, and Shelley Stamp, Introduction to *American Cinema's Transitional Era: Audiences, Institutions, Practices*, ed. Keil and Stamp (Berkeley: University of California Press, 2004), 1–11.

Keller, Susan, "Compact Resistance: Public Powdering and *Flânerie* in the Modern City," *Women's Studies* 40 (2011): 299–335.

Keller, Ulrich, "Conceptual and Stylistic Aspects of the Portraits," in *August Sander: Citizens of the Twentieth Century: Portrait Photographs 1892–1952*, ed. Gunther Sander and trans. Linda Keller (Cambridge, MA MIT Press, 1989), 27–39.

Kennedy, J. Gerald, "Toward a Poetics of the Short Story Cycle," *Journal of the Short Story in English* 11 (1988): 9–25.

Kerman, Cynthia Earl, and Richard Eldridge, *The Lives of Jean Toomer: A Hunger for Wholeness* (Baton Rouge: Louisiana State University Press, 1987).

King, Martin Luther Jr., *Why We Can't Wait* (New York: Harper and Row, 1964).

Kirby, Lynne, *Parallel Tracks: The Railroad Car and Silent Cinema* (Durham, NC: Duke University Press, 1997).

Kirstein, Lincoln, "Photographs of America: Walker Evans," in *American Photographs*, by Walker Evans (New York: Museum of Modern Art, 1988), 189–98.

Kittler, Friedrich, *Discourse Networks 1800/1900*, trans. Michael Metteer with Chris Cullens (Stanford, CA: Stanford University Press, 1990).

Kodat, Catherine Gunther, "To 'Flash White Light From Ebony': The Problem of Modernism in Jean Toomer's *Cane*," *Twentieth-Century Literature* 46.1 (2000): 1–19.

Komar, Kathleen L., *Pattern and Chaos: Multilinear Novels by Dos Passos, Döblin, Faulkner and Koeppen* (Columbia, SC: Camden House, 1983).

Koritz, Amy, *Culture Makers: Urban Performance and Literature in the 1920s* (Urbana and Chicago: University of Illinois Press, 2009).

Kracauer, Siegfried, "Girls and Crisis," in *The Weimar Republic Sourcebook*, ed. Anton Kaes, Martin Jay, and Edward Dimendberg (Berkeley: University of California Press, 1994), 565–66.

Kracauer, Siegfried, "The Mass Ornament," in *The Mass Ornament: Weimar Essays*, trans., ed., and intro. Thomas Y. Levin (Cambridge, MA and London: Harvard University Press, 1995), 75–88.

Kracauer, Siegfried, "Photography," in *The Mass Ornament: Weimar Essays*, trans., ed., and intro. Thomas Y. Levin (Cambridge, MA, and London: Harvard University Press, 1995), 47–64.

Kracauer, Siegfried, "Travel and Dance," in *The Mass Ornament: Weimar Essays*, trans., ed., and intro. Thomas Y. Levin (Cambridge, MA, and London: Harvard University Press, 1995), 65–74.

Kracauer, Siegfried, *Theory of Film: The Redemption of Physical Reality*, intro. Miriam Bratu Hansen (Princeton, NJ: Princeton University Press, 1997).

Krauss, Rosalind, "Photography in the Service of Surrealism," in *L'Amour fou: Photography and Surrealism*, by Rosalind Krauss and Jane Livingstone (New York: Abbeville, 1985), 15–56.

Krauss, Rosalind, "Sculpture in the Expanded Field," in *The Originality of the Avant-Garde and Other Modernist Myths* (Cambridge, MA: MIT Press, 1985), 276–90.

Kristeva, Julia, "Psychoanalysis and the Polis," in *The Kristeva Reader*, ed. Toril Moi (New York: Columbia University Press, 1986), 301–20.

Kuehl, John, and Jackson R. Bryer, eds., *Dear Scott/Dear Max: The Fitzgerald-Perkins Correspondence* (New York: Scribner's, 1971).

Kundu, Gautam, *Fitzgerald and the Influence of Film: The Language of Cinema in the Novels* (Jefferson, NC, and London: McFarland, 2008).

Lacan, Jacques, "Function and Field of Speech and Language in Psychoanalysis," in *Écrits: A Selection*, trans. Alan Sheridan (New York: Norton, 1977), 30–113.

Lassalle, Honor, and Abigail Solomon-Godeau, "Surrealist Confession: Claude Cahun's Photomontages," *Afterimage* 19 (March 1992): 10–13.

Latham, Aaron, *Crazy Sundays: F. Scott Fitzgerald in Hollywood* (London: Secker and Warburg, 1972).

Leperlier, François, *Claude Cahun: L'écart et la metamorphose* (Paris: Jean-Michel Place, 1992).

Levin, Jonathan, "'Entering the Modern Composition': Gertrude Stein and the Patterns of Modernism," in *Rereading the New: A Backward Glance at Modernism*, ed. Kevin J. H. Dettmar (Ann Arbor: University of Michigan Press, 1992), 137–66.

Lévi-Strauss, Claude, *The Savage Mind* (Chicago: University of Chicago Press, 1966).

Lewis, Sinclair, "Manhattan at Last!," review of *Manhattan Transfer*, by John Dos Passos, *Saturday Review*, December 5, 1925, 361. Accessed at http://www.unz.org/Pub/SaturdayRev-1925dec05-00361.

Locke, Alain, "The New Negro," introduction to *The New Negro*, ed. Locke (New York: Atheneum, 1992), xxv–xxvii.

Lomas, David, *The Haunted Self: Surrealism, Psychoanalysis, Subjectivity* (New Haven, CT, and London: Yale University Press, 2000).

Lowry, E. D., "The Lively Art of *Manhattan Transfer*," *PMLA* 84.6 (1969): 1628–38.

Macfadden, Bernarr, *Encyclopedia of Physical Culture*, 5 vols. (New York: Physical Culture Publishing, 1912).

Magny, Claude-Edmonde, *The Age of the American Novel: The Film Aesthetic of Fiction Between the Two Wars*, trans. Eleanor Hochman (New York: Ungar, 1972).

Mannoni, Laurent, *The Great Art of Light and Shadow: Archaeology of the Cinema*, intro. Tom Gunning (Exeter, UK: Exeter University Press, 2000).

Mao, Douglas, and Rebecca L. Walkowitz, "Modernisms Bad and New," introduction to *Bad Modernisms*, ed. Mao and Walkowitz (Durham, NC: Duke University Press, 2006), 1–18.

Mao, Douglas, and Rebecca L. Walkowitz, "The New Modernist Studies," *PMLA* 123.3 (2008): 737–48.

Marchand, Roland, *Advertising the American Dream: Making Way for Modernity, 1920–1940* (Berkeley: University of California Press, 1985).

Martin, Robert A., "Hollywood in Fitzgerald: After Paradise," in *The Short Stories of F. Scott Fitzgerald: New Approaches in Criticism*, ed. Jackson R. Bryer (Madison: University of Wisconsin Press, 1982), 127–48.

Mayer, David, "The Actress as Photographic Icon: From Early Photography to Early Film," in *The Cambridge Companion to the Actress*, ed. Maggie B. Gale and John Stokes (Cambridge: Cambridge University Press, 2007), 74–94.

McCabe, Susan, *Cinematic Modernism* (Cambridge: Cambridge University Press, 2005).

McCaffery, Steve, *Prior to Meaning: The Protosemantic and Poetics* (Evanston, IL: Northwestern University Press, 2001).

McCarren, Felicia, *Dancing Machines: Choreographies of the Age of Mechanical Reproduction* (Stanford, CA: Stanford University Press, 2003).

McCauley, Anne, *Industrial Madness: Commercial Photography in Paris, 1848–1871* (New Haven, CT, and London: Yale University Press, 1994).

McCauley, Elizabeth Anne, *A. A. E. Disdéri and the Carte de Visite Portrait Photograph* (New Haven, CT, and London: Yale University Press, 1985).

McGann, Jerome, *The Textual Condition* (Princeton, NJ: Princeton University Press, 1991).

McKay, Nellie. *Jean Toomer, Artist: A Study of His Literary Life and Work, 1894–1936.* (Chapel Hill: University of North Carolina Press, 1984).

McNay, Lois, *Foucault and Feminism: Power, Gender and the Self* (Cambridge, UK, and Malden, MA: Polity, 2013).

Metz, Christian, "Photography and Fetish," *October* 34 (Autumn 1985): 81–90.

Michaels, Walter Benn, *Our America: Nativism, Modernism, and Pluralism* (Durham, NC: Duke University Press, 1995).

Mickalites, Carey James, "*Manhattan Transfer*, Spectacular Time, and the Outmoded," *Arizona Quarterly: A Journal of American Literature, Culture, and Theory* 67.4 (2011): 59–82.

Millichap, Joseph R., *The Language of Vision: Photography and Southern Literature in the 1930s and After* (Baton Rouge: Louisiana State University Press, 2016).

Mintz, Susannah B., *Hurt and Pain: Literature and the Suffering Body* (London: Bloomsberg, 2013).

Mitchell, W. J. T. "Showing Seeing: A Critique of Visual Culture," in *What Do Pictures Want? The Lives and Loves of Images* (Chicago: University of Chicago Press, 2005), 336–56.

Mizejewski, Linda, *Ziegfeld Girl: Image and Icon in Culture and Cinema* (Durham, NC, and London: Duke University Press, 1999).

"Mlle. Anna Held Arrives: Naïve Talk of the Parisian Beauty and $1,500-a-Week Singer," *New York Times*, September 16, 1896. Accessed at http://query.nytimes.com/mem/archivefree/pdf?res=9B00E5DC1738E233A25755C1A96F9C94679ED7CF.

Moholy-Nagy, László, *Painting, Photography, Film*, trans. Janet Seligman Lund (London: Humphries, 1987).

Moholy-Nagy, László, "From Pigment to Light," in *Photography in Print: Writings from 1816 to the Present*, ed. Vicki Goldberg (Albuquerque: University of New Mexico Press, 1988), 339–48.

Mok, Michel, "The Other Side of Paradise, Scott Fitzgerald, 40, Engulfed in Despair," *New York Post*, September 25, 1936, in *F. Scott Fitzgerald in His Own Time: A Miscellany*, ed. Matthew J. Bruccoli and Jackson R. Bryer (Kent, OH: Kent State University Press, 1971), 294–99.

Moreland, Richard C., *Faulkner and Modernism: Rereading and Rewriting* (Madison: University of Wisconsin Press, 1989).

Moyer, Kermit W., "Fitzgerald's Two Unfinished Novels: The Count and the Tycoon in Spenglerian Perspective," *Contemporary Literature* 15.2 (1974): 238–56.

Mulvey, Laura, *Death 24x a Second: Stillness and the Moving Image* (London: Reaktion, 2006).

Mulvey, Laura, "Visual Pleasure and Narrative Cinema," in *Visual and Other Pleasures*, 2nd ed. (New York: Palgrave Macmillan, 2009), 14–30.

Murphet, Julian, "Gertrude Stein's Machinery of Perception," in *Literature and Visual Technologies: Writing After Cinema*, ed. Murphet and Lydia Rainford (Hampshire, UK, and New York: Palgrave Macmillan, 2003), 67–81.

Nadar, Félix, "*La première épreuve de photographie aérostatique*," in *Quand j'étais photographe* (Paris: Seuil, 1994), 95–122.

Nadar, Félix, *When I Was a Photographer*, trans. Eduardo Cadava and Liana Theodoratou (Cambridge, MA: MIT Press, 2015).

Nadell, Martha Jane, "Race and the Visual Arts in the Works of Jean Toomer and Georgia O'Keefe," in *Jean Toomer and the Harlem Renaissance*, ed. Geneviève Fabre and Michel Feith (New Brunswick, NJ: Rutgers University Press, 2001), 142–61.

Nadell, Martha Jane, *Enter the New Negroes: Images of Race in American Culture* (Cambridge: Cambridge University Press, 2004).

Nathan, George Jean, "Theater," *Scribner's Magazine* 102.5 (1937): 66–68.

Nanney, Lisa, *John Dos Passos* (Chapel Hill: University of North Carolina Press, 1998).

Nannicelli, Ted, *A Philosophy of the Screenplay* (New York: Routledge, 2013).

Newhall, Nancy, ed., *The Daybooks of Edward Weston*, vol. 1 (Millerton, NY: Aperture, 1961).

Ngai, Sianne, *Ugly Feelings* (Cambridge, MA: Harvard University Press, 2005).

Nielsen, Aldon Lynn, *Reading Race: White American Poets and the Racial Discourse in the Twentieth Century* (Athens: University of Georgia Press, 1988).

Niemeyer, Mark, "Hysteria and the Normal Unconscious: Dual Natures in Gertrude Stein's 'Melanctha,'" *Journal of American Studies* 28 (1994): 77–90.

North, Michael, *The Dialect of Modernism: Race, Language, and Twentieth-Century Literature* (New York: Oxford University Press, 1994).

North, Michael, *Reading 1922: A Return to the Scene of the Modern* (New York and Oxford: Oxford University Press, 1999).

North, Michael, *Camera Works: Photography and the Twentieth-Century Word* (Oxford: Oxford University Press, 2005).

Nowlin, Michael, "'A Gentile's Tragedy': Bearing the Word About Hollywood in *The Love of the Last Tycoon*," *The F. Scott Fitzgerald Review* 2.1 (2003): 156–85.

Novak, Daniel A., *Realism, Photography, and Nineteenth-Century Fiction* (Cambridge: Cambridge University Press, 2008).

O'Keeffe, Georgia, Introduction to *Georgia O'Keeffe, A Portrait*, by Alfred Stieglitz, n.p. (New York: Metropolitan Museum of Art, 1978).

Olin, Margaret, *Touching Photographs* (Chicago and London: University of Chicago Press, 2012).

Orvell, Miles, *The Real Thing: Imitation and Authenticity in American Culture, 1880–1940* (Chapel Hill: University of North Carolina Press, 1989).

Parr, Martin, and Gerry Badger, *The Photobook: A History*, 2 vols. (London: Phaidon, 2004, 2006).

Pasolini, Pier Paolo, "The Screenplay as a 'Structure That Wants to be Another Structure,'" in *Heretical Empiricism*, ed. Louise K. Barnett and trans. Ben Lawton and Louise K. Barnett (Bloomington and Indianapolis: Indiana University Press, 1988), 187–96.

Perloff, Marjorie, *The Poetics of Indeterminacy: Rimbaud to Cage* (Princeton, NJ: Princeton University Press, 1981).

Perosa, Sergio, *The Art of F. Scott Fitzgerald*, trans. Charles Matz (Ann Arbor: University of Michigan Press, 1965).

Petrovic, Paul, "'To Get to the Center': Recovering the Marginalized Woman in John Dos Passos's *Manhattan Transfer*," *Studies in American Naturalism* 4.2 (2009): 152–72.

Phelan, Peggy, *Unmarked: The Politics of Performance* (London and New York: Routledge, 1993).

Pinney, Christopher, *Photography and Anthropology* (London: Reaktion, 2011).

Poe, Edgar Allan, "The Daguerreotype," in *Classic Essays on Photography*, ed. Alan Trachtenberg (New Haven, CT: Leete's Island Books, 1980), 37–38.

Polan, Dana, "Brief Encounters: Mass Culture and the Evacuation of Sense," in *Studies in Entertainment: Critical Approaches to Mass Culture*, ed. Tania Modleski (Bloomington and Indianapolis: Indiana University Press, 1986), 167–87.

Price, Steven, *The Screenplay: Authorship, Theory and Criticism* (London: Palgrave Macmillan, 2010).

Rabinowitz, Paula, "Barbara Stanwyck's Anklet: The Other Side," in *Accessorizing the Body: Habits of Being*, ed. Christini Giorcelli and Rabinowitz (Minneapolis and London: University of Minnesota Press, 2011), 185–208.

Raiford, Leigh, "Lynching, Visuality, and the Un/Making of Blackness," *Nka: Journal of Contemporary African Art* 20 (Fall 2006): 22–31.

Raitt, Suzanne, "The Rhetoric of Efficiency in Early Modernism," *Modernism/modernity* 13.1 (2006): 835–51.

Riis, Jacob, *How the Other Half Lives: Studies Among the Tenements of New York*, intro. Luc Sante (New York and London: Penguin, 1997).

Rivière, Joan, "Womanliness as a Masquerade," in *Formations of Fantasy*, ed. Victor Burgin, James Donald, and Cora Kaplan (London: Methuen, 1986), 35–44.

Rosner, Victoria, *Modernism and the Architecture of Private Life* (New York: Columbia University Press, 2005).

Røssaak, Eivind, ed., *Between Stillness and Motion: Film, Photography, Algorithms* (Amsterdam: Amsterdam University Press, 2011).

Roth, Andrew, ed., *The Open Book: A History of the Photographic Book from 1978 to the Present* (Göteborg, Sweden: Hasselblad Center, 2004).

Rowe, John Carlos, "John Dos Passos's Imaginary City in *Manhattan Transfer*," in *Afterlives of Modernism: Liberalism, Transnationalism, and Political Critique* (Hanover, NH, and New Haven, CT: Dartmouth College Press, 2011), 61–74.

Ruddick, Lisa, *Reading Gertrude Stein: Body, Text, Gnosis* (Ithaca, NY: Cornell University Press, 1990).

Rusch, Frederik L., "Form, Function, and Creative Tension in *Cane*: Jean Toomer and the Need for the Avant-Garde," *MELUS* 17.4 (1991–1992): 15–28.

Saldívar-Hull, Sonia, "Wrestling Your Ally: Stein, Racism, and Feminist Critical Practice," in *Women's Writing in Exile*, ed. Mary Lynn Broe and Angela Ingram (Chapel Hill: University of North Carolina Press, 1989), 181–98.

Sante, Luc, Introduction to *How the Other Half Lives: Studies Among the Tenements of New York*, by Jacob Riis (New York and London: Penguin, 1997), ix–xxv.

Sawday, Jonathan, *The Body Emblazoned: Dissection and the Human Body in Renaissance Culture* (London: Routledge, 1995).

Scandura, Jani, *Down in the Dumps: Place, Modernity, American Depression* (Durham, NC: Duke University Press, 2008).

Scarry, Elaine, *The Body in Pain: The Making and Unmaking of the World* (New York: Oxford University Press, 1985).

Scharf, Aaron, *Art and Photography* (London: Allen Lane, 1983).

Schatz, Thomas, *The Genius of the System: Hollywood Filmmaking in the Studio Era* (Minneapolis and London: University of Minnesota Press, 2010).

Schmidt, Christine, "Second Skin: Annette Kellerman, the Modern Swimsuit, and an Australian Contribution to Global Fashion" (PhD diss., Queensland University of Technology, 2008).

Schmidt, Christine, and Jinna Tay, "Undressing Kellerman, Uncovering Broadhurst: The Modern Woman and 'Un-Australia,'" *Fashion Theory* 13.4 (2009): 481–98.

Schoenbach, Lisi, "'Peaceful and Exciting': Habit, Shock, and Gertrude Stein's Pragmatic Modernism," *Modernism/modernity* 11.2 (2004): 239–59.

Schulberg, Budd, Introduction to *Babylon Revisited: The Screenplay*, by F. Scott Fitzgerald (New York: Carroll & Graf, 1993).

Scruggs, Charles, "The Photographic Print, the Literary Negative: Alfried Stieglitz and Jean Toomer," *Arizona Quarterly: A Journal of American Literature, Culture, and Theory* 53.1 (1997): 61–89.

Scruggs, Charles, and Lee VanDemarr, *Jean Toomer and the Terrors of American History* (Philadelphia: University of Pennsylvania Press, 1998).

Seed, David, *Cinematic Fictions* (Liverpool, UK: Liverpool University Press, 2009).

Sekula, Allan, "The Body and the Archive," *October* 39 (Winter 1986): 3–64.

Seltzer, Mark, *Bodies and Machines* (New York and London: Routledge, 1992).

Senelick, Lawrence, "Eroticism in Early Theatrical Photography," *Theatre History Studies* 11 (1991): 1–49.

Shaw, Jennifer L., *Reading Claude Cahun's Disavowals* (Surrey, UK: Ashgate, 2013).

Sherrard-Johnson, Cherene, *Portraits of the New Negro Woman: Visual and Literary Culture in the Harlem Renaissance* (New Brunswick, NJ: Rutgers University Press, 2007).

Shigley, Sally Bishop, "Recalcitrant, Revered, and Reviled: Women in Jean Toomer's Short Story Cycle, *Cane*," *Short Story* 9.1 (2001): 88–98.

Shloss, Carol, *In Visible Light: Photography and the American Writer, 1840–1940* (New York: Oxford University Press, 1987).

Silverman, Kaja, *The Acoustic Mirror: The Female Voice in Psychoanalysis and Cinema* (Bloomington and Indianapolis: Indiana University Press, 1988).

Singer, Ben, "Modernity, Hyperstimulus, and the Rise of Popular Sensationalism," in *Cinema and the Invention of Modern Life*, ed. Leo Charney and Vanessa R. Schwartz (Berkeley: University of California Press, 1995), 72–96.

Sitney, P. Adams, *Modernist Montage: The Obscurity of Vision and Cinema and Literature* (New York: Columbia University Press, 1990).

Sliwinski, Sharon, "A Painful Labor: Photography and Responsibility," in *Representations of Pain in Art and Visual Culture*, ed. Maria Pia Di Bella and James Elkins (New York and London: Routledge, 2013), 64–74.

Smith, Joel, ed., *More Than One: Photographs in Sequence* (Princeton, NJ: Princeton University Art Museum, 2008).

Smith, Joel, "More Than One: Sources of Serialism," in *More Than One: Photographs in Sequence*, ed. Smith (Princeton, NJ: Princeton University Art Museum, 2008), 9–29.

Smith, Shawn Michelle, *Photography on the Color Line: W. E. B. Du Bois, Race, and Visual Culture* (Durham, NC, and London: Duke University Press, 2004).

Smith, Shawn Michelle, *At the Edge of Sight: Photography and the Unseen* (Durham, NC, and London: Duke University Press, 2013).

Snead, James A., "Repetition as a Figure of Black Culture," in *Black Literature and Literary Theory*, ed. Henry Louis Gates Jr. (New York: Methuen, 1984), 59–79.

Solomon-Godeau, Abigail, "The Legs of the Countess," *October* 39 (Winter 1986): 65–108.

Sontag, Susan, *Regarding the Pain of Others* (New York: Farrar, Straus and Giroux, 2003).

Sontag, Susan, *On Photography* (London: Penguin, 2008).

Spiegel, Alan, *Fiction and the Camera Eye: Visual Consciousness in Film and the Modern Novel* (Charlottesville: University Press of Virginia, 1976).

Spillers, Hortense J., "Mama's Baby, Papa's Maybe: An American Grammar Book," in *The Black Feminist Reader*, ed. Joy James and T. Denean Sharpley-Whiting (Boston: Wiley-Blackwell, 2000), 57–87.

Spindler, Michael, "John Dos Passos and the Visual Arts," *Journal of American Studies* 15.3 (1981): 391–405.

Stange, Maren, *Symbols of Ideal Life: Social Documentary Photography in America, 1890–1950* (New York: Cambridge University Press, 1989).

Steedman, Carolyn, *Dust* (Manchester, UK: Manchester University Press, 2001).

Stein, Gertrude. *Picasso* (New York: Dover, 1938).

Stein, Gertrude, *Paris France* (London: B. T. Batsford, 1940).

Stein, Gertrude, *The Autobiography of Alice B. Toklas* (London: Zephyr Books, 1947).

Stein, Gertrude, "A Transatlantic Interview, 1946," in *A Primer for the Gradual Understanding of Gertrude Stein*, ed. Robert Bartlett Hass (Los Angeles: Black Sparrow, 1971), 15–35.

Stein, Gertrude, "Composition as Explanation," in *Selected Writings of Gertrude Stein*, ed. and intro. Carl Van Vechten (New York: Vintage, 1972), 511–24.

Stein, Gertrude, *Everybody's Autobiography* (New York: Vintage, 1973).

Stein, Gertrude, "How Writing is Written," in *How Writing is Written: Volume II of the Previously Uncollected Writings of Gertrude Stein*, ed. Robert Bartlett Haas (Los Angeles: Black Sparrow Press, 1974), 151–60.

Stein, Gertrude, "I Came and Here I Am," in *How Writing is Written: Volume II of the Previously Uncollected Writings of Gertrude Stein*, ed. Robert Bartlett Haas (Los Angeles: Black Sparrow, 1974), 67–72.

Stein, Gertrude, "Portraits and Repetition," in *Lectures in America*, intro. Wendy Steiner (London: Virago, 1988), 163–206.

Stein, Gertrude, *Three Lives* (New York: Penguin, 1990).

Stein, Gertrude, *The Making of Americans* (Normal, IL: Dalkey Archive Press, 1995).

Stein, Gertrude, *A Play Called Not and Now*, in *Last Operas and Plays*, ed. Carl Van Vechten (Baltimore: Johns Hopkins University Press, 1995), 422–39.

Stein, Gertrude, "Lecture II," in *Narration: Four Lectures*, intro. Thornton Wilder (Chicago: University of Chicago Press, 2010), 16–29.

Stein, Gertrude, and Amy Feinstein, "The Modern Jew Who Has Given Up the Faith of His Fathers Can Reasonably and Consistently Believe in Isolation," *PMLA* 116.2 (2001): 416–18.

Stein, Gertrude, and Alice B. Toklas Papers 1837–1961, Clipping Book, 1909–1914, Series 1: Writings of Gertrude Stein, Box 77, Folder 1408, Yale Collection of American Literature, Beinecke Rare Book and Manuscript Library, Yale University, New Haven, CT.

Steiner, Wendy, *Exact Resemblance to Exact Resemblance: The Literary Portraiture of Gertrude Stein* (New Haven, CT: Yale University Press, 1978).

Stengers, Isabelle, *Power and Invention: Situating Science*, trans. Paul Bains (Minneapolis: University of Minnesota Press, 1997).

Stern, Milton R., "On Editing Dead Modern Authors: Fitzgerald and *Trimalchio*," *The F. Scott Fitzgerald Society Newsletter* 10 (December 2000): 9–18.

Stetler, Pepper, "'The New Visual Literature': László Moholy-Nagy's *Painting, Photography, Film*," *Grey Room* 32 (Summer 2008): 88–113.

Stewart, Garrett, *Between Film and Screen: Modernism's Photo Synthesis* (Chicago: University of Chicago Press, 1999).

Stewart, Susan, *On Longing: Narratives of the Miniature, the Gigantic, the Souvenir, the Collection* (Durham, NC, and London: Duke University Press, 1993).

Stieglitz, Alfred, "Editorial," in *Camera Work: The Complete Illustrations 1903–1917* (Cologne, Germany: Taschen, 1997), 660–61.

Stillinger, Jack, *Multiple Authorship and the Myth of Solitary Genius* (New York and Oxford: Oxford University Press, 1991).

Stimson, Blake, *The Pivot of the World: Photography and Its Nation* (Cambridge, MA: MIT Press, 2006).

Stubbs, Katherine, "Mechanizing the Female: Discourse and Control in the Industrial Economy," *differences: A Journal of Feminist Cultural Studies* 7.3 (1995): 141–63.

Suárez, Juan A., "City Space, Technology, Popular Culture: The Modernism of Paul Strand and Charles Sheeler's *Manhatta*," *Journal of American Studies* 36.1 (2002): 85–106.

Suleiman, Susan Rubin, *Subversive Intent: Gender, Politics, and the Avant-Garde* (Cambridge, MA, and London: Harvard University Press, 1990).

Thomas, Ronald R., *Detective Fiction and the Rise of Forensic Science* (Cambridge: Cambridge University Press, 1999).

Tichi, Cecelia, *Shifting Gears: Technology, Literature, Culture in Modernist America* (Chapel Hill and London: University of North Carolina Press, 1987).

Tomkins, Silvan, *Affect, Imagery, Consciousness*, 4 vols. (New York: Springer, 1963–1992.

Toomer, Jean, "The *Cane* Years," in *The Wayward and the Seeking: A Collection of Writings by Jean Toomer*, ed. Darwin T. Turner (Washington, DC: Howard University Press, 1980), 116–28.

Toomer, Jean, *The Wayward and the Seeking: A Collection of Writings by Jean Toomer*, ed. Darwin T. Turner (Washington, DC: Howard University Press, 1980).

Toomer, Jean, *A Jean Toomer Reader: Selected Unpublished Writings*, ed. Frederik L. Rusch (New York: Oxford University Press, 1993).

Toomer, Jean, "A New Race in America," in *A Jean Toomer Reader: Selected Unpublished Writings*, ed. Frederik L. Rusch (Oxford and New York: Oxford University Press, 1993), 105.

Toomer, Jean, *Cane* (New York: Liveright, 2011).

Toomer, Jean, "Song of the Son," *The Crisis: A Record of the Darker Races* 23.6 (1922): 261. Accessed at http://www.modjourn.org/render.php?id=1297796255203127&view=mjp_object.

Trachtenberg, Alan, *Reading American Photographs: Images as History, Mathew Brady to Walker Evans* (New York: Hill and Wang, 1989).

Trotter, David, *Cinema and Modernism* (Malden, MA: Blackwell, 2007).

Trotter, David, *Literature in the First Media Age: Britain Between the Wars* (Cambridge, MA: Harvard University Press, 2013).

Trumpeter, Kevin, "Furnishing Modernist Fiction: The Aesthetics of Refuse," *Modernism/Modernity* 20.2 (2013): 307–26.

Turner, Darwin T., "An Intersection of Paths: Correspondence Between Jean Toomer and Sherwood Anderson," in *Jean Toomer: A Critical Evaluation*, ed. Therman O'Daniel (Washington, DC: Howard University Press, 1988), 99–110.

Veblen, Thorstein, *The Theory of the Leisure Class: An Economic Study of Institutions* (New York: Dover, 1994).

Veitch, Jonathan, "Reading Hollywood," *Salmagundi* 126/127 (Spring–Summer 2000): 192–221.

Vickers, Nancy J., "Members Only: Marot's Anatomical Blazons," in *The Body in Parts: Fantasies of Corporeality in Early Modern Europe*, ed. David Hillman and Carla Mazzio, 2–21. (New York: Routledge, 1997), 2–21.

Wagner, Ann Middleton, *Three Artists (Three Women): Modernism and the Art of Hesse, Krasner, and O'Keeffe* (Berkeley: University of California Press, 1996).

Wagner, Linda W., "Dos Passos: Some Directions in the Criticism," *Resources for American Literary Study* 13 (August 1983): 201–206.

Walker, Alice, "The Divided Life of Jean Toomer," *New York Times Book Review*, July 13, 1980, 11, 16.

Walker, Jayne L., *The Making of a Modernist: Gertrude Stein from* Three Lives *to* Tender Buttons (Amherst: University of Massachusetts Press, 1984).

Watson, Jay, *Reading for the Body: The Recalcitrant Materiality of Southern Fiction, 1893–1985* (Athens: University of Georgia Press, 2012).

Webb, Jeff, "Literature and Lynching: Identity in Jean Toomer's *Cane*," *ELH* 67.1 (2000): 205–28.

Weiss, Allen S., *The Aesthetics of Excess* (Albany: State University of New York Press, 1989).

Wexler, Laura, *Tender Violence: Domestic Visions in an Age of U.S. Imperialism* (Chapel Hill: University of North Carolina Press, 2000).

Whalan, Mark, "'Taking Myself in Hand': Jean Toomer and Physical Culture," *Modernism/modernity* 10.4 (2003): 597–615.

Whalan, Mark, *Race, Manhood, and Modernism: The Short Story Cycles of Sherwood Anderson and Jean Toomer* (Knoxville: University of Tennessee Press, 2007).

White, Patricia, *Uninvited: Classical Hollywood Cinema and Lesbian Responsibility* (Bloomington: Indiana University Press, 1993).

White, Ray Lewis, ed., *Sherwood Anderson/Gertrude Stein: Correspondence and Personal Essays* (Chapel Hill: University of North Carolina Press, 1972).

Whittier-Ferguson, John, "Stein in Time: History, Manuscripts, and Memory," *Modernism/ modernity* 6.1 (1999): 115–51.

Whyde, Janet M., "Mediating Forms: Narrating the Body in Jean Toomer's *Cane*," *Southern Literary Journal* 26.1 (1993): 42–53.

Wiegman, Robyn, *American Anatomies: Theorizing Race and Gender* (Durham, NC: Duke University Press, 1995).

Williams, Linda, *Hard Core: Power, Pleasure, and the "Frenzy of the Visible"* (Berkeley: University of California Press, 1989).

Williams, Susan S., *Confounding Images: Photography and Portraiture in Antebellum American Fiction* (Philadelphia: University of Philadelphia Press, 1997).

Wilson, Edmund, *The Boys in the Back Room* (San Francisco: Colt, 1941).

Wilson, Edmund, *The American Earthquake: A Documentary of the Twenties and Thirties* (New York: Doubleday, 1958).

Wilson, Mary, *The Labors of Modernism: Domesticity, Servants, and Authorship in Modernist Fiction* (Farnham, VT, and Burlington, VT: Ashgate, 2013).

Wood, Amy Louise, *Lynching and Spectacle: Witnessing Racial Violence in America, 1890–1940* (Chapel Hill: University of Carolina Press, 2009).

Wright, Elizabeth, *Speaking Desires can be Dangerous: The Poetics of the Unconscious* (Cambridge, UK: Polity Press, 1999).

Wright, Richard, *Twelve Million Black Voices: A Folk History of the Negro in the United States* (New York: Viking, 1941).

Yaeger, Patricia, *Dirt and Desire: Reconstructing Southern Women's Writing, 1930–1990* (Chicago: University of Chicago Press, 2000).

Yochelson, Bonnie, and Daniel Czitrom, *Rediscovering Jacob Riis: Exposure Journalism and Photography in Turn-of-the-Century New York* (New York: New Press, 2007).

Index

Abbott, Berenice, 201n56
Adorno, Theodor, 17
advertisement, 24, 110, 127, *129*, 190–91, *192*
African Americanism, 25, 39, 65–72, 87–89,
    90–92, 94–95, 142
    and activism, 25, 67, 88, 92, 94, 98, 106
    and authenticity, 69–70, 72
    and modernism, 68
    and visual culture, 67–68, *90*, 90–92, *91*
Anderson, Sherwood, 67, 71–72, 75
Anthropology, 12–13, *12*
Aragon, Louis, 46
Atget, Eugène, 16, 201n56
auteur, 154
authorship, 26, 71, 153–59, 176, 186–87
    and collaboration, 151, 153–56, 158, 186
    See also screenwriting; textual editing

Balzac, Honoré de, 59
Barnum, Gertrude, 145–46
Barthes, Roland, 5, 10, 12–13, 28–29, 33–34, 38–9,
    41, 45–46, 65, 137, 157, 166–67, 195, 197n8
Baudelaire, Charles, 127
Baudrillard, Jean, 49, 157
Bauhaus school, 15. *See also* Moholy-Nagy, László
Benjamin, Walter, 9–10, 27, 77, 127, 132
Bergson, Henri, 22
Bertillon, Alphonse, 14, 46, *48*, 50
Blanchot, Maurice, 5, 159
blazon, 92–93, 95–96, 99
Brecht, Bertolt, 9
Breton, André, 46, 52, 193
Brouillet, Pierre André, 46–49, *49*

Cahun, Claude, 51–54, *53*, 58–61, *60*, *61*, 63, 100,
    151, 208n75
Cameron, Julia Margaret, 201n56
carte de visite, 10, 126–27
celebrity, 24, 26, 110–12, 120, 125–26, 130, 132, 149,
    162–63, 165–70, 179
    and photography, 26, 126–27, 132, 149, 167,
    226–27n101 (*see also* glamour shot)
Certeau, Michel de, 138–40
Cézanne, Paul, 34–35
Chaplin, Charlie, 161, 163, 184–85, *185*
Charcot, Jean-Martin, 46–49
chronophotography, 10, 13–17, 20–21, 134, 137, 162.
    See also Marey, Étienne-Jules; Muybridge,
    Eadweard
cinema, 12–3, 22–25, 77–79, 115–28, 149–55,
    161–65, 169–71, 181–83
    avant-garde, 23–24, 149, 153, 161
    classical, 149–50, 155, 161, 165, 169, 170–71, *172*,
    176, 179–80, 182, 187
    See also film; Hollywood
composite writing, 4–5, 7, 8, 11, 21–22, 25, 28–29,
    34, 65–66, 69–71, 103, 109, 117, 138, 140,
    147–50, 187, 195
    and textual frame, 33, 97, 107
    See also woman-in-series
criminology, 14, 46, 91. *See also* Bertillon,
    Alphonse
Cubism, 35, 76, 205n20. *See also* Cézanne, Paul;
    Picasso, Pablo

daguerreotype, 9, *9*, 59, 127, *128*
Dalí, Salvador, 46–47, *47*, 49–54, 63, 81

death, 34, 68, 83, 85, 95, 99, 100, 106–7, 143,
    166–67, 174, 178, 180–82, 187, 195
    scenes, 53–7, 62–3, 72–73, 85, 95, 98, 106–7, 174,
    181–82
    and photography, 5, 29, 56, 88–89, 137, 157,
    166–67, 181, 195
Debord, Guy, 137
Derrida, Jacques, 157, 172
Dickinson, Emily, 19–21, 32, 34
Disdéri, André-Adolphe-Eugène, 126–28, *128*.
    See also *carte de visite*
Dos Passos, John, 112–13, 115, 118–19, 132–33, 189
    Manhattan Transfer, 4–5, 7–8, 11, 21–24,
    108–48, 152–54, 166–67
    and modernist studies, 133, 219n68
    and theater, 112–13
    Three Soldiers, 217n34
    U.S.A. trilogy, 148, 216–17n21
dreams, 64, 147–48, 160, 175, 183–84, 195

Eisenstein, Sergei, 12, 23, 115, 173, 216n19, 217n21
eugenics, 1, 7, 37, 200n47, 221n99. *See also* Galton,
    Francis
Evans, Walker, 17, 188–95, *190, 192, 193, 194*

Faulkner, William, 26, 67, 150, 175
feminine masquerade, 6, 59–62, 180, 198n11
film, 12, 79, 150–51, 158, 162, 169, 171, 179
    theory, 22, 115
    technology of, 17, 22–23, 118, 159–60, 162,
    172–74, 184–87
    See also cinema; photogram
Fitzgerald, F. Scott, 148–49, 152–59, 173–76,
    184–85, 189
    "Babylon Revisited," 25, 149, 174–76, 177–78,
    183
    "Cosmopolitan," 4–5, 7–8, 11, 21–22, 25–26,
    149–51, 157, 174–87
    The Great Gatsby, 158, 174–76
    on Hollywood, 152–54
    The Last Tycoon, 4–5, 7–8, 11, 21–22, 25–26,
    149–52, 154, 156–61, 164–66, 169–76, 178
    Tender is the Night, 179
Foucault, Michel, 8, 26, 63, 87–88, 136, 139, 155.
    See also panopticism
fragmentation. *See* composite writing
Freud, Sigmund, 46–48, 64–65, 147–48, 150

Galton, Francis, 1–4, 6–10, 12, 14, 20, 28, 33, 39,
    189, 200n47
    and composite portraiture, 1–7, *2, 3*, 14, 80–1, 189
gaze, 78–79, 88, 102, 109, 125–27, 137, 140, 142–43
    male, 6, 24, 49–50, 79, 92–93, 125–27, 182
    oppositional, 88, 90, 94

glamour shot, 167–70, *168*, 172
grotesque, 98, 107, 170
    Southern, 99

Harlem Renaissance, 25, 66–67, 70, 72
    and modernism, 25, 67
Held, Anna, 111–12, *111*, 126
Hollywood, 26, 148–50, 152–55, 158–67, 171–75,
    180, 185, 187, 191
    and celebrity, 149, 165–67
    production, 127, 149–50, 160–62, *163, 173*
    (*see also* screenwriting)
    substitutability, 151, 162, 164–67, 178
hysteria, 46–50, *47, 49*, 52, 58

Joyce, James, 147–48

Käsebier, Gertrude, 201n56
Kellerman, Annette, 141
King, Martin Luther Jr., 99
Kracauer, Siegfried, 16, 20–21, 74, 121–22, 133–34,
    139, 194–95

Lacan, Jacques, 64, 183
Lévi-Strauss, Claude, 179
lynching, 25, 67, 74, 88–89, 92–100, 105–7, 109
    antilynching, 92, 94, 98, 102, 106
    photography, 25, 67, 88–89, 92–96, *96*, 98–99,
    102, 106, 126

MacFadden, Bernarr. *See* physical culture
    movement
machine culture, 133–39, 152–54, 171–72, 184–87
    body–machine complex, 110, 136
    "facialization machine," 194–95
    Fordism, 133, 148, 162
    Taylorism, 136–37, 162
    and the female body, 114–15, 133–36, 145
    and writing, 77, 80, 133–36
Marey, Étienne-Jules, 13–15, *15*, 20, 134–35, *135*
masks, 6, 49, 58–59, 180
medicalized encounter, 32, 50–51, 62, 188
miniaturization, 170, 184
modernism, 4–6, 26, 68, 75, 118, 148,
    162, 176, 187
    "bad modernism," 34
    and gender, 6, 8, 23, 25–26, 133, 176, 187
    high, 25, 117, 133, 149
    high and low, 23
    literary modernism, 4–6, 23, 26–27, 155, 187
    modernist writing, 7, 11, 23–24, 26, 147, 150, 187
    (*see also* composite writing)
    modern visual art, 34–35, 40–41 (*see also*
    Cubism; Surrealism)

and race, 6, 25, 26, 67–68, 75, 176, 187
and realism, 10–11
modernity, 33, 110, 117, 119, 121, 132–33, 139, 147, 195
Moholy-Nagy, László, 15–16, *16*
motion, 13–15, 20, 22, 78–79, 134, 138–39, 144–45, 161. *See also* chronophotography
Muybridge, Eadweard, 13, *13*, 16, 20–21, *21*, 134

Nadar, Félix, 16, 59, 193–94
nickelodeon, 116–17, 133
novel, 63, 68, 117, 119
realist, 8, 11, 31, 132

O'Keefe, Georgia, 74–76, 80–84, *82, 83, 84*, 93

pain, 62, 89, 92, 99
panopticism, 14, 125–26, 138–39, 144, 146, 189. *See also* surveillance
parataxis, 44–45, 50, 64, 147
Pasolini, Pier Paolo, 158, 160
performativity, 59, 106, 109, 180
photography, 1–6, 9–10, 14, 16–22, 35, 41, 54, 59, 74–77, 88–92, 94–95, 102–4, 108–10, 124–25, 130, 134, 137–38, 167, 195, 181
aerial, 139–40, *140*
and cinema (*see* still-moving field)
ethics of, 5–6, 27–29, 54, 88–90, 195
photographic encounter, 6, 28, 41–42, 42–43, 78, 81, 89, 99, 124–26
photographic essay, 17, 94–95
photographic frame, 24, 28, 89–91, 102–3, 191, 193
photographic indexicality, 4, 10–11, 24, 27–28, 33, 38–39, 42–43, 46, 77, 183, 193
photographic portraiture, 1–7, 14, *18, 19*, 59, 80–81, *90*, 90–91, *91*, 189, *193, 194*
photographic sequence (*see* serial photography)
serial photography, 2, 5, 8, *12, 13*, 14–17, *15*, 20–21, *21*, 37, 150, 189, 191, 201n56
Victorian, 10–11
photogram, 21–3, 25–26, 149–50, 159, 162, 164, 170, 173–74, 180–81, 184–85
and phonogram, 23, 200n37
physical culture movement, 70, 101–2, *102, 103*, 141
Picasso, Pablo, 40–41, 43, 58, 67
punctum, 12

realism, 10, 24, 31–35, 38–39, 62, 116, 132
neorealism, 32–33, 64
repetition, 33, 44–45, 50–51, 63–65, 118, 121–23, 147, 159, 161–66, 171–76, 179
and revision, 26, 150, 175–76, 179

resistance, 7–8, 24–25, 34, 54, 56–57, 62–63, 67–68, 85–88, 103, 110–11, 140, 146, 150, 180, 195, 197n8
Riis, Jacob, 37, *37*

Sander, August, 16–19, *18, 19*, 20–21
Schwob, Lucy. *See* Cahun, Claude
screenwriting, 149–56, 158, 160, 175–76, 184–86
Sontag, Susan, 10, 24, 27–28, 43, 46, 56, 88–89, 130, 191
sound, 172, 181, 183
spectacle, 99, 105, 118, 120, 137, 145
stasis, 22, 138, 140, 149–50, 161, 166–67
Stein, Gertrude, 38, 42–43, 72, 159, 169, 176, 189
Autobiography of Alice B. Toklas, The, 31, 34–35, 162–63, 165
and cinema, 161–64, 172–73
Everybody's Autobiography, 172
literary portraits, 40–41
Making of Americans, The, 32
and photography, 35, 40–43
Paris France, 42–43, 162
Play Called Not and Now, A, 163–64
and race, 25, 34–35, 36, 39–40, 42, 58, 64–65
and realism, 33–34
on Surrealism, 42
Three Lives, 4–5, 7–8, 11, 21–22, 24–25, 30–46, 50–51, 54–66, 70, 73, 76, 127, 147
stereopticon, 116–17
Stieglitz, Alfred, 40–41, 74–76, 80–84, *82, 83, 84*, 93, 212n49
still-moving field, 5, 11–12, 19, 22–24, 28–29, 62, 79, 118, 149–50, 200n37
Surrealism, 24, 33, 42–44, 46–52, 58, 65, 191, 193
and gender, 49
Surrealist photography, 10, 24, 33, 42–43, 46, 51
See also Dalí, Salvador; Cahun, Claude
surveillance, 24, 67, 91, 110, 125, 136, 138, 182
and film, 182
See also panopticism

textual editing, 155–58, 160, 169, 171
theater, 104–5, 109–16, 118–21, 125–29, 133–34, 142, 144
and photography, *111, 113, 114*, 126–27, *128, 129*, 135
See also spectacle; Ziegfeld Follies
Toomer, Jean, 68–72, 81, 189
Cane, 4–5, 7–8, 11, 21–22, 25–26, 65–74, 76–88, 90, 92–108, 182, 190–91
and photography, 74–76
and physical culture movement, 101–2, *103*
publication in *Crisis*, 92, 94
and race, 66, 69–72, 76–77

unfinished text, 149, 158–60

vanishing woman, 6, 56–57, 62–63, 83–87, 180–82
variety show. *See* theater
vaudeville. *See* theater
voice, 171–73, 176–77, 181–83, 187

Weston, Edward, 130–32, *131*, 162–63, *163*, 167
White, Minor, 17
whiteness, 25, 68, 99–101, 104, 143–44,
    226–27n101
    and spectatorship, 92–97 (*see also* lynching)

Wilson, Edmund, 156, 219n73
woman-in-series, 5, 7, 34, 65, 80, 109, 120, 143,
    147–49, 151, 165, 187, 195
Wright, Richard, 94–95

Ziegfeld, Florenz Jr., 110–13
Ziegfeld Follies, 112, 113–15, *113*, *114*, 118,
    129, *135*, 148
    Follies girl, 112, *113*, 113–15, 120–21, 127, 133–34,
        135, 142
    tableau vivant, 114–15
    See also spectacle; theater